Harry Chapin

The Music Behind the Man

Michael Francis Taylor

NEW HAVEN PUBLISHING LTD

First Edition
Published 2019
NEW HAVEN PUBLISHING LTD
www.newhavenpublishingltd.com
newhavenpublishing@gmail.com

Cover design ©Pete Cunliffe
pcunliffe@blueyonder.co.uk

Contents

Foreword by Howard Fields   4

Introduction   5

Acknowledgements   9

A Young Man on the Move   11

Band of Brothers   29

The Big Break   44

Heads and Tales   52

Sniper and Other Love Songs   74

Short Stories   97

The Ultimate Obscenity   117

Verities & Balderdash   127

Nights on Broadway   149

Portrait Gallery   159

Greatest Stories Live   179

On the Road to Kingdom Come   191

Dance Band on the Titanic   208

Living Room Suite   236

Legends of the Lost and Found   245

Sequel   257

One More Tomorrow   275

Last Stand   287

The Legacy   295

Album Gallery   310

For the Record   312

Foreword by Howard Fields

1975 was my first of seven years playing drums for Harry Chapin. I did not know him well at all yet, and so it was a surprise to find myself attending the Grammy Awards with him, his wife Sandy, and his dad Jim on the night of March 1st at the Uris Theater in New York City. Harry was nominated as Best Male Vocalist and would be performing 'Cat's In The Cradle' that evening. As we were approaching the doors leading from the lobby into the theater, the usher (young skinny guy around 20 dressed in usher red) noticed that Harry was overburdened with a guitar (not in its case), a handbag, and one or two other items. He offered to hold the guitar and Harry gladly gave it up. But opening the door for us, he accidentally dropped the guitar and simultaneously tripped in such a way that his foot came right down, hard, on the instrument. So... there the smashed guitar lay on the floor. It was not a pretty moment, and the next thing I remember was Harry putting his arm around a devastated and horrified kid, saying to him, "Don't worry about it bro". He could be like that.

Moments of kindness such as that were not uncommon in Harry's life. Many I witnessed myself. More are evidenced in this book. Those moments show qualities of the man less familiar, to most persons, than that of the musician, the songwriter, the poet, the singer, the humanitarian and the civic activist.

I stared at the back of Harry's head from the drumset for more than 900 concerts and it was an honor and a pleasure to have a front row seat to his creative process and abilities; to witness the way he'd piece together his stories of struggling underdogs and of dreamers who would never realize their dreams; to observe how he commingled his poetry with chords and melodies that perfectly complemented those stories; and all of that within the confines of a guitar style simple, unique and charming.

On another front, this book well documents the political challenges undertaken by Harry. I've many remembrances of quietly observing his joys and disappointments concerning his ongoing attempt to solve what many would refer to as the unsolvable problem of hunger in America. Had he lived, I've no doubt he'd still be fighting that fight.

Lastly, if a foreword could be dedicated, I'd be remiss not to dedicate this to the most important group of people in Harry's life, after his family and friends. His fans, those who Harry would refer to as "The only song I need", had a rare and unique connection to Harry and one that still lives on, as his songs will always remain prized gifts to those fans, their children and now their grandchildren.

Introduction

*"And as I wander with my music through the jungles of despair
My kid will learn guitar and find his street corner somewhere
There he'll make the silence listen to the dream behind the voice
And show his minstrel Hamlet daddy that there only was one choice"*

With the news of Harry Chapin's untimely death in July 1981, devoted fans throughout the world realized they had just lost one of the most original and respected talents in American popular music. For them, it was the ultimate tragedy - their hero taken from them at the peak of a short but illustrious career - but for many others it simply posed the question: "Harry who?" This seemed a little unjust for an artist who, in that short life, accomplished so much with so little and touched so many lives with his work, earning the respect and admiration of a sometimes cynical music industry.

Harry was a singer-songwriter who provoked contrasting opinions among his many critics. He was either greatly admired or passionately disliked. There was no middle ground. He appeared in books detailing the worst records ever made, and, by contrast, winning the praises of one music critic who voted one of his albums the best of 1977. But at the same time other critics were constantly dismissing his music as being over-sentimental, preachy, simplistic, and even careless.

The admiration for Harry Chapin, for those familiar with the man, divides between the music he made and the support he gave for numerous charitable and worthwhile causes during his life. Many saw him as a unique artist, unable to categorize his style of music making. He was not simply a songwriter; he was the epitome of a master storyteller - a kind of latter-day minstrel relating tales around a proverbial campfire. In doing that, he was virtually alone. Harry's story-song format owed much to his days in the film industry in the early 60s. As a result, the stories he told had a cinematic quality and were about the kind of individuals you could readily relate to. He wrote about ordinary people in ordinary situations, about the heartbreak of loneliness, broken relationships; of life's losers, outcasts and underdogs. But there was nothing ordinary in the songs. As with celebrated painter Norman Rockwell and poet Carl Sandburg, Harry used his songs as his medium to elevate and celebrate his subject matter, giving it a significance. What Rockwell and Sandburg achieved with their respective paintbrush and pen, Harry achieved with his guitar and heartfelt lyrics.

Harry felt he was following in the giant footsteps of singers he admired so much, notably Phil Ochs and his life-long hero, Pete Seeger. And like his heroes, he wrote about important social and political issues, but not always the

5

kind you would expect to hear about. Dipping into his catalogue of a dozen or more albums, you hear him bringing attention to subjects such as poor schooling, education, police corruption, teenage abortion, and self-abuse. Even some taboo subjects were given vivid awareness through his candid lyrics. In marked contrast, Harry was also a hopeless romantic, as evident in his emotive tributes to his wife and young family, as well as in his crafting of fine fables about love in all its complexities. The end result is that you often get a moral within the song, although he never tried to ram home his point. More often, you are caught by surprises and unexpected twists in the tale. Harry wanted to make music that mattered and that spoke of things he cared deeply about, whether it was commercial or not. He did not want to be remembered as a maker of three-minute pop records, which he looked upon as being like fast food – quick and easy to format, but not sustaining the listener for long before they moved to something else to whet their appetite. There was no lasting impression.

On his support for worthwhile causes, and for putting his talents, efforts, and money where his mouth was, no other artist has ever come close to what he achieved, nor can they boast the number of benefit concerts he performed in a recording career lasting barely a decade. Performing an unprecedented 200 or more concerts a year, almost half were benefits, with proceeds going to alleviate world hunger and dozens of charitable causes. He also led the way and encouraged others in the music business to organize all the wide ranging and now frequent and more fashionable charity concerts that have taken place since his death. Harry clearly wanted to make his mark, to try his hand at new things, and not leave a dream undone. He wanted us to see that there was so much more to life. He probably never achieved all he wanted, but he achieved a great deal, and it would be fair to say that he did manage to achieve one of his greatest desires. He once said in a radio interview, just over three years before he was killed: *"When I die, I would like it to be said that it mattered that I was alive."* Few people who knew the man, or simply know of his work, will disagree that he managed this.

Why then, after such an illustrious career, has Harry Chapin been largely forgotten by the music critics today? Although the immediate response to his death was overwhelming, a whole new generation have grown up unaware of who the man was, or what he had achieved. Many have a deep-rooted belief that all the good work that has been done to help combat world hunger originated with Mr Geldof in 1984, and that before he came along, no other artist had given a damn. Harry was often dismissed by a number of myopic critics as being somewhat tone-deaf outside a certain demographic, and as someone who tried to use a perceived overbearing personality to motivate and manipulate people's guilt in order to create what he saw as a better world. Maybe those same critics had never seen a child dying from hunger.

His music has always been open to criticism, as all music should be. Love it or loathe it, it cannot be ignored, and the facts speak for themselves. During his career, he made some of the finest introspective and personal albums of the genre, maintaining a high standard seldom seen in his contemporaries. He was not a unique singer, but his songs inspired and stirred emotions in a way that was unique at the time, and even today, perhaps only matched by a handful of artists like Bruce Springsteen. His concerts were modest affairs compared to today's theatrical events, but they generated an air of living room intimacy with his audience - 'the cheap seats' as they were affectionately referred to - that no one else was able to emulate. Harry's contemporaries included some of music's higher echelon of singer-songwriters - Springsteen, Joni Mitchell, James Taylor, Don McLean, Neil Diamond, Billy Joel, John Denver and Carly Simon, to name just a few - and they all had to pay their dues and work tirelessly to achieve success. Harry too paid his dues, sometimes even to the point of giving up on his chosen career, but once he connected with an audience, there was no going back. As he once said, *"If the audience understands, period, you've communicated."*

If ever a man deserved success it was Harry. He had immeasurable talent, and even if he had never chosen a path in music, he would have excelled in anything he chose to do. With a machine-like rhetoric and forthright views, he had the makings of a fine politician. Some say that in taking that path it could have eventually led him to the White House. Surely stranger things have happened. But in the end, as you will see here, of all the different roads he ventured down, in the end it was in his very DNA to be a performer. There only was one choice. But in choosing the path of a singer-songwriter, he selflessly offered advice to other performers. He cared for things that mattered, and he did something about it by persuading others to do the same. In doing this, he was able to reach out and touch so many lives, and as a result helped save countless numbers of lives too. Above everything else, this is the mark of a truly great man.

Harry Chapin was first and foremost a musician, and a fine one too. Music was in his blood, like his father before him, and all his early ventures and career switches only served as stepping stones along a path to becoming what he always was destined to be. Before he witnessed first-hand the cries of starving children, which for him would be a life-changing experience, he had written and performed songs prolifically with his two younger brothers, Tom and Steve. He may have lacked stage presence in his early days, often lumbering about in his everyday wardrobe or hunched on a stool, introducing each song in his own imitable style with his rasping voice and unconvincing laughter, but by watching others perform, he gradually learned to win over an audience. For him there was never any pretentiousness. What you saw with Harry was what you got, and he hooked and reeled these strangers in with his melodies until they became strangers no more; more like disciples, hanging on to every word, every chord, and completely engrossed in this minstrel and his tales. How could you define his music? The question is often asked, but the simple fact is no one really can. He was all things. He was simply Harry Chapin, a man whose story of a life, a life in which dreams were both realized and unfulfilled, was shared with the whole world in a uniquely evocative way.

Books about Harry's extraordinary life are few and far between; those solely about his music almost non-existent. Without taking anything away from this selfless humanitarian and tireless campaigner for a better world, it has always been his words and music that captivated me all those years ago, and so too thousands upon thousands of like-minded fans. With the question of *"Harry who?"* the answer from some middle-aged businessman with kids could very well be: *"You know, the guy who sang about that cat in a cradle."* Ask a New York cabbie of a certain age, and they will most likely start reciting the lyrics to one of Harry's seminal songs. Ask any radio DJ who was around at that time, and many will gladly tell you how one of Harry's songs became a mirror-image of his own life. Harry wrote about people like these, about what he saw and what he felt. How those songs came about is a story in itself, and one I can hopefully attempt to unravel and give the reader a flavor of what Harry the musician was all about. There are artists today who write and perform long story-songs that are still described by music writers as being "Chapinesque," which in itself seems a fitting tribute to the man.

In the following pages I will give an appraisal of Harry's songs, but I don't profess to be a music critic or reviewer - I'm just a fan, plain and simple. I will exhaust all adjectives in describing the songs that are nailed to my heart, but equally point out, maybe as Harry himself would appreciate, my disappointment or even dislike for a particular song. So, no brickbats please. I have also included the lyrics to a couple of dozen of what I consider to be his finest compositions.

This for me has been a labour of love, and the one person I really need to thank is Harry himself. It certainly mattered that he lived, and the world is a much colder place without him. His words and music seduced me as a teenager almost five decades ago, and I'm a better person for it.

Michael Francis Taylor
Broughton Astley
England
August 2019

Acknowledgments

To Sandy Chapin, Harry's widow, for her gracious comments and corrections.

To Jason and Josh Chapin, Harry's sons, for their invaluable help and advice, without which this book would have been so much harder to complete.

To Tom Chapin, Harry's brother, for his corrections and additions to the text.

To Pegge Strella at the Chapin Office for pointing me in the right direction.

To Teddie Dahlin and her staff at New Haven Publishing UK for bringing to life a book that she convinced me should be written.

To Howie Fields, Harry's only drummer, for his invaluable insight into recordings and concerts and for graciously contributing the Foreword.

To Steve Stout, photographer extraordinaire, for his permission to use his iconic images of Harry.

To the Joel Brodsky estate for their kind permission to use the cover photograph.

To Charlotte Mortimer at Warner/Chappell Music for permission to use Harry's lyrics.

To Linda McCarty, Mike Grayeb and Bill Hornung for permission to use their *Circle* newsletter articles.

To John H Robinson at Uncut for permission to use reviews and articles from *Melody Maker* and *New Musical Express*.

To my good friend James Court, established author in his own right, for urging me to follow in his footsteps.

To Angela, my own "dream lover of a lady," for tirelessly checking the draft and teaching me lessons in good grammar all over again

To all the "cheap seat" members of the Harry Chapin Fans and Harry Chapin Memories Facebook groups, too many to name, for all their comments and contributions over the last five months, but a special mention to Scott Sivakoff, Gerry Naughton, Jason Colannino and Brandon Walls. This book is dedicated to each and every one of you. Keep the change…

And finally, to the one man who touched my very soul four and a half decades ago - Harry Forster Chapin (1942-1981)

For further information
Harry Chapin Foundation – www.harrychapinfoundation.org
Harry Chapin Family Official Site – www.harrychapinmusic.com
The Harry Chapin Archive – www.harrychapin.com

9

WhyHunger - https://whyhunger.org
Long Island Cares - https://licares.org
Lyrics – www.harrychapin.com/music
Story of a Life: The Harry Chapin Family Album - Elspeth Hart, Sandy and Josh Chapin (Wading River Books)
Harry Chapin Fans Facebook group
Harry Chapin Memories Facebook group
Howie Fields – hfrockpaper@gmail.com

Music ratings
5 stars – Absolute classic
4 stars – Exceptional
3 stars – Good
2 stars – Average
1 star – Harry, it sucks!

A Young Man on the Move

"The story of my life is marked by the women who helped me. I owe a lot of the richness to certain people who cared a lot - cared about my dreams, I guess..."

Birth of an American Troubadour

Harry Forster Chapin is the second son born to parents James and Elspeth Chapin on Monday, December 7th 1942, at Sloane's Presbyterian Hospital, 168th Street, in the Washington Heights area of New York City. It is a country at war, and the first anniversary of the attack on Pearl Harbor. It is also barely a year following the birth of his elder brother, James Burke Chapin. Harry is named after his mother's grandfather, Harry Batterham, and his father's uncle, Harry Forbes. The name Forster comes from Forster Batterham, his mother's only uncle.

History records that the Chapins are direct descendants of one Deacon Samuel Chapin, born 1595 in Paignton, England, who sailed to America in the mid-17th century to become one of the founding fathers of Puritan Springfield, Massachusetts. Among the Chapin descendants are many illustrious names, including two US Presidents, as well as J P Morgan, Humphrey Bogart, Clint Eastwood and Amelia Earhart.

Harry's 23-year-old father James (Jim) Forbes Chapin is an athletic-looking man who makes a modest living as an accomplished jazz drummer, often being given the opportunity of playing with the Casa Loma Orchestra and for famous big band leaders of the time, such as Glen Gray, Tommy Dorsey, Tony Pastor and Woody Herman. Born in Manhattan in 1919 to James (Big Jim) Ormsby Chapin and Abigail (Abby) Chapin (nee Forbes), Jim leaves William and Mary College in early 1938 after skipping classes in order to indulge in his passion for drumming. Within a couple of years, he is playing opposite his idol Gene Krupa at the World's Fair in New York. In the early 40s he begins writing a book on jazz drumming techniques which is published in 1948.

Elspeth's ancestors also hail from the old mother country. In 1881, nineteen-year-old Harry Batterham leaves his modest home in Wisbech, in England's Fenland, to sail to America with his father William and begin a new life in rural North Carolina as indentured servants. With just two dimes between them when they arrive, father and son may have relatives already living in Raleigh, but they decide to settle and work in West Asheville, eventually earning enough money to set up a home. It is possible that other family members follow in their footsteps and emigrate to the New World.

William dies in 1885, and a few years later Harry hears about a young Lancashire-born woman called Nellie Forster, who lives two counties away. They meet, fall in love, and eventually marry. Among their children is Lillian (Lily) Mary Batterham, Harry Chapin's maternal grandmother, who later marries Kenneth Burke. (Jeanne) Elspeth Burke is born to them in New York in 1920. Known as 'Dutchie,' she is the first of three girls, and childhood is divided between winter months in New York City and summer months at the family home in rural Andover, New Jersey. After graduating Hunter College, she marries 21-year-old Jim Chapin, a long-time friend of Kenneth's.

For much of Harry Chapin's early childhood the family's home is a three-room apartment above a longshoreman's office at 353 West 11th Street, the last block before the Hudson River in Greenwich Village, and midway between the M&M Trucking Company and a Federal penitentiary. In 1943 his father Jim receives his draft papers and is sent for training at Fort Dix, near Trenton, New Jersey, but with his musical background he is selected to tour with service bands at various military bases across the country. Later transferred to the air force base at Charlotte, North Carolina, his musical talents are put to good use as snare drummer in the Morris Field Air Force Band. Although Harry sees little of his father during this time, Elspeth and the three boys take every opportunity to travel down to Charlotte and spend some months with him in a brick two-family house provided by the Air Force for the families of personnel. Their third son Thomas Forbes Chapin is born there on March 13th 1945. When the war finally comes to an end that summer, the family move back to Andover and West 11th Street. Jim continues his life on the road, playing with various bands, and leaves 25-year-old Elspeth to take care of her growing family, made even larger with the birth of a fourth son, Stephen Beal Chapin, in New York on December 30th 1946.

There are two great loves in Jim's life, his family and his career as a musician, but the constant touring and long periods away from home make it difficult to divide that devotion equally. Inevitably his errant nature fosters suspicion and mistrust at home, sadly leading to Jim and Elspeth parting ways in 1948. Although Elspeth is now left to bring up the children on her own, there is plenty of help at hand, in some cases literally just around the corner, and this will prove to be a turning point in the lives of six-year-old Harry and his three brothers. But the separation is taking its toll on their mother and, although she does her very best, the boys' saving grace comes in the shape of their two grandmothers, Abby Chapin and Lily Burke, two incredible women who now step in and help shepherd them throughout their formative years, injecting into them a strong will and self-confidence, traits that Harry will certainly take on board. Of all the brothers, it is Harry who is most like Abby, and she will have an enormous impact on his development.

While in Andover, Harry attends the Byram Township Consolidated School in Stanhope. His first-grade report card at age six shows that he has a good feel for storytelling: *"Harry works accurately and carefully. He is determined to keep at a task until it is finished. Makes good use of his leisure time.... storytelling is very good. Has imagination.... Harry has a shrill loud voice when playing excited in school and should try to speak in lower tones. Harry tries very hard. Is always attentive. He works independently and shows leadership in class."*

Abby has always been interested in the activities of her grandsons and becomes even closer to them once their parents are divorced. She takes them to museums at weekends and often attends the school PTA meetings. Now in her late 60s, Abby is still teaching English full-time in a New York school and caring for her seriously ill sister. She puts down to her New England heritage her ability to handle the added responsibilities. With Abby and Lily having been professional teachers themselves, these two matriarchs become the foundation on which the building blocks of the boys' lives are built. Even before their formal schooling, they all have a good grasp of the essential subjects. Harry's early education means he even manages to skip eighth grade in junior high school. Even though there is an assortment of family, friends and relations to play a part in his upbringing, Harry will always speak highly of the role his grandmothers have on his early life: *"They believed I was worthwhile long before the outside world did."*

But there is also music in the boys' blood. By the age of three, Harry, despite suffering serious bouts of asthma, can already play notes on his father's trumpet, and it is soon clear to see that they have inherited a large slice of their father's musical gene. Despite very little financial help from her errant husband, Elspeth manages to hang on to the family home, which is in his name, but only with the insistence and help of Abby.

The following winter brings added drama when Harry is knocked down by a taxi while running across Greenwich Avenue after school. Although not seriously hurt, Harry gets to have his photograph on the front page of New York newspapers, when reporters, standing outside the penitentiary waiting for a shot of convicted Soviet spy Judith Coplon, go to the scene of the accident to record the event as a "human interest" story. One description of the photo reads: *Unlucky Seven - His eyes badly puffed, tearful Harry Chapin, 7, of 353 W 11th St, is comforted by a passer-by after being hit by a car at W 10th St and Greenwich Ave.* His injuries are reported as not serious in St Vincent's Hospital. If anything is going to sap away whatever little self-confidence Harry has, this is an unfortunate good start. The four well-behaved, well-mannered Chapin boys are a close-knit group who rarely socialize, and they find it hard to be accepted into the rough-and-ready street gangs of the neighborhood, often becoming the target for ridicule and scorn when venturing outside. For Harry in particular, it creates a sense of social isolation. Outside of the warm bosom of his family, he finds it hard to fit in. Harry recalls: *"We were the strange kids on the block because we did things like read as well as throw stones."*

As well as helping out with the brothers' academic education, Abby also nurtures their growing interests in music and pays for them to have lessons at the nearby Greenwich House Music School on Barrow Street. Harry is keen to perfect his trumpet skills; Tom reluctantly has to learn the clarinet, and James and Steve choose the piano. All four boys also learn to read music. Not taking it too seriously to begin with, Harry eventually reaches a level in his trumpet playing where he will have the ability and newfound self-confidence to perform in front of small audiences at local talent shows, and even in front of the biggest critics of all at his school assemblies. In doing so, he is finding an easy way of bringing attention to himself, something he will later develop into an art form.

Harry remembers the music lessons:

"I'd taken trumpet lessons for a long time. I had a real hard ass trumpet teacher who thought I had some talent, pushed me like hell. I didn't enjoy it for the first 4 or 5 years until finally I got into it and I was glad he pushed me. I was 8 when I started. I had a guilt thing going with my teacher. He was one of those people who really is devoted to the instrument and if you didn't practice, he made you feel guilty and so I remember those first 4 or 5 years I was feeling guilty that I didn't work hard enough. Finally, I got on to it and I started practicing 2 or 3 hours a day and by the time I was 17 I could have gone on to become a classical trumpet player, that's the kind of stuff I was playing ..."

Away from performing, Harry still battles with his fears of isolation and loneliness. To counter this, he slowly develops an extrovert, full-octane and carefree persona that will make him the nucleus of the quartet of siblings. While older brother James is more introverted, shining brightly with his academic and intellectual abilities, a position which is never contested, Harry is the one who lacks focus. He is already the tallest (for now, anyway), the strongest, and the most outspoken sibling - brash, arrogant, and constantly striving to make himself heard. Even though he will look up to James as his moral compass, he will find the only real competition in these formative years will come from Tom, who will soon develop into a handsome all-American sportsman, excelling as a basketball player. And then there's young Steve, who slowly but surely will have the makings of becoming a serious musician.

Elspeth recalls the bond that develops between Harry and James: *"Harry and James were very close. They were only 13 months apart, and they sort of grew up together. When James was very young, he made up his own language, and Harry and he spoke in their own language. They had a word like 'lalloo' for water. They were always close and when they were really little, they were inseparable."*

(Mike Grayeb and Linda McCarty, *Circle*, Winter 2005)

The Chapins and the Burkes

As well as their two grandmothers, the Chapin boys are also encouraged and inspired by their two grandfathers. Born in Orange, New Jersey, in 1887, 'Big' Jim Chapin studies art in New York, Antwerp, and at the Royal Academy in London, before moving to Paris. Returning to the US in 1912 as an accomplished scenic painter, he takes on a variety of illustration work and book design, including having his work featured on the cover of *Time* magazine. Through contacts he is also chosen to illustrate some of Robert Frost's poetry books, leading to a lifelong friendship with the esteemed poet. While in New York Jim meets and marries Abby Forbes, a high school teacher. In 1919 she gives birth to Jim Chapin, Harry's father, but the couple divorce two years later. In 1924 Big Jim leaves New York to rent a cabin on the Marvin family farm in New Jersey, where he spends the next few years painting a series of portraits of the family which go on to have a significant impact on the art world. In the late 1930s he marries Mary Fischer while teaching in California and they have two sons, Elliott and Jed. In 1969 the family move to Toronto due to Jim's dissatisfaction with the escalating trouble in Vietnam. The subjects of Big Jim's paintings are often depicted as subjugated and downtrodden, and it is not surprising that some of the bleak settings and poignant characters portrayed on Jim's canvas will later be inspiration for some of Harry's finest poems and songs.

Harry's maternal grandfather, Kenneth Duva Burke, 'KB' to all who know him, is a Renaissance man and a giant in literary circles. Born in Pittsburgh in 1897, his talents range from author and poet to philosopher and musician. In 1919 he marries Lily Batterham and has three daughters, Eleanor, Elspeth and Frances. He will later re-marry and have two sons, Michael and Anthony (Butch). Moving to Greenwich Village in the 1920s KB makes his first mark in the literary world as a critic for *Dial* magazine and receives their award for distinguished service to American literature. The $2,000 prize money, along with a loan from father-in-law Harry Batterham, helps him purchase 150 acres of land just outside the town of Andover, New Jersey, where he will build the family home. Among his many celebrated works on analytical reasoning are *Language as Symbolic Action* and *On Symbols and Society*.

The affectionately-dubbed 'compound' at Andover provides a summer retreat and gathering place for both families and their close friends. Elspeth takes this opportunity to work in New York City, leaving her four boys with Lily at Andover and then going out there herself at weekends. While there, they live in a shingled house with no running water, an outdoor privy, and a pump on the back porch. On the overgrown farmland is a spring-fed lake, a natural clay tennis court, woods and a rocky hill - ideal playgrounds for the energetic Chapin boys. It is also a spiritual awakening for the young brothers as they enjoy several months of soaking up the cultural environment of the

Burkes and their many friends and relations who regularly gather there. Although not wealthy, the Burkes foster a wealth of creativity for the boys, and Harry finds a special life-long friend in his young uncle, Michael Burke.

Big Jim and KB, two highly talented and cultured men, can both see in young Harry the potential for great things, and also a strong drive to achieve his ambitions. But what exactly his goals are, not even Harry is sure.

Elspeth remembers: *"My father, Kenneth Burke, was a literary critic and a writer. But Harry grew up where it was assumed that men were creative, and there was not an emphasis on making money or arriving in the business world or anything like that. It was completely foreign to us. You supported your family, but it wasn't what seems to be now the emphasis on expensive cars and all that. It was a whole different emphasis. Somehow the all-American theme seems different than it did when I was younger. It was about making something or creating something or discovering truths."*

(Mike Grayeb and Linda McCarty, *Circle*, Winter 2005)

The Trouble with Henry Hart

It is 1950 and America is at war once again. At the age of eight, a new disturbing dynamic enters Harry's life. After a couple of jobs, Elspeth is now working in the city as editorial secretary to Henry Gideon Hart IV, managing editor of the new *Films and Review* magazine. A native of Philadelphia, Hart's claim to fame is that his great-great-grandfather is John Hart, one of the signatories of the Declaration of Independence from New Jersey. A romance follows. Although much older than Jim, Elspeth sees in Hart a disciplinarian and strong believer in upholding firm family values, hence the ideal father-figure for her family. But the truth will turn out to be far from that.

Two years later they are married and Hart moves into the cramped Chapin home on West 11th Street. Right from the start he looks on her four boys as being unrefined, socially-unacceptable Bohemians, and he makes it his crusade to get them to see things his way, with what turns out to be a draconian regime that brings with it heavy-handed punishment for not toeing the line. If there is ever a time when the brothers need each other, it is now, and Hart's attitude toward them, and, indeed, to their mother as well, serves only to draw them closer together. Steve tries to stand up to him, but often backs down. Tom, despite now being over six feet tall, is more placid and keeps out of his way the best he can. James keeps a level head and uses psychology, finding a way of deflecting Hart's temper by pretending to engage with him in often meaningless debates. Harry, of course, turns out to be the rebellious one, and Hart sees in him the biggest threat to his authority. Harry is a boy who craves approval in what he does and will go out of his way to please people, but being unable to hide his inner feelings, his attitude betrays his utter dislike for his

16

stepfather, and the consequence of this is that he feels the brunt of any punishment that is dished out. For these young boys, it is becoming a question of survival beneath their own roof.

Elspeth recalls there is never any animosity between the brothers: *"(Harry) was not a person that liked to fight in any way. He liked to argue and discuss. That may have had something to do with being brought up by women because the boys only saw their father occasionally and my father was around but he was writing. They would shove each other occasionally, but they'd never punch each other in the nose. It wasn't something anybody did. It was not a way to treat each other. My father was a great talker. He'd talk your head off. So there was much discussion going on all the time."*

(Mike Grayeb and Linda McCarty, *Circle*, Winter 2005)

It is now 1954. Ike is in the White House and the Korean War is over. Harry is twelve years old, but mentally a child no longer. In a way his stepfather is succeeding. Harry has fire in his belly and a fighting spirit that will shape the rest of his life. For the first time he has a reason to hate something, stand his ground, and try and do something about it. If Harry had anything to thank Hart for, perhaps even more so than his grandparents, it is for instilling in him a powerful determination to do something with himself. To overcome any odds. To be a winner.

Brooklyn Heights and Grace Church

Later that year, Hart buys a $16,000 four-story brownstone across the river at 45A Hicks Street, in the fashionable Brooklyn Heights area. Their first child Henry Gideon Hart V (Jeb) is born there. Three years later another son, John Barnes Hart, will come along. Elspeth is caught up in the middle of the continuing confrontations, her love divided between the six boys and her demanding husband. Luckily for the Chapin brothers, their father Jim is living close by and when he's at home his house becomes a welcome refuge. Sometimes they get to see him perform with a band in the local jazz clubs, dressed to the nines, and taking it all very seriously, but most of all, having a whale of a time. And that is something that these impressionable boys remember the most. Another avenue of escape is when William Everson, a friend of Hart's and a regular visitor to the home, brings with him copies of old movies for the boys to watch, as well as getting Harry interested in reading classic novels, thereby planting seeds for his future writing skills.

In 1956 fourteen-year-old Harry follows older brother James and enrolls at Brooklyn Technical High School, where he becomes a model student, excelling in math and history, and gladly volunteering for everything that's on offer. It is while at high school that Harry is given the unfortunate nickname of 'Gapin' Chapin' on account of his loud and brash personality. While there, his relationship with James grows even stronger, and he continues to look to him for guidance. In the meantime, Elspeth has seen an ad in the local paper for choir boys wanted at the local Grace Episcopal Church and she persuades Tom and Steve to join. Among the choirboys already in attendance are Robert Lamm, later one of the founding members of the rock group Chicago, and also a young soprano soloist by the name of John Wallace, who is destined to play a large part in Harry's life. John, already a choirboy for some three years, is two years older than Tom and three years older than Steve, and although friendships are hard to develop with the age difference, they get along fine and seeds are sown for what will later grow into a much closer and long-lasting relationship.

Elspeth remembers the start of their musical careers:

"When I moved to Brooklyn with the kids, I met a woman who told me that her little boy was going to the Grace Church and singing in the choir there three afternoons a week. And I was trying to figure out, having moved to this new community with these boys who were six, eight, ten, something like that, where they could play and what they could do. I took Tom down there when he was about eight. He was outraged by it. It was run by a choir director, who was a woman named Mrs. (Ann) McKittrick. Tom started in the choir and then Stevie joined. Harry, at that point, was in junior high school and was going on the subway back to the Village and was occasionally in it. But they joined not for religious reasons. It started out with me trying to put them in a place that would be wholesome. Then they did shows and they were playing their instruments together, making a group. Harry wrote a couple of the shows and got involved. Once a year they had a choir show, and they were always raising money. Harry was probably a teenager then. Stevie stayed on in the church and played the organ and kept up with it quite a bit."

(Mike Grayeb and Linda McCarty, *Circle,* Winter 2005)

John Wallace reflects on his early relationship with the Chapins:

"We were all serious about the choir and singing.... Harry knew where he wanted to go. Harry looked up to Steve for musical things. Harry had drive and will, but Steve is more laid back. Harry was a true extrovert... Steve can be extroverted and sociable when he wants. Tom is more solitary than the others and more self-contained. Harry was sociable but goal-oriented and trying to do things to get himself along. When I was living in New Jersey and wanted Harry to hear a song, I'd drag him over to my house to listen to a record. After couple of seconds, he turned the TV on with the sound down, and when a commercial came on he would change the channel. You had to work to get his attention. He'd talk about going through life round-shouldered, avoiding things that would get in the way. But the choir was a big deal for all of us. Harry was around it and it was focal point for all of our lives."

(Linda McCarty, *Circle*, Winter 2004)

Music is in the Genes

As a young teenager in the late 50s, Harry is being swept away by the burgeoning folk music scene, which is looked upon as a conduit for artists, through their simplistic music and thought-provoking lyrics, to take a stance on social and political issues of the day. Harry of course is attracted to it like a moth to a flame, and he listens with growing interest to the likes of the Kingston Trio, The Weavers, Oscar Brand and Peter, Paul and Mary. Tom recalls:

"I was 12, Harry was 14 and Steve was 11 when we heard a recording called The Weavers at Carnegie Hall. We found a simpatico where music and social action lived. It's what drew us to Pete Seeger and Woody Guthrie. Music could be about something real and help make some things come true that we cared about."
(Bill Hornung, *Circle* Fall 2003)

Harry has the urge to become part of this exciting new culture and begins efforts to make it happen. He takes more music lessons, this time using an old Jos Ricketts banjo that had once belonged to their Grandma Abby's brother, Harry Forbes, and with the help of Pete Seeger's essential guitar book teaches himself how to play a basic Sears-Roebuck store-bought guitar given to the brothers by Michael Burke. With a strong right hand and calluses galore, he manages to strum a tune in no time at all, and as he often says himself, he will soon realize that girls like guitar players much more than those who toot trumpets. For Harry, his newfound love for music might help build bridges with his father Jim. And it certainly does.

Folk music has also gotten under the skin of Tom and Steve. With small amounts of money raised from odd jobs they collect what basic instruments they need. Tom moves away from the clarinet and obtains a $50 plywood Kay guitar. In the meantime, Steve switches from piano to 10-strung ukulele and later upright bass. To begin with, Harry and Tom go through the learning process and play together songs of the Weavers. But soon they persuade Steve to join them as a trio, with Harry usually taking lead vocal and Tom and Steve using their choirboy skills to hone their vocal harmonies. They also have between them a meaty collection of folk albums to take inspiration from. But Harry doesn't just listen to these recordings, he gets his head inside the sound, analyzing it piece by piece, slowing it down to pick out more clearly the relevant parts that he can identify with and then play himself. But as long as he can strum a guitar, and strum it well, that will be good enough for him. He doesn't aspire to be the next Duane Eddy. His voice will always be his main instrument. As Harry says it himself, *"Folk music, the ultimate social weapon, becomes my full-time passion."* But there's one brother whose career will take a different path. Although joining them occasionally as keyboard and bongo player, James decides to opt out of any future musical career to continue with his studies in American history and politics. In that he will become very successful.

With the focus now on a trio rather than a quartet, the remaining Chapin boys spend most of the summer months, both at home and at Andover, rehearsing together. Harry is now quite proficient with his banjo techniques, but despite all his hard work, Tom proves to be the better guitar player. However, it is Steve who is turning out to be an all-round musician and arranger. He has honed his keyboard and choral skills by being allowed to play on the huge organ in Grace Church, and he now can turn his talented hands to a variety of instruments. But it soon becomes apparent to them that Harry's role will eventually be center stage and leading from the front. And their older brother also has another string to his bow. He has already been taking part in poetry writing competitions with Michael Burke at Grandma Lily's house. Now he is writing songs as well…

The Chapin Brothers Begin to Perform

In May 1959, billing themselves as The Chapin Brothers, the trio appear in public for the very first time when they perform before an enthusiastic hometown audience at the Grace Church Choir Show, an annual benefit to send Brooklyn kids to summer camp. In three-part 'pubescent harmony' they sing three songs, two of which are the Weavers' 'Come, Little Donkey, Come' and Woody Guthrie's classic 'This Land is Your Land'. This is followed by short, open-mike performances at the soon-to-become-legendary Bitter End in Greenwich Village, which are received quite well by what, after all, are non-paying audiences, and even despite some embarrassing ad-libbing among the boys on stage. More church concerts follow, as well as being asked to perform for $20 fees at neighborhood parties and social dances. As Harry recalls: *"We started out following the style of The Weavers. Of course, our voices hadn't changed yet, so we sounded more like the Chipmunks."*

This is their apprenticeship and schooling in their chosen performing art, and their music and stage presence improve with every appearance. In return they receive the much-needed appreciation from those watching, whether paying or not. Generally, the feedback is positive. At last they are reaching out and making contact. In a later interview Harry recalls: *"That was a watershed. It made us realize that we could be something besides an imitation of the Kingston Trio."*

Jim Chapin recalls those early days: *"The boys started playing together at the beginning of the summer of '57. Up until that time they had all played their own separate instruments. Harry, trumpet, Tom, clarinet, Steve, piano. That year, however, their young uncle Mike Burke bought a Sears Roebuck guitar and suddenly the trend was on. Harry started on guitar and banjo, Tom on guitar, and Steve on tenor guitar. They all had experience in singing prior to this, as both Steve and Tom had been boy soprano choir soloists at Grace Church in Brooklyn, and Harry sung in various school functions in and around Brooklyn Heights. Their first public singing engagement was at the Grace Church Annual Benefit Show in May of 1959. As time passed Steve started playing string bass, their voices changed, and the group began to have a more robust sound than the original 'Chipmunks.' By 1960, they were professional enough to start performing at dances and parties as paid entertainment. The boys were 13, 15 and 17 years old."*

Harry is about to savor new experiences. For the last two summers he has spent his time helping Michael Burke in some construction work and, as a result, has gained what will be a fleeting interest in architecture. Now he will enjoy a totally new experience as Grandma Lily takes him on an eight-week tour of Europe (she had already taken James two years before), and their journey takes in the delights of Britain, Italy, France and Switzerland. It is Harry's first taste of a world outside of New York. Even rural Andover cannot match this. On his return he goes back to school, now even more eager to learn, and he finally graduates in January 1960.

College Days and the Air Force Academy

Over the next few months Harry's relationship with his stepfather deteriorates. With James the peacemaker now away from home on a full scholarship at Hamilton College in Clinton, New York, the tension reaches boiling point, and with Harry no longer a dependent, he moves out of the house and goes back across the river to live with Grandma Abby at 50 Morningside Drive near Columbia University. The first thing he has to do is find some kind of paid work, and his first job is as a runner at the New York Stock Exchange on Wall Street. However, Harry cannot see his academic skills going to waste, and having attained impressive results in both English and Math he receives a scholarship to Cornell University in Ithaca, New York, where he will study architecture. But, more or less at the same time, and with the help of one of Hart's contacts in Congress, favors are called and he is awarded a second scholarship by the US Air Force Academy in far-off Colorado Springs. Hart sees it as the best possible opportunity to instill some discipline into his unruly stepson. It is time for Harry to make his first big decision. The perceived glamour of flying a jet plane is just too much for him to resist, although it goes against advice given by some other members of his family. Kenneth Burke sees it as just a training ground for the escalating conflict in Vietnam, and, in his mind, Harry will soon be going off to war.

Assigned to the 42nd Cadet Training Squadron, Harry's starry-eyed visions are quickly dispelled with the rigorous training and 'hazing' - the verbal abuse from upperclassmen he has to endure, almost from the moment he steps off the bus. It is the kind of abuse that makes his stepfather's tirades seem trivial in comparison. No matter how hard he tries, he finds it hard to conform to what he sees as a mean and arbitrary use of power. Although friendships are made, he again suffers bouts of isolation, but by August 1960 the stern and soul-destroying training is over and he is eventually accepted into the Cadet Wing. But by now Harry has become disillusioned and wants out. Seeking advice from the base chaplain, he is told that it will be a bad mistake to turn his back on a military career. In fact, he tells Harry that he will never be an achiever (a comment that Harry will keep in his pocket for future reference). After just three months his request to leave is accepted, although his final two weeks are made a nightmare until he is finally back at the sanctuary of Andover. Harry will later make a reference to his Academy days in the song **'Changes'**.

Harry recalls that time: *"I went to the Air Force and took basic training there – thought I wanted to be a flyer and discovered after doing a little flying it was sort of like super bicycle – you know the first time you're on a two wheeler it's a real turn on but then after a while it gets rather ordinary. Then went through basic training and got uptight not so much about flying but I couldn't ignore the fact that I was preparing for something that I hoped wouldn't happen, which was war…"*

By September Harry is back living with Abby, who now manages to get him readmitted at Cornell just in time for the fall semester. His love of architecture is dampened by the tedious learning process, and once again he struggles to focus on his studies. He spends that Christmas with his mother and has a chance to reconcile his differences with his stepfather, still bitter over him quitting the Academy. But nothing has changed, and once again it results in flaring tempers and heated words. That night Harry leaves the house and Hart for good. They will not see each other again for twenty years.

Finding Film Work and First Love

During his first summer break at Cornell, Harry takes a job at the *New York Herald-Tribune*-sponsored Fresh Aid Fund Camp for underprivileged inner-city kids in the town of Fishkill, north of the city. His brother Tom is already working there as a counsellor. While there, Harry meets and starts courting Clare McIntyre, an attractive socialite from affluent Scarsdale who has studied music therapy at a college in Poughkeepsie, and who is now working the summer months as a counsellor at nearby Camp Hayden. She is the daughter of Malcolm MacIntyre, a lawyer and corporate executive who, at the time, heads Eastern Airlines. Although they are poles apart in many ways there is instant chemistry between them. Both forthright and competitive, energetic and outspoken, their differences create sparks at times, but they share their thoughts for the future, their dreams and ambitions - of Harry becoming a successful music performer; of Clare becoming an actress or singer. Even though Harry has no direction in life and no money to achieve those dreams, he believes he has found his dream girl. However, Clare's parents are not keen on the budding relationship, and, as Tom Chapin relates, her father views Harry as something of a "ne'er-do-well", and not worthy of his daughter's affections. Even when it comes to seeing each other in New York, while Harry and his brothers take the subway, Clare's father gives her money and insists she always uses a cab.

Returning to Cornell that fall, Harry finds a platform to indulge in his growing passion for music when he's invited to play banjo and guitar for a twelve-piece a capella college singing group called The Sherwoods, whose members include fellow students Fred Kewley, later to become Harry's close friend and manager, and Rob White, a talented artist who will become part of Harry's road crew and go on to provide illustrations for some of his early albums. Even though at this stage the group find Harry's musical ability acceptable, his usual unkempt and awkward appearance on stage will prove another matter. His final year at Cornell finds Harry once again feeling out of place, lonely and depressed, although he finds some escape in improving his musical skills and also hustling dollars out of other students in games of pool. Failing in architecture, Harry now switches his major to English, but come January 1962, with grades slipping away and a tendency to skip more classes for his music (something that Jim his father did as a student), he finds himself kicked out of school.

Once again back with Grandma Abby, Harry is at a loose end, with no decent job prospects on the horizon. But fate once again plays its part. A phone call to one of his uncles, Ricky Leacock, ex-husband of Elspeth's sister Eleanor, brings an opportunity that will make an indelible impact on Harry's life. British-born Leacock works at Drew Associates in New York City, a company that specializes in making hour-long television documentaries. By the mid-60s Leacock has already played a pivotal role in making some of the most innovative documentaries of the decade, and has been instrumental in developing and using lightweight portable equipment, which has opened the way for genuine independent filmmakers. Ricky continues to be a presence at Andover and gets to know Harry very well. He manages to hook him up with his colleague Robert Drew and his production company. Harry's first job is packing film crates for $75 a week. Although the pay is modest, he finds himself soaking up this newfound creative environment, and his energy and enthusiasm soon gets him noticed. He finds a friend and father-figure in film producer Jim Lipscomb, who takes Harry under his wing and teaches him all there is to know about the film-making process. Lipscomb is thoroughly impressed by Harry's potential, and sees his protégé "hitting all the doors" of different career opportunities, any one of which will readily be opened for him. Harry's tireless efforts earn him steady promotion and by the fall of that year he becomes an assistant film editor. His very first assignment is editing *Aga Khan*, a documentary about the former Iranian prince, Olympic skier, and now religious leader. But before long Harry finds this type of work becomes unsettling and tiresome. Once again, he loses focus and wants out.

At the advice of Clare's father, Harry is persuaded to leave his job at Drew and return to Cornell, and with a recommendation from his former employer, he now pursues a degree in philosophy. Harry's and Clare's relationship continues, and they spend most weekends together, bringing with it for Harry a surge in creativity. He writes more songs and poems, even one dedicated to her called **'Stars Tangled in Her Hair'**, but by the summer of 1963 their romance is over. Clare goes off to Europe, which, according to Harry, is probably her father's decision as a way to draw a line under her relationship with someone he sees as a loser. When she finally returns, she leaves once again to go to university in San Francisco. Even though Harry writes to her often and speaks with her on the phone, Clare eventually settles down and gets married. The song **'The Mayor of Candor Lied'** is inspired by this episode in his life.

'Stars Tangled' is often cited as one of the first songs Harry composed. The lyrics offer an insight into his mindset at the time, and, despite its simple naivety, it's a foretaste of some of the more heartfelt and lovelorn ballads that will follow. Harry recalls: *"That summer I met a girl – the first chick I ever got really involved with and wrote a song about her called 'Stars Tangled in Her Hair' which strange enough people still ask for, they really like it, a very romantic song. Still holds up. Couple of bad rhymes. So, I was off and writing..."*

Tom Chapin reflects on their relationship: *"I wouldn't call Clare the love of his life, but she was certainly an early, formative love."* Harry would probably agree, but first love never dies. His young heart is broken. Of all the disappointments, knock-backs, and might-have-beens that have made their mark on his early life, this one hurts the most. With Clare, he has lost his fiery soul mate, and it's through her support and guidance that he has taken giant steps toward adopting the persona he needs if he's going to succeed in life. Her legacy is that it will inspire him to write one of his greatest ever songs, a song that will ultimately make him famous.

Lily, Abby and Clare are three important women who in individual ways help to shape Harry's life from childhood to adulthood, and give him the drive and energy to make changes to achieve his goals. But he is yet to meet the woman who will change his life forever.

Harry Gets Serious About His Music

Harry reflects on this stage of his life: *"By the end of '63, I am in love and thinking I should give one more shot at finishing college. But my second attempt at Cornell, and my first attempt at a love affair follow the same pattern – pyrotechnic beginnings followed by gradual decline. Ironically this educational and emotional merry-go-round makes a fertile climate for my first songs. They fall into the usual categories for young prophets: protest songs and lugubrious ballads of unrequited love. It takes four terms to bust out this time."*

Back on the Cornell campus, Harry again runs into 21-year-old Fred Kewley of The Sherwoods, who despite issues in the past is now becoming impressed with Harry's musical improvements, and as a result invites him back into the group, although some of the other members still have their reservations. What impresses Fred about Harry is his ability not just to play a song to you, but to *sell* it to you, like the super salesman he is destined to become. Over the last few months Harry has added harmonica to his repertoire, as well as traveling up to Harlem to study blues guitar with the Reverend Gary Davis. With all this comes a new self-confidence that enables him to do six-night solo stints at Johnny's Big Red, a popular college bar and nightspot, where he even steps off stage to go around the tables asking for requests. While performing there, he has the opportunity to watch another resident singer called Peter Yarrow (of Peter, Paul & Mary fame), and takes note of how he manages to hook the audience with his stage presence, something which Harry will soon adopt to perfection.

Sometime in January 1964 Harry and his brothers, wherever they may be, listen to their transistor radios and hear for the first time the opening lines to a song asking everyone to gather round and see for themselves how the waters around them have grown. It is, of course, Bob Dylan's 'The Times They Are A-Changin'', and his prophetic call to arms for the youth of America. It is like a shot of adrenalin in the arm of the stagnating folk scene, and, for Harry in particular, it relights the spark inside him. As he listens to these incredible lyrics coming over the airwaves, he is no longer able to focus on his studies, and something has to give. The following month it is not hard to imagine Harry and his brothers sitting in front of the television watching Ed Sullivan and seeing four smartly-dressed boys from Liverpool single-handedly changing the music scene forevermore in front of an audience of wild, screaming teenage girls. These two seminal moments in music must have an indelible impression on Harry, Tom and Steve, and in no small way will serve as key moments in their musical development. For Harry, in particular, anticipating once again being dismissed from college, he decides to leave anyway in the spring of 1964, to devote all his energies to the thing he loves the best. Already he has ambition. In an unedited typing exercise from February 1964, Harry writes: *"Yeah, I sing with my next two younger brothers, and we are going to make a million dollars, or so we think..."*

Meanwhile Tom is still up at Plattsburgh State College and Steve is studying in his final year at Brooklyn Tech, but they too are seduced by this double wave of stark, thought-provoking lyrics and electric guitar-driven pop, and come the summer months the three brothers are once again in demand and playing at a variety of venues in lower Manhattan and beyond, including regular appearances at the popular Bitter End and Café Wha?. They have also appointed as their first manager Alan Roth, another member of The Sherwoods, who, like Kewley, has been impressed by the demo tapes they have sent to him. Although not all their performances go down well, on the whole the reception is still positive, and some nights they are given the chance to open for more established acts like Bill Cosby, Tom Paxton, and Jim, Jack and Joan (the Joan being comedian Joan Rivers). Harry and Tom often compete for the audience's attention and enjoy stirring up an audience reaction with their friendly banter. However, it is becoming evident that they are three brothers with three individual tastes in music. There will come a point where some common ground has to be sought, or solo careers could very well be the future.

The end of the summer sees Tom and Steve resuming their education, and Harry once again returns to Cornell, this time auditing classes. To counter more bouts of depression, he finds comfort in the company of James, who is also now at Cornell studying for his masters in history. When Harry returns there, he now has the older brother he always looks up to now looking out for him. James refers to their relationship as "symbiotic" - *"He was action, and I was reflection; he was energy, and I was balance."*

But James is not the only one he can turn to. Harry has met another girl on campus called Jenny Gillette, who serves as an emotional crutch to help him pull himself together again. Although it's a short-lived relationship, he is spiritually awakened and ready for his next challenge, although unable to offer her total commitment. Like Clare had done before, she inspires him to uncover a deeper seam of creativity. Harry will go on to write poems and songs with Jenny in mind, but at that point in time is unable to see a long-term future with her, or truly understand the deeper feelings she has for him. As a result, the relationship soon comes to an end, and eventually she moves south to start a new life with her Florida-based fiancé. In 1967, just two years after getting married, 24-year-old Jenny succumbs to cancer. Months later Harry returns to the campus and feels an acute sense of loneliness as he walks around the grounds. Their brief relationship inspires him to write three of his most poignant songs, **'Sometime, Somewhere Wife'**, **'Winter Song'** and **'Old College Avenue'**. Harry recalls: *"The story of my life is marked by the women who helped me. I owe a lot of the richness to certain people who cared a lot - cared about my dreams, I guess..."*

The next challenge for Harry is not long in coming, and at the beginning of 1965 his old Drew colleague Jim Lipscomb offers his protégé the job as editor on a new short documentary called *The Big Guy*, the story of Minnesota-born heavyweight boxing contender 'Big Jim' Beattie. The work is completed in a matter of five months, but Harry decides that with summer around the corner, it's back to his music. More welcome news arrives when he learns that, after a torrid ten years, his mother Elspeth has finally turned her back on Hart and moved out of the house and up the road to live at 136 Hicks Street. Once again it becomes Harry's home and sanctuary. Elspeth leaves *Films in Review* and starts work at the Polytechnic Institute of Brooklyn, where she also takes night classes and eventually earns a masters degree in the History of Science. With her degree she later gets a job at the American Institute of Physics.

Kewley and the First Tastes of Success

With a new spring in their step, and with their friend Fred Kewley now on board as self-styled manager, the Chapin Brothers hit the road with a freshness and new approach that keeps pace with the changing music scene. This is the time of the so-called British Invasion and folk music has been pushed into the shadows. Not only is an electric guitar and autoharp added to their instruments, but Fred also sees to it that their vocals become more prominent. Best of all, he has them buy a brand-new van to drive them around...

Another change for the brothers is that they are no longer performing as a trio. Fred sees there is a need to give their performance a stronger beat and a more rhythmic feel. In other words, they need a drummer, and of course they don't have to look far. On Fred's advice they recruit their father Jim. In a match made in heaven, Jim readily throws himself into the role, keeping time and keeping his sons out of trouble, despite having to get used to the slowed-down pace of some of the gentler folk songs. Jim Chapin recollects a conversation Tom once had: *"Let me tell you what Tom said one time. He was asked by somebody.... 'You have all these brilliant people in your family.... geniuses, painters, writers, professors. How come you and the rest of the boys decided to pursue music?' Tom responded 'Well, dad seemed to be having more fun than the rest of them'."*

(Bill Horning, *Circle* Summer 2005)

The summer of 1965 brings a new experience for the Chapins, when, through Grandad Jim's contacts, they get the chance to appear on television. On August 4th they are invited on the prestigious *Merv Griffin Show*, a syndicated 45-minute television chat show that has musical guests. A fascinating glimpse of their performance is still out there on the internet, with all three brothers playing guitar (Steve on electric) and singing a live version of their **'Gotta Get a Daddy'**, a humorous jibe at their father's past errant ways, the same man who just happens to be sitting in the background, nonchalantly tapping away with his sticks. I'd like to think the song has his approval. Their profile is raised even further with a second appearance on October 19th. On October 14th and 21st the Chapins travel up to Canada to perform on singer Oscar Brand's CTV show *Let's Sing Out*, which broadcasts folk music from various college campuses, and also features as a regular guest a young singer called Joni Anderson, from Saskatoon, who will shortly change her name to Joni Mitchell. But despite this welcomed publicity, the brothers are still relatively unknown outside of the Big Apple.

The stage is now set for the next chapter in Harry's life. With an astute de-facto manager in Fred Kewley now on board, and with Jim's welcomed experience, the brothers can now offer their ever-growing and appreciative audiences a more professional stage performance with an enhanced sound and an expanded setlist of songs written by all three brothers.

The road to success is getting shorter day by day…

Band of Brothers

"We resolve to become full-time professionals. It's the summer of airborne dreams, potentials and performances, and yes, it felt like somehow, somewhere, sometime, we were going to make it."

Irv Kratka Senses an Opportunity

It is 1965 and Greenwich Village, just across the river from Brooklyn Heights, has changed with the British Invasion. What Harry and his brothers had once seen as a home from home has since lost some of its exuberance and vitality. Even Dylan has gone electric. Their whole act and type of music is in danger of becoming dead in the water and swallowed up by this tidal wave of rock music that kids are falling over themselves to listen to. But the brothers persevere, and, with more and more finely tuned and professional performances, are still holding on to their audiences. Harry recalls: *"I'm beginning to realize that I am not going to progress through life following the normal pattern. My brothers and I decide to get serious about our music. All the guitar playing that has been a crutch to our social lives, that had made us a couple of bucks on the side, that has given us something to do besides drinking beer on street corners, now is put to the test. We resolve to become full-time professionals. It's the summer of airborne dreams, potentials and performances, and yes, it felt like somehow, somewhere, sometime, we were going to make it."*

Fred Kewley has now moved into the Chapin house to enable him to give the brothers his full-time attention. Jim is still doing appearances in their half-hour acts, but when not available a steady replacement is found in Phil Forbes, another ex-choirboy from the Grace Church days. Embracing his long-overdue role as the caring father, Jim continues to offer his boys some tips on performance techniques and keeping faith in what they are doing. This naturally gives the brothers the urge to consider the next logical step in their careers – to record their music. With their television appearances seemingly dried up for now, and their summer performances beginning to wind down, they believe that they have sufficient experience and enough suitable material to record an album. But who to approach?

They have heard whispers that there have been some record company agents watching them perform during the summer, possibly even one from the giant Capitol Records, but their chance finally comes in a meeting with Irv Kratka, a fellow drummer and friend of Jim's. His claim to fame has been his earlier innovation, in which the sound of certain instruments is removed from a recording, to allow listeners to play their chosen instrument along with the recorded sound. The idea will later develop into a worldwide phenomenon, and Kratka's name will go down in the annals of music history as the 'Godfather of Karaoke.' Kratka owns Music Minus One, a tiny New York record company, whose novelty sing-along and play-along records will soon capture the market in a big way, but he also nurtures an ambition to be a record producer. He sees the Chapins as giving him that opportunity.

Things look quite promising for both artists and would-be producer, but the escalating conflict in Vietnam now threatens to turn the brothers' world upside down. It comes in the shape of draft papers. To defer their service, Tom and Steve elect to go back to college, but Harry's low college grades have made that impossible, and his stint in the US Air Force has already labelled him a veteran, to be called up for training as a reserve. Fortunately for him, a mix up with files results in him being given an honorable discharge. Their manager Kewley is not so lucky.

Elspeth recalls her fears about her boys being drafted: *"That was an enormous concern, and I moved Heaven and earth to keep the boys from going. We insisted they go and finish up college or something. I believed in college and felt that teenage boys should go to college. We were always news junkies who knew what was going on. People say they never listen to the news or read the papers. We read the New York Times. We knew about French Indochina and that we shouldn't have been over there. The whole family got together on that one, the Vietnam War."*

September 1965, and the brothers, along with Jim, meet with Kratka at his office and sign up to make their debut album. The label will be called Rock-Land Records, and all agree that the album will be titled ***Chapin Music!*** It is of course a folk album, recorded in less than a couple of hours in a studio so bare-boned that it has just two microphones that Kratka has patched together. But after all, Kratka is indulging himself in what is his tentative first step in the production business. Fortunately, he has Steve on hand to help with the arrangements, a skill that will eventually see him become a fine producer in his own right. Jerry Newman sits in as engineer. Tom sees the whole experience as something of a blur, remembering that it was just a case of standing in front of the microphone and replicating their live set, one song after another, and then moving on without any more extra dubbing necessary. Of the fourteen songs that are finally chosen (many arranged by Steve), two are written by Tom, four by Steve, and the remainder by Harry. As usual the vocals are shared between the three of them. Despite what the publicity photos indicate, Harry plays acoustic guitar and banjo, Tom acoustic and electric guitar, and Steve on organ and bass. With Jim out of town much of the time, the drumming on the album is mainly down to Phil Forbes.

***Chapin Music! ***
Rock-Land RR-66
Recorded: Music Minus One Studio, New York City Sept 1965
US Release date: Dec 1966
Producer – Irv Kratka
Engineer – Jerry Newman

Side 1: Baby Let Me Walk With You 2.40 (Tom) **, The Rains Come Down 3.05 (Steve) ***, When Do You Find Time to Breathe 3.40 (Harry) **, Someone Keeps Calling My Name 2.53 (Harry) ***, Thinking of Tonight 2.45 (Steve) ***, Ground Hog 2.20 (Harry) *, Foolish Games 2.25 (Steve) *

Side 2: Another Man 2.35 (Steve) ***, Stars Tangled (Harry) 3.05 ***, Come Back Strong 2.50 (Tom) ***. Blood Water 2.45 (Harry) **, Going, Going, Gone 2.48 (Harry) **. Let Me Down Easy 2.48 (Harry) ***, On the Road 3.05 (Harry) *

Despite the production difficulties, some of the songs do have a certain innocent charm. Tom's opener, **'Baby Let Me Walk With You'**, sounds similar to The Animals' 1964 hit 'Baby Can I Take You Home'; while Harry's **'Blood Water'**, a true story of student suicides from the Cornell days, not only showcases his banjo skills, but sets the tone with its spoken introduction, a precursor to what will become a trademark at his future concerts. The smooth Harry-penned ballad **'Let Me Down Easy'** shows the hidden crooner in Steve, while Steve's own **'Thinking of Tonight'** is embellished with sound effects. Harry's main contributions have been a staple part of the group's stage act for some time. **'Someone Keeps Calling My Name'** (later to be re-written for one of his solo albums and dedicated to his children) is an early showcase for their polished harmonies, while **'Stars Tangled'** is his old love letter to one-time girlfriend Clare, minus the first verse.

Tom gives his first impressions of the album: *"An album! After four years of writing and singing and thinking about it. We didn't want to do a quick taping and pressing. We waited for someone who understood what we were about. And we all knew it had to come. And now, finally, a concretion. Chapin Music is no longer just the three of us, a fleeting concert at Vassar College, or two sets a night at The Bitter End. Now there is this solid, plastic disc. In its grooves there is a lot of Chapin. Fourteen songs' worth of feeling. On it are the first two songs I ever wrote. They are always going to be sitting on this record, waiting to be played by anyone. Sorta pleasant as I think of it."*

Steve, sounding like the consummate music arranger he will become, also gives his views: *"It's going to be good to step back and listen to this record in a month or two. Right now, I am much too close to it. I keep hearing too little bass on this track, too much guitar on that, but all in all I have to admit*

31

it is pretty close to what we wanted when we started. (Of course, I do wish that Harry sounded a little less like a dirty old man on **'When Do You Find Time To Breathe'** *and there are a few places I would have liked to have used more of Tom's wild wails, but we've got other songs and other albums to go). I am glad we did get a wide variety of Chapin Music down. From my* **'Thinking of Tonight'**, *to Harry's* **'Blood Water'**, *to Tom's* **'Baby Let Me Walk With You'**, *is a pretty good indication of how far we reach. I hope so."*

And, finally, it's Harry's turn, in a philosophical style that already sets him apart from his two brothers: *"There is something in the singing of other poet's songs that only warm my mind when I'm alone. With no one close around, I search inside of other's words, and can rest in knowing something that they knew. But when you are gathered near, I do not speak another's words (they should do that telling, and gain your gathered answer). It is then that I make melodies of my own; (half our conversation), asking at your face and eyes, and listening for your voice in answer."*

Jim recalls his time playing with his sons: *"The best thing about the early days was when they asked me to play with them during the summer of '65. We just had a ball. Fred Kewley was manager at the time. Fred did very well in the beginning, but over time he didn't do as much managing as Harry did. But Fred did a good thing by keeping the peace — the boys had artistic differences. Stevie was the perfectionist; Tom was the best instrumentalist of the bunch and Harry wanted to put everything on right now. It would drive Stevie crazy."*

(Bill Hornung, *Circle*, Summer 2005)

Harry, Tom and Steve have experienced and enjoyed their first venture into recording their music, as basic as it is. They don't expect their album to threaten the charts, but time will tell how their hard work will be received by the music press at large. It will take over a year before its official release, so in the meantime they carry on performing. The following week they perform a concert at Hawkins' Hall in Tom's college at Plattsburgh, with their dad Jim coming on at the end of the first song to a standing ovation. Two days after the concert, the brothers are due in New York to audition for a new television show called *The Monkees*. With Steve taking the bus home, Jim, Harry and Tom drive back in Jim's Studebaker, with his drum kit on the roof and guitars in the back. Midway, Jim asks Harry to take over the driving (he has a learner's permit by now) and while on the highway a right tire bursts and the car rolls over twice. Harry breaks the steering wheel with his jaw, but Jim suffers a broken neck and damage to his spine that will leave him walking with a permanent stoop. It is a sad time for the family. Despite the traumatic experience the boys meet up with Steve in New York to do the audition at NBC's office. Despite finding out that Harry's guitar is broken due to the accident, they do their stuff, but despite showing some interest in Tom, it all comes to nothing. Somewhere out there lurk four young guys called Mike,

Mickey, Peter and Davy. As it transpires, these Monkees will go on to become a worldwide phenomenon.

The following year two songs from *Chapin Music!* are released as singles on the Rock-Land label: **'Come Back Strong'** backed with **'On the Road'** (RR-661), is followed by a promo single **'When Do You Find Time To Breathe'**, coupled with **'Someone Is Calling My Name'** (RR-663). Neither are successful, nor is **'The Chapins With Will Jordan and Friends: Old Time Movies'** (RR-664), a promotional record for Esquire Socks in cooperation with *Hullabaloo* magazine and featuring comedian Jordan, the famous Ed Sullivan-impersonator.

Los Angeles and More Film Work

With his brothers back at college, Harry now has time to concentrate more on his poetry and verse, and there is no better place for trying them out to an audience than at the home of Manny and Janet Castro, long-time friends of the Chapin family who live in nearby Remsen Street, and who enjoy hosting outdoor parties for friends and neighbors at which the boys often perform their songs.

Around this time 23-year-old Harry decides to try his hand as a guitar teacher as a way of earning some extra dollars, and he places an ad in the *Brooklyn Heights Press*. But while waiting for replies another job offer comes in from Jim Lipscomb at Drew and he begins another stint working freelance at the film company. While there, the boss at Drew suggests to celebrated photojournalist Cal Bernstein, currently in town looking for new filmmakers, that Harry will be an ideal choice as both writer and editor. Although Lipscomb disapproves, Harry accepts the offer and that September makes his first trip to Los Angeles, where he will spend the next six months working on what are just two airline commercials. Even though it is mundane work, it comes with an impressive salary of $250 a week. During that time Harry finds escape from the inevitable boredom by writing more poetry and songs, and even does some solo performances around the LA club scene, where he finds on the whole that the West Coast music fraternity just doesn't find him and his songs hip enough.

By the February of 1966 a depressed and disillusioned Harry bids farewell to the City of Angels, acquires a used car, and drives the 3,000 miles back home to New York. With the help of a new girlfriend, Harry now tries to get a book of his poetry published, but has it rejected. Another girl in his life at this time is an old friend called Gail Hollenburg, niece of the Castro family, whose house is now looked on by him as a home from home. Gail is now a single mother of a baby girl, having been married and divorced in the year since last seeing Harry, and their relationship now will be the inspiration for one of Harry's most sensitive and moving songs, **'And the Baby Never Cries'**. For Harry, relationships with girls have taken on a different perspective. Old flames Clare and Jenny have both left him heartbroken, and in order not to be hurt like that again, he becomes insensitive and hides his feelings beneath his brash persona. But in an instant that will now change forever.

Harry Finds His Dream Lover

While he has been away on the West Coast, Harry has forgotten all about his ad for guitar lessons, and when he gets back home his mother gives him the number of a lady who has shown an interest. Her name is Sandra (Sandy) Cashmore (nee Gaston), a married mother of three young children, who happens to be living just a few blocks away in a brownstone apartment at 14 Monroe Place. Six months after making her enquiry, she gets a call from Harry. Sandy is eight years older than Harry, a Bay State-born attractive and well-educated woman, who radiates class and has a keen sensitivity and a passion for arts and crafts. But she is also living an isolated life in a loveless marriage of seven years to Jim Cashmore, a controlling and detached alcoholic. What love she has is focused on her children - one-year-old Jason, three-year-old Jonathan, and five-year-old daughter Sarah James (Jaime). The one thing missing from her life, apart from a loving husband, is music. For her $10 lessons Sandy wants to be able to share those great American folk songs with her three children, and although already able to pick out songs on the piano, having taken lessons for five years, she feels that having her back to them at the keyboard won't have the effect she has in mind. Sandy then asks a friend in Brooklyn Heights who has connections with some music organizations to recommend a guitar teacher, and this woman just happens to be a friend and neighbor of the Chapins. She gives Sandy their number but, when she calls, Elspeth tells her that Harry is out in California and may be there for a while. Leaving her number, Sandy then tries a couple of other suggestions before eventually giving up on the idea.

So, six months later, when Harry makes the short walk to Sandy's apartment and they meet for the first time, it seems to her that her feeling of isolation is coming to an end. Teaching chords, singing to each other, and even reciting each other's poetry (Sandy being a closet poet herself), inevitably leads to a closeness that serves as a remedy for the loneliness they both suffer, and all this takes place while her husband Jim is often playing poker with his friends in the basement. Sandy recalls how this young, lean, and clean-shaven burst of energy sat there long after the allotted hour to play to her some of the songs he had written until she almost had to tell him it's time for him to leave. Meeting one another becomes a logistical challenge for them. Harry has his apartment in Brooklyn and Sandy, with divorce now on the horizon, moves into a rental beach house in Point Lookout, Long Island, from Memorial Day through Labor Day, where Jim comes down from the city to spend weekends with the family. Her three children are at school and she will shortly be studying at Columbia while holding down two part-time jobs, one as a secretary at the local community church and the other sewing sample dresses for a shop in New York City. At $12 for a finished dress, it just about covers babysitting and the gas to go and meet Harry.

Sandy sees in Harry everything that her husband is not, and, as time goes by, they are longing for each other's company. At first, she looks on his energetic and investigative mind as a stepladder to encourage her to be the same. While she waits for the right time to bring the sham of her marriage to an end, Harry remains patient. He knows in Sandy he has found someone very special. Once again, this whole episode will inspire another one of his more intimate vignettes in **'I Wanna Learn a Love Song'**.

By the spring of 1966 Harry is still on the lookout for regular work and has replied to an ad in the *New York Times* for a film editor, placed by a company called Big Fights Inc. He meets up with boss Bill Cayton and is offered the job, and for the next two years he works on the writing, producing and editing of a series of 45-minute documentaries called *Great Fights of the Century*, rehashing old footage of classic boxing bouts, as well as working on some 200 five-minute boxing 'knockout' films. Although he works closely with celebrated athlete Jim Jacobs, the 'Babe Ruth of handball', who, along with Bill, co-owns the archive of boxing footage, Harry finds the whole process once again routine and doing nothing to stir his creative juices. Here he is in this sterile, uninspiring nine-to-five job just staring at a screen. He needs a centre stage role, like the celluloid fighters he is being forced to watch eight hours a day. Like them, he craves the drama, emotion, and the raw energy that makes them winners and adored by a paying public. If only he could have the spotlight shining down on him. That's not his dream; it's his ambition, and he knows now he has the wherewithal to achieve it.

Toward the end of the summer Harry and Sandy are being drawn ever closer to one another. Somehow Harry gets her number at Point Lookout and makes occasional calls. In the meantime, Sandy has signed up for six weeks of poetry sessions at the YMHA in Manhattan, and when she tells Harry, he says "Sign me up. I'll pay you later." So begins their first kind of "dating." If Sandy is looking for a more meaningful life, she certainly finds it when she meets Harry's extended family of artists, poets, writers and musicians. While she begins divorce proceedings that fall, and despite any trepidations she may have, this shy, introvert woman, who herself has little money and an uncertain future, is finding herself falling in love with this outlandishly extrovert singer who appears to have neither money nor a future. There is a time when Sandy thinks that it isn't going to work, feeling she has to take care of her children

35

first and be more responsible, but on the verge of breaking up Harry presents her with a song he has written for her called **'It's You, Girl'**. There's something about this man that just melts her heart. Here is someone who never takes no for an answer and usually gets what he wants; the consummate pitchman.

Early the following year Sandy is divorced and she has enough money to buy a little house at Point Lookout on Long Island. Harry's love for her now generates in him a creative energy unparalleled until now. He writes more and more fluently, turning his feelings into poems, and poems into songs. His experiences in the film industry now give him a more cinematic approach to his writing, and his editing skills a more disciplined way to structure his work, deleting and swapping around words and phrases as he does so well with film shots. The end result is a whole spate of wonderfully crafted and atmospheric story songs that will come to define his musical career.

Legendary Champions and Ethiopia

While Harry and Sandy ponder over their future together, Harry finds himself back in the celluloid boxing ring when approached by Bill Cayton to write and direct a full-length documentary about the history of world heavyweight championship fights. It is to be a trilogy of films entitled *The Legendary Champions*, but once again Harry's heart isn't in the work and production runs way over schedule. As a result, only one of the three films is actually completed, covering the years from 1882 to 1929. Harry does however manage to persuade Bill to allow his brother Steve to compose the soundtrack and, along with Tom and his father, to record the music. By the beginning of 1968 the film is complete and opens at Kips Bay Theater in New York in October. Narrated by Thomas Rose, it is wonderful slice of nostalgia and a fitting tribute to some of boxing's earlier heroes, with clips of the fighters both in and out of the ring. From a technical point of view, Harry's innovative editing techniques of seamlessly mixing color clips with the grainy and faded black and white images, and cleverly interspersing them with darting shots of some of the era's most iconic celebrities, is well received by the critics. As a result, the documentary is nominated for an Academy Award in the category of Best Documentary Feature, although losing out to *Journey Into Self* at the following year's ceremony. It does, however, win first prize at both the New York and Atlanta Film Festivals.

As a much-needed break from what has become an energy-sapping job, Harry finds solace with his brothers, and at weekends he and Steve travel by bus all the way up to Plattsburgh College, where Tom is in his final year of studying, and they perform with him in a band called The Beautiful People, which Tom and Steve have put together. Harry finds himself filling in playing a very basic bass guitar. All this traveling to and from Plattsburgh by bus inspires Harry to write a song called **'Greyhound'**.

Turning his back for good on boxing films, Harry now finds himself editing short films with his old friend Jim Lipscomb, including a short film about controversial Alabama Governor and Presidential wannabe George Wallace, who a few years later will survive an assassination attempt. Harry then receives an invitation to travel with Jim to Ethiopia as his assistant to make a special documentary for World Bank, a global organization set up to help poorer nations develop their economy and fight poverty through sustainable sources. With Sandy's encouragement he leaps at the chance and spends the next month driving and flying across the fascinating land of contrasts. It will be Harry's first exposure to the grim reality of widespread hunger and starving children.

During the visit Jim and Harry even have a meeting with Emperor Haile Selassie and Harry recalls the experience in a letter home: *"Jim was sweating like a shower as he usually does when he is nervous, and our minds boggled when the gentleman leading us into the throne room bent down and kissed the floor. What to do? I didn't feel like a floor kisser! Just at about the time when a hard-eyed Emperor was coming towards us we heard the private secretary whisper, 'Bow your heads!' We did with relief, and old Haile barely nodded as we went by out of the room to leave us to our technical manipulations."*

In 1974 Harry and Sandy will spend a week in Haiti, where they visit the Albert Schweitzer Hospital and see the effects of hunger at its most extreme. Both these experiences will have an indelible impact on the rest of Harry's life.

Returning home from Ethiopia, Harry finally leaves his Brooklyn apartment and moves in with Sandy and they begin wedding preparations, but to his dismay he finds he has been replaced as bass player in his brothers' band, which is now being acknowledged as a creditable rock 'n' roll outfit. For Harry it is time to reevaluate his adult life. With both marriage and fatherhood around the corner, he feels he has enough creative talent to achieve success on his own. He has been writing songs for the last couple of years and has an idea to put them into a romantic musical which he will call *Buraka*, a mixture of Bermuda and Jamaica, and set in the Caribbean. The next three versions are set in the ghetto of New York, and another two "inside a guy's mind." After all versions are rejected, Harry will eventually give the project up, but the seeds are sown for what in seven years' time will become a relativity successful Broadway musical, giving new life to many of those songs. It will be called *The Night That Made America Famous*. But by then, Harry will already have achieved his success and become famous too.

In March 1968 James becomes the first of the Chapin brothers to marry when he weds Diana Derby, who later goes on to hold many prominent government posts in New York City. With James as best man and Steve playing organ, Harry and Sandy are married at Grace Church on November 26th 1968. He is soon to become a house-husband for a while when Sandy enrolls at Columbia University Graduate School to gain her PhD in aesthetic education, and he spends his time looking after the children while unsuccessfully trying to complete *Buraka*. With the acclaim heaped on him following the success of *Legendary Champions*, Harry is now much sought-after by the film industry as a writer, editor and even director, and his earnings are becoming substantial. Some of the money he makes goes to help subsidize the publishing of his father's prized books on jazz drumming techniques. Any rifts between father and son have long been mended.

The Chapins, Without Harry

In 1969, Steve, having married his girlfriend Ann Brown that January, finishes college and gets back together with Tom to form a new folk-rock band called The Chapins, with Phil Forbes on drums and his friend Doug Walker on electric guitar. Although not actually asked to perform with the band, Harry agrees to offer advice and to help write new songs, and with Steve putting the finishing touch to some of Harry's compositions, he gives the band a new dimension. In time they become the talk of the local clubs, particularly The Bitter End, where they soon earn their place as the resident house band and are managed by club owner Paul Colby. For Harry, the new band will become an ideal testing ground to see how his new songs are received, and as a result he begins writing new material at an unprecedented rate. Colby has the credentials and connections to get them a record deal, and with recorded demo tapes of their music sent out to various record companies, they eventually sign up (along with Harry as songwriter) with Epic Records, a subsidiary of Columbia. Their first two singles are **'Greyhound'** and **'Lady of the Highway'**, both written by Harry, but neither song manages to impress the studio executives and they fail to get released. Even though the main man at the record company likes the material, and despite never having seen them perform, he doesn't see Tom having the kind of personality to make an impact as the band's frontman. He even suggests that they team up with the more established Simon Sisters (Carly and Lucy) to become a new group called The Brothers and Sisters, but that too gets a negative response. Just as well; whatever becomes of Carly Simon?

Harry agrees with Colby that there is a problem with the band. Tom is finding it too hard trying to become hip and keep up with the changing times. What's more, their 'new' sound isn't that much different from the days of the Chapin Brothers. Harry is now able to see just how the music business operates and has a better awareness of what it requires to be successful artists. He looks at his brothers' band and sees it lacks both unity and identity - the essential dynamics that hook an audience like bands such as the Beatles or the Rolling Stones have achieved. There is also a dearth of their own material and too much reliance on Harry's songs, the melodies of which fit their image, but not so much his storyboard lyrics. As a result, many of Harry's new songs are rejected by the band, and they even refuse to sing again ones previously performed. They look on Harry as an overbearing coach rather than a musical adviser. Things go from bad to worse by the spring of 1970. Although continuing to perform at The Bitter End, Colby gradually loses faith in the band and fails to put greater efforts into promoting them, as any good manager should. Inevitably their relationship starts to deteriorate.

Meanwhile Harry also suffers another knock back when a screenplay he has written about his brother, called *Thomas Forbes Chapin and the Cold, Cold World*, fails to gain interest. Despite the prestige heaped on him since his Oscar nomination, he finds there are no film offers coming his way, and once more he is out of work. To earn some extra cash, he does some more freelance work for Jim at Drew, editing and co-producing a documentary for an ALCOA Hour special about sailing called *Duel in the Wind: In Defense of America's Cup*. He also writes and edits short films for Time-Life such as *Woodstock Nation*, *Cutting Loose*, *Oil Strike* and *The Deadly Road*, and begins editing and writing music for a Peter Gimbel Cinema Center Film Documentary called *Blue Water, White Death*. Harry still believes his film career is not taking off as he envisaged, and decides to take a six month break from work to concentrate more on his music projects, and gets more involved in community projects in and around Point Lookout. This includes Sandy volunteering him to work as literature director for Democrat politician Allard (Al) Lowenstein, who at the time is running for re-election for US Representative. A close friend of Donald Rumsfeld and closely aligned with Eugene McCarthy, he later raises his profile by spearheading the 'Dump Nixon' campaign, before being murdered by a deranged gunman ten years later.

Sandy recalls Harry's search for work: *"He had been working in film. That was how he made his living. Harry's plan at the time was to make enough money in 5 or 6 months that he would not have to work for 5 or 6 months, and during which time he would write screenplays, and he was going to write everything. He was going to have the Emmy and the Tony and an Oscar and a Grammy and so forth. He was going to write the Great American Novel, he had a lot of plans for writing... He needed a job, he wanted to still to be able to write, so he applied for a cab license. And I was something like 8 months pregnant. I felt very positive about it, because I thought, wow, it would be a great experience, because people in cabs will tell him stories, and he'll get all kinds of characters for songs. I think he was feeling pretty low about it..."*

Harry Considers a Solo Career

On March 21st 1971 Harry becomes a father for the first time when Sandy gives birth to a baby girl, Jennifer Elspeth. Later in the year, about the same time he reads about ex-girlfriend Clare's marriage in the newspaper, Harry applies for a hack license to drive cabs, but just days before reporting for his first 12-hour shift, several film offers suddenly come his way. Despite stories to the contrary, he never does become a New York cabbie. But with taxis and his time spent with Clare now firmly in his consciousness, the seeds of a song that will make him famous have well and truly just been sown.

Harry recalls those days: *"Last fall the bottom fell out of the film business and I started hustling my ass around, writing some film scripts and went and got myself a cab license in case it came down to it and the day I was supposed to start driving 3 film jobs came through, so I went back into films while the boys rented out the Village Gate for the summer. And when I finished the film, June 1st, I had nothing to do for the summer plus enough bread to get through and I decided to stick my neck out and try this idea out I'd been thinking about for about a year..."*

So Harry seriously considers becoming a solo singer. His family and friends who listen to him sing are all supportive, but after being thrown out of his brothers' band, he feels he must overcome a lot of voices who doubt his trajectory.

He first tries it out at The Bitter End but this turns out to be a dismal failure. Sandy is there supporting him and puts it all down to his appearance and his habit of lumbering around the stage in a clumsy fashion. Even Tom, never one to hold things back, calls the performance "lousy." Around this time Harry and Tom go to see rising star Kris Kristofferson perform at The Bitter End, his very first concert in the city. The opening act is Carly Simon, herself on the cusp of stardom. During the show Kris introduces two more up and coming artists by the names of Steve Goodman and John Prine, both soon to get their own record contracts. But when Kris does his own set, he performs his songs sitting center stage on a stool and introducing each one with a little story. The audience is transfixed, and so is Harry. Tom recalls: *"That night, I really feel like (Harry) sort of figured he could do this..."* Harry returns to the club after a couple of days and successfully tries it out. The audience seem engrossed in his songs, even the less mellow ones. Harry makes a decision there and then. He doesn't need his brothers to perform his songs. He has found the secret of how to succeed on his own.

Forming the Band

It is now the summer of 1971. With Harry thinking he will be working again with his brothers, he and Sandy rent out the property at Point Lookout for $3,000 from July 4th through to Labor Day, and move with the children to Andover. Out of the blue one day, Fred Kewley gets a call from Tom Chapin asking him, "Do you want to manage us?" The Chapins have just been released from their contract with Colby at Epic and they see in Fred the right man for the job. Fred readily agrees, later admitting it's one of the best decisions of his career. On June 29th, to get their careers relaunched, with the money earned from renting out the Point Lookout property Harry gets Fred to rent the downstairs room at the popular Village Gate club at 160 Bleecker Street in Greenwich Village for $400 a week for a period of five weeks, with the understanding that he is to supply more or less everything himself - advertising, tickets, sound system and drinks.

They are given the 10pm slot that follows the resident show *Jacques Brel Is Alive and Well and Living in Paris*. Fred also wants an opening act, and Harry suggests to him and the band that he can fill the spot. With the money he has just earned in the film industry, Harry plans to put together his own band of accomplished musicians - bass and electric guitarists, and surprisingly, introducing a cellist to offer a mellow counterpoint to what is after all his increasingly rasping voice. He probably gets the idea of a cello from listening to James Taylor's album *Sweet Baby James*. As Harry relates in a later interview at the Gate: *"I remembered an old thought that if you take a less than beautiful voice and add a beautiful cello, it frees the voice to do something else."* In his head it all sounds a good idea. No one in his brothers' band seems opposed to Harry's suggestion and Fred agrees to offer him the gig. Despite not drawing up any contract, Fred agrees with Harry's suggestion that if in the meantime he gets a record deal, he will split the money five ways.

Three weeks before opening night Harry places an ad in the *Village Voice* newsweekly for a cellist and a guitar player. In the meantime, he looks around for a talented bass player and calls on an old acquaintance, John Wallace, the ex-Grace Church choirboy and friend of the Castro family. Born in Utica, New York, in 1943, and raised in Brooklyn, Wallace has often played bass guitar along with the Chapin brothers at the Castros' parties, and since his choirboy days has been noted for his incredible five-octave-range voice. Harry hasn't seen Big John for seven years, but somehow gets his number and gives him a call. Now 27 years old, Wallace is a divorcee, and after living in Florida for a number of years is now back in New York working as a truck driver. He readily takes up Harry's offer of $10 a week, a five-way money split, and free lodging at Harry's mother's house. Big John recalls: *"It was kind of a no-brainer. It wasn't like my life was going so great anywhere else. I was married and my son - the oldest - was born in the spring of '71. It was pretty much around the same time. I was living in an apartment in Orange, New Jersey doing this trucking thing. It was just a pretty grimy kind of depressing life at the time."*

Next come the auditions for the other musicians, which are all held at Elspeth's house. Of the four cellists Harry chooses 21-year-old local musician Tim Scott. Tim is on the verge of going to City College when his actress-mother sees the ad in the paper that reads something like "Cellist wanted for singer-songwriter folk-rock group - Opening at prestigious Village club, six weeks." Although trained as a classical cellist he is enthusiastic about the chance to perform popular music with a real band.

For electric guitarist Harry takes on 36-year-old unemployed Ron Palmer from Syracuse. Ron has been playing one night a week in a local bar, the manager of which happens to be a friend of Fred Kewley's, and Ron sends a demo tape to Fred, which Fred then plays over the phone to Harry. Harry likes what he hears and offers him the job. Despite finding it hard to believe that Harry can't get hold of a guitarist in the city, Ron jumps at the chance, and as an out-of-towner, Harry offers him $20 a week, twice as much as the other band members, as well as lodging at Elspeth's home.

The Village Gate

The new band meet for the first time at Fred Kewley's New York office in Port Chester on June 22nd, just one week before their Village Gate debut. Of course, there are a number of issues. It becomes apparent that this odd-ball set of musicians are adequate at best; nothing really exceptional with their playing abilities. They are apprehensive about what's expected of them. Although Tim Scott is a good player, he cannot improvise, so Harry and Fred have to arrange the cello parts for him, as well as Fred having to arrange background vocals. At least Wallace and Palmer have good voices. As a result, Harry, with Fred's help, selects a setlist of eight of Harry's songs that the band will feel comfortable with. They are: **'Could You Leave a Light On Please'**; **'Dogtown'**; **'(And) The Baby Never Cries'**; **'Any Old Kind of Day'**; **'Greyhound'**; **'Sandy'**; **'Sometime, Somewhere Wife'**, and **'Everybody's Lonely'**. Harry also has a new song called **'Taxi'**, which is still a work in progress.

In less than a week the quartet conduct frantic rehearsals in a loft at Fred's office, scribbling down the parts for guitar, cello and vocals, and structuring each song to fit around the musicians' strengths and limitations. John Wallace recalls that first meeting:

"The band's first rehearsal was June 22, 1971 in Fred Kewley's office in Port Chester, New York (Kewley was Harry's manager). Harry hired Ron over the phone, and I hadn't met any of them before. We had only a week to

get ready and learn seven songs, including 'The Baby Never Cries' and 'Could You Put Your Light On, Please?' but we managed to do it. But I wasn't really a player at that point. It was tough for me. I had bought a used Fender six months before in a pawn shop. I had comprehension of it and wanted to play bass but had not been playing long at all. I was just learning notes and strings. It was not a fun time with the high pressure. We had to learn the songs, and I was not confident starting at ground zero."

(Linda McCarty, *Circle* Winter 2004)

On Tuesday, June 29th 1971, Harry's new band, calling themselves simply Harry to avoid any confusion with his brothers' outfit, make their debut at the Village Gate. Outside of the club Fred has had posters printed, craftily advertising the Chapins as *"The Best Band I've Seen This Year - Rock Magazine."* But there are no posters advertising Harry's band. They have half an hour to set up their equipment, and get the room ready. Friends and family are there to help, including taking the $2.50 tickets at the door. To work the lights, they have the help of Harry's stepbrother Jebbie Hart and ex-Sherwoods member Rob White. Fred, Tom and Steve have invited all their family and friends. Sandy too is there, along with Elspeth, KB, and Jim Lipscomb. Altogether there are some fifty people there, including a few persuaded to come in off the street to watch.

By 10pm the stage is set and the lights go down…

The Big Break

"I'm coming to you! I'm coming to the first people who believed in me.
Let's make Music!"

Harry Sings Gorgeous Ballads

The audience's reaction at the Village Gate is hard to judge. In a room that holds 225 seats, only a quarter are taken, and most of them are friends and family members, who, as expected, are doing their very best to appear over-enthusiastic in case there's someone in the audience who has record company connections. Over the next few weeks there are some nights when performers outnumber the audience, while some weekends the room is half filled. But Harry toughs it out, and even on bad nights, with unresponsive audiences, he takes on a different persona to gain their attention. Sometimes it works, but there are times it falls flat. But the regulars in the audience can see for themselves a growing confidence in the performances, particularly with the musicians. As for the songs themselves, their performance of **'Dogtown'** is the litmus test for the audience's reaction, as its structure and lyrical content serves as a fitting insight into Harry's emerging story-song makeup. If there are concert reviewers out there in the audience, they will pay particular attention to this song, which stands out in marked contrast to the rest of the set, with its controversial taboo subject, something that maybe even the keener listeners don't realize at the time. But it's a more theatrical, atmospheric approach and thought-provoking songs that Harry now focuses on to set his band apart from The Chapins. And it starts to work. As the weeks go by the crowds get larger, especially at weekends, and many come just to watch Harry's band and leave before The Chapins even come on stage. That must be a bitter pill to swallow for his two brothers.

Meanwhile Harry and his friends are trying their best to get the music press to come and watch them perform. It's not until July 22nd that Michael Jahn, the *New York Times'* first full-time rock journalist, announces he will be coming to see them perform that night. All the stops are pulled out to make the best possible impression. Family and friends are asked to greet each song with wild applause and finish each one with standing ovations. It works to some extent, but, like most critics, Jahn cannot be fooled. He's seen all this played out before. Dismissing the crowd's reaction, he focuses on the performance and is well and truly captivated by what he sees and hears. Two days later Jahn writes a glowing review on page 16 of the *Times*, fortuitously the same page on which the day's headline news of an airline hi-jacking is carried over, thereby making it even more noticeable: 'Harry Chapin Sings

Gorgeous Ballads'. In the short review Jahn is curious about how the songs switch from being charming to downright weird, especially **'Dogtown'**, but he is really impressed with songs like **'And the Baby Never Cries'** and **'Could You Put a Light On, Please'**. He refers to the whole set as being polished soft-folk and makes a point of saying how well Harry writes and sings. At last Harry and his band have had their first critical review, and a positive one at that, and now they have to milk it for all it's worth. Dozens of copies of the review are made and sent out to various record companies, followed by a rigorous charm offensive that involves calling companies direct and getting put through to anyone who sounds important. Harry often masquerades as manager Kewley, going out of his way to sing the praises of this "fantastic new act" that record companies are "queuing up to sign", and how it would be an "awful shame" if they missed out. Even though this is doubling the efforts to get results, there are times when he gets caught out, especially when Harry's voice is recognized from previous meetings with his brothers.

Harry recalls: *"We started using that to call record companies and it's absolutely impossible to get record companies off their ass I suddenly realized, especially in NY – if you were in Australia and they heard something about this wild new group they'd come and find you – but in NY and you have to take a taxi down to Greenwich Village you might as well forget it. Anything that close."*

Another positive article entitled 'Saga of a Brooklyn Heights Rock Group' appears in the *New York Times* on July 25th, profiling the band's background. With sheer hard work Harry's destiny is becoming fulfilled. Apart from his talent as an artist, which grows daily, he has the grit, determination and persuasive powers to make things happen behind the scenes. With Fred Kewley now focusing his own efforts on just Harry's band, the two of them make a formidable force. One is a laid-back, shrewd ideas-man, while the other is a tornado of manipulation and out-and-out scheming. They both can see success on the horizon, but Harry wants it now, and has his own ideas of getting it:

"I had figured out the worst thing about performing is, you do a great show some night – it was gone, you'd created something that was real but you had nothing left after, and that's when I decided it was OK. Write a book, you got that, make a film, you got that – but create magic in a room and it ain't there. ...Tom put together a group and they got a record deal with Epic, and it got terribly frustrating for me especially since I began writing more and more music and some of the things they wanted to do were different from some of the things I was writing and Stevie - the group is a little more rock orientated than I am. I'm more sorry - you know emotional. I'm involved with emotions."

45

Ann Purtill is Seduced by Harry's Music

But it doesn't come without help, and this arrives in the shape of a young woman called Ann Purtill, formerly a music staff writer at *Vogue* magazine and now a recent addition to Elektra Records' band of talent scouts. On seeing Harry perform for the first time to a packed house, like Jahn, she is seduced by his music. For her the whole performance has not been just a crowd-pleasing show; it has been a total dynamic "experience." Like always, the show opens with the lights turned out and Harry sitting centre stage singing the mellow **'Could You Put Your Light On, Please'**. Then the lights are on and the full band appear to continue the performance. To see an unrecorded artist who hasn't even got a contract do such polished, professional songs is truly mind-blowing, and to make it even more impressive Harry chooses this night to close the show with a debut performance of **'Taxi'**. The timing could not have been better. After the show Ann introduces herself to Harry and asks for a demo tape, although she admits to him that her label has enough artists already signed up. Ann knows that what she has just witnessed is something unique, but needs to convince herself that the performance isn't just a one-night sensation. Unbeknown to Harry, she goes back to see him three more times, and each time she is even more impressed. This guy is surely one of a kind.

In August Harry and The Chapins receive another positive review of their Village Gate performances, in a local paper: *"Separately or on a double bill, the Chapins show a singular talent. It's a talent which is reflected in their music and voices. It's a talent which reflects the individuality of each member of the group. Yet it is a talent which was developed in a uniquely gifted family."*

Sadly, all this sudden adoration for Harry's band has a detrimental effect on The Chapins, who are in danger of fading away into obscurity. At the end of the five week stint at the Village Gate, Tom and Steve feel that their profile remains as it was before, and with Fred Kewley now shifting his focus away from them, they depart on a short tour across the country to promote a single just released by Epic and sent out to various radio stations across the country. Produced by Rob Galbraith, it consists of two of Harry's songs, **'Working on My Life'** and **'The Only Thing (You Ever Really Have to Do Is Die)'**. How many stations play it will never be known, but it bombs. Giving the brothers a second chance, Epic release a follow up single, this time with two songs written by Steve, **'Hard Workin' Man'** coupled with **'You Deliver Me'**, but they too prove to be dead ducks. With the writing on the wall, Tom and Steve decide to break up the band.

While the brothers are touring, Harry has booked the Village Gate for a further five weeks, but now as the leading act billed as Harry Chapin, with various local bands providing the opening set. Steve Chapin recalls Harry *"going on a roll right after that, with record and booking offers. At first, he was terrible and then he was wonderful. He had found a way of self-expression and a marriage of personality and material."*

Make a Wish

Around this time TV producer Lester Cooper is looking for a host for a new half-hour children's show called *Make A Wish*, which is due to be aired Sunday mornings on ABC, replacing *Discovery*, a similar series for children. He has in mind someone with a warm, wholesome personality who can easily relate to young viewers and be able to write songs and perform them on the shows. The shows will have a different theme each week, with related songs, animations and on-location filming. On the day that The Chapins contract with manager Paul Colby expires, Colby tells Tom about the show and he goes for an audition. After a rigorous interview and screen test Cooper is unsure about him, but after passing on Oscar Brand and being turned down by John Denver and James Taylor, he comes back to Tom and offers him the job, not knowing that he will have Harry on board writing all the songs for him. Harry even re-writes part of the theme song composed by Bernie Green, but takes no credit for it. The show is first aired on September 12th 1971 and runs for five years. Many of Harry's songs have one-word titles such as **'Horse'**, **'Star'**, **'Fish'**, and **'Ball'**. One song called **'Circle'** will later become Harry's theme song and closing number in many of his concerts. Over the five years Harry is paid to write 160 songs for the show, with many given to Tom to learn just a few hours before a live recording session at the New York studios. The quick-cutting, stream-of-consciousness causes Tom Chapin years later to describe *Make a Wish* as *"a show for six-year-old speed freaks."*

Sandy also contributes to the songs for *Make a Wish*. While Harry is on the road doing the small clubs with his band, she comes up with ideas for songs and writes them down as free-verse poetry. Harry then teaches her the art of songwriting - rhyming lines, breaks, chorus, etc - and as a result she is able to write many songs for *Make a Wish*, and goes on to co-write with Harry some songs that will become classics. The series goes on to win a Peabody Award for Best Children's Series in 1971 and an Emmy award in 1975.

The Bidding War Begins

Meanwhile, despite the interest shown by staffer Ann Purtill of Elektra, Harry plays his first card with Vanguard Records, where he knows Dave Wilkes, an old friend and former manager of The Bitter End club, but they are non-committal about signing an artist whose avant-garde songs have had mixed reviews. They offer Harry a solo singles deal akin to what Epic had given The Chapins, but he turns it down. Although the giants in the game such as RCA, Atlantic and Capitol have shown a little interest in him, Harry dismisses them for now and turns his attention to Elektra. They have been around for just over twenty years, founded by Jac Holzman and Paul Rickolt in a college room for a joint investment of $300 each. Concentrating on folk music, the label has released albums by the likes of Oscar Brand, Judy Collins, Tom Paxton and Phil Ochs, all artists that Harry admires. But 40-year-old Holzman is a visionary and by the mid-60s had seized on the new wave of folk-rock and psychedelic rock with signings such as Love, Paul Butterfield's Blues Band and The Doors.

Just a year ago Holzman had sold Elektra for $10 million to what will become Warner Communications, but he elects to stay on as president of the label. He has recently signed Carly Simon and David Gates, two artists currently having success in the single and album charts. Harry sees Holzman and his reputation as a visionary as being the ideal home for his music. But now he has to convince him. The first step is to make a demo, and acting on Ann Purtill's advice, he decides to record some of his best work, which can then be sent out to various record companies, including Elektra. At a cost of some $2,000 he takes the band up to Media Sound Studios on West 57th Street to record a demo tape of seven songs: **'Could You Put Your Light On Please'**, **'Greyhound'**, **'Sandy'**, **'And the Baby Never Cries'**, **'Any Old Kind of Day'**, **'Dogtown'** and the just-completed **'Taxi'**.

It's now toward the end of August, and with the tapes sent out, it's back to performing. At the end of one of these shows Harry again meets up with a still-enthusiastic Ann and presents her with a copy of the demo tape she has promised to take back to her boss. With the knowledge that other labels are now getting keen to snap him up, she hastily sends a memo to Holzman. In it, she heaps praise on the musicianship, particularly the inclusion of a cello, as well as the performance as a whole, but criticizes what she describes as Harry's tendency to use a grating voice for effect, and also the unnecessary length of some of the songs. But these are trivial complaints. She sees him as a premier artist, likens him to James Taylor, and concludes with her recommendation: *"I really think he can be very, very major, and that he shouldn't slip by us because too many are pending. I will be heartbroken, of course, if you pass on him, but I'll feel better knowing you've seen and heard him."*

Holzman, who is as busy as he always is flying around the world, is not immediately sold on the idea, but while in New York a few weeks later, he takes the opportunity to go and see Harry perform at the Gate with his new advertising and publicity head, Bruce Harris. Still not having heard the demo tape, neither are impressed by what they see. Ann persuades Holzman to go and see him again, but still he remains unconvinced. Nevertheless, her bulldog tenacity eventually wears her boss down and he tells her to contact Harry and manager Kewley with an offer of a $3,500 advance.

In the meantime, the record giant Columbia have entered the frame. Their A&R man Paul Leka has already seen Harry perform at the Gate and listened to his demo tape. He also likes what he sees and sends a memo to company head Clive Davis suggesting he goes to see for himself Harry perform. On October 21st Davis and his entourage do just that and agree that Harry has something special. The astute Fred Kewley has also invited Ann along from Elektra so she can see the opposition sitting there, and maybe persuade her label to raise their offer. That same night Davis meets with Harry after the show and offers him a $5,000 advance. Ann gives Holzman the impression that Harry is still keen to sign with Elektra, and he comes back with what he insists is a final counter-offer of $7,500, which is more than double what he has given Carly Simon. Nothing can be decided just yet, as both record label bosses now go away on business trips. While hanging on for a better contract, Harry and his band can now only afford to rent the Village Gate a week at a time, and then only when there is a representative from a record company expected to be in attendance. They do however manage to earn a meagre $600 with performances up at colleges in Yonkers, New York, and Bennington, Vermont.

While on his business trip on the West Coast, Holzman has a chance to listen to Harry's demo tape in his car, and straight away is impressed with it. Maybe the sterile sound of a studio recording resonates better than the sound that comes through the inferior loud speakers at the Gate. Whatever it is, he is hooked, even seduced by the whole thing, especially **'Taxi'**, which for him is by far the standout track, despite its length. Back in New York a few days later, Holzman informs Ann Purtill that he is now desperate to steal him from under the noses of his competitors, and raises his final offer to an impressive $15,000. Harry, of course, is over the moon, and on November 4th, the same day his run at the Gate comes to an end after thirteen weeks and some eighty or so concerts, he finally meets with Holzman face to face and verbally agrees to the contract with a firm handshake.

Holzman wants to act fast and plans are set in place for Harry to choose a dozen or so songs for an album which will be recorded up at Elektra's studio at 1855 Broadway. In the meantime, the contract papers will be drawn up for him to sign within a week. Ann is in Boston while all this is happening, and when she returns a day or two later she finds on her office desk a tape and handwritten note from Harry that simply says: *"I'm coming to you! I'm coming to the first people who believed in me. Let's Make Music!"* She is beside herself with excitement. All her dogged determination and persuasive efforts to get her boss to stand by her intuition about Harry have paid off, but when she tries to get hold of him to give her congratulations he cannot be found, or worse, will not pick up her call. There's something wrong here. She smells a rat, and, deep down inside, suspects it's a Columbia rat. Her intuition is spot on. Fred has done no more than phone Davis at Columbia to tell him about the offer received by Elektra, but as yet no contract has been signed. Davis immediately doubles Holzman's offer to $30,000. Harry is now in a quandary. He wants to go with Elektra, but Columbia have the money and the biggest stars in the business. They even have Dylan. What will he do?

Before a decision is made, Ann has finally contacted Harry and Fred at the Burke home in Andover. She calls Holzman and through her he arranges for them to meet him at Kennedy Airport, where he is due to fly out to Los Angeles. Face to face, he makes them a further offer of $25,000 and leaves it to them to sleep on it and get back with an answer.

Now the bidding war between Holzman and Davis, two of the most powerful men in the industry, seriously takes off. As before, Fred phones Davis about the new offer, which Harry considers close enough to sway his decision to go with the company they prefer. But Davis is tenacious and now offers $50,000. After another call from Fred, Holzman reacts with an offer of $40,000. Not to be outbid, Davis's final offer is a staggering $80,000, a figure he thinks they simply can't refuse, and Harry tells Holzman just that. Is Harry being shameless, relentless? Not at all, he is learning to be an astute businessman.

Jac Holzman Gets His Man

The Elektra president is not about to give up the chase and the next morning flies back to New York and goes straight to Sandy's house. Harry is there. Holzman admits he cannot match Columbia's offer, but he puts his cards on the table and offers what he considers an unprecedented, once-in-a-lifetime deal, with a commitment to personally supervise and produce the recording of his album, and channel all resources into making it a success. Jac says he is not leaving until a deal has been struck. Harry is won over by the business proposition and by midday he agrees to go with Elektra. It turns out to be the biggest ever contract for a new artist in the history of the label:

A ten-album deal over five years
$40,000 advance
$20,000 advance on the second album
$25,000 advance on the third album
$5000 increases on each six subsequent albums
Free studio time at Elektra's facilities (an estimated initial saving of $25,000 per album)
No other album to be distributed by Elektra during the first month following release date of his album

Full promotional effort to be given the album for the first month following release date.

Harry's right to terminate the contract six months after release of his second album.

This is indeed an unprecedented step in the music business. No artist is ever given free studio time. Even Davis at Columbia admits that Holzman's generous deal is unbeatable in what it has to offer their brash new signing. Even though Holzman never ups the deal, only matching it in terms of the front money, his creative genius with the other clauses in the contract eventually help to get his man. Caught up in the wake of all this, of course, there is Ann Purtill, understandably feeling aggrieved and bitter over Harry reneging on his handshake agreement with Holzman. But she soon realizes handshakes mean very little in the music business. Harry may not realize it, but he has lost perhaps his most stalwart and loyal supporter, and, despite him going on to apologize and give her credit on almost every future album, it will take many years for her to forgive him, if she ever does. Harry sums up these incredible last few months: *"The funniest thing about this summer is I have been having ideas. It's the first time that the timing of something I've come up with seems to have come at the right time and it's been absolutely incredible summer in that way."*

On November 18th 1971 Harry signs the contract with Elektra in Holzman's New York office, and gets to meet some of the invited main players in the music industry. They are all impressed by what they hear, and all have big expectations from this singer, approaching 30, who Holzman has gone out on a limb to sign up. Sandy sees the signing as Holzman's swansong, the last artist he is going to get while with Elektra, and that can only be good for Harry's career. But will he be able to deliver? In an interview the following year, Harry relates: *"We were beating on record company doors, making phone calls, and sending our reviews to all the companies. We just bombarded the bastards, and since there was more than one outfit competing for us, it was fun to watch the dollars soar and the presidents' egos get involved. I tried to approach the problem of getting a contract as hard-headedly as possible. It depends upon talent, of course, but other than that it's pure logistics."*

As for the recording of the album, Holzman decides it will not take place in New York after all, but out on the West Coast, and a week or two after signing the contract has Harry and the band, along with Fred Kewley and all their families, board the company's Lear Jet and head off for Los Angeles to begin making the debut album. It will be called ***Heads and Tales***.

Harry no longer has both feet on the ground. He is well and truly flying high...

Heads and Tales

"I'm always sticking my neck out, sometimes making an ass of myself - a fact of life you have to accept if you're going to be a performer. But occasionally it works out for me, this seems to be one of those times"

Los Angeles, January 1972

Jac Holzman's faith in Harry has brought him to Studio A at Elektra Sound Recorders at 962 La Cienega Boulevard, a sixteen-track state-of-the-art facility that has all the latest technology that money can buy. This is where just eleven months before The Doors had recorded their *Morrison Hotel* album. Harry is thinking of his early days spent there in the film industry. He remembers his time with Clare. As well as **'Taxi'**, he will have her in mind for another song to be included in the new album. Harry could not be more impressed, and although Holzman himself has never set foot in the LA studio before and has no idea of how to use the equipment, he is quick to learn, and has on board to handle the technical stuff sound engineer Bruce Morgan, son of Hite Morgan, famous for being the Beach Boys' first producer. Harry's band are equally impressed by the set-up, having never seen anything like it before, and Harry himself cannot help but compare it with Kratka's makeshift studio in New York. With Holzman doing his best to look and act the part of producer, much of the hard work is done by Harry and Fred Kewley, but before long even Holzman is getting more involved, and no one there wants to burst his ego.

In a November interview with Jerry Gilbert in the British *Sounds* magazine, Harry gives a wry explanation to his rapid rise to success, saying that this is the first time an idea of his has worked out just fine, and that the reason he signed for Elektra in the first place is not due to money, but due to Jac Holzman's personal commitment.

Due to the length of several songs, they agree on a nine-track album, with **'Taxi'** easily being earmarked as the standout song and pencilled in to be the theme for the album's cover illustration, which will be designed by the talented New Jersey-born artist Robert L Heimall, who has already worked on albums by The Doors and Carly Simon. The band have no trouble with the sessions, as they have been playing most of the songs for months. Steve Chapin is also on hand to play piano, while drums are in the capable hands of the experienced session musician Russ Kunkel, who has already contributed on soon-to-be-iconic albums such as James Taylor's *Sweet Baby James* and Carole King's *Tapestry*. John Wallace sees how Kunkel helps to bring a sense of calm, a professionalism that holds everything together in the studio. But for

John it also seems that with everything he plays it's like being under a microscope, being scrutinized; he's therefore apprehensive about making mistakes in the studio. Tim Scott is also impressed by the professionalism of Kunkel, and particularly that of Holzman, and recalls how he personally engineers the song **'Same Sad Singer'** in the middle of the night, having him lay down three tracks of the cello. Within three weeks, with overdubs completed, **_Heads and Tales_** (often misspelt in articles and reviews as _Heads and Tails_) is ready to go.

The opening track will be the mellow **'Could You Put Your Light On, Please'**, the song that often opens their live concerts, and this will lead into the lengthy **'Greyhound'**, two songs poles apart in structure and style, before side one rounds off with three of Harry's more melancholy songs. Side two will have just four tracks. The much-anticipated **'Taxi'** is selected as the lead track, followed by the beautiful **'Any Old Kind Of Day'**, a gentle song in stark contrast to what follows. Despite having reservations, the controversial **'Dogtown'** will no doubt get the critics' tongues wagging like the dogs' tails, and before they try to unravel the meaning behind the lyric, **'Same Sad Singer'**, another heartfelt ballad and a last-minute addition, brings the album gently to a close. Surprisingly there is no place for the poignant ballads **'And the Baby Never Cries'** and **'Sandy'**.

In a promotional ad for the album Holzman writes: _Harry is a storyteller and if I may coin a word, an evocateur. His songs, in which **'Taxi'** is a superb example, are a marvelous unity of memorable melody and finely wrought lyrics. Harry's album, which we are now completing, will be ready to ship February 15. He is a major discovery and we expect him to have the same kind of initial public impact as did Carly Simon. Harry's album marks my return to the studio as a producer._

Heads and Tales (1972) *****
Elektra EKS 75042
Recorded & mixed: Studio A, Elektra Sound Recorders, LA Dec 1971-Jan 1972
US Release Date: March 11th 1972
Producer – Jac Holzman
Engineer – Bruce Morgan

Could You Put Your Light On, Please ***
When Harry was a guest on Tom Snyder's _Tomorrow_ show, this song was played as an intro from a commercial break. Harry explains that the title comes from his wife one night in 1971 as they are about to go to sleep. She turns to him and asks him to put the light on, and he does, and writes a song from that one line the next day. It is Harry's attempt to prove he can write more than just story songs, and thoughts of unfulfilled dreams and lost love echo strongly

in the lyrics. Wistful and introspective, it is the epitome of a break-up song and well-chosen to be the opening track on the album as it is also the opening song in live concerts, often sung in complete darkness before the band join him on stage. The song is one of the seven chosen to be on the demo tape sent to Elektra in late 1971, but unlike the demo tape the album version begins with the chorus. In a review for *Rolling Stone*, Ben Gerson, although critical of the *"risky"* story songs on the album, describes this evocative song as being *"contemporary rockabilly"* and likens it to contemporary songwriters such as B J Thomas and Joe South. The following month, Ann Tan of *Words and Music* is impressed by the song's subtle key changes and with *"rocking spirited rhythm"* that contrasts sharply with its heartfelt lyrics; while *Sounds*'s Penny Valentine describes it as simply being *"gently painful."* Whether listened to with the lights on or off, this is hauntingly beautiful.

Greyhound ****

One of Harry's earliest story songs, written in the summer of 1969, primarily for his brothers' band The Chapins. Although recorded as their debut single by Epic Records it is never released. It is later included in the demo tape Harry sends to Elektra prior to signing with them. It is inspired by the numerous journeys he makes with the eponymous bus company to see his brothers and girlfriends around the various college campuses. This is not the first time Greyhound has figured in a lyric, as previously it has been namechecked in songs like The Drifters' 'On Broadway' and Chuck Berry's 'Promised Land'. In the latter, Berry's journey through the South ends when *"Halfway across Alabam' and that 'hound broke down and left us all stranded in downtown Birmingham."* Harry also resurrects the name in **'Bluesman'** in 1977.

In Harry's song it's past midnight when the narrator boards a Greyhound bus for what for us is an unknown destination. He just needs to get away from where he is without a thought or care for where he's going to. Of course, the bus is late; maybe Harry's subtle dig at past experiences of an erratic schedule:

It's midnight at the depot
And I drag my bags in line.
Travelin' light, I got to go
But the bus won't be on time.
Everybody's looking half alive.
Later on the bus arrives.

They punch my ticket I find a seat
And we move out past the lights.
Come on Driver, where's the heat?
It's cold out in the night.

I keep telling to myself that I don't care.
Come tomorrow, I'll be there.

In the four-line chorus that follows Harry soon dispels any ideas the bus company may have of cashing in on the song:

Take the Greyhound.
It's a dog of a way to get around.
Take the Greyhound.
It's a dog gone easy way to get you down.

During this cold overnight journey, he is physically and mentally restless:

Tired of watching this night go by
So I look across the aisle.
The window's frosted, I can't sleep
But the girl returns my smile.
She reminds me of someone I knew back home.
So I doze. So it goes.

But he doesn't sleep for long. The bus pulls in at a rest stop; a change of scenery for the narrator, but nothing really changes:

I'm wrinkled on my stool at the rest stop.
The waitress being cozy with the highway cop.
My coffee's tasting tired.
My eyes roll over dead.
Got to go outside and get the gas out of my head.
Oh, to be in bed.

He's now back on the bus, the exhilarating pace of the music urging it along to its destination. Unable to sleep, his mind is restless and his thoughts become more anxious as the music - a driving drumbeat and jangling banjo - reaches a crescendo. Maybe this journey is just one that's taking him from one dead-end town to another; from one depressing and lonely slice of life on to the next:

You got me driving.
I'm on your Greyhound bus and you're driving.
But there's nothing new about Greyhounds.
Nothing new about feeling down.

Nothing new about putting off
Or putting myself on.

Looking to tomorrow is the way the loser hides
I should have realized by now that all my life's a ride.
It's time to find some happy times and make myself some friends
I know there ain't no rainbows waiting when this journey ends.

Suddenly all is calm, and as the narrator reaches his destination, he also reaches a conclusion that the journey itself is better than reaching the final goal.

Stepping off this dirty bus, first time I understood
It's got to be the going not the getting there that's good
That's a thought for keeping if I could
It's got to be the going not the getting there that's good

In an interview about the song in October 1975 Harry explains its meaning: *"I feel that life is not a goal, it's a process so many people get confused about. It's a physiological fact that psychologists say that man can adapt to any new situation within 72 hours and that's what makes him an incredible animal. Have you ever been on vacation for a week and by the end of that week it seems like you've spent your whole life there, and then when you come home you say, 'Where's this strange place' and you adapt back to it. Well if life was just a goal, think that whenever you arrive at a goal, within 72 hours it becomes the normality, so in a sense what you've got to do is illuminate your life by the methodology of what you're doing, the method and in the ways you do it rather than the actual places you're going..."*

Ben Gerson of *Rolling Stone*, no fan of Harry's long story songs, comments that they are the worst kind of song, and that songs like **'Greyhound'** and **'Taxi'** lack both structure and an incomplete resolution. Alan Bradley, another reviewer, applauds Harry's mockery of the bus company, but points out that it shouldn't take over five minutes to express what he thinks of the journey. Allegedly, the Greyhound Company catches on to the tagline at the end of the song, and approaches Harry for permission to use it for an ad slogan, but soon change their mind when they see in what context it is being used. But the song does nothing to damage reputations. Greyhound buses, along with baseball, apple pie, and hot dogs, still conjure up visions of what Harry himself would see as a country that is still holding on to its dream.

From the cheap seats:

Hank Naisby - *It's summed up in the line, "it's gotta be the goin', not the getting' there that's good." Life hands us lots of issues. We need to enjoy the ride no matter what is dished out.*

Ernie Zahrn - *Having spent 48 hours on a Greyhound getting home for Christmas 1968, I immediately identified with this song immediately. From boredom to leg cramps, it was a Dog of a Way to get around! Spend another day of my leave finding a flight back to Fort Huachuca Arizona. Thanks to my parents for buying my ticket with money they needed for other things.*

Everybody's Lonely ****

Another of Harry's songs originally written for The Chapins, reflecting the angst of human existence, and, for Harry, the isolation suffered throughout his childhood and teenage years, of love lost and found. Maybe it's about ex-girlfriends Clare or Jenny. But in the song, he knows now what to do with his life and has it all figured out. Ron Palmer's guitar provides a short but exquisite bridge and the chorus, equally short, is truly outstanding, with the melody and Harry's vocal elevating what originally appears to be a simple singalong lyric. The song is later re-written by Harry for his musical ***Somethin's Brewin' in Gainesville***, later re-launched as ***Cotton Patch Gospel*** in 1981. Re-titled '**One More Tomorrow**' it is one of the show's many highlights. This song, and the two that follow it, is why Harry is so essential to me. Take away the hard-hitting, soul-searching, and thought-provoking story songs that will soon become his trademark, you tend to forget his gift of writing such melancholy and emotive songs such as these. These are coming straight from a heart that's being worn on the proverbial sleeve.

Sometime, Somewhere Wife ***

Written in the winter of 1971, with Harry now married and deeply in love with Sandy, but it's all about ex-girlfriend Jenny. The narrator is reminiscing over the break-up of a long relationship, one that could have led to marriage if he had only asked this girl who loves him. It seems he will never be able to shake off from his mind the might-have-beens of past relationships. The song even ends with the repeated line, *"I've got to find her..."*

Empty ***

Another song about one of Harry's failed relationships with a girl he took for granted and now regrets she has gone. This may have been written before he meets Sandy, but of course we are still left to guess who it's about. Not as poignant as the previous track which shares the same subject, it does have a sublime, almost indiscernible counter-vocal heard towards the end, with the line, *"Guess I gotta be like the circus man, swallow the knife as well as I can."*

Taxi ***

Just another simple tale of loneliness, but arguably Harry's greatest song. This sad ballad, about a former couple with deferred dreams meeting by chance in a taxi cab, is one of his most cinematic compositions. Completed by the spring of 1971, just in time for its debut at the Village Gate, 'Taxi' is nothing more than his paean to his first love, Clare MacIntyre. Having just read in the paper of her marriage to a rich businessman, he writes about how they might meet again by chance. In Harry's mind the setting has to be San Francisco, the place where, in real life, Clare went off to university to study music therapy, thus signaling the end of their relationship. In this tale Harry sees himself almost at rock-bottom, a simple cab driver and one of life's losers. In perhaps the most recognizable two verses of any of Harry's songs, he picks up his last fare of the night, with Ron Palmer's atmospheric guitar imitating the falling drops of rain:

It was raining hard in 'Frisco
I needed one more fare to make my night
A lady up ahead waved to flag me down
She got in at the light.
"Where you going to my Lady Blue
It's a shame you ruined your gown in the rain."
She just looked out the window
She said, "16 Parkside Lane"

Just then, Tim Scott's cello kicks in in dramatic style, perhaps coming as quite a surprise to first-time listeners to Harry's music. Of course, as many Chapin fans know, the address is purely fictitious, as there is no such place in the city. However, we now have two people who look familiar to each other, and it doesn't take long before there is a connection:

Something about her was familiar
I could swear I'd seen her face before
But she said, "I'm sure you're mistaken"
And she didn't say anything more

It took a while, but she looked in the mirror
And she glanced at the license for my name
A smile seemed to come to her slowly
It was a sad smile, just the same

And she said, "How are you Harry?"
I said, "How are you Sue?
Through the too many miles

And the too little smiles
I still remember you"

How many years it has been is uncertain, but they begin to reminisce about their fairytale romance of long ago and the big dreams they both shared back then. We get to share those dreams – for Harry a dream never realized, the perceived glamour of being a pilot (harking back to his time in the Air Force Academy), and for Sue who now appears to be "flying high" with her dream fulfilled:

It was somewhere in a fairy tale
I used to take her home in my car
We learned about love in the back of the Dodge
The lesson hadn't gone too far

You see, she was gonna be an actress
And I was gonna learn to fly
She took off to find the footlights
And I took off to find the sky

Whether in conversation with her, or giving the listener his own life-assessment, Harry's voice becomes more agitated as he sees himself just biding his time in pursuance of his dream:

Oh, I've got something inside me
To drive a princess blind
There's a wild man, wizard
He's hiding in me, illuminating my mind
Oh, I've got something inside me,
Not what my life's about
Cause I been letting my outside tide me,
Over 'til my time runs out.

It's the frustration of what people realize when they can't attain the success they dream of, that life itself has now become something less than they hoped for. But for Sue there is an air of uncertainty. It is said that she dropped her dreams and married a rich man because she was afraid to take risks. Sue is now walking a tightrope, afraid to fall. The uncertainty is echoed beautifully in Big John's wonderful angelic voice. (It is alleged that these four lines are attributed to the American poet and novelist Sylvia Plath (1932-63), but an examination of her work finds no basis for the claim).

Baby's so high that she's skying,
Yeah she's flying, but afraid to fall.
And I'll tell you why Baby's crying,
Cause she's dying, aren't we all?

At the end of the ride Harry drops Sue off at what appears to be a luxury address in an affluent part of the city:

There was not much more for us to talk about
Whatever we had once was gone
So I turned my cab into the driveway
Past the gate and the fine trimmed lawns

And she said we must get together
But I knew it'd never be arranged
And she handed me twenty dollars
For a two fifty fare, she said
"Harry, keep the change"

By keeping the change from a $20 bill - perhaps the one line that will be ingrained in cabbies' minds forevermore - Harry feels no anger or hurt, just regret. When he says other men wouldn't have let her go, or wouldn't have taken the money, we know of course he's talking about an earlier version of himself:

Well, another man might have been angry
And another man might have been hurt
But another man never would have let her go
I stashed the bill in my shirt

As the song draws to an end, Harry, who had wanted to be a pilot, justifies his life by saying that he still gets to fly high when he's stoned in his cab. Sue had dreamed of being an actress and now lives a relatively affluent life and gets to act, looking like she is satisfied with it. In one sense, they have both got what they wanted:

And she walked away in silence
It's strange, how you never know
But we'd both gotten what we'd asked for
Such a long, long time ago

You see, she was gonna be an actress
And I was gonna learn to fly

She took off to find the footlights
I took off for the sky

When he was younger maybe he could have fought to stop her getting away, but now, without hope, he sees the money as buying himself another chance to get flying high (a not so subtle reference to drugs) and continue his dreaming:

And here, she's acting happy
Inside her handsome home
And me, I'm flying in my taxi
Taking tips, and getting stoned
I go flying so high, when I'm stoned

In a later interview, Sandy explains that the song had been written with little editing and that Harry had this vision that after telling people about all his dreams, one of them years later would get into the cab he was driving, and it would turn out to be an old college girlfriend of his. Niles Siegel, one of Elektra's promotional team, remembers the battle they had getting the record played in San Francisco, one of the major markets in the country in terms of the Top 40. As the name 'Frisco' is considered by them derogatory, the promoters had to plead with the radio stations there to play **'Taxi'**. Sebastian Stone, program director in the city, and a good friend of Siegel, told him straight: "Niles, I can't play this record. They're going to chew me up and spit me out here if I play this record, calling San Francisco 'Frisco.' I can't do it." As it turns out the record soon begins selling so well that they have to play it.

Is **'Taxi'** a depressing song? In an interview with British DJ Noel Edmonds in December 1977, Harry gives us his views:

*"I've been accused of writing a lot of depressing songs. I guess **'Taxi'** was the first one everybody heard, and in fact it's probably true. It goes back to recognition. When you're feeling good, it's the last time in the world you need other people. You can just wander down the street or take your skateboard or surfboard and get on a wave and just float away. The time you need communication is when things aren't going well. It's time when you need that sense of communion or a sense of everybody else in the same boat. Anybody's who's been to one of my concerts, even though I sing sad song after sad song...sometimes happy songs, does not go out depressed. Number one, I am usually a positive person. I was born that way. The fact is the times I am most pushed to create are when I'm trying to come to terms with some of the things that tend to crunch those positive things and in the act of encompassing them defeat them. So, **'Taxi'** is about a guy and a girl who sold out their dreams. But in that sense of recognition, even though he's flying so high when he's*

stoned at the end of the song, other people listening to that song make the next step."

Harry also refers to the song in an interview with Britain's *Melody Maker*:

"I'm not at all surprised it wasn't big here. I was surprised it did well in the States. It sold 700,000, they tell me, though I don't know if they are telling me the truth. You know how much hype there is in this industry. But look at the things it had against it - One, its length. Two, it doesn't have a chorus. Three, it's not about young kids, it's about this old guy and this old married woman. Four, there's apparently a drug reference in the last line, though as a matter of fact I'm not a druggie."

Critics are divided over the song. *Billboard* describes it as exploding *"with vast musical depth."* Ben Gerson of *Rolling Stone* calls it the second or third worst song on the album, accusing Harry of banality and using superfluous and irrelevant detail in his lyrics that disrupt the song's narrative flow. In short, he writes, it's poorly produced and contains a catalogue of mistakes, both melodically and lyrically. Music journalist Peter Doggett writes: *"Few debut singles have ever summed up an artist's strengths so clearly."* Alan Bradley writes that Harry has written a story song with sensitivity and perception, and quotes the great George Bernard Shaw - *"There are two tragedies in life. One is not to get your heart's desire. The other is to get it."* Another reviewer, perhaps missing the point, calls it *"a bittersweet and extremely revealing tale of the youth-drug culture."*

Incredible as it sounds, this is a debut album from a band who have been together less than seven months, and in **'Taxi'** we have a fiercely original tonal and cinematic masterpiece, with Harry already close to his creative best with a unique song that can stand on its own magnificence. It manages to touch on a real, personal meaning to so many of us - plans made, but never realized, goals set but never achieved, and great loves that come into our lives that are then lost. If ever a story needs a sequel, it's this one…

From the cheap seats:

Brandon Walls - *This great group of musicians come together to form a masterpiece of a song. An art form of a song. Poetically, the sequel to his first song was also his last song.*

Alan L Geraci - *Harry enjoyed writing songs about journeys, not destinations. 'Taxi' is the epitome of the story of lost journeys and twisted detours. 'Taxi' ends, "I go flying so high when I'm stoned," and reminds us to find a path back to the journey by escaping from present reality.*

Tony Bentivegna - *It's his magnum opus. Nothing like blasting it in the car (the **Greatest Stories** live version) and when it gets to the end I sing a high harmony on top of the last lines, "I go flying so high when I'm stoned." Gets me every time.*

Richard Barbato - *It was the first story song I ever heard. It was reminiscent of watching a movie. It had a beginning middle and end. I still rooted for Harry and Sue to get together no matter how many times I heard the song, even though I knew they wouldn't. It was also the longest song I'd heard since 'American Pie'.*

Jason Colannino - *The birth of the 'Keep the Change' catch phrase that the audience would shout during every time this song was played. The phrase that Harry would sign my autograph with. The song itself gave Harry an identity. The blue-collar common man we could all relate to. Ironically Harry himself never kept the change for himself, he gave it all away. I met Harry in 1976 when I was 7. He signed his autograph that read, 'To Jason, a great name. Keep the change!' I visited his grave in 1999 for the first time. I left him a note that read 'To Harry, a great name. Keep the change.'*

Any Old Kind Of Day *****

Dream-like ballad with a melancholy touch. The feeling of loss at the passing of uneventful time, devoid of anything memorable, is expressed beautifully in this sentimental, reflective song. Written in the late 60s during a surge in creativity and brought about by the wonderful time Harry spends with the Castro family, the close friends who have taken him to their bosom, a time when they hold regular parties at which he can perform his songs to an always supportive and appreciative audience. This introspective song continues the album's theme of loneliness and isolation. The narrator is a singer and for him things haven't been going too well in the past. We find him lying awake in bed at night in what we take to be a run-down city hotel room. But this is just a normal day in what he sees as an empty monotonous lifestyle:

Turning on my pillow, thinking kind of strange
The color is of midnight in this room
The cars outside are coughing and it's kinda hard to sleep
and there's neon out the window, not the moon.

In the chorus he contemplates how time is slipping by him like the beating of his heart.

And it was just an any old kind of day
The kind that comes and slips away
The kind that fills up easy my life's time
The night brought any old kind of dark
I heard the ticking of my heart
Then why am I thinking something's left behind?

63

Daytime brings some relief from the tedium as he jauntily walks the city streets to wherever it is he's going, but it seems like his life is on a never-ending loop, and he ponders whether things will turn out differently:

I whistled round today and I skipped a footloose jig
to the hurdy-gurdy music of the street
I looked past those rooftops and I saw that cloudless sky
But I keep on asking why
my life is passing by
And I'm left up high and dry
But it ain't no good to cry
So I shrug the useless sigh
And I trust to things that other days will meet.

Night comes around again and we're back in the solitude of his darkened hotel room, with a mocking rain outside now seemingly adding to his sorrow; he hopes that sleep will get these negative thoughts out of his head, and starts thinking positively that eventually his life will turn around.

Night has had its laughing when the street lights blind the stars
So now it's shedding rain to sing it's sorrow, sorrow
It's time for me to sleep and to rest these thoughts away
There's gonna be another day
When things will go my way
And there's other things to say
And there's other songs to play
And there'll be time enough for thinking come tomorrow.

It's a chillingly beautiful song with a depth of sorrow that shows Harry as a master of writing plaintive, soul-searching ballads. Superbly produced by Kewley and arranged by Steve Chapin, it opens with just Harry's acoustic guitar before being joined by Steve's gentle piano, which eases us into the first chorus, now effortlessly supplemented with Wallace's base and Palmer's riffs. The second verse and chorus are just amazing to listen to, introducing Scott's gentle and evocative cello and sublime angelic backing vocals, which come into their own on the final verse, especially with Wallace's incredible range. An early version of the song was included in the demo tape sent to Elektra in late 1971. The album cut will now be chosen as the flip-side to the forthcoming **'Taxi'** single. In October 1976 The Chapins also record their version of the song on New York DJ Peter Fornatale's radio show, while promoting Tom's debut album *Life is Like That*. The tapes are lost for 30 years until finally unearthed by Fornatale. It's interesting to hear how their close Weavers-style harmonies offer a folkier take on this beautiful song.

For once-dubbed "adequate musicians," this is a fitting showcase for how they have developed into a tightly-knit professional band. Holzman could easily have insisted on Harry using all session musicians like percussionist Kunkel, but now he must truly appreciate that these guys are really good. But there is also Harry's tender voice that perfectly complements the lyric, and stands in complete contrast to the track that will follow this.

From the cheap seats
Simone Moore - *This is one of my favorites; always a reminder that there will be another day, things will get better and that though we have regrets there will be other loves, other songs.*

Dogtown *****
During this creative boost of the late 60s, Harry is writing with more maturity, and as well as introspective and semi-autobiographical songs, he is developing some of his very first story-songs, extracting episodes from his personal life and constructing a narrative that relays the same emotions felt, but relocated to a different setting, whether real or make-believe. **'Dogtown'** is not only his first fully-fledged story-song and a fine example of his craft, but it will become one of the most controversial songs of his career. It is also one of the songs presented on the demo tape given to Elektra in late 1971. But where does Harry get the inspiration for such a dark story? On a trip with Sandy to visit her parents' summer address in Gloucester, Massachusetts, north of Boston, she takes him to visit the famous remains of an old, long-deserted settlement at Cape Anne. First settled in the late 17th century, legend has it that the village gained its name from the dogs that the women keep while their husbands are away fighting in the Revolutionary War. Over the years a number of reasons bring about its demise, and with a dwindling population and alleged practices of witchcraft, by 1828 it is finally abandoned, leaving just packs of wild dogs to roam around the ruins. Harry is inspired by what he sees and he comes away with a story developing in his fertile mind. He sees it as a New England whaling saga. But Harry's focus is not on the whalers, but on the wives left behind for months on end with just their dogs for company while their husbands sail the oceans in search of blubber.

In the opening verses Harry sets the scene and references why the place is given its sobriquet:

Up in Massachusetts there's a little spit of land.
The men who make the maps, yes, they call the place Cape Anne
The men who do the fishing call it Gloucester Harbor Sound
But the women left behind, they call the place Dogtown.
The men go out for whaling past the breakers and the fogs
The women stay home waiting; they're protected by the dogs

A tough old whaler woman who had seen three husbands drown
Polled the population and she named the place Dogtown.
And these grey faced women in their black widow's gowns
Living in this graveyard granite town
You soon learn there's many more than one way to drown
That's while going to the dogs, here in Dogtown.

As this bride of just ten days begins to relate her story, we begin to see a darker picture:

My father was a merchant all in the Boston fief
When my husband came and asked him for my hand
But little did I know then that a Gloucester Whaler's wife
Married but the sea salt and the sand.
He took me up to Dogtown the day I was a bride
We had ten days together before he left my side
He's the first mate on a whaling ship, the keeper of the log.
He said, "Farewell, my darling, I'm gonna leave you with my dog."

This is made even more eerie in the haunting chorus that follows:

And I have seen the splintered timbers of a hundred shattered hulls
Known the silence of the granite and the screeching of the gulls
I've heard that crazy widow Cather walk the harbor as she raves
At the endless rolling whisper of the waves.

With her husband's ship months overdue, we share the woman's darkest thoughts:

Sitting by the fireside, the embers slowly die
Is it a sign of weakness when a woman wants to cry
The dog is closely watching, the fire glints in his eye
No use to go to sleep this early, no use to even try

My blood beats like a woman's, I've got a woman's breast and thighs
But where am I to offer them, to the ocean or the skies?
Living with this silent dog all the moments of my life
He has been my only husband, am I a widow, or his wife?

Yes, it's a Dogtown and it's a fog town,
And there's nothing around 'cept the sea pounding granite ground
And this black midnight horror of a hound.

As we come to the last verse the woman is on top of a cliff, resigning herself that her husband is lost at sea, maybe contemplating suicide herself, but leaving us with one chilling thought:

I'm standing on this craggy cliff, my eyes fixed on the sea
Six months past when his ship was due, I'm a widow-to-be
For liking this half-living with the lonely and the fog
You need the bastard of the mating of a woman and a dog.

In his review, *Rolling Stone*'s Ben Gerson writes about **'Dogtown'**, and, surprisingly for him, is emotionally drawn to the subject matter, in what he sees as an episode in his country's history left too long in the shadows. Of course, it is all simply conjecture; there is no evidence that acts of bestiality had ever taken place. Although Harry's brothers had once been skeptical of having it in their playlist, Holzman is ensnared by its captivating drama and has no qualms about its inclusion on the album. *Billboard* rates both **'Dogtown'** and **'Taxi'** as *"masterpieces,"* having *"the sweep of classical music"* and *"the vibrant surge of rock,"* and predicts a fast rise to stardom for the singer. In an interview with Britain's Noel Edmonds in December 1977, Harry gives his thoughts on the song:

"It is one of the most desolate spots. The day I went it was raining...it was like a typical English day. I suddenly had a vision of what it must have been like for a woman, left behind by her husband, after she was newly married. He's going off on a trip that would take at best a year, probably two years, and she's standing there six months after he's supposed to have come back and there's no sign of him. She's left behind with a giant, black dog and all the urges of humanity. What do you do? Well that's what the song is about."

Despite the eeriness of the subject, the song is filled with fine musical moments as the story unfolds - Kunkel's atmospheric but dirge-like drumbeats; Palmer's understated guitar; Steve Chapin's keyboard mimicking a woman's heartbeat, and Scott's seemingly distant but haunting cello. But to top it all, there's Harry's unashamedly convincing vocal. He knows full well that many listeners will be repelled by the whole idea but he never holds back with his passionate delivery. Lyrically, it remains a profoundly thought-provoking and evocative tour de force, but in the end it's just another simple song about loneliness, or, as Harry refers to it, *"rather a sensational way of resolving it."*

From the cheap seats
Scott Sivakoff - *I've always said that I thought the song was a little on the weird side, but if you listen closely to the words you really get a sense of what I think Harry was trying to say. I believe that there is some truth in the song and even though it has a shocking and odd hook at the end, the message*

is interesting. To me there is certainly a message of loneliness, but there is also a message of loyalty and love. The woman in the story knew that the guy had a dangerous job but married him anyway and really holds out hope. The tragic nature of it is when sheer desperation kicks in and she turns to her only other companion... the dog. In modern days the dog could be a metaphor for an alternative option. But in the timeframe of the song, my guess is that such things probably happened. Again, it's tragic. The song does a great job of painting the picture of desperation and loneliness but I think also says something about loyalty and love.

Alan L Geraci - *'Dogtown' captures the true perils of loneliness. Harry focused on loneliness in his early years in many of his lyrics. It not only creates a troubling image of loneliness during the early whaling days of New England but the music reinforces the message with its loud heart beats and minor key riffs. I love the effect, the story and the lesson.*

Herb Walsh - *I played this song in a bar in St. John's, Newfoundland, Canada in 1992 the day a crab boat hand had drowned. I had just returned from a week at sea as a deckhand on a longliner. The audience was as rapt listening as I was singing it. Harry captured the realities of life in ways others can only dream of. Coincidentally there were a lot of Newfoundlanders who migrated to Massachusetts in the mid 1800s.*

Mark Charlesworth - *I love this song to me it's kind a saying until you know the background of a person's story don't be too quick to judge. Men and women go through tough things in their lives and it sometimes takes us down paths I never thought we could go.*

Same Sad Singer **

Whereas **'Taxi'** is a song inspired by Clare, this last-minute addition to the album is undoubtedly all about her, and perhaps the last song he writes with her in mind. He's reaching out to her, wherever she may be, to tell her that he's finally achieved his ambition, an ambition that he feels ultimately ended their relationship. Not as melodic as his other songs of lost love, nor lyrically as engaging, it is the album's weakest track. Maybe it's Harry finally drawing a line under past relationships. It would be nice to think that. As this song had been chosen over **'Sandy'**, his first love letter to his wife, he now needs to write songs more with Sandy in mind. Maybe this is where it will change....

The Promotional Campaign Gets Underway

Now begins Holzman's promised promotional campaign. With a release date pencilled in for the second week of March 1972, the ideal place to introduce the band and the album is at the record label's very first national sales convention, held at the Riviera Hotel in Palm Springs from January 6th-9th. In attendance will be over 300 of Warner Communications' leading members responsible for the marketing side of the business. Holzman goes out of his way to impress his parent company, so rather than just sending out promo copies of the album to the relevant company salesmen, he seizes this opportunity of bringing all the marketing staff together and getting Harry to perform to them in person. Not only that, his label stablemates The Doors and Carly Simon will also be there to perform songs from their recently released albums. Holzman has Harry and Carly headlining Saturday night's big event, but will his gamble with Harry pay off?

Fortunately for Holzman, things cannot go better. Harry's performance, particularly his rendition of **'Taxi'**, goes down without a hitch and receives a standing ovation from the inquisitive audience, many of whom are seeing and hearing their latest signing for the very first time, and they come away impressed with Holzman's new protégé. A month before the album's release, the promotional work is in full swing. Bob Heimall's artwork for the front cover of what is a gatefold sleeve is both simple and evocative, and has a photo of a relaxed and smiling Harry, taken by Frank Bez, leaning out of the door of a New York cab and framed by their iconic yellow and black-and-white checkered livery. The same format is used on the back cover, with Bez's image of the four band members looking pensively through the window of what looks like a diner, again framed by the cab colors. To give the listener a better understanding of the songs, a special six-page full-color lyric folio is included, all songs copyrighted to Story Songs Limited.

Holzman keeps his word to Harry by swamping the media with all kinds of promotional paraphernalia. Record stores are sent eye-catching preview booklets, cardboard cut-outs of Harry, posters, banners, and even bumper stickers to put on display. Radio stations are inundated with newly-mastered demo records of **'Taxi'** and **'Could You Leave Your Light on, Please'**, both chosen to be the first single releases. Harry, of course, is at the forefront, and uses all his charm, drive and energy to help things along, even making personal calls and visits to radio stations to persuade them to play **'Taxi'**, despite it being over twice the length of what is deemed an acceptable running time. He even makes it his mission to seek out all the heads at Elektra responsible for any aspect of the marketing and selling of the album, sitting in on their meetings, firing questions at them, and getting to know all there is to know about the business. And at the same time, they are also getting to know what this singer is all about.

It doesn't take long for **_Heads and Tales_** to start making money, and after some 30,000 copies are pre-ordered just for the LA area alone, by February the total sales come in at $75,000. As promised in the contract, Holzman also helps to organize a promotional tour around the country, although it turns out not to be as glamorous as Harry and the band visualize. Many of the venues are low-key at best, and the pay is modest. Much of the traveling is done by cars or crammed into one van, and as well as the band members on the road, there is also Kewley and the two young unpaid volunteer roadies, Rob White and Jeb Hart, to share food and budget motel rooms. The record company does provide a modest amount of expenses, but until they get a return on their investment, money remains tight. Harry takes on two roles, one as a performer, one as a marketing man, and in every town they go to he continues his hustling of local record stores and radio stations. He is slowly coming to realize that the music business is all about money, period. As he sees it now, the reason he has come this far is down to one thing: it's nothing to do with any artistic aspect, it's all about making someone else a lot of money. No one knows that more that Jac Holzman, and to his credit, he does his best to find more prestigious venues for the band. He gets in touch with Arlene Rothberg, manager of Carly Simon, to have Harry open for her at Boston's Symphony Hall on February 12th, and again the following night at the Veterans Memorial Auditorium in Providence, Rhode Island. In the hour-long sets for both shows Harry is received with wild enthusiasm by the audience, a reception that some say even outdoes Carly's performance. For Harry and his band, that is another welcome sign of success.

Harry recalls later that year: *"I'm a storyteller and a communicator, and I try to figure out better ways of performing all the time. I've found the best thing you can do as a performer is to give clear signals yourself in order that you receive clear signals back. I'm not a completely unconscious lifestyler type of musician, and I'm gratified that the majority of critics like me."*

On March 11th 1972 **Heads and Tales** is released and spends 27 weeks on the *Billboard* 200 charts, peaking at #60 in July. The single **'Taxi'** is not expected to do well, as it runs to nearly seven minutes, and most AM radio stations rarely play records of more than two minutes, three at best. But progressive FM stations are now becoming more in fashion, playing longer songs and even full albums. Despite its length, the single **'Taxi'** has a supporter in WMEX-Boston radio DJ Jim Connors who gives it plenty of airplay on the East Coast and sees it lasting 16 weeks on the *Billboard* Hot 100, peaking at #24 on June 3rd (the day The Staple Singers are heading the charts with 'I'll Take You There'). Eventually **'Taxi'** is ranked the #85 top single of the year, even reaching a creditable #5 in the Canadian charts. It also becomes the most requested song in the States for ten weeks, thanks to it finally receiving airplay on the more conservative AM stations (despite the perceived references to drug use).

Harry's concerts begin to receive glowing reviews. After a performance at The Bitter End on April 5th, one critic is so impressed with the band's sound, especially Tim Scott's cello playing, that he concludes: *"Quite simply, Chapin's singing - and Chapin's group - were unexpected delights. They should be heard.*" The same critic applauds the new album as a whole as a *"superb recording,"* and recommends it to lovers of quality music.

John Wallace recalls the first time the band appears in public following the success of **'Taxi'** on the radio: *"It was Banana Fish Park in Brooklyn and Urbana, IL. What a huge difference that made! We'd been doing gigs here and there with polite applause, but it was the first place it was on the radio and people went nuts. Now we're in a whole new level of magnitude. It was really exciting but funny because it was like before, but the only thing different was that people had heard it on the radio. We walked out and people went nuts, and there was a standing ovation, and we hadn't even done anything. We got carried away to a certain extent, but I was 28 and Ron was 36. We were more settled and it would have been worse if we were younger. It was the Mason-Dixon Line back then - on the radio or not on the radio. Of course, 'Taxi' made Harry a legit player."*

(Linda McCarty, *Circle*, Winter 2004)

Ben Gerson of *Rolling Stone* sums up the album, rating several of the shorter, less risky songs, for which he feels Harry is just playing safe, but at the same time having one last dig at **'Taxi'**, implying that as Harry had once worked for a stock broker, he should write a story song about that too. Ann Tan of *Words and Music* writes: *"It is a solid piece of professional music as was ever laid down on wax, and the production itself is excellent...These songs are a kind of trip into self-discovery land, and somehow, after hearing the album, one emerges a little bit wiser."* Penny Valentine of *Sounds* concludes that it is *"well worth having for those moments of rare calm,"* and that Chapin displays a feeling of *"relaxed personal contact"* in his singing.

To music critics and record company bosses alike, Harry remains an oddity. In what turns out to be boom decade for singer-songwriters, he is being likened to contemporary artists such as Gordon Lightfoot, James Taylor and Tim Buckley, but he cannot be buttonholed into any one category. His connection with an audience is unparalleled for a singer-songwriter; no one has divided critics' opinion of someone as much as him. Yes, he is unorthodox and difficult to be classified. There's no one around that writes or performs songs the way Harry does.

The touring continues. The end of March brings with it a three-night engagement opening for soft-rockers the Pousette-Dart Band, at the Stonehenge Club, an old colonial building in Ipswich, Massachusetts, well noted for its impressive acoustics. The following month will see them supporting comedian David Steinberg in a two-week engagement at the rebuilt Mister Kelly's nightclub in Chicago, despite receiving a modest fee of just $500 a week. Following engagements at the prestigious Troubadour nightclub in West Hollywood, Harry goes east once more to appear on May 20th at the

Capitol Theatre in Passaic, New Jersey, in support of English guitarist John McLaughlin's new band, the Mahavishnu Orchestra.

Going Public - National Television at Last

The following month, Harry is given the chance to boost his exposure with a brace of television appearances. On June 5th, the day after a four-night stint with fellow singer-songwriter Ronee Blakley at My Father's Place, a club in Roslyn, Long Island, he is invited to appear on ABC's late night television slot, *The Dick Cavett Show*, and although not performing, is interviewed by the host, along with fellow guests, including actor Alan Arkin and comedian Dick Gregory. A few weeks later, on June 28th, he finally gets the chance to do a solo performance on national television when he guests on Westinghouse's *The David Frost Show* and sings **'Taxi'**, his first television performance since appearing with his brothers on Canada's *Let's Sing Out* in 1965.

But the biggest showstopper occurs a week later, when, on July 6th, he appears as the musical guest on NBC's prestigious *The Tonight Show with Johnny Carson*, whose other guests that night include actors Ed Asner, Robert Blake and Shelley Winters. His evocative performance of **'Taxi'** has the studio audience transfixed, but the biggest response comes from the viewers, and after the show, the station is inundated with telegrams and phone calls offering their praise. For Carson and his production team, this is unprecedented. After the show the band are in the parking lot, loading up their equipment, when Fred de Cordova, the show's producer, comes over and says, "Guys, we have absolutely never done this before, but what are you doing tomorrow night? Can you come back tomorrow night and do it again?" Of course, Harry agrees, and performs the following night, reportedly the first time on the show an artist is asked back in such a way, and he will go on to appear on the show a further thirteen times during his career.

In July, Harry supports Arlo Guthrie, son of the legendary Woody, at the Schaefer Music Festival in Central Park, the first of what will become an annual event for Harry, and this is followed by a six-night engagement at the popular Cellar Door in Washington D.C. During this period of constant touring, Harry manages to get home to Sandy and the kids for two or three days each month. Pregnant with their second child, and still studying hard on her thesis at Columbia University, she feels like they are beginning to live separate lives, in separate worlds, and with little communication. Like Harry in his past life, it's now her turn again to suffer the pain and frustration of feeling alone.

For Sandy and those that know him, Harry is now seen as a different person. John Wallace sees it too: *"Part of that was the fact that it had been the four of us in the band, and after a while Harry drifted away and rightly so. He had so many things going on, so it was like leaving a cat or dog home alone. It was more like being abandoned. He wasn't ours anymore; he belonged to everybody. Harry never did anything maliciously to cause you grief. If it happened it was inadvertent on his part."*

(Linda McCarty, *Circle*, Winter 2004)

No longer just a part of a tightly-knit circle of family and friends; they are now outsiders. Harry has become a commodity. He now belongs to his public.

Sniper and Other Love Songs

"I've been around the world long enough to realize that it's not all down to dollars and cents – it's the personal commitment you need, and I'm just terribly happy with the way everything is going"

Tension and Disharmony

The constant touring in the summer months of 1972, along with Harry's time-consuming preoccupation with self-promoting, means that his band has little time for rehearsing together, and this inevitably leads to a strained relationship and clashes of egos. With money now lining their once empty pockets, there is a new dynamic within the band. They have lost touch with their roots. These unsettling vibes find their way into the recording studio that summer, as work begins on the second album. For Harry it will be a frustrating time. Although many of the intended songs have been written, he grows impatient with the process, preferring the concert stage to the rigorous demands of recording the songs. His band members are not the same eager, naïve, wide-eyed musicians they were when they stepped into the recording studio seven months ago. Now there appears to be an underlying air of individual self-importance, rather than a determination to work in harmony. Harry's continued absence on his promotional crusade often creates tension with the other band members, and rehearsals often have to go on without him, especially now he has invited Sandy and the children over to Los Angeles. Cracks are beginning to appear. Where the first album was the result of a pleasant, close-knit, and mutually-fulfilling effort by all involved, this time it could very well be a case of just get in there and get the job done, but only after dogged and uninterrupted hard work. Many look on a second album as being a make-or-break indication of an artist's future success, and it's not hard to imagine that that's exactly what's on Harry's mind. Apart from the positive reaction to the release of **'Taxi'** as a money-making single, its parent album has so far only brought in what can be called moderate sales, rather less than anticipated, and certainly something that Elektra are taking notice of. With this in mind, Harry realizes that this, his sophomore album, has to do so much better. If it fails, who knows? He just might have to terminate his time with Elektra, something, of course, that is written into the contract.

In the meantime, the touring continues, and August finds them as busy as ever. On August 3rd they are invited back on *The Tonight Show with Johnny Carson*, where they perform one of Harry's new songs called **'Sniper'** to a jaw-dropping audience. A week-long engagement at Paul's Mall in Boston is soon followed by more television appearances, both taped the same day on

August 19th. The first is Dick Clark's legendary *American Bandstand*, aired on ABC, and filmed at their LA studios. Harry performs **'Taxi'** and **'Could You Put Your Light On, Please'** in front of an enthusiastic studio audience. Their second appearance is on a pilot for NBC's new 90-minute show called *The Midnight Special*, which will be screened late on Friday nights before the Carson show. In this, Harry sits and chats briefly with guest host John Denver about the story behind **'Taxi'**, before turning in a sublime performance of the song, one of the best ever to be screened. That same night they play in support of label stablemate David Gates and his group Bread at The Blossom Center, an impressive outdoor amphitheater at Cuyahoga Falls near Cleveland, Ohio, before going on to Chicago to perform at the Arie Crown Theater on Lakeside Drive, another regular venue in the years to follow.

The Making of a Masterpiece

In between concerts, Harry has been working on his next project all summer long and writing songs at an impressive rate. What he has in mind is a concept album that relates to a young man's journey to an anonymous city where he meets a diverse collection of lonely characters, all with traumas of one kind or another, and struggling for answers in the concrete confines of their urban environment. As Harry later puts it: *"The album was about a young man who comes to the city, any city, and the kind of people me meets. One, he tells of their stories and conditions; two, the things he wants; and three, his relationships with women."* Sounds interesting, but as Harry has some twenty songs or more as candidates for inclusion, he visualizes a double album with the catchy title of *Sweet City Suite*, but then changes the title after songwriters and producers Cashman & West record the near-eleven-minute-long, New York-themed, 'American City Suite' for their album *A Song or Two*, released on Dunhill later that summer. Undeterred, Harry decides to give his album the contradictory but eye-catching title of ***Sniper and Other Love Songs***.

But how to sell this idea to Holzman? Back in the studio, the band rehearse the songs, old and new, and record a demo tape. Of the twenty songs selected, a few of them are ones scribbled down by Harry a number of years ago, and only now seeing the light of day, while several others are simply revised versions. But of the new ones, written during the summer months, two will stand out as what many consider to be his best-ever work. Surely the time and cost involved in a double album will be out of the question. With the proposal and demo tapes of the intended songs put in front of him, Jac Holzman meets with his team at his New York office, where they listen to the tapes and discuss each song at some length. Harry and Fred Kewley arrive, expecting to take part in the conference, but are asked by Holzman to wait outside the office. It is a nerve-racking, nail-biting time for both. So much depends on this. Like the previous album, it will also include some lengthy songs, no doubt to be deemed unsuitable for single release and a source of extra revenue. The private meeting held by Holzman has in attendance his general manager Bill Harvey, along with Mel Posner, head of sales, and the one person who has made this all possible, Ann Purtill. Each one is asked to listen to the songs and give their opinion in as few words as possible. Harry is on tenterhooks, and even before the final song comes to an end, his burning frustration gets the better of him, and he walks uninvited into the room, where, to his relief, he is allowed to remain for the final judgment. Ann, for one, is not too happy about this not-unexpected turn of events. With so many negative comments on his songs going around the table, Harry realizes that they are not going to share his plans for a double album, and his reaction to it shows. What he doesn't know is that he is also losing their respect.

In the months spent aggressively targeting and haranguing record company staff, radio station bosses, record store owners, and even his own band members, Harry has become what many see as "a pain in the ass". But that is the nature of the man, and the more forceful and bull-headed he appears, the more people he seems to alienate. Do people still want to help him achieve success when he acts like this? After all, they have other artists who they are only too willing to support. So, it is decided - there will be nine songs, one single album. With the decision made, the band return to the studio to finish off the chosen songs.

To his credit, Holzman agrees to give the new album an impressive cover, with gatefold sleeve, artwork once again handled by Bob Heimall, and photography by Frank Bez. The difference this time is that instead of an inserted lyric sheet as on the previous album, the lyrics will now form the main feature of the inside jacket, with wonderfully surreal cameo collages for each song drawn by the talented Rob White, still the enthusiastic and welcome young member of Harry's road crew. Once more the band are featured on the back cover, this time with their instruments, and a silhouetted Harry facing them in the foreground.

Sniper and Other Love Songs *****
Elektra EKS 75042
Recorded at Elektra Sound Recorders, Los Angeles, Summer 1972
US Release Date: October 1972
Producer - Fred Kewley
Engineer - Bruce Morgan

The front cover has the following introduction: *"...Being some assorted scenes from the 'Movie of my life' wherein Farley Higgins comes to the city to make his fortune, meets with mixed success and a rather wide range of people of different conditions and finally learns the truths that were there to be seen all along...*" The running order gives the listener a helter-skelter ride of emotions. The optimism found in **'Sunday Morning Sunshine'** turns to tragedy in the epic heart-wrenching saga that is **'Sniper'**, followed by a chance to catch your breath in the poignancy of **'And the Baby Never Cries'** and the utter sadness in **'Burning Herself'** - four completely different songs that are a fitting showcase for Harry's development as a master songsmith. Side two doesn't hold back on the emotional pull either, and opens with **'Barefoot Boy'**, a truncated version of an earlier song. Then it's tissues ready as we are engrossed in the bittersweet **'Better Place to Be'**, before humming along to the anthemic **'Circle'**, an old *Make a Wish* offering. The controversial subject of **'Women Child'** gives pause for reflection on a highly sensitive subject, before the gentle **'Winter Song'**, another autobiographical paean to lost love, brings the album to an all-too-soon conclusion. With nine diverse songs in the can, as on the previous album, and with a total running time of just thirteen minutes more than before, so much depends on this. Will it be the make-or-break moment they fear?

Sunday Morning Sunshine ***
A nice bouncy introduction to the album in the folk-based "your love gives me life" vein, and one that on first listening appears to set the tone for more to come. The narrator is in fact introducing what is to follow. Initially the only song on the album that looks suitable for release as a potential single. After its release the band perform a wonderful a capella version of the song to open their concerts. In the meantime, first-time listeners will be getting comfortable in their chairs listening to the album expecting Harry's usual blend of lonely souls and lost love to follow this track. They are in for a rude awakening.

From the cheap seats
Bob Clare - *Beautiful love song. Ron and John very present. Incredible use of a Sunday choir too.*

Sniper *****
A love song? Really? Straight away we have a contradiction in an album full of contradictions. What exactly are we expected to love here? The subject matter is as controversial as **'Dogtown'** was on the previous album in its risqué implications, but the big difference here is that this is all so terribly real. On August 1st 1966, 24-year-old Harry is probably working in the office, editing *Legendary Champions*, when he first hears the news transpiring down in Austin, Texas. After stabbing his wife and mother to death the night before, a 25-year-old former US Marine, Charles Whitman, takes an arsenal of weapons to the top of a clock tower on the campus of the University of Texas, where he is studying architectural engineering on a Naval scholarship. Over the next ninety minutes he opens fire and eventually kills 18 people and

wounds another 31 before cops storm the tower and shoot him dead. At the time it is one of the country's deadliest mass shootings. The evening before Whitman climbs the campus tower, he writes a goodbye letter, which begins: *"I don't really understand myself these days. I am supposed to be an average reasonable and intelligent young man. However, lately (I can't recall when it started) I have been a victim of many unusual and irrational thoughts."* An autopsy carried out on Whitman discovers that an undiagnosed brain tumor may have caused his violent impulses, a tumor that was growing so fast it probably would have killed him in a few months. There is speculation that it somehow had a marked effect on his personality and prompted his actions. In his book *A Sniper in the Tower*, Gary Lavergne has a different view and believes Whitman assumed the role of a killer as he could not respect or even admire himself, and had become more or less everything he despised in other people. He could not live with that, and set out to die in a way that would get his name in the headlines by taking other lives with him.

The tragic event has a marked effect on Harry, and within days of hearing the story, he begins to ask himself questions. What was going on in this killer's head? What psychological makeup did he have that could explain these terrible actions? Those questions evolve into a poem based on the real event, and from poem it soon turns into a song. The killer is now anonymous, the victims fictitious, but the storyline parallels the real events, and the result is a bleak but riveting ten-minute conceptual work, ambitious in scope, which plays out like a sinister movie screenplay. Using a variety of instrumental techniques and vocal characterizations, Harry describes the unfolding story, building the tension to its bloody climax, and along the way the time shifts back and forth with news reports of witness statements, and even getting into the mind of the killer, past and present. In a little under ten minutes we also get into the mind of a great songwriter who's at the very top of his game.

The song begins with the words *"She said not now"* repeated over the threatening opening chords, before the music then settles down to allow the narrator to set the scene. But who is this "she" the song refers to? For those listening to this song, not familiar with the real-life story, the title itself is a harbinger for what could transpire, and in the first two verses there's no guessing what's inside these suitcases. But why is there so little time to do what he has in mind?

It is an early Monday morning.
The sun is becoming bright on the land.
No one is watching as he comes a walking.
Two bulky suitcases hang from his hands.

He heads towards the tower that stands in the campus.
He goes through the door, he starts up the stairs.

The sound of his footsteps, the sound of his breathing,
The sound of the silence, for no one was there.

The narration is abruptly interrupted by what will be the first of a series of after-the-event news interviews in which a selection of individuals give brief but candid impressions of this person they once knew, or think they knew. Harry's distorted vocal enables the listener to single out these anonymous interviewees:

I didn't really know him.
He was kind of strange.
Always sort of sat there.
He never seemed to change

As the narrator resumes the story, there are early indications of the killer's mental state. In just four lines, we find him in a world that appears to be one of solitary isolation, unknown to anyone, even to whatever God that should be watching over him. He is questioning his very existence.

He reached the catwalk. He put down his burden.
The four-sided clock began to chime.
Seven am, the day is beginning.
So much to do and so little time.
He looks at the city where no one had known him.
He looks at the sky where no one looks down.
He looks at his life and what it had shown him.
He looks for his shadow, it cannot be found.

This is followed by another short witness statement:

He was such a moody child, very hard to touch.
Even as a baby he never smiled too much, no, no.

Following another witness statement, we have a glimpse into his background, and the first time we hear from the killer about a fragile relationship with his mother, his voice at first sounding agitated, but then gradually softening:

"You bug me," she said,
"You're ugly," she said,
"Please hug me," I said,
But she just sat there
With the same flat stare

79

That she saves for me alone
When I'm home.
When I'm home.
Take me home.

The tension is mounting, and so too his anger, as we begin to see what he is planning to do. He has an arsenal of weapons and his "questions" and "answers" and the "conversation" he seeks now reveal the horror of their true meaning:

He laid out the rifles, he loaded the shotgun,
He stacked up the cartridges along the wall.
He knew he would need them for his conversation.
If it went as it he planned, then he might use them all.
He said, "Listen you people I've got a question.
You won't pay attention but I'll ask anyhow.
I found a way that will get me an answer.
Been waiting to ask you 'til now.
Right now!"

While remaining unanswered, his anger reaches boiling point. In his turmoil, he begins to ask himself pointed questions that he alone knows the answers to:

"Am I?
I am a lover who's never been kissed.
Am I?
I am a fighter who's not made a fist.
Am I?
If I'm alive then there's so much I've missed.
How do I know I exist?
Are you listening to me?
Are you listening to me?
Am I?"

With that, the killing spree begins. But the narrator gives fictitious names to the victims, giving them the kind of anonymity that makes their fate seem secondary to the primary message of the song. And he doesn't hold back in his graphic description of their fates:

The first words he spoke took the town by surprise.
One got Mrs. Gibbons above her right eye.
It blew her through the window wedged her against the door.

Reality poured from her face, staining the floor.

Once again, the sequence of events is interrupted by a witness statement:

He was kind of creepy,
Sort of a dunce.
I met him at the corner bar.
I only dated the poor boy once,
That's all. Just once, that was all.

Three more victims fall before his answers finally come in the shape of bullets:

Bill Whedon was questioned as stepped from his car.
Tom Scott ran across the street but he never got that far.
The police were there in minutes, they set up barricades.
He spoke right on over them in a half-mile circle.
In a dumb struck city his pointed questions were sprayed.

The flow of the song suddenly changes again as the narration switches to spoken words:

He knocked over Danny Tyson as he ran towards the noise.
Just about then the answers started coming. Sweet, sweet joy.
Thudding in the clock face, whining off the walls,
Reaching up to where he sat there, answering calls.
Thirty-seven people got his message so far.
Yes, he was reaching them right where they are.

As the victim count reaches horrendous proportions, the cops get ready to storm the tower. The news is spreading fast as his deeds are now being broadcast - surely one of his aims. Following the final witness report we have the four-worded question that the media are asking – the very essence of the song:

They set up an assault team. They asked for volunteers.
They had to go and get him, that much was clear.
And the word spread about him on the radios and TVs.
In appropriately sober tone they asked "Who can it be?"

One final witness statement, and then we're back inside the killer's head. Will he find the answers he craves? Will we find the answer? He's becoming almost delirious now, intoxicated with the morbid ferment of his own doing.

81

He knows the end is near, and as we share his thoughts, it lets us into a deeply troubled, tormented mind. We find there is a want of love and kindness from the one person in the world who should have given it to him. As his world is about to end, his thoughts turn once again to his mother in a series of tender pleas for her love, but like a thunderbolt he is jolted back to reality and the burning truth that she is the root cause of all the demons in his head.

They're coming to get me, they don't want to let me
Stay in the bright light too long.
It's getting on noon now, it's goin to be soon now.
But oh, what a wonderful sound!

Mama, won't you nurse me?
Rain me down the sweet milk of your kindness.
Mama, it's getting worse for me.
Won't you please make me warm and mindless?

Mama, yes you have cursed me.
I never will forgive you for your blindness.
I hate you!

He now knows his fate is at hand as the answers come thick and fast. Shot to pieces, in his dying breath he gives us the one final and chilling reason for his actions.

The wires are all humming for me.
And I can hear them coming for me.
Soon they'll be here, but there's nothing to fear.
Not any more though they've blasted the door.

As the copter dropped the gas he shouted "Who cares?"
They could hear him laughing as they started up the stairs.
As they stormed out on the catwalk, blinking at the sun,
With their final fusillade his answer had come.

Am I?
There is no way that you can hide me.
Am ?
Though you have put your fire inside me.
Am I ?
You've given me my answer can't you see?
I was!
I am!

And now I will be
I will be

Take away the tragic real-life event the song is based on, and we are left with what surely is Harry's most cold and vivid depiction of what loneliness and being unloved can ultimately lead to. Some listeners will no doubt feel empathy with this, but find it difficult to condone the killer's actions. Others will be abhorred to even think Harry would give this subject matter such significance. But how does this stand up to being a love story? Unlike Whitman, the real killer, there is no brain tumor here. But is it right to try and humanize or even legitimize what Harry's character has done? The victims in the song - some 37 at the last count - don't seem to figure as much as the reason why they are dead. The lyrics are cleverly woven to show an uneasy sympathy with the perpetrator. The flashbacks certainly divulge a life of abject loneliness, totally devoid of love; his own thoughts betraying a boiling hatred of how his unhappy life has led him to this campus tower. From the mouths of those who think they knew him we get a picture - *"Kind of strange," "Moody," "Creepy," "Dunce," "Taciturn," "Dull Boy,", "Not much of a joiner"* - that when put together paint an image of a short fuse just waiting to be ignited. He wants the world to know who he was, who he is, but the world is not listening. Now he has found a way to get attention, and for evermore they will surely know what he will become. Harry's anonymous individual easily fits the bill for two of his favorite subjects - loneliness and being unloved. Maybe to ignore such people is a crime in itself, leaving us the culprits and the ones to blame for what transpires... But Harry isn't really saying that. In what after all is a fictional tale, inspired by but not based on what happened, he's leaving it to us, the curious listener, to pass judgment: Was the killer human or inhuman? Was he a tragic victim here, as well as the dead and dying left on the ground? That's what makes this great divisive song stand out, perhaps in a way that none of his other work has quite managed to do.

The song's musical and vocal complexities are reminiscent of Jethro Tull's epic *Thick as a Brick* album, released earlier that year and surely an obvious influence. Apparently over the intervening months since writing the song, Harry makes at least twenty or so changes to the tempo and melody, all to heighten the drama and give added impact, and the recording of the song has been described as tough going, considering what it involves. John Wallace, recognizing a masterpiece in the making, recalls the recording of the song: *"We learned that song in pieces in the studio, and it was so big we couldn't learn it all at once. Remember, **Sniper** was just our second LP. We tried to do it and would take it one second at a time. It's music first for me. Words are like placeholders. There's a lot to think about on stage, and then I get lost in it and become part of it."*

(Linda McCarty, *Circle*, Winter 2003)

Harry recalls the effect the song has in his interview with British DJ Noel Edmonds in December 1977:

"At a concert in Illinois I sang a song called **'Sniper'***, which I am very proud of. I think it is one of the best things I've done. Half way through the song a distinguished gentleman with a beard, sitting in the third row, jumped up and ran out, evidently in some distress. I asked about it later and nobody knew, until I asked one person, who said, 'Oh, didn't you know? That's the head of the English Department here. His son was killed by that sniper, the guy Charles Whitman in Texas. He became an alcoholic for three years, was an absolute wreck, but he pulled himself back together and is now a fantastic teacher...' Here's an example where if you're trying to write serious material, it's amazing how you can sometimes have an impact you didn't necessarily want to have. In general, I have to say Harry Chapin is the villain in almost all of his songs. I'm not writing from a superior point of view, especially in the male-female relationship. It's usually I'm the one doing something dumb. Frankly, I give that as a lesson to young songwriters. If you're going to say something nice about somebody, make it somebody else in your songs. If you're going to say something nasty, make it about yourself. Automatically people will trust you more."*

Not surprisingly most reviews of the song are mixed. One of Harry's severest critics, Stephen Holden, refers to it as *"grotesque"* and *"pretentious"* and even an *"all-time low in tasteless over-production."* Yet Alan Bradley is full of praise, admiring Harry for his risky approach to such a controversial real-life tragedy and viewing it as a perfect example of *"psychological commentary."* In another review of the song in January 1973, one critic calls it *"a kind of condensed modern opera in construction. An operetta...a combination of Oswald, Sirhan, and Manson."*

Harry later sings **'Sniper'** in a televised *Soundstage* concert in 1975, arguably his greatest performance captured on film, in which he appears almost maniacal at times, totally possessed by the subject matter, and leaving the audience applauding politely and seemingly stunned by what they have just heard and witnessed. Almost fifty years on, mass shootings are becoming more commonplace around the world, and hundreds of innocent victims die at the hands of "crazed" gunmen. We try to analyze why it happens; we study the perpetrators' background for a key to unlock their mindset. We look for hidden answers in the complexities of the human mind and what it might take to set off a sequence of events that lead to such devastating consequences. Maybe the answers have always been there...

From the cheap seats

Gerry Naughton - *Chapin provides an insight into the mind of the killer. Mass shootings don't just happen but are often the unleashing of an anger caused by an emotional and psychological breakdown. Every person has a need for love, social acceptance and a self-profile. An examination of Chapin's character the Sniper depicts a man who was rejected and isolated throughout his life. Thus, it is a very important song in that it highlights a major causation of anti-social behavior, criminality and destruction.*

Mary Ferri Kral – *I have always loved 'Sniper'. The way Harry could be in this guy's head was amazing to me. The music and how it changed throughout the song. The passion in it. Just everything. I was blown away the first time I heard 'Sniper'. Harry was a genius.*

Scott Sivakoff - *This album was one of the ones I wound up buying later in my discovery of Harry's music. I remember talking about Harry with a friend and we got on the topic of this song. At the time I hadn't heard it yet so it was hard to be part of that conversation, but I remember being told about how powerful the song was. When I finally heard the song, I remember being amazed at the power that it had. Not just lyrically but musically and arrangement too. Harry really was a musical genius but more than that he knew how to deliver a message and did so brilliantly with this song. The final part at the end is in my opinion the best piece of music on any of Harry's songs. The story is sadly still relevant in present day. We all want feedback and sadly those on the fringes sometimes opt for short, quick glory rather than a lifetime of nothing... but it is one of Harry's definite, true masterpieces.*

And the Baby Never Cries *****

The perfect counterpoint to the track that's gone before. A song that harks back to a brief relationship Harry has with Gail Hollenborg, niece of Manny and Janet Castro, the long-time family friends back in Brooklyn Heights, and of the times he charms her with his songs of love. Their brief relationship ends, and it's not until a year later that he sees her again, in which time she has been married and divorced, and is now living in an apartment, a single mother of a baby girl. Harry has Gail firmly in mind when writing the lyrics. Introducing the song in concert at Harper College in Palatine, Illinois, in April 1973, he relates the story:

"These singing evenings in these strange towns, for us always end up a little strange. You end up with very funny feelings....When you leave, half up and half down, you don't know what to do with yourself, and that time of night you have really basic urges, I guess the most basic thing is to have a good woman in your arms. A couple of years back I had a rather wild and wonderful wacky relationship with a young lady I used to go and visit at about 3am. She lived a couple of blocks away from the club I was singing at. She had a baby

from a prior relationship, and when I get there the baby was always asleep, so called this song about her."

As in Gail's case, we find the woman is separated from her husband and is now living alone as a single mother. In the final verse he writes of a tree brushing her bedroom window when the wind is blowing - quite removed from the story, but nevertheless so evocative, in keeping with the mood of the song. The chorus is seductively sublime, relating how in this brief moment of tranquility, they communicate in whispers, and how he makes her feel *"reborn."* The song was originally written as **'Baby Never Cries'** and included on the demo tape sent to Elektra in 1971, and also penciled in, but never selected, for inclusion on *Heads and Tales*.

Burning Herself ****

A tragic tale of a man in love with a woman who has the compulsive urge to self-harm, scarring her body with cigarettes, and in doing so reflecting the scars in her mind, a cry for help. Apparently, this is a true story about a woman Harry meets at Cornell, a story he relates while introducing the song at the Palatine concert in Illinois:

"So, we had a third date and I got very clever. I showed up and took her out in the morning, instead of worrying about curfew later on, and brought her back to my place around seven, and after some pleasant fumbling I got her blouse off. That's when this story turned rather crazy because there on her chest... there were some cigarette burns... I asked the obvious question – I said 'how?' And she said she had done it to herself. I asked her 'why?' She said that, after thinking about it for a while, 'Because I had to.' As I said, in true life those things that become funny situations can end up being little horror stories. I was really shaking and I ran out of there with her, dropped her off at the door, didn't kiss her anywhere, and tried to forget about the whole thing. About seven or eight months ago I was in LA. We were about to do the second album and I suddenly thought about this whole thing in a completely different context, because here in this day of women's lib I realize I spent about 30 or 40 hours with this girl because my mind was on one particular goal and I really had no inkling of how much trouble she was in, so I didn't like myself at that moment, and I wrote this rather strange, confused song."

Harry transforms the tragic story into a beautiful song. Is she preferring her passion for pain to the reality of her own empty existence? He can't think of anything that can help, and as a result feels he is letting her down. All in all, the song is an intelligent treatment of self-harm which of course is rare in songwriting, especially when the subject is a woman, and Harry approaches it in a gut-twisting, blunt manner that may not sit well with some listeners. Surprisingly, the song will be chosen as the flip-side to the **'Sunday Morning Sunshine'** single.

Cliff Geismar - *Harry was not afraid to deal with real issues, no matter how dark or tragic. It was one of the things that set him apart from many other artists.*

Scott Blitz - *Back in Harry's day self-mutilation was misunderstood and not really discussed. As a father of a child who self-mutilated for over a decade back in the 90s I learned that it was still a topic much in the dark. Harry covered it better than her therapist 18 years later. He didn't back away from any topic he wanted to shed light on and always did it in a classy up-front way. And shedding light on a subject, no matter how dark, is how real understanding and acceptance begins.*

Patricia Ehrich - *Harry was never afraid to tackle the darker side of the human condition.*

Barefoot Boy ****
With its innate simplicity, this imagery of an urban concrete landscape replacing the countryside is both prophetic and thought-provoking. This is another song evolving from an earlier eight-minute version that may have been excluded from *Heads and Tales*. In the longer version, there is an additional six minutes that has all the makings of a country jamboree, complete with the sound effects of lumberjacks, birdsong, train whistles, and even what appear to be *Deliverance*-style dueling banjos – altogether creating a sonic tapestry of a long-gone slice of American rural life. All this builds up to the final chorus, and a tender vocal almost drowned out by a church organ. The wistful music heard toward the end will resurface as the opening melody of the classic '**Mail Order Annie**' on Harry's next album, *Short Stories*. It's sad that the longer version isn't included on this album, but what we are left with is as evocative as they come. The album version is inexplicably listed as '**Barefoot Lady**' on the 2002 CD release on the Wounded Bird Label. However, to the fans' delight, the long version eventually surfaces as a bonus track on the double-CD *Heads and Tales / Sniper and Other Love Songs*, released on Elektra in 2004.

From the cheap seats
Keith W. Stanger - *I love this song... a song of keeping life simple and not getting caught up in the rat race. So many times, I turned to this song when the world was becoming complicated and stressful.*

Better Place To Be *****
The song that puts Watertown, New York, on the map. Written while Harry "spent a week there one afternoon," this is the epitome of a story-song which, like '**Sniper**', evolves from a poem and is perhaps his greatest statement on the heartbreaking subject of loneliness, the theme for so many of

his compositions. Recalling the many times he spent traveling from Brooklyn to visit brothers Tom and Steve at their colleges in upstate Ithaca and Plattsburgh, Harry writes about one of those journeys when he stops for a couple of hours at a roadside bar and grill in Watertown. While there, Harry gets into a conversation with an elderly man, who tells him he works as a night watchman for the J R Miller clothing company and reminiscences about the time he had a one-night stand with a beautiful lady. Dripping with pathos, Harry turns this into a bittersweet melodrama:

It was an early morning barroom,
And the place had just opened up.
And the little man came in so fast and started at his cups.
The broad who served the whiskey was a big old friendly girl.
Who tried to fight her empty nights by smiling at the world.

And she said, "Hey Bub, it's been awhile since you been around.
Where the hell you been hiding and why do you look so down?"
But the little man just sat there like he never heard a sound.

Her smiling face is itself a thin veil disguising her own empty life, a life in which she is acutely self-conscious of her own appearance.

The waitress, she gave out a cough, and acting not the least put off,
She spoke once again, "I don't want to bother you, consider it's understood.
I know I'm not no beauty queen, but I sure can listen good."
And the little man took his drink in his hand
And he raised it to his lips.
He took a couple of sips.
And he told the waitress this story

As the man begins to tell her his story, the waitress listens intently. As the storytelling now switches from narrator to this anonymous little man, we are transported back in time to a magical moment in what seems an otherwise downbeat life. Instead of mentioning the real-life company, the narrator has him working at a factory with a similar, but fictitious, name.

"I am the midnight watchman at Miller's Tool and Die.
I watch the metal rusting, and I watch the time go by.
A week ago at the diner I stopped to get a bite.
And this here lovely lady, she sat two seats from my right.
And Lord, Lord, Lord, she was alright!
"Well, she was so damned beautiful she could warm a winter's frost.
But she was long past lonely, and well-nigh kinda lost.

Now I'm not much of a mover, or a pick-em-up easy guy,
But I decided to glide on over, and give her one good try.
And Lord, Lord, Lord she was worth a try.
"Tongued-tied like a school boy, I stammered out some words.
But it didn't really matter much, 'cause I don't think she heard.
She just looked clear on through me to a space back in my head.
It shamed me into silence, as quietly she said,
'If you want me to come with you, then that's all right with me.
'Cause I know I'm going nowhere, and anywhere's a better place to be.'

We never do get to know what the man says to her, but we kind of imagine it's a real bad chat-up line, and that this woman is not looking for conversation, just an opportunity to satisfy a desire, a long-felt need, to have someone to connect with physically as a short-term remedy for her own empty life.

"I drove her to my boarding house, and I took her up to my room.
And I went to turn on the only light to brighten up the gloom.
But she said, 'Please leave the light off, Oh I don't mind the dark.'
And as her clothes all tumbled 'round her, I could hear my heart.
"The moonlight shone upon her as she lay back in my bed.
It was the kind of scene I only had imagined in my head.
I just could not believe it, to think that she was real.
And as I tried to tell her she said 'Shhh.. I know just how you feel.
And if you want to come here with me, then that's all right with me.
'Cause I've been oh so lonely, lovin' someone is a better way to be.
Anywhere's a better way to be.'
"The morning came so swiftly as I held her in my arms.
But she slept like a baby, snug and safe from harm.
I did not want to share her or dare to break the mood,
So before she woke, I went out to buy us both some food.
"I came back with my paper bag, to find that she was gone.
She'd left a six-word letter saying 'It's time that I moved on.'

And that's where his story ends. The waitress is an emotional wreck by now and, putting herself down once more, offers to take the place of this woman and share their lonely lives together:

The waitress took her bar rag, and she wiped it across her eyes.
And as she spoke her voice came out as something like a sigh.
She said. "I wish that I was beautiful, or that you were halfway blind.
I wish I weren't so doggone fat, I wish that you were mine.
And I wish that you'd come with me, when I leave for home.
Cause we both know all about loneliness, and living all alone."

And the little man,
Looked at the empty glass in his hand.
And he smiled a crooked grin,
He said, "I guess I'm out of gin.
And know we both have been so lonely.
And if you want me to come with you, then that's all right with me.
'Cause I know I'm goin' nowhere and anywhere's a better place to be."

Maybe rather than continuing to look at his life from the bottom of a glass, he accepts the waitress's offer, and they go off together, leaving us to imagine the outcome. The woman in the man's story remains a mystery, much as Sue does in **'Taxi'** (at least until the sequel). We know nothing about her apart from her loneliness. Some have suggested she's a call girl with a conscience; others just a sad lonely heart. But we will always remember the *"rotund"* friendly waitress with the big smile that's almost as big as her breaking heart, and we hope that for the two of them their time together will have a deeper long-lasting meaning, as loneliness is a hard and hollow place.

Whatever the unanswered questions, it remains one of the most talked about songs of Harry's career, and certainly top of the list for many of his devoted fans. *Rolling Stone*'s Stephen Holden is as horrified with this song as he was with **'Sniper'**, and compares it to a *"Saroyanesque barroom soap opera."* Another critic writes that Harry does not simply use his characters to make a point, but has the ability to portray them in all their different complexities, which in reality is often hard to achieve in song. The truth is it's just a bittersweet story of loneliness, like so many of Harry's songs, likely to bring large lumps to many throats. Although there are three people in the story, we all root for the little guy and the waitress. The other woman's loneliness seems fleeting, a temporary fix at best, but it's nice to imagine that these two lost souls will now go off to have a more permanent bond. Like many of Harry's story songs, it begs for a sequel.

In concert, Harry often cites this as one of his favorite songs, and when performed live it remains, along with a certain song about bananas, a permanent fixture on the setlist. Despite its length, it is the only other song on the album to be released as a single, first as a two-parter and then backed with **'Winter Song'**, but it only reaches #118 in the *Billboard* 100. A live version from the 1976 album ***Greatest Stories Live*** does slightly better, reaching #86.

From the cheap seats
Kelly Barry - *First, it's a story about a man telling a story. It's filled with loneliness and people's attempts to escape it. For these two truly lonely people, the escapes are destined to be temporary, but it's better than always being alone. The music is filled with pathos and emotion - perfect for the inevitable finish. I cry as often as not when I listen to it - and it can't just be*

heard in the background, it must be listened to for true appreciation of this Harry gem

Mary Jo McDonough - *Harry's songs are so visual and personal. And I think music videos are almost an insult... as if they are supposed to make up your mind for you. '**Better Place to Be**' is particularly visual and personal. Every time I listen to it, it's as if a mini movie plays in my head, but it's MY mini movie. I am so glad that Harry lived when he did, before music videos became, what's the word, de rigueur.*

Ellen Gordon Klein – *Love this song. It's a beautiful story about both the man and the waitress. There are so many lonely people in this world, and when they can find each other, even for a night, the pain of the loneliness can be forgotten. One of my very favorite stories*

Circle **

This is maybe the only song written for Tom Chapin's *Make a Wish* television show that makes it into a recording studio. Originally titled '**All My Life's a Circle**', Tom takes up the story:

"After the gigs at the Gate, we usually met, ate, and rehashed the evening at Maria's Diner in Brooklyn Heights. It was late Sunday night, and we were going to be shooting the episode for 'Circle' early on Monday morning, and he promised me he'd have it done. So at 6:00am Harry called me and played the first verse and chorus over the phone while I took down words and scratched out the tune." (*Circle*, Spring 2003)

The producers of the show are impressed with the song, and within a matter of hours Tom is performing it on camera, as he strolls around the Cinderella fountain in Central Park. For a while the song exists only as the first verse and chorus, and it's hard not to imagine children across America who watch the show humming the tune to themselves in the days and weeks that follow. One person who is really impressed with the song is Harry's mother Elspeth, who encourages him to write more verses. Not wanting to disappoint his mother, Harry does just that and in no time at all this song will become his anthem, performed perhaps more times in concert than any other song, usually as an encore and later coupled with the equally touching '**You Are the Only Song**'. Surprisingly it is never issued as a single, although it becomes one of the most covered of Harry's songs, recorded by artists as diverse as Roy Orbison, Edith Brickell and Siouxsie and the Banshees, and even achieves top ten chart success in the UK when covered by The New Seekers that same year.

Woman Child **

With mass murderers and self-harm already covered on the album, it's no surprise that it doesn't end there, and we are soon back to dealing with controversial issues. This time the subject matter is teenage abortion. With still a year to go before the Supreme Court legalizes abortion, Harry tackles it in a way that might surprise some listeners. The narrator of the song, also a singer, is in a relationship with a girl we assume is much younger. The story begins with the teenage girl walking the streets one night. Not knowing what to do or where to go, she calls the narrator in the early hours of the morning to tell him she is pregnant. But he doesn't think it is his. Although offering money for an abortion, he refuses to go with her, but assures her that at the clinic she won't feel a thing, but have *"the sweet salvation that little knife can bring."* When it's all over, she can go home and rest, not feel any guilt, and he can get on with his singing and put it all down to a *"two-hundred-dollar mishap."* But it's in the last line of the chorus that the true tragedy of the story hits home, when the narrator asks the girl, *"What will you tell your teddy bear?"* These insensitive remarks will of course be looked upon in horror by many, but this is just Harry once again provoking a reaction and not in any way based on any personal experience.

Ron Palmer's guitar playing on the second verse is outstanding, along with Steve's subtle piano and the shimmering sound effects towards the end, but once again it's Harry's strong vocal that elevates the song and gives it that extra punch that the hard-edged lyrics require.

Winter Song **

Another touching song, this one is inspired by old flame and fellow Cornell student Jenny Gillette. Although their relationship is brief, he writes fondly about her as each season passes by. Performed with just acoustic guitar and cello, this is a fitting end to the shock, sorrow, and sympathy of all that's gone before. It will be chosen as the flip-side to the **'Better Place To Be'** single when released later in the year. **'Old College Avenue'** on the next album will also have his time with Jenny in mind.

The War with the Critics Begins

In September 1972, with royalty cheques for his first album now coming through, Harry and his family are able to move from Point Lookout to live in a large 80-year-old, multi-room house in Huntington, Long Island, overlooking the waters of Long Island Sound. Harry often refers to it as the *"Make a Wish* House," as royalties from the show help pay for it. The following month Harry makes his first brief visit to Great Britain, where he appears at the Queen Elizabeth Hall on London's Southbank, supporting two other Elektra signings, Ian Matthews' new folk/rock band Plainsong, and Nashville singer-songwriter Mickey Newbury, whose most recent album includes the classic 'An American Trilogy', and who will write many

Chapinesque-style story-songs in his career, the most notable being the tear-inducing 'San Francisco Mabel Joy'.

In early October ***Sniper and Other Love Songs*** is finally released. As expected, the reviews are either very good or very bad, mostly the latter. Harry's very own bête noire, Stephen Holden of *Rolling Stone*, writing on December 7th, is reviled by what he refers to as Harry's bawling, off-pitch voice churning out a *"wretched excess"* of *"emotional diarrhea."* Admitting to the fact that the energy and feeling expressed in the songs may evoke some measure of sympathy, it is dampened somewhat by Harry's overbearing self-pity.

Melody Maker carries two positive reviews of the album: *The first time you listen to a song by Harry Chapin, let me give you a bit of advice: close your eyes and let the pictures come. I guarantee they will come. Perhaps its because he's been a film director good enough to be nominated for an Academy Award or perhaps because he's so conscious of the singer-songwriter's story-telling role that his music publishing company is called Story Songs Ltd. They come, even with a schlock song like **'Circle'**, which suddenly becomes less of a schlock song and more of a, well, philosophical statement when Harry Chapin himself sings it...*

One critic compares Harry to Dylan, while the *Brooklyn Spectator* declares that *"few have the perspicacity and imagination to create a prose story line set to music. Thanks to this singer, a new term joins the musical glossary: Chapinesque."*

Harry will always focus on the negative reviews, and it hurts. Even his brothers Tom and James view the album as being full of doom and gloom, and the white collars at Elektra fear that if people don't make a connection and relate to the songs, it will ultimately fail. Yes, they admire its artistry, even its audacity, but when it comes to sales number crunching, there are real concerns. Without a hit record that AM radio stations can play, how are people even going to be aware of him? It all comes back to the record industry's maxim: only hit records make money, not pretentious artistic statements. Always seemingly at loggerheads with the critics who rubbish his music and performance, Harry is fighting a losing battle. He needs a champion to fight in his corner. Unlike contemporary singer songwriters like Carly Simon, Neil Diamond and Elton John, who are well on the way to superstardom, he feels his career is beginning to stagnate before it's even given a chance to lift off. He considers his new album his best work, the songs the best he's ever written, and despite that it's being slated. Many of the music critics of the day just don't get Harry, or refuse to admit they do. Some tend to review the music without even considering the lyrics, and rate his musical style as average at best. Those who do try to analyze the words come up with a variety of adjectives to describe their views, using pretentious and kitschy phrases to mock the very thing they are guilty of doing themselves.

Harry himself confesses: *"My sound is really like anything else. It's developed from several things, with the result that I like to write all different kinds of songs. Lyrically, I find I must have some experience of what I'm writing about, if not literally, then at least emotionally. The people in my songs must know about what they speak. I have written songs where that innate honesty doesn't come across, but I've never released them."*

So why has Harry become a target for such hostility and the beneficiary of toxic reviews from some critics? New York radio DJ Pete Fornatale, considered "the father of FM" and a big supporter of the singer, nails it when he suggests that Harry has a habit of always telling it like it is, without thinking it through first, and by doing so just rubs people up the wrong way. Some look on him as just a self-important phony, while others may be a little jealous of the close relationship he is developing with his audience, who not only celebrate his live performances but now participate in them too. So, if people like this are having a problem with the man himself, they are not going out on a limb to praise his music. This never-ending tussle to have his music recognized will continue to go on for years to come. Only after his untimely death in nine years' time will their plaudits come flooding in. However, unlike those for television or movies, music reviews don't always impact on sales. As long as a record gets sufficient airplay, the listeners out there will have the final say on how much money it's going to make.

Sniper and Other Love Songs was always going to be a financial risk, but it stands as Harry's most underrated work and his finest musical achievement, a prime example of a cinematic style of storytelling that defines the genre. Self-indulgent, perhaps, pretentious, maybe; but like the minstrels of old he captivates the listener and leaves them with some thought-provoking and candid imagery of a darker, somewhat sinister slice of American life and the complexities of the human soul. Nearly fifty years after its first release opinion is changing, and it now receives the credit it deserves. That year, Harry will have the last laugh, when the success of ***Heads and Tales***, and **'Taxi'** in particular, earns him a Grammy nomination for Best New Artist of the Year, losing out to the band America. He also has recognition from *Billboard* magazine by being presented with their Trendsetter Award *"for devising a storytelling style of songwriting with a narrative impact rare to popular music."*

So, there it is. Two albums, one hit single, and a mixed bag of critical reviews, both good and not so good. Not an auspicious start when it comes to commercial success, but with his time in the recording business not even a year old yet, Harry has managed to write half a dozen songs that will be considered among his finest work. The likes of **'Taxi'**, **'Dogtown'**, **'Sniper'** and **'Better Place To Be'** will showcase just what a gifted songwriter Harry really is, with some people in the industry placing him well above some of his contemporaries. Whether he can keep this standard up remains to be seen, and certainly he will have Elektra asking that same question. Although some will say his best is yet to come, these two albums alone cannot be surpassed in their creative impact. This is not the prosaic pop fodder that is rife around this time; this is putting the dynamics of a story and weaving them into song in a way seldom done before. This is in essence a new art form, and it belongs uniquely to Harry Chapin.

Frustrating Times for both Sandy and the Band

On November 13th Harry and the band are once again invited on *The Tonight Show with Johnny Carson* and they do a fine performance of **'Greyhound'**. A few days later Sandy is driving Harry to JFK Airport for the start of a week-long engagement at the Great Southeast Music Hall in in Atlanta. En route she suddenly goes into labour and is rushed to hospital, where she gives birth to their second child, Joshua Burke Chapin, two months early. After Harry departs for Georgia, complications set in and Joshua goes into special care. Although missing the birth of his son, Harry flies back from Atlanta every night after the show to be with them.

The end of the month finds Harry doing a six-night stint back at The Troubadour in West Hollywood, supported by Hall & Oates, whose impressive debut album *Whole Oats* has just been released. During the concert Hall & Oates manage to persuade Harry to come on stage during their encore and join them in one of their songs called 'Whistling Dave'. After spending Christmas at home in their new Huntington home, it's not long before Harry is out on the road again. Following another performance on the *Carson* show, in which they promote the soon-to-be-released single, **'Better Place To Be'**, they play several nights at the popular Boarding House in San Francisco. February finds more television work, and on the 23rd the band tape two shows, *The Midnight Special*, in which they perform **'Sunday Morning Sunshine'**, **'Sniper'** and **'Taxi'**, and also two songs for a return visit to the *Carson* show. Both of these are followed that night with a college concert in New Rochelle.

It is indeed a busy time for all concerned, no more so than for Sandy, who now has baby Josh to worry about, and the added news that her father has been taken seriously ill. On April 15th, while Harry is down in Philadelphia co-hosting an episode of the *Mike Douglas Show* and unable to get away, Sandy's father dies, and a part of her life has gone forever. Meanwhile, the growing unrest in Harry's band results in its first casualty. Sixteen months after first auditioning for a cellist in the back room of Elspeth Chapin's house, Tim Scott decides to quit the band for a career in classical music, later citing personal and artistic differences with Harry. The disorganized, haphazard approach to rehearsing and recording, Harry's often-bullish egotistical nature, bad time-keeping, and even a dislike for some of the music they are making, just doesn't fit in with his idea of a solid professional way of working, and the recent strains of completing this last album seems to be the final straw. Tim will carry on until June, giving Harry time to get a replacement, and even participates in some of the recording sessions for the new album.

Sandy's frustration with Harry is evident in the many poems she is writing at the time. While in the process of putting together songs for **Sniper** Harry has asked her for ideas, and when Sandy suggests something about a father-son relationship, he doesn't really see it as hit material and rejects the idea. But Sandy isn't about to give up. Instead she re-writes it as a complete lyric that he can turn into a song. She calls it **'Cat's in the Cradle'**. It is a subtle way of telling Harry how she now feels about their relationship, and more importantly the failing relationship he is having with his children. When she shows the lyric to him a few weeks later, while home on one of his usual short visits, he looks it over but chooses to dismiss it as a potential song. Harry still isn't getting the message, and this situation will remain so for many more months.

Those next few months will see their relationship reaching breaking point.

Short Stories

"Music is a cruel mistress. You're putting your ego out there for a shot and you've got a lot of people judging you, and sometimes the verdict isn't as nice as you'd like it to be"

Enter Paul Leka

Michael Masters is a more accomplished cellist than Tim Scott, having attended the Julliard School of Performing Arts in Manhattan for the best part of seven years. Hailing from Columbus, Ohio, and in his late twenties, Masters can easily be mistaken for being John Wallace's kid brother; tall, bearded and bespectacled. He also has no trouble settling into the band, at least for the time being. Wallace sees an immediate improvement with Masters on board. But for Harry and the band there are even bigger changes just around the corner. By April 1973 Harry is busy writing and re-writing songs for the next album, with brother Steve doing a fine job with some of the arrangements, and a few of the new songs are tested at live concerts to gauge the audience reaction. On April 19th a concert at Harper College in Palatine, Illinois, is recorded for posterity, and it showcases some early versions of songs like **'They Call Her Easy'** and **'Mr Tanner'**, both of which will grace the new album. The full setlist is as follows: Sunday Morning Sunshine, Greyhound, Empty, Talkin' Bout Love (Steve), Better Place To Be, Pigeon Run, And the Baby Never Cries, They Call Her Easy, Mr Tanner, Could You Put Your Light On Please, Burning Herself, Any Old Kind of Day, The Old Greasy Spoon, Taxi, Sniper.

The new album will be called ***Short Stories*** (although the "short" may be a little misleading). With the dismal failure of the last album hanging heavy on his mind, and for that matter, on Jac Holzman's too, Harry needs to look at solutions to the underlying problems. What did go wrong with what he thought was his best work to date? To begin with, he looks at the production. Holzman had done a good job with producing ***Heads and Tales***, but the decision to hand production of ***Sniper*** over to Fred Kewley is now looked upon as a mistake by both Harry and Holzman. The answer lies in getting a top professional on board. Fred has no qualms about giving up production duties, as he can now devote all his energies into the band's management. His first assignment is to find a producer to fit the bill. He remembers Paul Leka, the young songwriter and producer at Columbia Records, who back in the Village Gate days had come down to watch Harry perform and recommended him to his boss Clive Davis, who subsequently lost out to Holzman in the bidding war to sign Harry. Fred now gives him a call.

97

Leka has music pedigree. Already a multi-instrumentalist, successful songwriter, and producer of hits like the Lemon Pipers' 'Green Tambourine', and more recently co-producer of REO Speedwagon's first two albums, he has a sound understanding of record production, working for one of the biggest labels in the land, although not quite yet considered at the top of his game. But Leka is not all that happy working at Columbia, and he is waiting for the opportunity to go it alone. The timing is just right. Not only does Leka agree to produce *Short Stories*, but he also offers the use of the sixteen-track Connecticut Recording Studios, located above a five and dime store on Main Street, Bridgeport, which he co-owns with partner Billy Gross, and he's also brought along the experienced Billy Rose II as sound engineer. Harry is impressed. Not only can he now put the bad memories of recording on the West Coast behind him, Bridgeport is just a two-hour drive from his home in Huntington. New surroundings; a new producer and studio; home every night with Sandy and the kids - it couldn't be better.

Bridgeport Studios - Recording Closer to Home

With everyone settled into their new surroundings and now closer to their homes, work begins in earnest in their new studio. Leka is looking for a fuller sound and brings in a handful of session musicians and backing singers. Drummer Buddy Salzman has already played on many of the Four Seasons' biggest hits and more recently on Melanie's smash hit single, 'Brand New Key'. Bobby Carlin is also on hand with fresh sticks, as well as Harry's dad Jim. Harold Keinz will add a variety of brass and woodwind instruments to the mix, as well as a thirteen-piece orchestra arranged by Irving Spice. Last but not least there will be harmonicist Dave Armstrong. As a bonus for Harry, brothers Steve and Tom will also be on hand to help. But the move comes with a problem. By switching locations, it forfeits the free studio time agreed to by Holzman for using his LA facilities, and now Harry has to pay the rent himself, and the anticipated six-week recording schedule he has in mind could cost him an estimated $35,000. To keep the cost down Harry uses the studio through the night and following morning at a lower rental rate.

Meanwhile tour dates have to be met. After appearing once again at the Great Southeast Music Hall in Atlanta toward the end of April, the band perform at a number of venues, including benefit concerts in Rochester and Philadelphia, and on May 9th they make another appearance on *The Tonight Show with Johnny Carson* to debut a song called **'Mr Tanner'**, destined to become the highlight of the new album. With rehearsals and recordings well under way, there comes another bombshell. It is announced that the former owner of Asylum Records, David Geffen, is to be the new chairman of Elektra/Asylum, and that former president Jac Holzman is considering either resignation or retirement. Harry is in danger of losing his friend and mentor. Although the contract Harry signed with Elektra back in November 1972 guarantees to record, release, and promote his first three albums, there is of course an option for him to renegotiate after the second one, especially if it comes to having issues with the label. The option also applies if Holzman decides to leave the company. This of course puts Harry in a strong bargaining position, and astute manager Fred Kewley sniffs an opportunity here. Why not tout the new album to other record labels and see what happens? If no offers come in, it still means Elektra have to honor the contract and produce *Short Stories*. In another heated meeting in the New York office, this time with Holzman, Ann Purtill and soon-to-be label boss Mel Posner in attendance, Harry and Fred tell them their intentions, but nothing is resolved, and the meeting ends with an angry Holzman saying that there will be no work done on the new album if they get into talks with rival companies. Harry does no more than call his bluff and begins the process of selling his new album to another label. Several turn him down, including Warner Brothers, who, by belonging to the same parent company as Elektra, are only too aware of what a financial disaster *Sniper and Other Love Songs* continues to be. Of course, Holzman soon finds out about Harry's touting effort from Warner boss Mo Ostin, and by some accounts is enraged. In the meantime, Harry gets his producer Leka to contact a friend and ex-Columbia man, Kip Cohen, now one of the bigwigs at A&M Records. After listening to the almost-complete collection of songs for the album, Cohen is more than impressed, and gladly offers a contract. Eventually the whole idea comes to nothing, when Harry manages to settle his differences with Holzman and Geffen after an emotion-filled meeting. For Fred Kewley it leaves a bitter taste in his mouth, feeling his position as manager is now being undermined. In his opinion it will be a mistake to stay with Elektra when there are hard-working labels out there that can offer a better deal. One day, but not now, he will be proved right.

So, with business matters settled, at least for now, the focus is back on the music, and Elektra do their bit to make the third album a much-needed success. With Harry writing and re-writing songs up to the last minute, ten are selected for the final cut. One of them will prove another turning-point for both Harry and the label. The album cover, of course, needs to stand out, as there is a market out there for people who buy albums more for their attractive cover than the musical content. Impressed by his artwork on the inside jacket of *Sniper*, road manager Rob White is again called upon to deliver another surreal visual interpretation - a graphic image in which the faces of the band members, along with their instruments, are seemingly being engulfed in an erotic, writhing sea of naked bodies, glaring eyes, snakes, chess pieces, and even dogs both small and very large (a nod to **'Dogtown'**, perhaps?). Yet another gatefold sleeve includes both lyrics and three of photographer Ruth

Bernal's images, one of which is an intimate glimpse of Harry holding up his young daughter Jenny.

Short Stories (1973) *****
Elektra EKS 75065
Recorded: Connecticut Recording Studios, Bridgeport, CT. Spring-Summer 1973
US Release Date: December 1st 1973
Producer - Paul Leka
Engineer - Billy Rose II

The album will produce three of Harry's most iconic songs. The eponymous title track is followed by **'W.O.L.D.'**, soon to become the darling of middle-aged radio DJs and the first UK hit single. Three introspective tracks, **'Song For Myself'**, **'Song Man'** and **'Changes'** bring side one to a thought-provoking close. The second side of the album is a tour de force, with the first three tracks, **'They Call Her Easy'**, **'Mr Tanner'** and **'Mail Order Annie'**, being story-songs that are often cited among Harry's best work. The album rounds off with **'There's a Lot of Lonely People Tonight'** and the wistful **'Old College Avenue'**, familiar songs about loneliness and lost love.

Short Stories ****
Great opening track and a short metaphor for the human condition. The narrator asks his lover rhetorical one-line questions, believing that the mixed emotions they experience are just simple "short stories," nothing more than chapters of their past and future life story. A strong opening song, with clever wordplay, and Harry's voice putting his views across in a dynamic way. Although having the potential to be a hit in its own right, it is chosen for the flip-side to the single **'W.O.L.D.'**

From the cheap seats
Thomas Dolan - *Harry, I believe, saw life as a series of these short stories. Seemingly unconnected tales that, only upon reading/living all of them, reveal a common theme. Harry reveals that he has lived all of these lives...After living these stories, he/we can find himself / our self... After we realize we are all connected. The song ends with one meaningful human connection... the building block of all love. That's what I've got.*

Alan L. Geraci - *Our lives are a patchwork of short stories. Stories that when stitched together are the values that make us whole. "I have found a smile in the midst of tears. I can find a heart in the midst of fear."*

W.O.L.D. *****

The song that makes Harry an international star also serves as this author's introduction to the singer, when played for the first time on UK radio in early 1974. And what a song it is. Like **'Taxi'** had done almost two years before with cab drivers across the country, it will do the same for the growing army of middle-aged radio disc jockeys still hanging on to their careers, both home and abroad. One or two of them will claim to have been the inspiration for the song. One story relates Harry meeting and listening to Jim Connors of Boston's WMEX radio station, a fan of his music, making a phone call from the studio to his ex-wife Linda. This leads to Harry and Connors having a deep conversation that allegedly provides the background for the song. In a later interview, Linda recalls: *"He let Harry Chapin listen to a phone conversation between him and myself, and he took it and ran with it. It was a sad, personal conversation that led Chapin to write the song. The conversation was about the way he did not come back to see his children.... He called and told me, 'just to give you a heads up, there's a song out about us.' I said ok, and then I heard it on the radio."*

In the song the aging DJ is calling his wife on the phone in Boise, Idaho. He's back in town again and now working as a morning jock for the local radio station W.O.L.D. The opening lines will be omitted from the single version, with listeners not even realizing he's making a phone call.

Hello honey it's me...
What did you think when you heard me back on the radio?
What did the kids say when they knew it was their long lost Daddio?

And this is where the single version starts off:

Remember how we listened to the radio
And I said 'That's the place to be'
And how I got the job as an FM Jock the day you married me?
It was two kids and I was into AM rock
But I just had to run around
It's been eight years since I left you babe
Let me tell you 'bout what's gone down

The chorus follows, with the narrator trying to convince his wife how his exciting career makes him feel young-at-heart:

I am the morning DJ at W.O.L.D.
Playing all the hits for you wherever you may be
The bright good-morning voice who's heard but never seen
Feeling all of forty-five going on fifteen

101

The drinking I did on my last big gig it made my voice go low
They said that they liked the young sound when they let me go
So I drifted on down to Tulsa, Oklahoma, to do me a late night talk show
Now I've worked my way back home again here to Boise, Idaho
That's how this business goes
I'm making extra money doing high school sock hops
I'm the big time guest MC
You should hear me talking to the little children
And listen what they say to me
I got a spot on the top of my head, just begging for a new toupee
There's a tire round my gut from sitting on my ***
But it's never gonna go away

Although he tries to convince his wife how successful he still is, he cannot escape the fact that his age is becoming a handicap. He is now close to home, and he has a dream of finally settling down. But it depends on one thing:

Sometimes I get this crazy dream
That I just take off in my car
But you can travel on ten thousand miles and still stay where you are
Thinkin' that I should stop this jocking
And start that record store
Maybe I could settle down if you'd take me back once more

So, it's not the first time he's asked her to take him back. How many times? Again, this is where the single version omits these next four lines and goes straight into the chorus, depriving those particular 45rpm listeners of a few seconds it takes to get his wife's response and complete the story of how she's now met someone else:

Okay honey I see.
I guess he's better than me.
Sure old girl, I understand.
You don't have to worry, I'm such a happy man

He's now become the **'Cat's in the Cradle'** man, traveling around the country from one radio station to another, from talk shows to high school dances, and all that time he's getting older and out of touch with current trends and, even worse, getting out of touch with his wife and family. But he's kidding himself and the *"happy man"* that his radio persona has always portrayed is a thin disguise for how he must really feel - his career and marriage have both been failures and it seems he has no future.

Harry has his own view of these aging jocks: *"The guys saw the world as their apple and there were those in their prime. The older guys were hanging on by their fingernails...I flashed out what it would be like to be forty-five going on fifteen because the disc jockeys had to keep young listeners while they were getting older."*

In an interview on Noel's radio show three years later, Harry reflects on the song: *"'W.O.L.D.' is really a song that was triggered by 'Taxi'. After 'Taxi' came out, my record company sent me all around the country to meet disc-jockeys. And there were three types. There were the young-comers, who saw the world ahead of them as a giant apple, ready to be juicily bitten into. There were the guys in their prime, who stood astride the business. And there were older guys, who were holding on by their fingernails, desperately trying to relate, forty-five going on fifteen. I met a bunch of those. We all go there, but it how we continue relating."*

Unbeknown to Harry at the time of writing, somewhere in the backwoods of Virginia a tiny radio station is operating under the letters W.O.L.D. Now they are suing him for $25,000. Harry remains calm: *"I'm not worried at all. There's no way they can win that case. Before they filed the suit, they were even asking me if I'd give them an interview. The funny thing about that station is they haven't even got a morning DJ...Every radio station in the States adopts three of four letters as its name. The ones in the east start with the letter K, those in the west with the letter W. All I did was to take the word OLD – because the song is about a DJ aging – and add it to the letter W."*

For any radio hams out there about to burst a blood vessel, yes, you are correct. It would be impossible for Harry's W.O.L.D. station to be based in Boise, Idaho, as the call letters of most radio stations west of the Mississippi begin with "K" and not "W." But when performing the song around the country, Harry usually replaced the name in the last verse to the call letters of the local radio station, much to the audience's delight.

Harry compares the life of a disc jockey to that of his own career as a performer: *"It's a lot less glamorous than it seems. You spend all your time in some tiny room eight feet by ten trying to hold a one-man party on the air. No matter how bad you feel you've got to sound exciting. Apart from the occasional phone call from a listener, you don't get any feedback, so you have to wait three months for the ratings before you know whether you're doing okay or not...Both deal with audiences younger than themselves and both face a tremendous strain on their life as a result. They also share a certain sense of insecurity arising out of the fact that neither have much longevity in their careers. There are three types. The newcomers who are all set to go, the ones in their prime, and the older guys who are just hanging on by their fingernails...No one complains it's inaccurate. When I first wrote it, I guessed that some DJs would look upon it as a downer, but fortunately most accept it. Some even go as far as to say it's about them."*

103

Sandy Chapin has her own views on **'W.O.L.D.'** and sees the character as a composite person. As Harry likes to do his self-promoting, he meets up with a lot of radio station jockeys and program directors across the country, and while launching the *Sniper* album Harry holds a big party at their Huntington house and invites lots of radio station people who he gets to know quite well. The **'W.O.L.D.'** character is based on some of these people, but no one in particular. However, the song reputedly helps inspire writer Hugh Wilson develop the idea for his 1978 television sitcom *WKRP* in Cincinnati, starring Gary Sandy as the aging boss of a struggling radio station. I'm sure if he was asked, Harry would have gladly re-written the song as its theme tune.

Released as a single in the US in December, backed with **'Short Stories'**, it peaks at #36 on the *Billboard* Hot 100 chart, and #26 on the Cashbox Top 100, but it seems to do better in Canada, reaching an impressive #9 in their Adult Contemporary chart, and #14 in their RPM Top Singles listing. In Europe it receives enough airplay to see it reach #4 in the Dutch Top 40 and #30 in the UK's *New Musical Express* charts at the beginning of June 1974, making it Harry's most successful single in that country.The song's success in the UK is mainly down to Noel Edmonds, the BBC's very own "morning deejay" radio presenter, who chooses it as his record of the week and gives it sufficient airplay to get it charted. *Melody Maker* later laments on the poor chart showing for one of the album's best-known songs: *"By now it should be deemed a case of criminal neglect that Harry Chapin's 'W.O.L.D.' is not in the top ten, or even higher, because it's a classic of a kind, combining a neat moralistic storyline with an appropriately catchy, schmaltzy melody. Doubly a pity because one might recommend this album from which it's taken if it weren't for the fact that the single is far and away the best track here…"*

From the cheap seats

Cindy Funk - *To me it shows that sometimes show business is not what it's cracked up to be. You'd think that being a big-time DJ would be glamorous. But in reality, it's an ageing guy with a good voice in a studio, totally alone*

Mark Trottier - *It's the story of a man who always lived for today and refused to grow up; until, suddenly, it was tomorrow and he was nowhere man. He just has to keep telling himself he is happy*

Jason Colannino - *Any other song writer of the day would dare to write a song about the trials and tribulations of a morning DJ? It sure seemed like a dream job didn't it? Playing your favorite records getting to meet famous entertainers getting those free concert tickets. And hopefully you're being heard by millions of people. Harry brought a glimpse into the personal life of a radio DJ whose job is pretty much on the line at all times. As soon as those ratings slip just a little bit you not only lose your job you have to pack your*

104

things and go to a completely different town or even a completely different state and do it all over again, taking a toll on your personal life

Song For Myself ***

The first of a trio of back-to-back introspective songs. Here he is in an apprehensive and philosophical mood, and asking his girl rhetorical questions whether they should worry more about the future of their country in light of the Watergate scandal. The reply of *"I don't believe it!"* confirms he is no believer in Dylan's misguided optimism that there are answers somewhere out there, *"blowin' in the wind."* In trying to believe in himself, his thoughts even challenge the in-vogue answers found in popular songs of the day – that love is the answer, that to be nice to people is a better way forward. Again, the cry comes back, *"I don't believe it!"* In fact, at the time of writing the song, there had been a few protest songs written since 1963, including Thunderclap Newman's 'Something in the Air', Buffalo Springfield's 'For What It's Worth', and Neil Young's 'Ohio', to name just a few. Nevertheless, Harry is telling his girl that it's time something was done. No, he doesn't want to force his views on her. She doesn't have to listen to this. After all, it's just what's going on in his own mind. It's a song for himself.

For any songwriter it is a rhetorical question. One reviewer suggests that if the subjects are unhappy, flawed, and unable to hold on to love or even appreciate what love is, *"it's the reality that's left in the wake of the 1960's overweening idealism."* As one critic sees it: *"The door of the past has finally been closed and sealed, it seems."* This is the first track on the album with a political theme, and another will follow shortly. Harry is becoming more aware of the sorry state his country is in, an awareness that will grow more acute in the years to come.

Song Man ***

Love song for Sandy, and in some ways an apology to her, in which Harry references two fellow singer-songwriters, Leon Russell and Elton John, who both wrote love songs for their "special girls." Without mentioning song titles, it's most likely referring to Leon's 'Song For You', written for his estranged lover, and featured on his eponymous second album, and Elton's 'Your Song', with lyrics by Bernie Taupin, which is also from his sophomore album; both songs were recorded in 1970. *Melody Maker*'s Michael Watts writes: *"Even clever little touches like the brief snatch of Elton's Your Song introduced as an illustration of his own attempt to write a song to a girl, can't overcome the dreariness of the melody..."*

Changes ****

Harry's first real protest about America's changing values, and specifically aimed at the Nixon administration that runs the country from 1969 to 1974, and, at the time of writing the song, is wrapped up in a scandal that will, within less than a year, bring it crashing to its knees. Harry is a Democrat and an active supporter of the "Dump Nixon" campaign, and he blames the Republican administration for the country's vanishing values that he once held in the highest esteem. These changes also alter Harry as a person. The "drowning man" in the song is a reference to Phil Ochs, the Texas-born singer and political activist whose songs have become anthems for the anti-war movement during the last decade, but by the early 70s the so-called "singing journalist" has become disillusioned and depressed with Nixon's policies. As a result, his writing dries up and his popularity goes into decline. Within a couple of years, he will take his own life, not by drowning, but by hanging himself. After his death, Harry will give tribute to him in the song, **'The Parade's Still Passing By'**, featured on the 1976 album *On the Road to Kingdom Come*. In the song Harry also derides his short time in the Air Force Academy, when his aspirations of a better country were shattered. But if Harry had changed as a result of his country changing, maybe it was because the whole world was changing too.

From the cheap seats

Lucy Lambert - *I always felt it referred to the human heart and spirit being one of trust and desire to be a part of the solution. As time went by, the singer/writer found disillusionment and shame in the country in which he had so much hope. We don't have any of these kinds of lyrics today. No more seven-minute time frames to build a truly heartfelt idea.*

Ellen Klein - *Your taste in music changes, and as you mature your opinions change. What you once believed so strongly in, is not so important now.*

They Call Her Easy *****

A song that links the basic human need of companionship with the issue of abject loneliness, and is reputedly about an early relationship Harry has in around 1963 when he joins his brother Tom as a summer camp counsellor up in Collegetown. While performing together at Camp Deerfield, Harry meets and starts dating a girl who is a horse-riding teacher, with very liberal attitudes towards casual sex. Of course, the relationship is only fleeting but it sows the seeds for a later composition.

In the song the narrator is at a loose end as he wanders around a strange town, but as he goes into a bar for a drink he gets into a conversation with the old barman who knows a local woman who can help him – a woman they call "easy," and someone who doesn't like to *"spend her nights alone."* The narrator finds her on the street where the barman says she will be, and she takes him back to a run-down farmhouse where they have sex. Like the barman said, no money is asked for, and the following morning the narrator hastily takes his leave as the woman lies there crying. When he meets up with the barman the following day he brags about just how "easy" she was, but the barman pulls him up and regrets the narrator feels that way about her, adding that wouldn't it be a better world if everyone was free with their love like she is.

There is an interesting early version of this song with different lyrics performed in concert at Harper College on Palatine, Illinois in April 1973, some eight months before the album's eventual release:

I was new in town and in need of a friend
I never thought I'd see myself smiling again
Looking in the place for a woman to hold me
And this is what a red-faced barman told me

There's a crazy girl and she lives in town
She only comes out when the sun goes down
I guess she doesn't like to spend her nights alone
If you find her she will take you home

We call her Easy
'Cause you know it's not a way that a woman should be
We call her Easy, she is giving out her love for free

After they make love in the run-down farm, it is the woman who sings the chorus:

They call me Easy
They say it's not the way that a woman should be
They call me Easy
For giving out my love for free.

The final verses also shed a different light on the story:

Next day I was walking around in town
When the bartender saw me, and he waved me down
Tossed the ball back and forth bright and breezy
Laughing about how she was so easy

And she left next week on a cross-country bus
No more lonely nights when she feels rough
You think it's only right we let her be
But we still all laughing at Easy.

107

When you rearrange the pieces of the puzzles of the past
When you sigh at all the heartaches, relive the laughs
Remember moments that you made a mark
And a few special faces that lit up the dark

But then Easy left a lesson that I hope will remain
Lots of lonely people and there's plenty of pain
To say what a fine world it would be
If we were free with our love like Easy

Incidentally the lines *"When you rearrange the pieces of the puzzles of the past / When you sigh at all the heartaches, relive the laughs"* will be used again for the beginning of the wonderful song **'Babysitter'** on the *Portrait Gallery* album. Putting an emotional or monetary price on love happens a lot in rock music, but Harry's view of what a relationship could be, but often fails to be, allows him to tell a story about a subject of which there is little else left to say. Harry will approach the subject of female loneliness in a number of his songs. Perhaps the woman in **'Better Place to Be'** is "easy" with her love. Certainly, the one in **'Mercenaries'** fits the bill only too well, and possibly even Sue, the **'Taxi'** girl herself, after she had fallen on hard times in **'Sequel'**.

With Harry there will always be so many unanswered questions.

From the cheap seats

Thomas Dolan - *The women is representative of the "better us". She is what Harry hoped we all could be...open, honest, welcoming, loving...but without fear of being taken advantage of. Hence the old man's reproach when the singer brags of his conquest. Key line: "Dream of the kind of world it could be if we were with our love like Easy." Next two lines are the lesson learned. A hidden gem*

Kelly Barry - *No way was she a prostitute. She was a kind, open, loving person who gave of herself. The music is so tender - to match the lyrics - that she has to be part of the open loving movement. I played this song often the day Harry died - it really touches a nerve.*

Larry Wood - *You have to consider the era we all felt a lot different about sex. We all have been lonely and I have taken refuge from loneliness with another lonely soul. I am widowed and truly could see my place in a 'Better Place To Be'*

Mr Tanner *****

Along with **'Better Place to Be'**, this is unquestionably one of the most popular songs in Harry's live performances, and one of a handful actually based on headline-making real events. Harry had read a short article on page

108

63 of the Sunday edition of the *New York Times*, dated March 28th 1971. It was about Martin Tubridy, a bass-baritone from Weston, Connecticut who had saved enough money to rent Carnegie Recital Hall to make his New York debut two days before. The music critic is not impressed and rates the performance as falling short of professional standards, with emphasis on a voice that lacks tonal steadiness and adequate phrasing. Harry must keep this story in mind, when almost a year later he reads another *Times* article, dated February 17th 1972, a short piece on page 32 written by Allen Hughes. This time it's about a second performance in the city by Tubridy, this time at the Town Hall. Nothing has changed. Hughes writes that the singer's voice again is limited in flexibility and range, and despite coming well prepared and singing conscientiously, the performance once again was not up to an *"acceptable professional standard."* Harry connects the two reviews and has the makings of a great story. Here is a man with a gifted voice who has a dream and stakes everything on one shot at the big time, only to have his performance slated by critics and have that dream torn to pieces. By changing the name and places, but using actual words and phrases taken from both reviews, Harry pieces together one of his greatest story songs. He calls his singer Martin Tanner:

Mr Tanner was a cleaner from a town in the Midwest.
Of all the cleaning shops around he'd made his the best.
He also was a baritone who sang while hanging clothes.
He practiced scales while pressing tails and sang at local shows.
His friends and neighbors praised the voice that poured out from his throat.
They said that he should use his gift instead of cleaning coats.

In the chorus that follows, sung by Harry, we have John Wallace emulating Tanner's bass-baritone voice with a soaring counter-melody of a piece from 'O Holy Night', the well-known Christmas carol composed by Adolphe Adam in 1847 to the French poem 'Minuit, chrétiens' (Midnight, Christians) written by wine merchant and poet Placide Cappeau (1808–1877). Surely Big John's finest moment:

But music was his life, it was not his livelihood,
and it made him feel so happy and it made him feel so good.
And he sang from his heart and he sang from his soul.
He did not know how well he sang; It just made him whole.

Counter-melody:

Fall on your knees
O hear the angels' voices

O night divine
O night when Christ was born
O night divine o night
O night divine

With his God-given gift of a voice, and finally being convinced to take a shot at the big time, he summons up the courage to do it. But is this really what he wants? We all fear the worst…

His friends kept working on him to try music out full time.
A big debut and rave reviews, a great career to climb.
Finally they got to him, he would take the fling.
A concert agent in New York agreed to have him sing.
There were plane tickets, phone calls, money spent to rent the hall.
It took most of his savings but he'd gladly used them all.
The evening came, he took the stage, his face set in a smile.
And in the half filled hall the critics sat watching on the aisle.
But the concert was a blur to him, spatters of applause.
He did not know how well he sang, he only heard the flaws.
But the critics were concise, it only took four lines.
But no one could accuse them of being over kind.

With a background of swirling music, Harry reads out the critics' response, using certain words and phrases from the original *New York Times* reviews:

Mr. Martin Tanner, Baritone, of Dayton, Ohio made his Town Hall debut last night. He came well prepared, but unfortunately his presentation was not up to contemporary professional standards. His voice lacks the range of tonal color necessary to make it consistently interesting. Full time consideration of another endeavor might be in order.

He came home to Dayton and was questioned by his friends. But he smiled and just said nothing and he never sang again, Excepting very late at night when the shop was dark and closed, He sang softly to himself as he sorted through the clothes.

The song ends with a much slowed down chorus, allowing us to hear Big John's voice in all its glory.

Tubridy does go on to perform with moderate success, but he is not aware that he has been the inspiration for the song until being told in the mid 90s. In 2016, now well into his 70s, he is approached by the Chapin family to sing the

'O Holy Night' part of the song at a special concert for the Harry Chapin Foundation at Fairfield University. Neil Steinberg of the *Chicago Sun-Times* is there to interview Tubridy, and the singer talks about what for him is a surreal moment: *"It doesn't seem like this could actually happen. A standing ovation. Incredible, really."* One reviewer of the performance writes: *"There really is only one thing left to say: Mr. Martin Tubridy, baritone, of Weston, Conn., sang the 'O Holy Night' counter melody in 'Mr. Tanner' with a fullness, strength and conviction which, while at one point hard to hear over the audience cheering, was consistently interesting. Particularly, at the very end, when the lyrics are, 'He did not know how well he sang, it just made him whole,' but you hear."*

In an interview in October 1975 Harry reflects on the song: *"In the rock business if you get bombed by critics – the Times' critic said Mick Jagger had a horrible voice, it wouldn't mean anything, it couldn't ruin his career – but if you're a classical singer come to New York and sing at Carnegie Hall or Town Hall for the first time and you get bombed with four lines like that, and you've spent fifteen years training your voice, at that point you can just imagine how devastating it would be…I was one of those musicians who never made it. I spent about ten years around the edges and you wonder how they come to terms with their attempts at being talented. Music is a cruel mistress. You're putting your ego out there for a shot and you've got a lot of people judging you and sometimes the verdict isn't as nice as you'd like it to be."*

The song is so powerful it can almost move the listener to tears. In reality it's all a metaphor for Harry's personal battle with his critics. For all of his success and his growing popularity, he is still hated by many critics. To them he is still Martin Tanner.

From the cheap seats

Rodney Stewart - *Mr. Tanner to me is about how you sometimes have to protect the pieces of yourself that you love. Also though, because I'm a realist, it's about the realities of professional performing. It's not enough to be good. You truly have to be great to succeed in a business as rough as music.*

Cliff Geismar - *Beautiful story of a man whose music meant more to him than any critics review - magical song about living a dream.*

Ellen Gordon Klein - *As a wannabe singer/actor for a time, I know the struggles of thinking you are really good, dreaming of a big career, friends urging you on, only to find you are really good, but there are so many others. You are average; maybe not Carnegie Hall quality. This song rips at my heart every time because I can feel Mr. Tanner's feelings and can identify with the high of the concert and the low that followed. I, too, went back to my 'office' job, and still dabble here and there. It's a heartfelt song of a cross section of life and that little shot at fleeting fame.*

Sandy Austin Goldstein - *There are people that try and succeed, people that try and fail, people that never try at all...what makes people choose what they do is fascinating to me. When you are rejected, do you keep trying? For me, the answer is yes.*

Melba Davis Nickoles - *Thank you Mr Tubridy, Mr Tanner, Big John, and Harry Chapin for giving us a glimpse into the world of someone who chose privacy over that horrible light that the public can shed on someone who just tries and is beaten like a prize fighter, by words not fists. You live on with us. The ones who loved Harry and are proud of every time he maybe, got punched but got up to do it one more time. Until Harry won that fight. And we are so glad we knew a little of you all.*

Mail Order Annie *****

Harry's tribute to some of the neglected and unsung women that helped build the American West - mail order brides. Many European-American men ventured west to make their fortune in the latter part of the 19th century but lacked the essential thing to raise a family - a wife. Very few single women lived out west at the time, so the men searched for women by putting personal ads in magazines and newspapers. And there were many young women willing to take the opportunity - single or widowed, divorced or runaways - and the temptation to gain financial security and the curiosity of what life would be like on the frontier seemed an attractive prospect. Many would enclose a photograph of themselves with the reply, and then the courtship would commence in writing, until these "picture brides" finally agreed to marry the man they had never even met.

It has been said that Harry wrote this song while waiting for Sandy to pick him up at a train station, and it gets him thinking of another man, waiting in a station for a train to arrive, somewhere way out west on the Dakota plains, a hundred years ago. Harry not only sees the romance of these stories, but also the challenges facing both husband and new bride in what is an unforgiving way of life. Like in a number of his songs, Harry uses his own name for the narrator. Here he is Harry Crane, a North Dakota farmer, waiting on the platform of the remote station as the train pulls in from its long journey west.

At first I did not think it could be you.
But you're the only one that got off the train.
So you must be my wife Miss Annie Halsey
I must be your husband – Yes, I'm Harry Crane.
Mail Order Annie, never mind your crying.
Your tears are sweet rain in my empty life.
Mail Order Annie, can't you see I'm trying
To tell you that I'm glad you're here...
You are the woman who's come to be my wife.

112

Although pouring on the charm in the chorus, Harry does a terrible job of welcoming this city girl to the neighborhood. No wonder she is crying. But Annie must be made of stronger stuff, otherwise she would have got back on board the train.

You know you're not as pretty as I dreamed you'd be,
But then I'm not no Handsome Fancy Dan.
And out here, looks are really not important, no, no.
It's what's inside a woman when she's up against the land.
You know it's not no easy life you're entering.
The winter wind comes whistling through the cracks there in the sod.
You know you'll never have too many neighbors.
There's you babe, and there's me, and there's God.

In the next verse we get some indication of the reason she is there, having been *"thrown out on her own,"* maybe the result of some personal tragedy back home, maybe even an unruly daughter to someone, but whatever it is she has mentioned it in her correspondence.

You know I'm just a dirt man from the North Dakota plains.
You're just one girl from the city who's been thrown out on her own.
And I'm standing here not sure of what to say to you
'cepting Mail Order Annie, let's you and me go home.

Harry sounds almost apologetic for what he has to offer her, and is unsure of what else to say to her. But Annie doesn't say anything; she's heard all she wants to hear. This is her future now, their future, and, on a larger scale, it's also the future of America. Whatever it takes, together they will make this their home. We never do get to hear about Annie's response. Another candidate for a sequel that is never to be….

The song is underscored by Ron Palmer's beautiful acoustic guitar and Mike Masters' evocative cello, but will always be best remembered for the haunting solo from session musician David Armstrong, bringing a touch of added pathos to the heartfelt lyrics. The same refrain can be also be heard at the end of **'Barefoot Boy'** on the previous album.

From the cheap seats
Gerry Naughton - *This is a very poignant and underrated song. Another Chapin masterpiece! The story is about history, humility and fortitude. We can envisage the bleak landscape of the 1800s American mid-west. We imagine the main character Harry Crane toiling the land as part of settlement and prosperity but being isolated and lonely. Annie's arrival is probably more about practicality as it is about love. Chapin, himself, said that any good song*

should be about asking questions! The listener is left with numerous questions about the lives of the two people in the song – and, in particular, Annie. As Harry is the only one who speaks, one gets the impression that Annie is a somewhat demure person. "You're one girl from the city who's been thrown out on her own", begs the question if Annie came from an orphanage or a woman's institution. We are left to wonder if Annie has the same need for life stability and a relationship as her husband-to-be! We know Harry's first impression of Annie, but we don't know about Annie's feelings upon meeting this man. We are also left to wonder about the future of the couple. Probably their meeting was the single most important event in their lives. The endeavor of Harry to work the land and of Annie to arrive on the train in the first place suggests that they will succeed in their life together. There is the sense of endearment and a sense of enduring in Harry's words. Love and humility will prevail.

Debby Di Donato Sorrick - *I wanted this song before I walked down the aisle at my wedding. I was marrying a man from California and would have to leave my life, family, friends and Sussex County NJ. All the things I desperately loved.*

Alan L Geraci - *Harry encapsulates the emotion of loneliness by embracing the rugged ride of America's expansion period of manifest destiny*

There's a Lot of Lonely People Tonight **

Singalong stuff here, pleasant enough. For a subject like loneliness, it lacks the empathy to make it want to stay in the memory for long.

Old College Avenue ****

No, this is not Big John singing - this is indeed Harry, with a particularly unusual high voice. Along with **'Winter Song'** on the previous album, this comes from Harry's brief relationship with Jenny Gillette, a fellow student he meets while attending Cornell in the early 60s, and the same girl he falls in love with, but never gets around to telling her how he feels about her until it's too late. Another plaintive story of lost love. As Harry wanders through the campus grounds he is probably coming to realize that his destiny lies elsewhere. The music slowly fades in with acoustic guitar, cello and piccolo (courtesy of Harold Keinz). It is fall and the narrator is revisiting the old college campus one night, fondly reminiscing about the time they shared a one-bed room together, and of how she had gently put his life back together again. He remembers it all so clearly, even *"the tangled trails of time"* that eventually leads to their parting. He is full of regret. Two years after this album is released, Jenny dies from a brain tumor at the age of 24.

From the cheap seats

114

Gerry Naughton - *The song tells us that the relationship was important to Harry. Perhaps the most poignant line: "And you took my future with you, and you left my past behind" was an admission that the relationship did have a long-term potential, and that it also helped Harry to overcome the negatives of his past.*

"Reviews are Free Advice"

In June 1973, long before the album's release, Harry talks about the reasoning behind his music:

"Some people think I'm nothing more than a stoned-out cab driver. But anyone who follows through my albums knows better. The rock press either hate what I'm doing or love it, which to me means I'm doing something right. I get letters from all kinds of people. What impresses me more than repeated chart success is the fact that there are English and drama teachers going through my lyrics in their classes. That is an achievement. I'm not playing to get off on commerciality. To have people sit down and take the time to listen is better than any screaming crowd. Most of the music press doesn't understand my attitudes. To them, a song that isn't 'Fire and Rain' or 'I Want You Babe' isn't a song. But the situation that creates an attitude is what constructs a good story. There's nothing terrible with intellectual discipline, but save it for someone else. Reviews are free advice. And like anything else, there's some you should listen to and some you shouldn't."

During the fall of 1973 Harry and the band begin a promotional tour throughout the East and Midwest, as well as another appearance on *The Tonight Show with Johnny Carson* in September, performing **'They Call Her Easy'** and **'Song For Myself'**. This is followed in October with a week-long engagement at The Bitter End club in New York. ***Short Stories*** is released on December 1st, eventually reaching #61 on the *Billboard* 200 and a creditable #39 on the Canadian album charts.

Paul Gambaccini of *Rolling Stone* writes a positive review, calling the album a *"major achievement,"* admiring him for tackling subjects too weighty for other performers to attempt, but also fearing that its *"depressing quality of desperation"* will have an effect on its success. Jerry Gilbert of *Sounds* magazine is not so impressed and feels that overall it's not as good as the previous album. He finds the lyrics written down on the sleeve like the short stories the album title suggests to be quite stirring, but in song form they seem to lose impact and almost go by unnoticed. In summing up he wonders whether Harry is a better short story writer than he is a songwriter. Another reviewer for *Melody Maker* points out that the lyrics on Harry's last two albums are not even written down in verse, but are paragraphs like passages from a book, and each telling a tale conjured up in Harry's fertile mind, with some embellishing thrown in for good measure. Harry is much like his contemporaries James Taylor and Jim Croce, observing a melancholy side of life through his self-contained character portraits.

Harry agrees that the lyrics to his songs are more important than the music, but explains that his stories are mainly written from some personal or real-life experience, no matter how vague that reference may be: *"I try to have some emotional reality. That's the key. It doesn't necessarily literally have to happen to me. It's something that I understand. The quality I look for in my songs is what I call a grounding which is having the person in the song knowing about what he speaks."*

That December, Elektra decide to release **'W.O.L.D.'** as the next single, backed with **'Short Stories'**, and copies are sent off to radio stations across the country. Harry knows that he has a potential hit on his hands. After all, it's about the job those guys who get to play his music do every day for a living, and it has to resonate with many of them. The first station he targets is WRKO, the "voice of Boston" and soon to oust its Boston competitor WMEX as the city's sole AM Top 40 station. To enlist help Harry calls on an old Boston friend, William 'Zeke' Marsden, a railroadman who he met after a concert there in the summer of 1972 and struck up an instant friendship with his large family, a friendship that lasts a lifetime. Harry does no more than get Marsden and his whole family and friends to inundate the radio station with written requests to play **'W.O.L.D.'**, many of the letters using false names. The plan works and without the station raising suspicion, the song gets onto the nationwide RKO playlist, reaching #9 within a fortnight. On March 23rd 1974 **'W.O.L.D.'** peaks at #36 on the *Billboard* 100, remaining on the chart for over 15 weeks. Harry actually visits WRKO and comes clean about the rigged letters to the excited station boss.

January 1974 gets under way with a fine performance of **'W.O.L.D.'** on *The Tonight Show with Johnny Carson*, followed in February by concerts in Missouri, Kentucky and Ohio, and a return to the popular *Mike Douglas Show* to perform a full-version **'Taxi'**, and snippets of **'Circle'** and **'Sunday Morning Sunshine'**. At the show at the Kiel Opera House in St Louis on February 2nd an upcoming singer-songwriter opens for Harry. His name – Billy Joel.

Harry has done what Elektra needed. With a hit record and album sales looking promising, he finds himself back in their good books and once again elevated to one of their top five artists. More and more people now want to come and see him live. But he isn't able to sit on his laurels for long, however. Elektra, as is their wont, are already calling for fresh material.

The Ultimate Obscenity

"You want to know what is really obscene? Hunger.
Hunger is an obscenity and hunger in America is the ultimate obscenity"

Father Bill Ayres to the Rescue

Harry, although enjoying the resurgence of his music career with the album *Short Stories* and the international success of the single **'W.O.L.D.'**, now finds that his personal life has hit rock bottom when Sandy, tired of his chameleon persona and unsettling lifestyle, tells him to move out. Moving back into his mother's house, Harry now takes stock of his life, asking himself questions that only he can answer. Most of all, what will it mean to lose the one person in his life who really matters?

Help is on its way in the shape of Father Bill Ayres, Catholic priest, songwriter, and fellow-Long Islander. Already known to Tom and Steve, Bill had become a priest in 1966 for the diocese of Rockville Center, Long Island, and for the next ten years serves at St James Church in Seaford, New York. But Bill also has a passion for radio broadcasting. In 1968 he has his first radio stint on Long Island's WGSM station, working alongside Pete Fornatele, and five years later is given his own weekly talk show called *On This Rock* on New York's WPLJ-FM, as well as having a Sunday morning show on WABC. Most of the interviews are with rock and pop musicians who are asked about what spiritual meanings their songs give them, and the show also invites calls from listeners and offers advice on a wide range of issues, whether it be personal, social or spiritual. After being interviewed on one of his shows, Harry strikes up with Bill what will become a lifelong friendship, and with Sandy's agreement, Bill holds a number of sessions with the couple in their Huntington home which eventually help to reconcile their marital differences.

For Harry it's not just a case of rebuilding his relationship with his wife, but reassessing his own life and values. Sandy has often posed the question to him - what is the true meaning of success? Is it the ego-inflating buzz of being a successful artist or the ability to use that fame to improve society? In the end, Sandy, being the born persuasive teacher she is, manages to make Harry see things her way.

Everything is now up to Harry.

A vital lesson has been learned. From now on Sandy insists that Harry devotes more of his time to meaningful activities, not the star-tripping, self-seeking lifestyle of a celebrity performer. He also has to reconnect with their children, who, due to the constant touring and promotional duties, have been growing up without him. Harry agrees to all this. He will change, whatever it

117

takes. Harry will reflect on this period in the song **'Star Tripper'** on a future album. He is also asked to immerse himself in Sandy's tireless community work, such as raising funds through organizing and performing in cultural 'Lively Arts' festivals each spring for the cash-strapped Huntington Arts Council and also the Performing Arts Foundation of Long Island (PAF), based in Huntington, which fosters arts-in-education and professional theatre. Harry puts his energies into all these new projects and even arranges what will later become annual benefit concerts for PAF held at Huntington High School. Invited to join the board, he will go on to become its chairperson. Harry is returning to reality. He has come close to losing everything he loves. He will not be so foolish as to risk it again. In the past it has all been about him. From now on he will live in Sandy's world and be grateful he is a part of it.

Around this time Harry and Sandy decide to take in fifteen-year-old Dana and her sister Gail, who come from a previous relationship his father had that didn't work out. With a total of seven children of varying ages to bring up, Harry can now easily see where his priorities lie. It terrifies him to think he could once again become the **'Cat's in the Cradle'** father, that with him out of the picture it would seem that the kids don't matter anymore to him, and in doing so he wouldn't matter at all to them. Harry now makes sure with his manager that there are no more long-distance concerts held near the West Coast, and that he keeps them closer to home, no more than a three-hour flight away. He keeps his word (at least for the time being) and for the rest of the year no concerts are held further west than Missouri and Kansas, and then only a handful. Harry recalls:

"So here I was, a new career going strong, faced with the question of what to do with it. All my brave words of the 60s about the social responsibility of successful people became bluffs to be called. I believe that success brings responsibility. It also does not bring immunity to the consequences of our quickening march toward oblivion. The bottom line is that all of us should be involved in our own futures to create a world that our children will want to live in."

Why Hunger?

But when did Harry get involved with the issue of world hunger? In October 1973, while Bill Ayres is interviewing Harry on his radio show, the question comes up: *"If you could choose one cause and make a lifetime commitment to bring change, what would it be?"* They both agree on the issue of hunger. After the interview the *"two action-oriented men,"* as their friends refer to them, decide to see what can be done to alleviate hunger. Even during the marital meetings with Sandy and Bill the subject also crops up. Bill recalls: *"In the beginning, I was the one who knew about hunger. I'd feed him books*

118

and after a while he started feeding me books. I mean he really got into it and he became very, very knowledgeable, very articulate, and a great spokesman..."

Apart from Harry now regularly attending PAF meetings, he also begins holding informal talks at schools and colleges with various student bodies about all manner of subjects, including music, ambitions, and even politics, but due to the current televised news coming out of drought-stricken Africa, the topic of world hunger is also debated. For the next two years Harry will speak at some forty-odd schools and colleges in the Long Island area, and the hunger crisis is an ever-present topic. For Harry it must also bring back memories of what he experienced first-hand while filming in Ethiopia with Jim Lipscomb. Maybe subconsciously it has already become his most important social commitment, and more than anything else, will now change his life forever.

Gerald Grossman is a 15-year-old high school student at Great Neck, New York. Years later he recalls a visit by Harry:

Throughout that day, though, as Mr. Chapin visited our high school in Great Neck and spoke in open workshops that were to precede an afternoon benefit concert he was giving in our auditorium, it became apparent that he was no ordinary pop star. In fact, becoming a pop star seemed to be way down on his list of priorities. Instead, Mr. Chapin spent the day passionately describing to all who would listen what he said was the pressing problem of worldwide hunger... Harry Chapin had touched a nerve. He touched nerves with his music all the time, but on that spring day he saw an opportunity to influence and help shape young minds, and he seized it. Harry Chapin's cause was one of simple human decency: He sought to combat world hunger. He saw people all over the world, children much like us, who did not have enough to eat, and he wanted to do something about it.

The Long Crusade Begins

During the spring of 1974 Harry and Bill begin to research hunger issues in much greater detail, holding discussions at Harry's home with politicians, economists and so-called experts on the subject, and only when given the facts represented in cold hard statistics, a truer picture emerges of what is, and has always been, a human crisis of unparalleled magnitude. Among the invited guests are Harry's brother James, now a professor of American Diplomacy at Rutgers University, and Long Island Congressman Tom Downey. Bill is impressed with Harry's energy and commitment. One of Harry's favorite sayings at the time is *"Give a man a fish and he'll eat for the day; teach him to fish and he'll eat for a lifetime."* Bill will take that a step further, saying that a man not only needs to know how to fish, but to have the freedom to do it and a place to do it. *"That's where community comes in. We have to help each other, and we feel government has a very important role therein."* What follows is a long crusade to get the government and the United Nations to take action.

There have already been concerts for hunger victims, like the recent one for Bangla Desh in New York, which raises nearly half a million dollars, and Harry and Bill approach a number of artists to help organize a similar event for the relief of starving people in the drought-stricken sub-Sahara region of Africa. Harry calls some friends, among them Art Garfunkel, Seals and Croft, Don McLean, Crosby Stills and Nash, and John Denver, who, according to Harry, all agree to participate. Michael Viner, aide to John Scali, US Ambassador to the United Nations, is appointed to spearhead the search for other artists who are willing to take part. Concert plans are announced at a press conference on June 18th, where Scali stresses that his involvement is that of a private citizen, and not as an official of the government. In his speech he hopes that the planned concerts will raise sufficient money to *"focus world attention on this tragedy. I hope the concerts can bridge the communications gap in a way that no government organization can."*

Sketchy plans for three 'Concerts For Africa' get under way, with dates pencilled in for the Houston Astrodome (August 22nd), Los Angeles Forum (23rd) and Madison Square Garden (25th). A telegram from Viner announcing the press conference has a star-studded list of artists who have agreed to participate, and as well as those already contacted by Harry, it now includes Helen Reddy, Roberta Flack, Harry Nilsson, Ringo Star, Richie Havens and comedian Richard Pryor. But the truth is that some of these artists never actually give Viner their commitment. Even John Lennon's name makes the list, which Viner later confesses was just "an oversight." Apparently, he had only agreed to listen to the idea. Some of the people involved in the planning have already voiced off-the-record reservations about Viner's commitment, reservations that are now sadly proving to be justified. While all this is going on Harry takes his family on a much-needed summer vacation to Greece and hands the reins over to Viner, who is also president of Pride Records, chairman of the event and also co-chairman of the planning committee along with concert promoter Bill Graham. Both Scali and Viner announce that the benefits will raise money through ticket sales (up to $25 each), television rights, record sales for a planned double album, and all the assorted merchandise that goes hand-in-hand with such events. Even a movie deal is being negotiated. But when Harry returns from vacation, he finds Viner has not managed to book a single act.

The Origins of World Hunger Year

Harry comes to realize that even if they manage to raise a million dollars through spontaneous Bangla Desh-style concerts, it could only feed several thousand starving people for one day. He reaches the conclusion that this "event psychosis" of dollar donations is not the answer. He points to the political and corporate dynamics that oil the mechanisms of the planet, from the blatant corruptness of unstable regimes to the unbalanced distribution of land and wealth, which makes it impossible for some poorer countries to have the ways and means to feed themselves. That's where both the problems and solutions lie. It's all about international politics. Harry's brother James recalls: *"Harry understood these causes required a lifetime investment psychologically. You don't just do one good deed, then the battle is won. The fat lady never sings."*

Harry and Bill come to see that it will take more than benefits, charities and the hunger-relief efforts of organizations like UNICEF to eradicate world hunger. They see the roots to a long-term solution lie in training, education, and raising public and political awareness. The next step is to create their own non-profit organization to combat the root causes of hunger, poverty and exploitation prevalent around the world, with the aim to establish communities and programs across the world to foster self-reliance through education in farming, agriculture and food nutrition, but most of all to develop the political will to get it all done. They will call the organization W.H.Y. (World Hunger Year); not just a short-lived project as the title suggests, but an ongoing year-on-year commitment to resolve all the issues. This selfless commitment between two best friends pays off. With the help and expert advice from several politicians (even Ralph Nader, the controversial social activist and champion of consumer protection laws, offers his help) involvements are secured, and finally in September 1975 W.H.Y. is launched. Through his persistent lobbying of Congressmen, Harry finally persuades President Carter to create what becomes America's only Presidential Commission on Hunger. Harry has used his success, personality, talent, and reputation and turned it into a weapon that gets people moving into action. Although looked upon by some as a pushy pain in the ass, his forceful and irascible methods move mountains into getting an apathetic government to finally act. Few individuals could ever have done this.

On November 10th 1976, before leaving Los Angeles and the recording for the **Greatest Stories Live** album, Harry appears on the television show *Good Morning America*, and over the Thanksgiving weekend co-hosts with Bill Ayres what will be the first of three annual 'Hungerthons' on New York's avant-garde WNEW-FM radio station, where all regular Sunday programming and commercials are suspended in order to publicize the issue of world hunger. The show has mainly an all-talk format, although Harry does occasionally sing, and invited guests include experts on medical, nutritional, and agricultural issues. Although station manager Mel Karmazin has reservations over devoting 24 hours of air time to one single topic, he is assured it has no connection with promoting Harry's music, and all his staff who know Harry vouch for his integrity. As it turns out, the show is a qualified success, reaching out to an estimated one million listeners, many of whom, with Harry's urging, will write some 1,500 letters and telegrams and even begin to lobby politicians themselves to get them to take action. On April 14th 1977, two days after his televised concert in Germany, Harry is back in the States and arranging a meeting with the President's son, Chip Carter, at the White House. Whatever is said, it has positive results, and in days President Carter and some of his officials have watched for themselves Harry's emotive film on world hunger, and the President writes to the National Security Council advising them to address the crisis and come up with initiatives, and gives his son the job of coordinating it.

The Lobbying Begins

Sometime in May, Harry invites Bill Ayres and Congressman Downey to a meeting at his Huntington home to discuss the issues of world hunger. Harry is alarmed when he hears that despite numerous government agencies spending billions of dollars each year on the problem, it has had little effect. Between them they consider presenting to Congress a bi-annual report on just what effect this money is having on the problem. But Sandy suggests going one better and lobbying for an actual Presidential Commission to be set up. Harry is at first skeptical, thinking of the dozens of similar commissions that end up being white elephants, but then he begins to see its feasibility. The next step is to get politicians on board to sponsor the idea and then present the idea as a resolution to put before Congress, and, if passed, put before the President. Harry meets with Senator Patrick Leahy of Vermont and Minnesota Congressman Rick Nolan, and his commitment wins their support. To draw up the resolution they get the help of agriculture and nutrition expert John Kramer. Sandy recounts Harry's usual strategy when lobbying for the Presidential Commission: *"Harry would hang out in the bathroom. He knew, sooner or later, everyone would be there. When a Senator walked in the door, he'd strike up his guitar and say, 'I'm Harry Chapin. I want to talk to you about hunger.'"*

At the end of July, Harry meets up with his W.H.Y. coordinators in Washington before meeting John Kramer in his office at the Capitol to hear about how the resolution for a Presidential Commission has been received. Great news - it has been passed unanimously. At the meeting with Kramer, Harry goes into verbal overload explaining why setting up a commission is important, and with a few suggestions of his own, gives it his full support. Chapin then meets up with Leahy and Nolan and begins the process of drafting a four-page resolution that proposes a two-year commission, with the first year spent fact-finding and auditing all of the current government hunger agencies in order to present to the President an interim statement, and with the second year raising public awareness through education before finally issuing their recommendations. The cost of all this will be an estimated $5 million, but all it requires now is Congress's approval. Thus begin weeks of Harry and others lobbying congressmen to win their support. He also appears on a number of television chat shows to raise the topic in his own inimitable style. Within a couple of months, they have amongst their supporters such luminaries as Senators Edward Kennedy, George McGovern, and Robert Dole to endorse the resolution, which is presented to Congress in a number of different bills, as the law states that no more than twenty-five congressmen can sponsor an individual bill.

On the day the bills are presented, Harry performs a free concert on the steps of the Capitol, which is actually filmed by some of his old Drew Associates cameramen, who happen to be there setting up to do a documentary on the energy crisis. The resolution is a resounding success, passed by a vote of 364 to 38, with the Senate voting unanimously. It will take five months for President Carter to give his verdict, but in a matter of just five months Harry has initiated his idea, drawn it up, lobbied politicians for its support, and even serenaded them outside the Capitol in order to get it put through. This unprecedented action will go down as perhaps his greatest achievement.

On October 15th, Harry stages a huge benefit to raise enough money to set up what will become the Food Policy Center, set up to deal with the lobbying side of W.H.Y. in Washington. Dubbed 'Four Together,' the concert is held at the Olympia Stadium in Detroit and also has Harry's friends and fellow artists James Taylor, John Denver and Gordon Lightfoot on the bill. The concert raises an impressive $156,000, with a third of it going toward the purchase of an office building in the capital and the rest in support of W.H.Y. To raise additional funds Harry is also involved in launching a bi-monthly magazine called *Food Monitor* which carries news and articles on food and hunger issues, to which he also contributes a few of his own articles. This is followed by more concerts in Kentucky, Ohio and Georgia before ending the month with another solo benefit at Huntington High School alongside benefit-stalwarts Richie Havens and Oscar Brand.

President Carter Signs the Commission

With the first sessions coming to an end on January 27th 1978, Harry takes a break from recording to keep to his touring schedule. On February 2nd, he is doing back-to-back concerts in Hamilton, Ontario, knowing that the next day President Carter will be meeting up with sponsors of the Presidential Commission resolution at the White House and reaching his decision. After the last show, which finishes at 1am, Harry and his team drive down to Buffalo in a raging blizzard to catch a chartered plane to Washington. After a nerve-jangling flight and hardly any sleep, Harry arrives in the capital at 5am and manages to get a couple of hours' sleep in a hotel near the Capitol before heading to Senator Leahy's office to meet with the sponsors in preparation for the meeting with the President. After that they head straight for the White House. At 9.45am President Carter arrives and the meeting begins, with Harry sitting three seats to his left. Harry's opening speech overruns the allotted two minutes, but Carter admits that he admires his enthusiasm. In no time at all he responds by saying: "Yes, I think it's a good idea. Let's go ahead with it." The room falls silent for a few seconds as the President's reply hasn't sunk in straight away, but then everyone looks at each other and smiles. Harry Chapin has pulled it off.

Senator Leahy is full of admiration for Harry: *"Harry would not stop. He continued to hammer the reasons for it into the president. Carter sat there trying to explain that he agreed, but Harry wasn't going to let him off that easy. He wanted not only for him to agree, he wanted him to be committed. That's the difference between Harry Chapin and those who simply give lip service to a cause."*

On September 5th 1978, after some wrangling over who to choose to be on the commission, President Carter finally signs the executive order establishing the 20-member Commission on Domestic and International Hunger and Malnutrition. It not only predicts a global hunger crisis in the next two decades, but also recommends a change in government foreign policy - a two-fold increase in its foreign aid (currently $7 billion), a focus on "self-reliant growth" to enable undeveloped countries to feed themselves through more equitable land ownership and smarter methods of farming nutritional foodstuffs, and, perhaps most importantly, recognizing poverty as the primary cause of hunger, both home and abroad. This last recommendation is a bone of contention amongst the politicians who fail to see any connection. Harry puts it down to the selection of the Commission members, who had a distinct lack of the necessary expertise required to deal with the issues. Apart from Harry, those who were selected failed to attend all the fifteen or so scheduled meetings.

Maybe Harry has got the timing all wrong. After all, 1980 is a Presidential election year, and with Reagan and the Republican Party breathing down Carter's neck, Harry's pet project is being side-lined for the election campaign. However, many of the Commission's recommendations will be put into legislation, and in September 1981 the Hunger Elimination and Global Security Act is presented to Congress, sponsored by Oregon senator Mark

Hatfield, which *"expresses the sense of Congress that the United States should make development of poor countries and the eradication of poverty and hunger the primary objective of U.S. foreign policy,"* and *"directs the President to designate certain foreign aid programs as Hunger Relief and Prevention Assistance."* However, it is never enacted. Walter Falcon, a member of the Commission, recalls how they tried to finish the March 1980 report before Carter left office, but it ends up falling "between the cracks" of the outgoing and incoming administrations, and as a result Reagan never picks up on it.

The Ongoing Success of W.H.Y.

Harry will remain committed to his goal of ending world hunger and poverty for the rest of his life, raising untold amounts of money in concerts to fund the work of the organization. In 1975 there were just 28 emergency food providers in New York City. Today there are roughly 1,200. Since Harry's death, the unceasing work will continue to be his everlasting legacy. Almost five decades after his death, the Chapin family, along with Bill Ayres at the helm, are continuing the fight. At the time of writing WhyHunger has grown to work with some 8,000 community-based groups across the globe, working together to eradicate hunger, educate, give support to find employment, provide health care and housing for people in need, and a myriad of other functions.

Bill Ayres recalls: *"Harry was big on empowerment. The idea of World Hunger Year isn't simply to put food in people's mouths, but to help them change their lives, to get people involved in their own desire to help themselves. Harry wanted to reach both people who are hungry and people who feel left out of the political process. He did not want to motivate people through guilt; he wanted to combine a sense of awareness of responsibility with a sense of life."*

With Reagan succeeding Carter in the White House, the Presidential Commission turns out to be largely ineffective. Harry's commitment to his ideals and dreams will ensure that a congressional body will remain in place, and at the time of his death there are more plans being made to introduce hunger legislation and other food-related initiatives.

On June 30th 1980 Harry receives the following letter from President Carter: *I want to express my appreciation for your contributions to the development of public policy as a member of the Presidential Commission on World Hunger. You have my assurance that the Commission's thoughtful and challenging report will be the beginning of a continuing effort to strengthen our programs in this area. As we go forward with measures recommended by the report, I hope you will continue your efforts to build public support for action to overcome world hunger.*

Years later Bill is asked if the Presidential Commission had been successful: *"Yes, it was, in the sense that it finished its work and it published all these findings, which if Carter would have been President, he would have put into effect. At least I hope he would have. But most of them did not get put into effect because Reagan won. It was a heartbreaker. But a lot of people got influenced by it and some very interesting pieces of legislation and policy came as a result of it, even though it didn't take root in the way we hoped it would."*

To this day Harry's children are all involved in charitable endeavors. Jaime and Jason have spent most of their working lives in the non-profit sector, while Jono serves as a community leader in Middlebury, Vermont. Daughter Jen, herself a successful singer-songwriter and activist, is an enthusiastic supporter of community issues, particularly food issues, in her Brooklyn neighborhood, and regularly does benefit concerts as well as serving as chair on the board of directors for WhyHunger, the new name for W.H.Y. Although memories of Harry's music career will ebb and flow, the legacy of what this charismatic individual has done to make it a better world will last an eternity.

Verities & Balderdash

"I have a distant early warning system, who's very close to me, whenever Harry Chapin gets off on some crazy situation gives me a kick in the pants"

The Making of a Hit Record

With the sudden increase in benefit concerts that they are having to perform, the strain is beginning to show on both Harry's band and manager Fred Kewley. With something like a third of all performances going unpaid and the chosen venues often lacking in adequate facilities (even a stage in some places), Harry's relationship with them begins to deteriorate. But Harry is a changing man. For him it is no longer about making hit songs and bringing in the dollars, it's about saving his marriage and proving to himself that what he is doing matters. He needs to regain his self-respect. The intimacy and harmony that had been forged together as a band six months ago is fading away. The change in Harry's persona is reflected in his songwriting, and for inspiration on his next two albums he will look nearer to home, to his wife and family. With Harry now taking the role of fatherhood more seriously, he looks again at Sandy's father-son lyric and at last it finally resonates with him. Within days he turns it into a song, adding the nursery line chorus, and for those who hear it for the first time, they know with **'Cat's in the Cradle'** he has a hit record on his hands.

Sandy recalls that the idea for the song came from a combination of things. From listening to an old country song in which an elderly couple, while sitting together having breakfast, look out at the garden at an old rusted swing and sandbox and think back to younger days when all the children and grandkids were around, and how time passes by so quick. One minute they are there, and the next they are gone. And then there's a story about how her ex-husband Jim was treated by his father when she first met him, and how he was so busy trying to get his son a job in politics that there was no other communication between them until he went off to law school and then joined the Air Force Judge Advocate Corps. Then it was too late. And now there is Harry, who is spending so much time away from home, and has even missed his son Josh being born. All these things have resonance, and Sandy takes a little piece of each one and crafts them into a beautiful song.

In the spring of 1974 Harry returns to the Connecticut Recording Studios in Bridgeport with enough new material to make what he hopes to be his first double album. It will be called *Verities & Balderdash* (basically meaning "truth and nonsense.") Once again, due to the escalating costs, the label turns him down. Geffen rates the songs highly, but the idea of making two albums for the price of one is once again considered commercially unviable. On May 25th the band perform at the Capitol Theater in Passaic, New Jersey, with the following setlist: Sunday Morning Sunshine, W.O.L.D., Mr Tanner, Six String Orchestra, Better Place To Be, Lesson #18 (Ron), Experience #9 (Ron), Experience #12 (Ron), Country Medley, 30,000 Pounds of Bananas, Mail Order Annie, Taxi, Sniper, What Made America Famous.

Harry's intention is to make a more upbeat album with high production values. For this he needs to give it a more professional sound, and on producer Leka's suggestion, he dismisses any input from his band and instead has the producer bring in experienced session musicians, including the highly respected and much-sought-after guitarist John Tropea, as well as bass player Don Payne, keyboard player Don Grolnick, and drummer Allan Schwartzberg. Brothers Steve and Tom will also be on hand to help, as well as their ever-eager father Jim.

Verities and Balderdash (1974) *****
Elektra 7E-1012
Recorded: Connecticut Recording Studios, Bridgeport, CT. Spring 1974
US Release Date: August 24th 1974
Producer: Paul Leka
Engineer: Billy Rose II

Once again, the design for the album cover is eye-catching. The artwork by Glen Christiansen, with illustrations by Bill Hoffman, is of a collection of watercolor images in the shape of a guitar, with a painting of Harry on the front cover imitating the pointed finger of the Uncle Sam military recruiting poster (later to be recreated in an iconic photograph by the late Joel Brodsky). The wry smile on Harry's face some way reflects the contradictions found among the songs. Although it is the first album not to have a gatefold sleeve, it still retains a pull-out lyric sheet with photographs once again taken by Ruth Bernal. Of the nine songs chosen for the album, only four are new compositions. Side one has the potential to yield at least a trio of hit singles, **'Cat's in the Cradle'**, **'I Wanna Learn a Love Song'** and **'Shooting Star'**, all of them about family, and none of them lengthy story songs that the label may have issues with. There is also one of Harry's first attempts at musical slapstick, **'30,000 Pounds of Bananas'**, written quite a while ago and once favored for inclusion on one of the previous albums. It will be destined to become a firm fixture of his live concerts. The laughs then die down with the mellow and melodic **'She Sings Songs Without Words'**, another long-overdue apology to Sandy for his recent behavior. Side two has a harder edge to it, with its opening track **'What Made America Famous'** being one of Harry's best lyrical works to date. Its highly charged finale then leads nicely

128

into the more serene and gentle **'Vacancy'**, one more tale of loneliness, before our senses are once again stirred as Harry delves into the subject of mid-life crisis with **'Halfway to Heaven'**, a song originally selected for a previous work. The album closes on a happy note with another slice of well-constructed Chapin humor in **'Six-String Orchestra'**, also previously side-lined.

Cat's in the Cradle *****

Without a doubt Harry's most famous song, but most of the credit should go to Sandy, whose poem about a father-son relationship, which evolved later into a lyric, leads to both its recording and a life-changing moment for the singer. It becomes the single that propels the album's success - a tale of a hard-working father who is idolized by his young son but due to his job commitments becomes inattentive toward him, and by the time he realizes that their relationship is damaged; it is too late. A simple tale, perhaps, but it resonates with so many people, who see this same situation developing and happening every day of their lives.

The song begins with the well-meaning but career-oriented narrator having just become a father:

My child arrived just the other day
He came to the world in the usual way
But there were planes to catch and bills to pay
He learned to walk while I was away
And he was talkin' 'fore I knew it, and as he grew
He'd say "I'm gonna be like you dad
You know I'm gonna be like you"

And the cat's in the cradle and the silver spoon
Little boy blue and the man on the moon
"When you comin' home dad?"
"I don't know when, but we'll get together then,
You know we'll have a good time then."

As the child grows this career that keeps him away from home makes him miss precious moments like his boy talking for the first time and taking his first steps. But when he does come home, his son always tells how much he can't wait for him to come home again to *"have a good time,"* but, more than anything else, wants to grow up to be just like him, the father he adores. On his tenth birthday his dad gives him a present but is too busy even to play a simple game of catch with him. His son doesn't show any disappointment. This is still his hero, the father he aspires to become.

My son turned ten just the other day
He said, "Thanks for the ball, dad, come on let's play
Can you teach me to throw?" I said "Not today
I got a lot to do," he said, "That's ok"
And he walked away but his smile never dimmed,
And said, "I'm gonna be like him, yeah
You know I'm gonna be like him"

Almost a decade passes and the roles begin to be reversed. His son is now on the threshold of adulthood, and his father makes what is a belated attempt to sit and talk with him. But we never do find out what the conversation would have been about because his son has his own agenda now. Father-to-son chats will have to wait.

Well, he came from college just the other day
So much like a man I just had to say
"Son, I'm proud of you can you sit for a while?"
He shook his head and said with a smile
"What I'd really like Dad is to borrow the car keys
See you later, can I have them please?"

By the end of the song the tables have been well and truly turned. The father now has all the time in the world to devote to his son. But his son has now moved away, married with a family of his own. Now his son is too busy to find the time for him.

I've long since retired. My son's moved away
I called him up just the other day
I said, "I'd like to see you if you don't mind"
He said, "I'd love to Dad, if I can find the time.
You see my new job's a hassle and kids have the flu
But it's sure nice talking to you, Dad
It's been sure nice talking to you"

Too late. The father finally realizes what has happened. His son has mistakenly learned what is most important in life from watching his father's example.

And as I hung up the phone it occurred to me -
He'd grown up just like me
My boy was just like me.

In a 1977 interview with British DJ Noel Edmonds, Harry recalls:

"The lyrics of 'Cat's in the Cradle' come from a poem of (Sandy's) that was zinging me for running around the country, worrying about being successful and not enough about the kids. So, I have a distant early warning system, who's very close to me, whenever Harry Chapin gets off on some crazy situation gives me a kick in the pants… I'd done that as a propaganda piece it would have been 'fathers pay attention to your children or else they won't pay attention to you,' and it would have been a goddamn bore. But done on an emotional basis, not from me being in an enlightened position, but rather being in a sense the fool that all this is happening to, being blind as it unfolds. That freshly, emotionally implanted a truth that was already there, or re-implanted a truth that everybody knew and put it in such a way, that I got 175 separate letters from clergymen alone, saying they used it as a basis for a sermon in the United States."

On Dec 21st **'Cat's in the Cradle'** hits the #1 spot on the *Billboard* 100, taking over from Carl Douglas's 'Kung Fu Fighting', and stays there for a week until being replaced by Helen Reddy's 'Angie Baby' on the 28th. Not only does it remain in the Top 40 for nineteen weeks, it also reaches the #1 spot on the Cashbox 100 chart and #6 on *Billboard's* Adult Contemporary chart. At the end of the month it will be certified gold, a little over a week after its parent album receives the same accolade. Sandy later remembers the song's impact: *"That was the kind of song that people bought to deliver to other people. We were really surprised to find out that it had been used in church services and marriage counseling. American parents seem to think they can buy out their relationship with their kids. The song proved them wrong."*

Someone once dubbed this song *"the most timeless tearjerker ever."* **'Cat's in the Cradle'** will indeed remain timeless, because its fundamental message will go on to haunt families for generations to come. Thanks to Harry and Sandy's song, America's children, and their children's children, will have a better understanding that one of the primary aspects of raising a family is to not lose touch with your kids. And so too will parents around the world. In 2011 **'Cat's in the Cradle'** is inducted into the Grammy Hall of Fame.

From the cheap seats
Bob Smith - *My gateway song to Harry and still one of my favorites. I tried to raise my son opposite of the song and think I did a good job however I'm older now as well as my son and find myself like the father in the song with his son grown.*

Scott Blitz - *Exactly my story. I wanted to and was the opposite. I not only had the catches but became the coach of every team my son was on from 7-16. But it ended just as the song does. He moved to California and I live in Maryland. I see him about once a year. When it first came out I didn't relate as I saw my dad almost every day and I was the opposite parent, completely* involved. But it still ended up in the exact same place as the song...I have to approach it from a personal view. When it came out it sounded like the most commercial of Harry's songs and I thought it was just ok. Is Harry selling out? A bit of a cliché. I was a young father and didn't get it. Now all these years later and my kids are grown I realize as I sit and wait for any communication from them how spot on he was. Not a day goes by that I don't think about the irony of the song and how it's a reflection of my life.

Scott Sivakoff - *This is the song that got me hooked on Harry. In particular, the version on* **Greatest Stories Live** *was the actual one that did it. I remember my father playing the song for me as a kid (many years later he told me that he heard this song on the day I was born). As a freshman in high school I was given an assignment to find and report on a song about family. At that time, my father suggested this song and I was hooked from that moment on (turns out I couldn't use the song as another student had already used the song, but when her copy of the tape (remember tapes?) failed in class, I had a copy on me that we were able to use). Anyway, the song started me on a wonderful journey through life and music as I discovered more and more of Harry's music and met more and more fans (thanks internet). This song is also the first song I learned to play on guitar and to this day is such a joy to listen to and/or just pick up the guitar and play!*

Konrad Craig - *'Cat's in the Cradle'* *is a story within a story. It is pertinent to all fathers and sons, but considers the changing of the guard within all families and the dynamic changes that happen to us all. It always makes me think when I see my own children growing up, how will it always make me think when I see my own children growing up, how will this love change as we all grow old?*

Stephen Shilman - *It certainly hits me harder than most because my eldest son has passed away. I live in Europe and he lived in the States. The saddest, most difficult days of my life. I'm crying as I write this & it's been a long time since it occurred.*

Cliff Geismar - *A remarkable commentary on family life of the 1970s. In my opinion no one has ever captured the essence of the interaction between family and the struggle to earn a living so succinctly and elegantly*

I Wanna Learn a Love Song *****

The story of how Harry meets Sandy, a song especially written for this album. There's no poetic license here, this is almost exactly how it happens almost ten years before, an intimate glimpse into Jim Cashmore's brownstone apartment at 14 Monroe Place, Brooklyn Heights, where Harry comes to give her guitar lessons and plays to her his own *"backlog of hobo stories and dilapidated dreams."* For $10 an hour, once a week, Harry gets to sit with this 32-year-old lady who will become the love of his life. Some bargain! Of course, there is no record of how many lessons it takes, but with a lot of wooing by Harry, they become inseparable. The one problem, of course, is her husband. The lessons turn into deep, meaningful conversations. She enjoys listening to his whispered songs. He reads poems she has written. And all the time something's burning inside of them. Inevitably, they crave each other's company, and as the tension builds, so does the passion. The connection has been made: if not physical, then certainly spiritual. These two lonely people have found a love for each other that will last a lifetime, and Harry puts his feelings for her into words.

According to Sandy, the *"concrete castle king"* description given to her husband is metaphorical. Jim Cashmore was in fact a lawyer, but the description may come from the fact they lived in a castle-like four-story brownstone apartment in Brooklyn Heights. Or, as she likes to admit, it's probably "whatever fit the poetry". Sandy seldom speaks of her ex-husband, but Harry has his own opinions of him and will put his feelings toward him in the songs **'Poor Damned Fool'** and **'I Wonder What Happened To Him'**. Elektra will eventually release **'I Wanna Learn a Love Song'** as a single in February 1975, backed with **'She Sings Songs Without Words'**, and it eventually reaches #44 on the *Billboard* 100 and #7 on their Adult Contemporary chart.

Shooting Star *****
The inspiration for this lyrically vivid song is hard to pin down. Harry's son Josh recalls: *"My father swore to my mother that this was about his grandfather, literary critic Kenneth Burke, and his wife Lily. Sounds like it could have been about my parents as well."* It could very well be about KB, a literary giant whose muses and inspirations were often well outside what was considered the societal norm, and maybe as a result looked on by some as a little *"crazy"* at times.

He was crazy, of course
From the first she must have known it
But still she went on with him
And she never once had shown it
And she took him off the street
And she dried his tears of grieving
She listened to his visions
She believed in his believing

He was the sun, burning bright and brittle
And she was the moon shining back his light a little
He was a shooting star
She was softer and more slowly
He could not make things possible

133

But she could make them Holy, Holy

Listening to this opening verse and chorus, the words can also be interpreted as being about Harry's relationship with Sandy, and, like **'Star Tripper'** on the *Portrait Gallery* album, see Harry's skyrocketing career as an artist almost leading him to lose the one thing in his life that really matters. However, the remaining verses surely bring us back to KB's relationship with his wives. He married twice, divorcing Lily Batterham, Harry's maternal grandmother, to marry her sister, Libby Batterham.

He was dancing to some music,
No one else had ever heard
He'd speak in unknown languages
She would translate every word
And then when the world was laughing at his castles in the sky
She'd hold him in her body
Till he once again could fly

Well, she gave him a daughter
And she gave him a son
She was a Mother and a Wife,
And Lover when the day was done
He was too far gone for giving love
What he offered in its stead
Was the knowledge she was the only thing
That was not in his head

He took off East one morning
Towards the rising sun's red glow
She knew he was going nowhere
But, of course, she let him go
And as she stood and watched him dwindle
Much too empty to be sad
He reappeared beside her saying,
"You're all I've ever had"

Although surprisingly never considered for a single release, it is fondly remembered for being sung by legendary rock star Pat Benatar at the Carnegie Hall Tribute Concert, perhaps the outstanding performance of the evening.

From the cheap seats
Beth Waggenspack - *Putting on my rhetoric professor hat here: if Harry said it was about Kenneth Burke, I will agree. The first line of that song is "He*

was crazy of course." That describes some of Burke's theory and concepts (for me, at least, not necessarily my colleagues). The other line that has to be a reference to Burke (or his ideas) was "Reality is only just a word" (Corey's Coming). Whenever I teach Burke, I humanize him by playing the latter.

Alan L Geraci - *I love this song. As a tribute to his grandparents, Harry captures the essence of their relationship and their dynamics of fulfilling the needs of the individual while elevating the oneness of the couple.*

Carmen Regan - *He was the Sun burning brightly which tells me that he was the leader in the relationship, the decision maker and had big dreams for his life. She was the Moon reflecting back the very best of his qualities feeling protected but at the same time steering him gently towards all that was practical and kind without ever taking away from the beauty or respect of their relationship.*

30,000 Pounds of Bananas **

Only two stars? This will no doubt outrage almost every die-hard Chapin fan in the world who has screamed for Harry to sing this in concert (and he always did). As a novelty song, it does have some particular charm, and Harry always had an acute sense of humor, using it as an occasional counterpoint to his more dark and sombre tales. But that humor can sometimes backfire. It is based on a true story about an accident in Scranton, Pennsylvania, where a driver loses control of a truck full of bananas he is delivering and is killed in the crash. It's only after learning of that little-known fact that we should reappraise the song's misguided humor. Harry is told of the story a few months later by a local man while riding a Greyhound bus out of Scranton. According to Sandy, it is written as a serious poem to highlight society's morbid preoccupation with the numbers coming out of Vietnam, without thinking of the human tragedy behind them. The point Harry makes is that the number of spilt bananas involved seems more important than the life that has been lost.

And the story is truly heartbreaking. On March 18th 1965, 35-year-old Scranton truck driver Eugene Sesky, an employee of Fred Carpentier, a small Scranton truck company, was on his way back home with a 15-ton load of bananas that he had collected from the boat piers in Weehawken, New Jersey. He was driving a 1950s Brockway diesel truck tractor with a 35ft semi-trailer. The bananas were destined for the "wholesale block" on the western edge of Lackawanna Avenue, possibly Halem Hazzouri Bananas, which at the time was the premier seller in the area. Sesky was driving along Route 307, which contains a two-mile descent extending from Lake Scranton to the bottom of Moosic Street, an elevation that drops more than 500ft in less than a mile and a half. Due to mechanical failure while negotiating the descent, Sesky lost control and the truck ran into town at close to 90mph, colliding with a number of vehicles before turning over (maybe intentionally) and hitting a house close to the bottom of the hill, just short of running into a gas station and a crowd of pedestrians, although some sixteen people were injured when their cars were struck as the truck went past. Some witnesses claimed that the driver did everything he could to avoid hitting anyone, even climbing out onto the running board and shouting warnings. Sesky was thrown from the cab and killed.

To begin with Harry takes the story seriously, the words often just spoken in solo performances, but turning it into a song, and with the band backing him, a humorous side to the story begins to develop, and the audience reaction cements the song as a staple part of his live concerts.

Perhaps the most notable live performance is in California in November 1975 and featured on the **Greatest Stories Live** album. Harry performs two alternate endings that he says he had originally had in mind for the song, both dismissed by brothers Tom and Steve who give their honest opinion, *"Harry, it sucks!"* It becomes a frequent heckle from the audience in future concerts. Maybe sometimes it is done because some people feel, like we should all feel, that beneath this veneer of spontaneous laughter, there is still that morbid reality of what the song is actually about. Allegedly, due to some comments made in the press, Harry promises to donate royalties for the song to Sesky's widow. Whether he does or not, he continues to perform it to raucous audiences for the rest of his career. By not singing it, he risks life and limb....

In his interview with Noel Edmonds in December 1977, Harry speaks about the effect **'Bananas'** had on Sesky's family: *"I first wrote the song as a poem and it was a comment on the Vietnam body count. We got so involved with statistics that we didn't think of the human story behind it. So it was a piece of black comedy. The point is very simple. The song seems to have a bizarre life force within its craziness. But the original urge was very simple. I was coming through Scranton, Pennsylvania in 1965. An elderly gentleman did get in and tell me the story of this event, and to put a weird little kick on it, to show you how life can come around double-edged, I got a call about two years later from a lawyer. The lawyer was calling for the sister of the guy who was killed in the story. He had no legal basis to ask, but he said, 'You're coming to Scranton and they're using **'Bananas'** on the radio program as promotion for the concert. Could you ask him to stop it?'"*

The album version is almost like hearing a Chapin Brothers recording again, with Tom on banjo, Steve on piano and Jim back on drums, but in concert Harry usually turns this less than six-minute-long song into a fifteen-minute-plus saga, complete with alternate endings and all the banter that goes on in between. For what is probably a small minority in the audience, it must grate on their teeth or give them a chance for a restroom break. And he will go on to do this in almost every single concert for the rest of his career. Maybe just once in a while he could have dropped it and used those fifteen minutes to treat the audience to other songs that he seldom performed live - songs such as **'The Rock'**, **'She is Always Seventeen'**, **'Country Dreams'** and

136

'**Vacancy**'. But then again, the audience would probably never let him get away with it, with screams of "Bananas…give us Bananas!" Taking the tragic real-life aside, though, the song does have its humorous moments. Just the thought of the runaway truck *"smearing"* down the road once brought a smile to this author's face, but only the once…..

From the cheap seats
Brandon Walls - *The subject isn't divisive, but the song is. Most people love it (I do). But some believe that Harry shouldn't have made a song out of it, or at least not have made it as jokingly. But that's the song.*

Ellen Gordon Klein - *I Love 'Bananas,' but the first time I heard it and certainly after I heard it in concert with all the endings, and so comedic, it always gave me pause because it's a true story and a man died. I looked at it as a black comedy (original ending specifically).*

She Sings Songs Without Words *****
Where '**I Wanna Learn a Love Song**' tells us about how Harry first meets Sandy, this is undoubtedly one of his finest and most melodic love letters to her. Seldom in a song has Harry crafted together words so intimate and so eloquent in describing his wife of just six years. In three sublime verses Harry uses clever alliterative phrases that highlight his poetic prowess.

I was thrown on the cobblestones, tossed at her feet
My fool's mouth was filled with the dust from the street
An out of work court jester with nowhere to go
And no need to speak, for she seemed to know

The chorus that follows has Harry comparing Sandy to the great romantic poets of history, the same poets that he himself is trying to emulate, with well-chosen words that express such deep sensual and passionate feelings:

She sings the songs without words
Songs that sailors, and blind men, and beggars have heard
She knows more of love than the poets can say
And her eyes offer something that won't go away

The final two four-line verses are arguably the finest lyrics Harry has ever written in describing the woman he loves:

This mad mocking town and its dishonored guest
Disappeared in the colors that danced on her dress
She led me to safety in a forest of green
And showed my stale eyes some sights never seen

137

She spills magic and moonlight in her meadows and streams
And seeks deep inside me and touches my dreams
The morning comes smiling and I laugh with no sound
And snuggle in silence in the sweet peace I've found

It is worth comparing this to **'Sandy'**, one of Harry's first love letters to his wife. Where that song's beauty lies in its innate simplicity, this magnificent dream-like ballad is built on a bed of angelic backing vocals, and with Steve Chapin's wonderful piano accompaniment expresses so much gentleness and devotion that it stands in stark contrast to the much harsher tone of the album. In the corner of the album's back cover, almost going unnoticed, is written: *"This album is dedicated to Sandy, who has been more than dedicated to me for 8 years. May I be someday be what she sees in me."* With this Harry is rubber-stamping his newfound commitment to his wife. He will dedicate a number of love songs to her throughout his life, but there are none more beautiful and heartfelt than this one. The song is fittingly chosen as the flip-side to the single **'I Wanna Learn a Love Song'**, making it a double-sided romantic tribute to his wife.

What Made America Famous? *****
Written around 1970, this song proves to be a milestone in Harry's music career. It is inspired by true events that happen in Point Lookout, Harry and Sandy's home before moving to Huntington. One night there is a report of a suspicious fire at a so-called welfare house in town occupied by black families, but it takes the volunteer firefighters two hours to respond. In Harry's story the setting is a nameless town with its strait-laced, church-going inhabitants.

It was the town that made America famous
The churches full and the kids all goin' to hell
Six traffic lights and seven cops and all the streets kept clean
The supermarket and the drugstore, and the bars all doing well

There's something a little unsettling in the line *"the kids all goin' to hell."* Maybe all is not as serene as it seems. The focus of the song now turns to the town's fire department, run by volunteers, all with their own day jobs.

Now they were the folks that made America famous
Our local fire department stocked with short-haired volunteers
And on Saturday night while America boozes
The fire department showed dirty movies,
The lawyer and the grocer seeing their dreams

138

Come to life on the movie screen
While the plumber hopes that he won't be seen
As he tries to hide his fears and he wipes away his tears
But something's burning somewhere
Does anybody care?

One of these firemen, an overweight plumber, is seemingly embarrassed to be there, and afraid his shame may be noticed by his more macho and bigoted colleagues. But outside there is a growing tension in the air... The nice upstanding residents have a problem with one group of undesirables that are spoiling the image of their picture-book town, but now it's their turn to state their case. These long-haired *"dropouts"* are at loggerheads with the very community they live in:

We were the kids that made America famous
The kind of kids that long since drove our parents to despair
We were lazy longhairs dropping out, lost, confused, and copping out
Convinced our futures were in doubt and trying not to care.

We lived in the house that made America famous
It was a rundown slum, the shame of all the decent folks in town
We hippies and some welfare cases
Crowded families of coal-black faces
Cramped inside some cracked old boards
The best that we all could afford
But still too fine for the rich landlord to ever tear it down
And we could hear the sound
Of something's burning somewhere
Is anybody there?

Constantly harassed by the cops, these kids lash back with an incendiary stunt that will have consequences:

We all lived the life that made America famous
Our cops would make a point to shadow us around the town
And we love-children put a swastika
On the bright red firehouse door
America, the beautiful - it makes a body proud.

One night a fire breaks out in the cramped house, either accidentally or deliberately (even one of the angered firemen perhaps?). We never do find out. But all their lives are now in danger:

139

And then came the night that made America famous
Was it carelessness or someone's sick idea of a joke?
In the tinder-box trap that we hippies lived in
Someone struck a spark
At first I thought that I was dreaming,
Then I saw the first flames gleaming
And heard the sound of children screaming
Coming through the smoke
And something's burning somewhere
Does anybody care?

The alarm is raised, but instead of the firemen racing to the scene like they always would, the story takes a dramatic turn:

It was the fire that made America famous
The sirens wailed and the firemen stumbled, sleepy, from their homes
And when then plumber yelled, "Come on, let's go"
They saw what was burning and said, "Take it slow
Let them sweat a little, they'll never know
And beside, we just cleaned the chrome."
Said the plumber, "Then I'm going alone."

The remainder of the story is taken up by the narrator, as he and his family await rescue from the burning building. We are not sure if these are the only ones who have not managed to get out of the house:

Well he rolled on up in the fire truck
And raised the ladder to the ledge
Me and my girl and a couple of kids
Were clinging like bats to the edge
We staggered to salvation, and collapsed on the street
And I never thought that a fat man's face would ever look so sweet.

This plumber has become a hero, not just to this young family, but hopefully to the townsfolk he serves.

I shook his hand in the scene that made America famous
And he smiled from the heart that made America great
We spent the rest of that night in the home of this man
That we'd never known before
Its funny, when you get that close, its kind of hard to hate.

The song ends with this same man dreaming of a better country for his kids. But it doesn't end there. The same thing is still happening across the country - something's burning somewhere. Does anybody care?

I went to sleep with the hope that made America famous
I had the kind of dream that maybe they're still trying to teach in school
Of the America that made America famous
And of the people who just might understand
That how together, yes we can,
Create a country better than
The one we have made of this land
We have the choice to make each man
Who dares to dream, reaching out his hand,
A prophet, or just a crazy Goddamn dreamer of a fool,
Yes, a crazy fool

And something's burning somewhere
Does anybody care?
Is anybody there?
Is anybody there?

Heroes are people who you'd never suspect, or ever know. But the plumber in this story is no super-hero. He's an ordinary guy who has simply done what anyone with a conscience would do and has had the emotional courage to stand up and be counted, put aside any differences, and just get the job done. This, in essence, is Harry's dream for a better country. It serves as a warning to people that if they persist in being antagonistic towards others, whoever they are, they may not be able to control the "burning fire" that's inside of them. The song manages to exude a preachiness that most of Harry's better story songs steer clear of. According to critic Alan Bradley: *"It's not that long-hairs and bigoted foremen failing to understand each other is an unfit subject for songwriting, it's rather than a man capable of* **'Better Place To Be'** *and* **'Mr Tanner'** *must by virtue of his ability be considered on a higher level than* **'What Made America Famous'** *permits us to consider him."* Another critic points out that Harry has *"shamelessly"* borrowed the lines *"Is anybody there? Does anybody care?"* from a song in Sherman Edwards' 1972 Broadway musical *1776*.

Harry recalls: *"***'What Made America Famous'** *basically comes out of a thing where my wife was saying 'You should write a song about a volunteer fire department and name it Answering the Call.' Now, I took it to a whole other place, but I'm a believer in recognizing good ideas. My wife happens to be a fantastic poet and I've been very lucky to have her with me."*

141

In an interview with Sandy, Linda McCarty writes how the song has its origins in the community of Point Lookout: *"In the late 1960s when the Chapins lived there, the local realtors had an unwritten agreement that they would never rent to African-Americans. 'They were trying to avoid what they imagined: 10 people to a room and bottles all over the sidewalk,' she said. Then, the owner of the business block rented the apartments to African-American families, she added. Soon, there were meetings about condemning the building. 'I learned more about poverty in that one year,' Sandy said. 'My kids went out to stand on the corner for the school bus. The black kids were on one side of the street and the white kids on the other side. So, I asked Jaime to go stand with the black kids.' The fire happened in December, a few months after the Chapins had moved to Huntington, but they heard about it from a distance. Was it an accident or deliberately set? 'When there's been such an effort to condemn the building and get people out, it makes you wonder,' Sandy said."*

(*Circle*, Summer 2004)

Like **'Taxi'** had been, **'What Made America Famous'** is more of a request hit than a big seller. Where Jerry Peterson of KHJ in Los Angeles claims he got more requests for **'Taxi'** than any other song except Led Zeppelin's 'Stairway to Heaven', he pays Harry a more unusual compliment by selecting **'What Made America Famous'** as the only current track that year programmed on the KHJ Memorial Day Solid Gold Weekend's Firecracker 500. Released as a single in July 1974, with **'Old College Avenue'** on the flip-side, it peaks at #87 on the Cashbox Top 100.

Harry's song certainly strikes a chord with some of the leading lights in the music world, and talks with Broadway producers will soon get under way. For Harry it will be the answer to another long-nurtured dream.

From the cheap seats

Nancy Rothstein - *I always thought it was about the ever-burning generational war, favorite quote that pops into my head frequently is 'it's funny when you get that close, it's kind of hard to hate.' Lesson learned.*

Bob Smith - *I think whether it's generational, race, religion, sexual preference or anything else that divides this country when the chips are down, and someone needs help like the fire in the song; America helps despite the hate/differences. The song is very dated, in its wording, but still holds true today.*

Vacancy ****

A song about a motel owner must have raised a few eyebrows in the Elektra boardroom. But this poignant tale of loneliness and a vain attempt to establish human connection is judged good enough to be chosen for the flip-side of the **'Cat's in the Cradle'** single. The inspiration for the song may possibly have come from the motel scene in the 1968 Broadway play *Morning, Noon and Night*. Once again Steve Chapin's keyboard skills do justice to Harry's finely-crafted lyrics. In the song, the nameless and solitary owner of the roadside motel is longing for people to come and stay the night and fill up his empty rooms. But this isn't Norman Bates. There's no drama about to unfold. His daytimes are empty, devoid of human contact, and the only way he can find solace is in these brief nighttime encounters, where the only connections made live in his imagination of what clandestine things may be going on behind the closed doors of the motel rooms. As checkout comes around in the morning and his guests leave, he goes to tidy up the rooms, cleaning or taking away things that hold clues to their stay, much like detective's leads.

A faultless, crystal-clear production makes this pleasant but pedestrian song sound even better than it is, and manages to evoke memories for anyone whose has visited a motel, coaxing the listener to imagine themselves what stories lie behind the tell-tale ashtrays, sheets, and towels. But for the motel man and his guests, they are, after all, just spectator and participants in an endless dance of despair. The song is a fitting flip-side to the number one single **'Cat's in the Cradle'**.

Halfway to Heaven *****

Another great song that in its original form fails to make the final cut on *Sniper and Other Love Songs*. Written sometime in 1972 it is inspired by a conversation Harry has while waiting in a railroad station for a train, with a man sitting next to him bragging about having an affair at work with his secretary. By putting himself in the man's shoes, Harry gives his view on the perils and pitfalls of having a mid-life crisis. Still in his early thirties when he writes this, he can't really consider himself having reached that point just yet. He can only imagine how it might affect him. In the song the narrator is delayed in his journey home from work, giving him time to ponder and take stock of his life. Married for fifteen years, with two boys, he feels he's already lived up to his promises, but knows now there's something missing in his life. He looks to his wife. Whatever morals he once may have had have changed with the times. The world is now a different place from when he was young. His sheltered upbringing by an overprotective mother has left him devoid of any loving relationships until he married the first "good" girl he meets. At work he gets friendly with his new young secretary, perhaps half his age, and the signals she gives off indicate a mutual attraction. He knows what this can lead to, and never doubts that she will be only too obliging. His mind is made up. This girl is too much of a temptation and he invites her out for dinner.

Harry's highly-charged vocal, and Leka's polished production, make this one of the highlights of the album, and a marked improvement on the original version recorded by the band. With Allen Schwartzberg's machine-like drumming and John Tropea's blazing guitar work in the finale, this is solid justification for the decision to have experienced session musicians on board.

The original version of the song is mistakenly labelled 'Highway to Heaven' on the 2004 double-CD, ***Heads and Tales / Sniper and Other Love Songs***.

From the cheap seats

Gerry Naughton - *Chapin didn't make a moral statement in '**Halfway to Heaven**', but he adroitly described the trap between old-fashioned family values with the lure of sexual desire. The song doesn't question morality, but rather it makes us reflect on changes in lifestyle habits and what has become socially more tolerated: "How the World's accepting now, what they once would not allow". Neither does Chapin, by way of his central character, consider the possible negative consequences of the impending affair, such as marital breakdown, separation from children and complications in the workplace. Chapin based many of his songs on real-life situations without making judgement – and this is one of them!*

Bruce Morgan - *One of his songs where he touched on every middle-aged man's fantasy and now being good all his life, does he do it?*

Jim G Phynn - *I don't think this song has held up very well over the years. What the narrator of this story is considering doing, is undoubtedly workplace harassment and, in light of the MeToo movement, it's not a good message to be sending. That said, I'm not entirely unsympathetic to the narrator. He was born a little too early to be able to express himself in a manner consistent with the changing norms and mores of the 1960s (the sexual revolution), and he's not wrong for resenting the fact that he wasn't afforded the choices someone marginally younger would have been permitted to make. We see the same thing today in people who are vocally homophobic, and yet get caught in a gay tryst. They were told from a young age how 'wrong' it is to be gay and have difficulties in reconciling that against both their own feelings and a new reality that's more accepting.*

Tony Bentivegna - *Harry apparently did not allow vices to consume him or compromise his obligations or causes. But it's really the great storytelling that matters to me as a fan. And it's honest because, after all, the fantasy of taking the young secretary "out to dinner" is real to many middle-aged men. You will find such themes in many great works of literature, and readers rarely criticize those authors for it.*

Cliff Geismar – *I refuse to consider anything in the song as harassment. Love this song...and will not condemn anything he did or said 35-40 years ago. We know that his "macho" character was part of hidden charm. It is also undeniable that he respected men and women whether they were easy, cheesy or sleazy. Enough said.*

Melba Davis Nickoles - *Someone asked the question about Sandy being offended by the song. Is Stephen King's wife afraid to go to sleep with him at night? No. They are all just fiction. Except the ones he says are based on true events. Sandy, herself, said in an interview, she found his slips of paper with songs written on them all the time. I don't believe she was offended by a fictitious song that might be real to someone else. We all (most of us) have an imagination, think thoughts that we are glad no one else can hear. He took his imagination, and made a wonderful career for himself, a great living for Sandy and their family and left a mark on those of us who loved him that will only go away when we cease to live. I talk to my husband about Harry all the time. He isn't offended. He knows, listening to Harry is something I enjoy. Like reading a good book. These 'story songs' are almost real to us, but not real enough to interfere with our everyday lives.*

Six-String Orchestra ***

Rounding the album off this has Harry in semi-autobiographical mood, pointing a finger of fun at himself in a light-hearted parody of how he dreams of being a better musician. In the song he is a young guitarist whose lack of talent is much in evidence from what we hear. Even his mother agrees there's room for improvement. To add emphasis to that claim, he begins the song by making false starts and then plays out-of-tune notes on his six-string guitar before he finally gets some sort of rhythm going and begins to tell his story, even making a wisecrack at Eric Clapton's expense. As he continues to practice, he imagines what he would sound like with other musicians helping him along. One by one, on cue, we have other instruments being introduced - bass, lead guitar, drums, and strings - until it sounds to him like a symphony orchestra. Along with the music, his singing also improves with each line, but by the end of the chorus, his dream has evaporated, and we are back with just him and his fumbled attempts at playing guitar. He sings of playing at talent shows, writing love songs to impress a girl, sending a demo tape to record companies, and even taking up guitar lessons, but in each case his efforts are thwarted, and he continues undeterred with his dream, convinced that becoming a fine musician is his destiny.

The message is simple: if you don't succeed, try and try again until you do. Much of the song parallels Harry's early career as a singer, from taking up guitar, attending talent shows, writing love songs to get the girls, and eventually joining up with his brothers to form a band and getting rejected by record labels until getting the break. But there are also shades of **'Mr Tanner'** in the song. Whether in record company replies or critics' reviews, their advice is the same - pursue another career. The song is actually a studio recording with canned laughter added to give it the effect of a live performance. Once more Jim Chapin is given the chance to sit behind the drums, while Tom is on banjo, and Paul Leka himself plays piano. The song will become a popular part of future concerts, with Harry often dedicating it to "all the bad guitar players in America."

The Trouble With Harry...

On July 24th Harry performs once again at the Schaefer Music Festival in Central Park, entertaining the enthusiastic New York crowd in a rainstorm, or, as Harry puts it, *"a picnic gone awry."* The setlist is as follows: Sunday Morning Sunshine, Greyhound, Talkin Bout Love, Better Place To Be, Pigeon Run, Lesson #18 (Ron), Experience #9 (Ron), Six String Orchestra, W.O.L.D., Hillbilly Medley, 30,000 Pounds of Bananas, Lesson #36 (Ron).

A month later the album is released and there are strong indications of it being a success. Harry is eager to promote the song **'What Made America Famous'** and get it released as a single, although he realizes its length will prove difficult to get AM radio stations to play it. Demo copies of the full 6.53-minute song are rushed out to radio stations, and Harry follows it up by once again making personal visits, even singing it live to the station bosses. A repeat effort of forging written requests to Boston's WKRO station fails when it is figured out what is being done. Although the reception to the song is generally positive, it doesn't get the anticipated airplay, and is dropped as a potential single.

But there is always **'Cat's in the Cradle'**. Harry isn't all that happy with the recording, believing the tempo is too fast, but before he gets the chance to go back into the studio to re-record it, Elektra release the original as a single on October 1st, with **'Vacancy'** on the flip-side, and in no time at all it is shooting up the *Billboard* 100 chart. Harry's usual detractors continue to be reticent. Stephen Holden in *Village Voice* calls the whole album *"nauseating,"* while *Rolling Stone* even declines to review it all.

Melody Maker issues a critical review of the album: *"The man from W.O.L.D., with a collection of interesting little tales, often wry and with a moral to tell. There's something charmingly old-fashioned about Chapin's music-songs which are complete tuneful stories, delivered with an unlikely intensity and importance, scarcely used since the days of Tommy Roe and Del Shannon...Chapin's not exactly a good singer and his melodies and song structures aren't stunningly original, but there's character and he gives it all it's worth. The worth isn't too great and consequently a nothing song like* **'Vacancy'** *sounds faintly ridiculous, while* **'What Made America Famous'** *and all its ironic national pride is overdone to the point of losing its credibility...."*

During that fall, Harry appears twice at the Capitol Theater in Portchester, New York, and one reviewer is at least more positive: *"An evening with Harry Chapin proved to be one of the finest concerts I have ever witnessed...An intimate atmosphere created an inner glow in everyone. Something I thought*

146

could never be kindled in concert again. It seemed Harry had invited us all into his living room, feeling comfortable..."

Following a concert at New York's Avery Fisher Hall, a review appears in *Melody Maker*: *"The trouble with Harry is that he's such a goddamn regular guy. The way he handles himself onstage, for instance. Like a scoutmaster, wholesome and good-intentioned, addressing his young troops, words of wisdom in bull sessions around the campfire...Harry is a nice person. Really. You could take your mother and she wouldn't throw up...Harry begins to get through to me. He may be earnest, and so enthusiastic he turns red-faced from strumming his acoustic, but at least the guy cares."*

On November 4th Harry appears with his band on *The Mike Douglas Show* and performs **'Cat's in the Cradle'** and **'I Wanna Learn a Love Song'** to a nationwide audience. A month later on December 3rd the fourth Chicago-based WTTW television production of *Soundstage* is aired on PBS television, with Harry and his band (Wallace, Masters and Palmer) performing for the hour-long taped special entitled *The Book of Chapin*. In an intimate setting in front of a small audience in Studio A, they perform a selection of songs, as well as a brief question and answer section. Harry begins the set with a stunning version of **'What Made America Famous'**, initially sung in an empty studio, but by the end of the song, when Harry is asking "Is anybody there?" the audience somehow magically appears (making you think that two versions were actually performed). This is followed by superlative performances of **'W.O.L.D.'**, **'Mr Tanner'**, **'Six String Orchestra'**, **'Mail Order Annie'**, **'Cat's in the Cradle'**, **'Taxi'**, and a rare live performance of **'She Sings Songs Without Words'**. But the highlight of the show has to be his powerful and emotional nine-minute-long rendition of **'Sniper'**, surely one of his greatest vocal performances ever to be caught on film. (In 1978 Harry is invited back to host a *Soundstage* special, showcasing a variety of performances from the first five years, including Harry's own performances of **'Cat's in the Cradle'** and **'Circle'**). As a result of the *Soundstage* broadcast, radio stations continue to be inundated with requests to play some of the featured songs, but it's **'Cat's'** that most people want to hear.

John Wallace remembers the highs and lows of those early days:

*"Harry never lacked confidence. The first time I heard **'Cat's In The Cradle'** I thought, 'This song is good.' Harry was standing in front of me with his foot on a chair and banging out chords, and I thought, 'This is great and this is a hit.' We just went with the program, and not even six months later it was a rocket. After four months we were flying in Elektra's corporate Gulfstream with Holzman himself and recording in Elektra's own studios. We never lost respect in terms of who we were. We were humble and knew we had a lot to be humble about. We got carried away by the trappings but not so much Harry. Harry was more goal-oriented, didn't even smoke cigarettes, no drinking - not involved in that stuff. It was a brutal schedule in those days, but*

you use whatever help you can. We were doing 20 nights a month at that point. No bus, no limo. We drove or flew and you don't always eat right on the run. We were lucky to get to sleep at three or four in the morning and were up at seven. The lifestyle is important because of what happens to people and bands. You have to work at keeping people together under those circumstances."
(Linda McCarty, *Circle* Winter 2004)

The impact on Harry is monumental. The success of this one song not only raises his profile enormously, but he is now developing a new persona, one that will slot nicely into what is considered to be mainstream music. With **'Cat's'**, and songs like it on the album, he is no longer looked on as the unorthodox or unconventional singer of such heartbreaking and tragic songs found on previous albums. He is now Harry Chapin the family man, the singer of radio-friendly pop songs. The critics may not care for him, perhaps even less so now for this sudden success, but the public adore this song, and their adoration will make him a very rich man. The popularity of **'Cat's'** means that it is added to the setlist of many established performers and Harry is in constant demand to do interviews, commercials, and more television appearances. Within four months of its release *Verities & Balderdash* will have sold over 600,000 copies and earns Harry his first gold record. He is also nominated for a Grammy in the Best Male Pop Vocal Performance category for **'Cat's'**, and in March 1975 will sing it at the awards ceremony, although losing out on the night to Stevie Wonder's album, *Fulfullingness' First Finale*. Harry's success lies in the fact that he manages to feel the emotional pulse of the everyday person. People can easily relate to the feelings his songs portray. With his sumptuous melodies he works his magic to make his tales of love and hate, discovery and disenchantment, and success and failure, that little less painful and easier to accept. He has become a working man's hero who maintains a close and intimate relationship with his audience using his remarkable energy to pull at their heartstrings.

But Harry now has other things on his mind. Apart from his ongoing commitments to W.H.Y. and helping Sandy out with projects closer to home, he finds that he can no longer see the light of the moon outside his bedroom window. There's only neon. And it's the neon lights of Broadway.

Nights on Broadway

"I think that there were some things for me to learn, and, I think, the next time I do something like that, I'll be closer to having it make a real major impact"

The Lure of the Theater

It is a difficult time for Harry. On one hand he now has the opportunity to cash in on the burgeoning success of the ***Verities & Balderdash*** album and its hit single, with Elektra expecting a lucrative nationwide tour and media appearances to boost record sales, but on the other hand, over the last few months, he has had his sights on a new venture. Back in the spring of 1974 Harry had taken the song **'What Made America Famous'** to a couple of New York theater producers, Joseph Beruh and Edgar Lansbury (the latter the brother of actress Angela Lansbury) with the idea of using it as the basis for a musical. Along with nearly thirty other songs he has written, Harry envisages a unique and sweeping multimedia-type musical history of the country spanning two decades from the 60s into the 70s, and using all the latest theatrical film, lighting techniques, and innovative ways of stage production, to give it both a uniqueness and impact. Beruh and Lansbury are well respected for bringing new ideas to the stage, and already have strong credentials in musical theater with the likes of *Gypsy* and the recent smash hit *Godspell*. A new musical revue with the emphasis on America is much to their liking, and will be the embodiment of Harry's long cherished idea of bringing to the stage his views about how the young and defiant youth of the 60s, who dared to take a stand through their music and marching to pursue their elusive America Dream, are now becoming a fast-fading memory, fueled by their now middle-aged apathy and conservatism. It has all the hallmarks of being a success.

For one thing this is no record label that Harry has to convince and make compromises with; these are two of Broadway's top producers, and they want to make this musical as much as Harry does. With little hesitation they give him a one-year contract in which he will receive 10% of the gross takings, and the Ethel Barrymore Theater at 243 West 47th Street is chosen as the ideal venue. Depending on its initial success, they hope for a six-month run. Lansbury and Beruh both put $75,000 each into the production, in partnership with the so-called Shubert Organization which invests another $150,000. Among a dozen or more other contributors, Angela Lansbury herself donates $8,000. Harry also foots the bill for scenery props to the tune of some $5,000. With a little over seven months to prepare, Harry begins working with Gene

Frankel, an avant-garde director who has previously won three Obie Awards for *Volpone, Machinal* and Jean Genet's *The Blacks*, which ran for an incredible 1,000 performances. Often referred to as one of the founders of the off-Broadway movement, he is also founder of the Berkshire Theater Festival where he originated *Waiting for Godot*. For Broadway, he has directed *Lost in the Stars, The Lincoln Mask* and *An Enemy of the People*, as well as the 1969 non-musical *Indians*, which garners the Burns Mantle Award for Best Play. Harry and Sandy have already seen *Indians* and are highly impressed with Frankel's conceptual treatment.

The name given to the revue will be ***The Night That Made America Famous*** and it will be due to open at the end of February 1975. Covering events over the last fifteen years, Harry chooses for material eight songs from his four studio albums released so far - **'Taxi'** from ***Heads and Tales***; **'Sunday Morning Sunshine'**, **'Better Place To Be'**, and the title track from ***Sniper and Other Love Songs***; **'Mr Tanner'** from ***Short Stories***; and **'Six-String Orchestra'**, **'Cat's in the Cradle'**, and **'What Made America Famous'** from ***Verities & Balderdash***. The remaining songs are either new compositions (including **'Bummer'**, which will be on the next album), or ones originally written for his aborted ***Buraka*** project of some seven years before.

In July 1974 both Rob White and Jeb Hart, Harry's road crew for over two years, decide to quit and pursue their own careers. While Rob goes on to have a successful career in art, Jeb, having learned along the way from Harry and Fred Kewley a great deal about road management, takes on that role with a band called Mt Airy, which had been formed around 1971 by guitarist Eric Weissberg (best known for his banjo theme to the movie *Deliverance*), and now includes both Tom and Steve Chapin, friends of fellow band member Bob Hinkle. Two new road crew members are subsequently recruited for the upcoming show and future concerts - Jeff Gross, who will handle lighting, and Michael Solomon as sound technician. Although Mt Airy go on to have moderate local success, releasing an eponymous-titled album on the Thimble label in 1973, they fail to get a major recording contract and break up in late 1974. Harry of course wastes no time in bringing on board his two brothers for the forthcoming shows, with Tom also standing by as Harry's understudy if needed (he never is).

By the end of the year, after some three and a half years and countless concerts, lead guitarist Ron Palmer also announces he is quitting the band, citing growing differences with Harry and his disillusionment with the whole record business. He will continue to make music until his death in 2019 at the age of 84, but his valuable contribution to songs like **'Any Old Kind of Day'**, **'Taxi'**, **'Greyhound'**, **'Dogtown'** and **'Sniper'** will never be forgotten.

John Wallace is not surprised by Ron's departure: *"Ron thought it was ridiculous that just as **'Cat's In The Cradle'** had hit number one, Harry had locked himself up for two years with the show when he was about to cash in* *on concert revenues. Ron was bitter, and we weren't involved in the decision, so he quit. He didn't regret it. Fortunately for Harry's career, the show only lasted 6 weeks (12 with rehearsals). We came out of it with Steve, Tom and Howie Fields. It became a six-piece band with the new configuration, and we started doing concerts again."*

(Linda McCarty, *Circle*, Winter 2004)

Ron is indeed upset about the Broadway show. On the back of the success of **'Cat's'**, concert bookings have come pouring in and their fees have risen from around $2,500 a night to $7,500. According to John, *"Harry had this kind of bug up his ass to do Broadway. Right at the peak, he shuts everything down and goes to Broadway."* Fred Kewley too has tried his best to dissuade Harry from doing the show. With dollar signs in his eyes, he is convinced that he has the potential to increase his performance money from $10,000 a night to maybe something like $40,000, but eventually resigns himself to the fact that it is, after all, Harry's chance to fulfill one of his dreams, whatever the cost may be. As a replacement for Ron, Harry gets his brother Steve, as musical director, to get in touch with his old friend Doug Walker, ex-member of The Chapins from the Village Gate days. Seldom out of work since then, Walker had formed The Performing Band with his friend and ex-Chapins drummer Phil Forbes, but the band lacks the essential ingredients to make a success of it and eventually folds.

Big John and Mike Masters retain their roles for the shows, but a versatile drummer is also needed. In conversation with Steve, Doug Walker suggests he gets in touch with Howie Fields, a young Brooklyn musician. After attending James Madison High School, Howie had received his BA in Music at Long Island University, and had played in various bands during his college years. More recently he performed alongside Doug with The Performing Band.

Harry announces that the show will be a meeting place of a musical and rock concert, with thirty songs, sixteen of which are new compositions. The show also has the first six-figure budget of any similar Broadway project. Harry points out: *"I think I write for real people. My vision is evidently shared by many people. There is no humanity market in a sales sense, which is why some of my records make it and some don't."* But on the whole, it is a misguided vision. Harry's idea that his story songs will successfully transfer onto stage with a little choreography thrown in is ill-conceived. Despite characters living within each song, the production will have no plot and no narrative. For all the superficial razzamatazz, it will simply be looked upon as Harry Chapin in concert.

But there is optimism. Not only will the show be the first time anyone from the world of popular music has taken a concert show to Broadway, it will also be the first time the three Chapin brothers have performed together since the late 60s. Harry will work with Solomon to bring a whole new sound to the theater. Against Frankel's advice, he installs an expensive state-of-the-art quadrophonic sound system and, perhaps for the first time in a Broadway theater, has microphones set up on stage. As a result, it becomes cluttered with cables and wires. To Frankel it must indeed seem like this is turning into another Chapin concert, not a musical revue. But he has faith and is willing to indulge him. Although Harry himself will be singing nine of the featured songs, there is the need to bring in some established singers who have the kind of big voice that can do credit to some of the show's hard-hitting numbers. As many of the songs Harry had written for *Buraka* were intended for female voices, Frankel manages to get hold of two of Broadway's rising stars.

In 1972 Santa Fe-raised singer Kelly Garrett made her Broadway debut in the musical *Mother Earth* at the Belasco Theater, and, despite its short run, won a Theater World award. The previous spring she returned to Broadway to perform in Sammy Cahn's musical revue *Words & Music*, and was nominated for the 1st Annual Comedy Awards. This was followed by a starring role in the CBS television show *Your Hit Parade*. Prior to her audition for Harry's show, she sang at the prestigious Rainbow Grill in New York and was a guest singer on various late-night chat shows. Having recently signed a lucrative record contract with RCA, her first single 'As Far as We Can Go' has just been released.

Delores Hall is a black gospel singer who was one of the original members of the 1969 Los Angeles production of the celebrated musical *Hair*, notable for her roles as Sheila and Hud, and with her signature pigtails opening the show with a glorious soul rendition of 'Age of Aquarius'. Three years later she appeared as the character Bread in the short-lived Broadway rock musical *Dude*, as well as performing in George Harrison's Concert for Bangla Desh. She then had a part in the musical *Godspell*, before taking time off to record her first album for RCA. She has only just returned to the cast when she is offered a role in Harry's show.

Another lead male singer is also sought for the show, and Frankel chooses the talented black singer Gilbert Price, who has already received acclaim for three New York musicals, *Six*, *Promenade* and *Lost in the Stars*. His resonant baritone was critically acclaimed in his performance in the Civil Rights musical *Jerico-Jim Crow* in 1964, for which he received a World Theater Award. He also won an award for 1965's long-running musical, *The Roar of the Greasepaint, The Smell of the Crowd*. Later he had his own show on Canadian television and was a regular guest on *The Mike Douglas Show*, as well as touring with Harry Belafonte. With his incredible five-octave range, at least it means that John Wallace can rest his vocals for a while.

Bill Starr has featured in a number of stage musicals and television's *That's Life*, before appearing in the award-winning stage production of *A Woman in the Life of a Man*. Among the other performers chosen are Lynn

152

Thigpen (stand-in for Hall), Alexandra Borrie (stand-in for Garrett), Sid Marshall (stand-in for Price), and Ernie Pysher (stand-in for Starr). The choreographer for the show is Doug Rogers, who has worked with Frankel on the acclaimed project *Split Lip*, and among the talented troupe of dancers is Mercedes Ellington, granddaughter of the famous jazz musician. For set design Frankel turns to award-winning Kert Lundell, who has worked on *The Lincoln Mask* and *The Sunshine Boys*.

Daily rehearsals for the show commence on January 13th 1975 and are held at the New York School of Ballet on Broadway and 82nd Street. During the next four weeks Harry works his socks off, and as well as rehearsals and meetings for the show, he still has to make a number of trips to Washington to make the final time-consuming arrangements for setting up W.H.Y., and keeping his promise to Sandy by performing benefit concerts for PAF, and making personal appearances at local schools and colleges, including a solo benefit for Sag Harbor Youth at East Hampton High School on January 17th. Six days later he co-hosts an edition of *The Mike Douglas Show*, along with singer Vic Damone. On top of all this he is about to go back into the studio to record his next album. Harry's non-stop energy is impressive, but surely, he can't continue like that for much longer. Something has to give.

The First Previews

On February 26th 1975 **The Night That Made America Famous** has its first preview. Drummer Howie Fields recalls: *"After just a few weeks of rehearsal under the direction of Steve Chapin, we made our way over to this celebrated Broadway Theater with a show that contained eight known songs from pre-existing LPs of Harry's... There were also additional song fragments and poetry of Harry's, either performed live or on tape. It was a motley collection of band members made up of long-haired, hippie, rock/folk/pop heads plus Big John, combined with a nine-person cast of young, sophisticated Broadway types with impressive backgrounds in legitimate show music, cabaret, opera, classical, and gospel. I already knew guitarist Doug Walker (formerly of The Chapins) from a Brooklyn group I had played in '73 and '74 called The Performing Band. It was great getting to know Steve, Tom Chapin, Big John Wallace, percussionist Jim Chapin (the dad), and Harry's cellist Mike Masters."*

Harry explains the background to the show in an interview for *Melody Maker*: *"People say my songs are like mini-movies, and I've been able to combine this with film script writing, the theatre and the sort of multi-media pop concert that we've got in this show. The basic question I'm asking in the show is how does a thinking human being, who's gone through all the ups and downs and heartbreaks and hopes of the last 15 years, come out with*

153

something to face the next 15. I'm what they call a hard-assed liberal, and I've been trying to look at the ills. If you've got cancer, you should cut your leg off or wherever the cancer is: do something about it rather than dance while Rome burns or flee the city...Obviously any artistic endeavour has a lot of patchwork to it, so I had to include some of my better known ones. **'Taxi'** is actually three songs stuck together, anyway. In my performance I act out my songs, like **'Sniper'**, but maybe I do it a little more in this show. I have more dramatic leeway in this context so we utilise it...I have no idea whether it'll last six months at all. I don't know what the effect of reviews are these days, but I do know that many shows that get bad reviews have very long runs. We've had some bad reviews and some raves so we'll just have to see. That's the suspense in it."

Although the theme of the show is evident, there is a distinct lack of plot. Some of the chosen songs fit in quite well, but there are some like **'Taxi'**, **'Cat's in the Cradle'** and **'Better Place to Be'** that are completely out of context, confusing members of the audience by making it look like they're watching a separate Harry Chapin concert, totally unrelated to the rest of the show. Some just don't get it at all. Harry's show is all about war and politics, something the audience know only too well, having been saturated with it on television every night, and they surely don't need to be reminded now just how repressed their country is. They don't need another political sermon; they want to escape from that. They have come here for an emotional experience and just want to be entertained.

But the show does have its moments. Harry's rendition of **'Sniper'**, which brings Act One to a close, is sung to a backdrop of film clips of the assassinations of JFK, Malcolm X and Martin Luther King, while members of the cast act as bystanders being interviewed by TV reporters. In **'Mr Tanner'** Harry is joined by Price who does an excellent baritone version of the "skying" segment, and in an evocative version of **'Taxi'**, Harry is joined by Kelly Garrett to play the part of Sue. As well as dramatic lighting and visual dynamics, the show also has members of the stage crew using hand-held cameras to project images onto a giant closed-circuit television screen. On some nights things do go wrong, embarrassingly wrong, but on the whole they get away with it. The two female lead singers add their professional touch and experience to bring energy to the performances, and the choreography is, as expected, well up to the mark. The finale of Act Two, with Harry singing the title song, is an emotional powerhouse, and on some nights for an encore he is joined by Tom and Steve on stage, along with father Jim, where they and the cast perform a rousing rendition of **'Circle'**, just to add fuel to the thoughts of skeptics that they are indeed watching one of Harry's concerts. Theater critic Clive Barnes of the *New York Times*, a man whose reviews have been known to make or break Broadway shows, writes on February 27th that although it bears some similarity to Jacques Brel's sellout show, it is convoluted and distinctly lacking in freshness. He sees that Harry tries to get his points across in his songs but they are just too overworked. Nevertheless, he admits the show has energy and the production values are high, but remains dubious about whether there will be enough people who want to come and see it.

"The Show Is A Success, No Doubt About That"

With the preview shows over, the official opening is held on March 9th, and Harry waits in anticipation for the reviews to come in. Once again, they are mixed, with the older critics deriding it, and younger ones being more positive. Martin Gottfried of the *New York Post* writes that despite its pretentious overdressing, it is still full of life.

Melody Maker also reviews the show that month: *"Harry Chapin, the singer who tells stories rather than sings songs, has recently moved his craft a giant leap forward with the opening of The Night That Made America Famous, an off-Broadway musical named after one of his songs, and featuring around 25 of his compositions. It put the art of the singer/songwriter on a different level than the concert...Here he was, in a small, intimate theatre, surrounded by dancers, moving props, revolving stages, multimedia projection on to a white screen and musicians who weave in and out of scenery on moving podiums...At the end, when the carefully rehearsed routines are over, Harry stays for encores that drop the formality of the rest of the concert, eventually encouraging his audience to join in, introducing his two brothers and father (who plays drums in their band) and even bringing on the theatre doorman who just happens to be a genius at playing the musical saw. The show is a success, no doubt about that..."*

Another critic writes: *"Chapin himself overcomes a limited voice and unexceptional presence with a contagious amiability that survives the ardor of his liberalism. More to the point of the show, his music should catch the spirit of anyone willing. It is good at long last to have a contemporary musician on the Broadway stage, fortunate that it the lyrical, catchy, exciting music of Chapin, and even more fortunate that Frankel could pull the vague idea together with stage discipline. It may be dressed up, but its heart is beautiful and it sure is alive."*

The Broadway shows continue, one each weekday, Tuesday through Friday, and then two shows each day at the weekend. On Saturday March 1st, Harry completes the last of the two shows and heads off with Sandy, his father Jim, and drummer Howie to attend the 17th Grammy Awards at the nearby Uris Theater on West 51st Street, where he has been nominated for Best Pop Vocal Performance for **'Cat's in the Cradle'**.

As the weeks pass it becomes obvious that the show's days are numbered. Misleading publicity by the producers and fluctuating attendance figures have an effect on both cast and crew. Harry even begins to waive his royalties and the cast also take pay cuts in an attempt to keep the production alive. To supplement the band's earnings, Harry hits on the idea of doing regular concerts on Mondays, their one day off from the show. On the afternoon of March 26th Harry and the band go to Philadelphia to appear on *The Mike Douglas Show*, co-hosted by diminutive child actor Mason Reese. As they get ready to perform **'Cat's in the Cradle'**, Reese unexpectedly begins to cry and has to be consoled by Douglas. Five days later on Monday, March 31st, they travel to Chicago to perform a one-off show at the Aerie Crown Theater in front of a sell-out 3,500 audience. With Tom now a part of the touring band (at least for the next six months or so), he will open the shows with a short set, followed by Harry's. These two performances, one televised, one a live concert, are the first live outings for Harry's new regular line-up, which now consists of John Wallace, Doug Walker, Michael Masters, Howie Fields, Steve Chapin, and of course, for the time being, Tom.

In her review of the Chicago performance, rock critic Lynne Van Matre of the *Chicago Tribune* writes that Harry puts on a good lively show, and despite some of the songs deemed as *"trite"*, she is in awe of the crowd's reaction to his over-dramatic performance of **'Sniper'** and concludes that *"nothing succeeds like emotional excess."*

"A Real Shock Test For The Critics…"

Unfortunately, this Monday night concert will be the last. On April 1st the producers of the Broadway show issue a closing-down notice. Harry gets news of this later when reading a paper on board a flight from Washington to New York, after holding meetings for the W.H.Y. project. There will be just five more performances before the final curtain. On April 9th, a week after another appearance on *The Mike Douglas Show* to perform **'I Wanna Learn a Love Song'** and **'Tangled Up Puppet'**, the Broadway show finally comes to an end. In its seven-week run, in which there have been fourteen preview shows and forty-five regular performances, it has resulted in a financial disaster, losing something in the region of $400,000. But for Harry it comes as a relief. It has been an exhausting dream fulfilled, and now he can pour all his energies into completing his next album and taking his new band out on the road to play to more receptive audiences and raising funds for W.H.Y. and PAF, the latter alone requiring some $15,000 a month to keep it alive.

In a 1977 interview Harry has his own ideas why the show ultimately fails: *"I felt that modern folk/rock/pop music had not really been utilized on Broadway. There was Hair of course, and there had been concerts, you know*

- *Neil Diamond, Alice Cooper or Bette Midler, but no one who was a major artist had brought a concept show to Broadway. So, I decided to do a show that was part theatre, part concept, part multimedia experience. It was a real shock test for the critics - everyone under 40 loved it, everyone over 40 hated it. I think that basically that's my fault, because a really persuasive artistic experience is able to seduce all age groups, and I think 'Cat's in the Cradle' can turn on kids of seven and grandfathers, and hippies and hard hats, and college professors. So, I think that there were some things for me to learn, and, I think, the next time I do something like that, I'll be closer to having it make a real major impact."*

Tom Chapin seems to believe the whole thing has been a mistake: *"Nobody wanted to do it except Harry. He just had a number one hit in America, and now instead of touring and doing television specials and being 'the guy,' he does a half-assed Broadway show. And it didn't work."* Never one to hold back on his criticism, he looks back on the show and admits, *"It really sucked."* Howie Fields remembers how Harry felt at its closure: *"I think it was a bittersweet thing for him. He wasn't thrilled with the show closing, but I think hitting the road again made him happy as well."*

Harry already has plans for the immediate future. In an interview with *Melody Maker* he discloses that he wants to tour Europe when the Broadway show comes to an end: *"I'd like to go over and take my family, because my ancestors came from England hundreds of years ago. 'Cat's in the Cradle' hasn't done that well over there, so I don't know whether we could arrange a tour or not. 'W.O.L.D.' was a minor hit, 'Taxi' never got played, and 'Circle' was the only song that made it, but that was by the New Seekers. I really want to get there, though."*

Despite its failures, the show picks up a total of three Tony nominations: Gilbert Price for Best Featured Actor in a Musical and Kelly Garrett for Best Featured Actress in a Musical and also Outstanding Featured Actress in a Musical. Price is also nominated for a Drama Desk Award for Outstanding Featured Actor in a Musical. All eventually lose out to the stars of the successful Broadway musical *The Wiz*.

In 1975 Harry's first book of poetry ***Looking...Seeing*** is published by Thomas Y Crowell. It contains forty poems and fourteen song lyrics, and is illustrated by Harry's former road crew member Rob White, now a talented sculptor and artist. By June of that year Harry has been elected chairman of PAF for the next three years, meaning that he has to take on a more hands-on role and not just rely his benefits to raise money. With that in mind, Harry insists that all the trustees of the organization also commit themselves to organizing fund-raising activities, while he himself makes a personal goal of raising some $50,000 a year. In order to revitalize the community playhouse into a more regional professional theater, it needs to have a professional producer in charge, and Harry seeks out and employs Jay Broad, an

157

accomplished New York playwright and stage director, to organize its transformation and into a theater that only promotes original plays. One of these new productions will be **The Zinger**, written by Harry and Sandy, which will open in March 1976. But Broad's hunger for perfection leads to rapidly increasing costs, and increasing costs ultimately lead to Harry and his band doing even more benefits.

On being asked by an interviewer if he is still happy, Harry replies: *"Look, I'm enjoying all this; my success. That's the reason I'm smiling a lot. But I was a Joe Slob all my life and just because people cheer now doesn't mean I'm not a Joe Slob anymore."*

Portrait Gallery

"I would like to say that when I die, from an external point of view, that it mattered that Harry Chapin was alive"

"A Working Man's Hero"

Even while **The Night That Made America Famous** is still running on Broadway in the early spring of 1975, Harry is in the process of writing and rehearsing for his fifth studio album at Connecticut Recording Studios at Bridgeport, a two-hour drive up the coast from Huntington. Many of the songs for the album will actually be written on the journeys back and forth. Now with Broadway just a memory, the band once again hit the road. May brings concerts in New York, Missouri and Illinois, as well as Harry taping for a whole week of co-hosting *The Mike Douglas Show* in Philadelphia, to be broadcast the first week of July. On June 2nd the band play their first outdoor concert at the JFK Memorial Stadium in Bridgeport, Connecticut, along with Rita Coolidge, Kris Kristofferson and Billy Swan, all three of whom are later invited to participate in the recording of the new album. Four days later the band play in support of Seals & Croft and country singer Michael Murphey at the Providence Civic Center in Rhode Island.

Their performance at the Temple University Music Festival in Ambler, Pennsylvania on June 14th receives a glowing review: *"Now in the process of completing his fifth album, he continues to increase the size and demographics of his audience without sacrificing his artistic standards and goals. He is an artist who sells without having sold out. Chapin's success seems to lie in the fact that he feels the emotional pulse of the everyday person – his songs portraying feelings that many can easily relate to. Throughout those beautiful melodies, he works magic, making the insights about love and hate, success and failure, and discovery and disenchantment, less painful and a bit easier to accept...Chapin is truly a 'working man's hero,' an upfront performer who is not aloof, but has close contact with his audience. He plies a dynamic yet sensitive set, packed with both energy and emotion."*

On June 18th Harry and the band perform again at the Schaefer Music Festival in Central Park, sharing the same bill with Bob Marley and the Wailers. The outdoor venue is where some of the world's top artists have performed over the past few years, and drummer Howie Fields can't help but be awed by the experience in this, his home town: *"Doug Walker and I drove through Central Park with our credentials, following the map that was provided, passing the early-birds who were already queued up on a line that I myself had been on so many times. We finally made our way over to the*

159

artists' load-in area. I remember being fascinated by the on-stage mirrors suspended high over the performers so that stage lights, at the rear of the stage, could be aimed at the performers' image in the mirror and thereby illuminating them."

From June 30th to July 4th Harry's five consecutive appearances on the *Mike Douglas Show* are aired, with performances on the first three shows of **'I Wanna Learn a Love Song'**, **'W.O.L.D.'** and **'Cat's in the Cradle'**. His brother Tom and father Jim also appear with him on one of the shows, along with actors Tony Randall, Richard Pryor, Barry Newman, and George Hamilton, and music from The Pointer Sisters.

On July 12th Harry and his family are saddened by the death of 84-year-old 'Big Jim' Chapin, his inspirational grandfather. Jim and his second wife Mary moved to Toronto in 1969 to be with their son Eliot, and a few months before Jim died Harry, Tom and Steve pay them a visit after playing a concert there. Jim has always been proud of his boy and the success he has achieved.

In an interview with Noel Edmonds in December 1977, Harry recalls what his grandfather says to him just before he dies, and the effect it has on him: *"I would like to say that when I die, from an external point of view, that it mattered that Harry Chapin was alive. From an internal point of view, I would like to be able to say what my two grandfathers can say, one who passed away last summer, aged eighty-eight. He said about three weeks before he died, 'You know, Harry, all my life I've wanted to be a painter, and do you know what I've been? I've been a painter. Some days I've gone to bed with what I call a "bad tired." I've struggled at the wrong things and when I've hit the hay I toss and turn. Other days, even though I may not have been successful, I go to bed with what I call a "good tired." I've struggled at the right things and when I hit the hay I say "take me away" and I sleep the sleep of the dead. I'm eighty-eight years old, you can take me away. And that sense of peace, that sense of having used whatever the little neurons, molecule sand electrons and all the chemical reactions and electrical reactions that make up a human being is important, since I don't believe in the after-life. I wish I did. Every time I desperately approach religions to say "do I believe," I still don't.' But that sense of peace that my grandfather, Jim Chapin, achieved, and my other grandfather, Kenneth Burke, he has it too. God almighty, what a seductive concept. That in your life you can use it to that extent, and that's where the saying 'when in doubt, do something' comes from. So the combination is, number one, to have a personal affirmation and use the things you have and to reassure myself that all these struggles have been at least note-worthy of others' attention."*

A couple of weeks later, on July 26th, they band performs at Washington Park in Homewood, Illinois, along with Janis Ian, who at the time is enjoying renewed success with the song 'At Seventeen', and two days later they appear at the Performing Arts Center in Saratoga, New York, where guitarist and singer-songwriter Steve Goodman (famous for his song 'City of New Orleans') opens the show for them. August finds Harry back in the Midwest performing at the Mississippi River Festival at the Southern Illinois University in Edwardsville on the 11th with the following setlist: Dreams Go By, Could You Put Your Light On, Please, Saturday Morning (Tom), Short Stories, On the Road to Kingdom Come, I Wanna Learn a Love Song, Mr Tanner, Someone Keeps Calling My Name, Better Place To Be, Let Time Go Lightly (Steve), Cat's in the Cradle. Four days later they appear at the Mesker Music Theater in Evansville, Indiana, again in support of Seals & Croft. On the 17th they make their first trip to Canada's capital to do a one-off concert at the National Arts Center. Later that month dates closer to home culminate on the 28th with a free open-air concert at the Government Center in Boston, in front of an estimated crowd of 50,000.

On September 9th Harry is invited onto *The Tonight Show with Johnny Carson* where he debuts his new song, **'Tangled Up Puppet'**, and dedicates it to his daughter Jaime. Over the next couple of weeks, the band play in Wisconsin, Kentucky and Arizona before returning to the USAF base in Colorado Springs for another performance and another chance to reflect on an earlier career. On September 22nd he again appears on the *Mike Douglas Show*, this time co-hosting with singer Eddie Fisher for five consecutive nights. In the meantime, the recording of the next album has gotten under way at Bridgeport. Once again Harry has enough material - some 24 new or revised songs - to warrant a double album, but once again the idea is rejected by Elektra. The title for the new album is **Portrait Gallery**, and of the ten songs to make the cut, six are family-orientated. Like in the previous album, Harry is determined to keep it personal. Unlike the recording of **Verities & Balderdash**, which was fraught with disagreements and disharmony among the band members, the only thing this time is the amount of stress they find themselves under. Some of the songs are rehearsed and recorded following the Broadway shows, usually between the hours of midnight and noon to keep costs to a minimum, and Harry's tired voice is now sounding ever hoarser. It also becomes custom for Harry to record his very first demos of the songs without making time to refine or re-write them. Three of the songs that fail to make the final cut – **'The Shortest Story'**, **'Love Is Just Another Word'**, and **'She Is Always Seventeen'**, as good as they are, eventually turn up on the **Greatest Stories Live** album the following year.

Producer Paul Leka is again at the helm and employs the same list of session musicians as before, although Steve, John and Mike contribute on some tracks, and manager Fred Kewley is invited to do the cello arrangement on a couple of songs. Leka also drafts in brothers Frank and George Simms, two of the most sought-after session singers in the business, as well as inviting several of Harry's fellow artists to appear on two of the tracks. However, following disagreements with Leka, Harry becomes determined that this will

161

be the last album he works on. Even at this stage he brings in Fred to handle production of the album before it is mastered. Leka is apparently horrified with the result.

Artwork for the album is again handed to Glen Christiansen and Milton Glaser, the latter most famous for designing the "I ♥ NY" logo a couple of years later. With a gatefold sleeve and lyrics on the inside jacket, there is also what appear to be assorted little jigsaw pieces which when put together make up parts of the front and rear cover image of Harry. An inscription on the rear cover reads: *"A Portrait Gallery should be filled with those we know, those we would like to know, and those we should not ignore."* Side one of the album consists of five tracks, three of which, **'Dreams Go By'**, **'Tangled Up Puppet'** and **'Someone Is Calling My Name'**, as the album's title suggests, are portraits of Harry's family, while the remaining two, **'Star Tripper'** and **'Babysitter'**, focus on Harry himself, one a candid retelling of an episode from his adolescence, and the other his own reflection on where his rapid success has led him to. Apart from just one family-orientated song, **'Sandy'**, and a couple of throwaway singalong tunes, side two is dominated by two classic story songs, **'The Rock'** and **'Bummer'**, and although seemingly out of place on this album, they are nevertheless as gripping and soul-searching as they come.

Portrait Gallery (1975) ****
Elektra 7E-1041
Recorded: Connecticut Recording Studios, Bridgeport, CT. Summer 1975
US Release Date: September 27th 1975
Producer: Paul Leka
Engineer: Ron Bacchiocchi

Dreams Go By ***
Certainly, one of Harry's most popular sing-along songs and, as a result, a concert favorite, with audiences attempting the impossible to whistle along in harmony over the catchy *Godfather*-like mandolin intro. In this melancholy song, both whimsical and yet cynical, the narrator is singing to his wife about the multiple dreams they have had at various stages of their lives, and how they are never realized. While still at school, she aspires to be a poet, and he a baseball player; but he figures they will have to wait until they finish their education before those dreams come true. As they watch their dreams fly away as the years pass, he reminds her that maybe someday they will be able to dream again. On their wedding day he feels some guilt that by marrying him she has forsaken a career in medicine to set up their home; while he also makes a confession that his dream of becoming a successful painter has had to be put on hold, as raising and supporting a family must now take precedence. Finally, as grandparents, they look back one more time on lost dreams, and the narrator

confesses that dreams are best imagined when you're young, before the realization that you may not always get to touch them because life just gets in the way.

Apart from the Simms brothers, the background vocalists include fellow artists Kris Kristofferson, Rita Coolidge and Billy Swan, on loan from their respective labels, who also appear on the album's final track, **'Stop Singing Those Sad Songs'**. Harry always feels that this was the one song on the album that has surefire hit potential, and a demo record is sent out to radio stations, with both stereo and mono versions. It is officially released as single in July, some two months before even the album itself comes out, and with another album track, **'Sandy'**, on the flip-side. To Harry's disappointment, it fails to get sufficient airplay, although subsequently makes #33 in Billboard's Adult Contemporary Chart.

Colin Irwin of *Melody Maker* is not impressed by the song: *"A cheerful observation of the passing of time to please society - grow up, get a good job, married, kids, live happily ever after. Oh well, it is summer and Chapin has such a bright, unusual voice, he can afford a little banality. A Miss."*

Tangled Up Puppet *****

The first of a handful of songs written specifically for one of Harry's children. With lyrics written by Sandy, this is a wonderful tribute to daughter Jaime, the eldest of her three children from her previous marriage to Jim Cashmore. Jaime is about 12-13 years old at the time the song is written, the same time when, according to Sandy, she is turning from tomboy into a teenage girl. The song serves as a fitting companion to **'Cat's in the Cradle'**, but instead of missing his son growing up and becoming an adult, in this case it is the daughter gradually ignoring her father, the narrator. Harry laments how she is growing up before his very eyes and becoming more independent. In the first two verses of the song Jaime is perhaps five or six years of age and the bond with her dad is solid. But as the years roll by, he begins to notice subtle changes. Slowly he begins to feel he is losing the close bond they once had, that loving entrapment he felt as she was able to wrap him around her little fingers and make him dance to her tune. As the song moves on, Jaime is now a teenager, finding her way in the world, and perhaps feels it isn't so cool now to play games with him. But there's one magical moment when she forgets herself, and in an all-too-brief game of tag with her dad she remembers the happy times of her childhood and is that young girl once again. Once again, a priceless, intimate vignette.

Like the son in **'Cat's in the Cradle'**, Jaime has her own agenda now. The privacy of her bedroom is her safe haven, not having to share her secret thoughts with anyone, lost in her dreams, and slowly becoming her own woman. The father capitulates. He admits he has lost his little girl, but realizes

163

he has gained this *"brand new woman"* and reminds her that he will always be there for her in the years to come.

The message is clear enough. Like **'Cat's in the Cradle'**, parents need to treasure and make the best of the time they have with their children, because that time soon passes. Both songs are a tribute to Sandy as an accomplished poet and lyricist in her own right.

Where **'Cat's'** serves as a subtle hint to Harry to be more hands-on with his kids, Sandy's words in **'Tangled Up Puppet'** are full of the warmth and love of devoted parents, and Harry has turned her words into one of the most emotional and heartwarming songs of his career. Singer Terri Klausner reflects tearfully on the song that she later has the honor to sing at Harry's Tribute Concert at Carnegie Hall, and calls it *"just a beautiful, beautiful story."* A demo record sent out to radio stations with both mono and stereo versions is subtitled 'A Song For My Daughter.' A follow-up single, still with the subtitle, is released in January 1976, and, backed with the dire **'Dirt Gets Under Your Fingernails'**, fails to make the charts.

From the cheap seats

Char Stanley - *When I first heard that song, I was a teenager and didn't have any children. My daughter is 29 now. When she was a teen, I made her listen to it. 13 is a hard age for both child and parent. When she heard 'Tangled up Puppet' she understood that even though we didn't know what (or how) to say what was on our minds - the underlying unconditional love was there. My daughter tells me that when she has a daughter, she will have her listen to it, too. My daughter is my best friend now. I thank Harry for that.*

Melba Davis Nickoles - *A one arm around your shoulder hug has replaced hours on your lap. It is considered a successful story of raising a child. But, after they leave, and go to the house that they now call home, you sit alone. Sometimes you cry. You clean up dishes now instead of toys. And, as successful child rearing goes. This is life. You have done what you set out to do. They will be doing the same thing soon. You hope that you have instilled in them the same love for their child that you had for yours. That little boy or girl who just drove away. In their car instead of on their tricycle. A success story. But that success story sometimes hurts a little. Harry knew. He helps us all. Me anyway. He can't bring back that little child, but he helps me remember.*

Erika Kilborn - *I think my favorite song from Harry is 'Tangled Up Puppet'. The first time I heard it, I cried. It still makes me teary. I always wished that my father felt that way about me. Harry really had a way of getting to the heart of the matter.*

164

Star Tripper *****

Harry's take on the effect that large egos can have, and serves as a fine example of his lyrical craft. Very similar in style to **'Shooting Star'** on the previous album, this is written by Harry around the same time he works on Sandy's **'Cat's in the Cradle'**. The ethereal music at the beginning of the song, courtesy of Ron Bacchiocchi's synthesizer, brings to mind the calls of humpback whales. In the opening verse the narrator sees himself as a singer who sees his career has taken off much like an astronaut on a celestial path, not quite yet reaching ultimate stardom, but well on the way to achieving it, and all the time totally engrossed in the journey:

I have made a little music in some corners of the land
I have fused some crystal images from common grains of sand
And if I haven't reached the heavens, then I've surely learned to fly
And been caught up in the soaring and the touching of the sky

But in the chorus that follows, he reflects on the sacrifices made that placed him on that road to success. He has spent too long away from the most important things in his life - his wife and family, too blind to see the effects it may have had on them, and his biggest fear is that he may have lost them. In an attempt to put things right, he is coming home.

But the startripper's coming on back home now
It's a crazy blind man's journey he's been on
The star tripper's lost and all alone now
And it's your face he'd like to look upon
Yes, he's praying that you won't be long gone

He looks at what it is that has led him there, how the music industry has packaged him as a commodity, not a person, churning out his records, carving him *"into plastic"* and promoting him into a world that will mold him into something he feels he's not. Assured that he was doing the right thing, he now sees that the journey to stardom has left him feeling empty and alone.

They put you in a capsule, they send you towards the sun
They carve you into plastic before your orbit's done
And all the scribes and seers they chorus out your name
And though the photographs and headlines change the story stays the same

I thought that I was soaring like an eagle
I thought that I was roaring like the wind
I thought that I had surely reached the end now
But I can't remember anywhere I've been

165

In the final verse he regrets what he's done. Unable to find the answers, it at least makes him realize that in his egotistical quest for glory he had lost touch with the one thing that really matters.

Was I looking for a star or something out behind it?
Whatever I was looking for, I surely did not find it
And for all my sky-high journeys the only thing I know
Is that you almost always lose yourself when you let yourself go

Hypnotically beautiful song, and lyrically up there with the best of Harry's work. But it is also a musical tour de force with Paul Leka bringing out the very best in the talented musicians he has on board. It is released as a single in Feb 1976, with **'The Rock'** on the flip-side, but fails to chart, despite perhaps being the best pairing for any of Harry's singles.

From the cheap seats
Scott Sivakoff - *I love this song. The live versions are better than the studio version (in my opinion). When I first heard this song, I took it literally. I thought it was about an astronaut's journey. As I listened to it more and got older, I found myself interpreting it in a very different light. I have come to believe that it is about now losing yourself in your own ego. Harry talks about it a little on the **Bottom Line** concert CD, saying how he wrote it shortly after he and Sandy co-wrote **'Cat's In The Cradle'**. I find more little nuggets of brilliance in the lyric to this each time I hear it. Such as the second verse: 'They put you in a capsule, they send you towards the sun. They carve you into plastic before your orbit's done. And all the scribes and seers, they chorus out your name. Though the photographs and headlines change, the story says the same!' Wow! Amazing lyric. You work hard to make it in life. Sometimes, if you are lucky, you can succeed and you think that it is the best thing ever. In some cases, people may even notice, but at the end of it all, it's just same old same old and onlookers, if they notice you at all, always move onto the next shiny capsule. You have to make yourself satisfied with your own accomplishments. You have to come back to realize what's really important so that you don't miss out on the important things in life.*

Babysitter ****
A song that may have had the potential to be a misstep for Harry, but he manages to turn what would be nothing more than a locker room tale into a beautiful and poignant coming of age story of first love, and how that experience impacts on the rest of his life. In the introduction to the song, the narrator sounds a little apprehensive to relate a story that he's never told to anyone before, a story harking back to his youth, except that now he will pour

his heart out to the girl (now a woman) who it's all about. In the first verse we are given their ages - the sixteen-year-old girl in question is the narrator's babysitter, while he is just twelve, and probably the eldest of his mother's children who the girl is being paid to look after while she is out. Without having to spell it out, the chorus leaves nothing to the imagination of what then transpires.

Once again, like so many times in Harry's songs, we find in the girl a lonely heart aching to be loved, much like the barmaid in **'Better Place to Be'** or the single mother in **'And the Baby Never Cries'**. Harry relates a similar story of adolescence in the song **'Manhood'** on the 1977 album *Dance Band on the Titanic*.

From the cheap seats

Thomas Dolan - *I truly worry that I am going to sound redundant; however, much like 'Better Place To Be' and 'They Call Her Easy', if you remove the sexual content, it's about making love, something people give without expecting something in return. The Babysitter gave the singer something as a gift. She expected nothing in return. He values the gift. I think Harry saw love as more of a gift people can give one another without making it transactional. Did it happen? Who knows? The message is about a person recognizing a need in another and being a giving person. Hadn't tied these three songs together, but I'm seeing the connection now. 'Sometimes I don't know what I'm thinking until all the words come out.' A paraphrase, but I've found out it to be true.*

Melba Davis Nickoles - *He said she was 16. We were all 16 at some point. Now, the part about him being 12 is disturbing to me as a grandmother but those were different times. My husband has some aunts who were 15 or 16 when they got married or had children. I have never listened to this song, but this is the way things were. I know. We have, as time has gone by, made laws, rules, some that are good, some bad. The thing that bothers me is a 12-year-old. But if it's his story, it's his story.*

Someone Keeps Calling My Name ***

Harry delves deep into his back catalogue, with a re-write of one of the brothers' early compositions. In its original form it appears on the album *Chapin Music!* Where the original and much shorter version is in the tradition of The Kingston Trio, Harry turns the song into a family portrait by adding verses about each of their four children, Jenny, Jason, Jonathan and Jaime. In a cleverly worded song Harry puts words into their mouths to reflect their outlooks on life. It starts with young Jenny, Harry and Sandy's first child, just four years old, but right away we see she has a strong personality and is not afraid to face challenges. In the second verse Jason, the youngest of Sandy's children, is ten years old, and Harry has him reflecting on his parents' broken

167

marriage. Then we come to Jonathan (Jono) who it seems is about twelve and a half (*"fifty seasons"*), and the middle of Sandy's three children (where in fact they are just 16 months apart). Harry sees him pretty much like himself. Finally, we have fifteen-year-old Jaime, the oldest of the children but now, as we have seen in '**Tangled Up Puppet'**, blossoming as a teenager.

The Rock *****

One of Harry's most atmospheric story songs and a gripping analogy of what Harry sees as society's tendency to react to disasters and not have the vision to prevent them from happening in the first place. In Harry's story, a young man repeatedly warns the townspeople that the large rock that hangs over the town is about to come crashing down on everybody, but they are dismissive of his claims, knowing that the rock has been up there on the mountain for many thousands of years. Without help, the boy will take matters into his own hands and spend the rest of his life figuring out ways to stop the rock falling. The song's pulsating violins set the tone for the drama to unfold. For the young boy, it begins with a nightmare - a recurring vision of the giant rock breaking free and rolling down the hill to crush the town - and a cry in the night: *"The rock is gonna fall on us!"* But his dismissive mother tries to ease his worried mind by relating the centuries-old children's folk-tale of how the paranoid Chicken Little is hit on the head with something and then spreads unnecessary alarm among his animal friends by repeating *"the sky's a-gonna fall!"* Of course, it never does.

Each subsequent verse has the boy growing up with the fear still deeply embedded in his mind. The next person to ridicule him is his teacher after he tells his classmates of what he sees as an impending disaster. And then as a young adult, with a reputation around the town as being nothing more than an alarmist, he is brought before the magistrate to explain himself. Convinced now that no one is listening to him, much like the deranged gunman in '**Sniper'**, he decides to takes drastic action, although the townsfolk seem quite prepared to let him go ahead. To them he has become *"a crazy fool"*, a *"madman"* deserving nothing more than their mockery. He spends days up on the mountain working out ways to prevent a disaster, until one night a tremor causes the giant rock to move. But the rumbling noise that brings the townsfolk out of their homes soon subsides. If it was a tremor it's all over now and there's nothing to worry about. The rock is still up there, where it was, and, in their minds, where it always will be. Some worry about what may have happened to that *"crazy"* kid who was last seen on the mountain, but any concern is met with scorn and laughter.

We assume our tragic hero is dead, as people now refer to him in the past tense. Harry may be symbolizing the townsfolk as being as hard and *"unfeeling"* as the rock itself. They are unaware of the sacrifice the man has made to save many lives, and for them life will now go on *"as usual round here."* Death is not for them to think about. But this is Harry Chapin. And there's no way the story ends there. There's always a final twist. As the sound of the violins begins to fade, the listener can hear the distant rumbling of the rock that is now beginning to slide.

This is no Chicken Little fantasy. This is turning into a nightmarish reality. But in another sense, we have this young man refusing to be *"chicken"* and having the courage to face his fears and sacrifice his own life to save many others. Like the gallant plumber in **'What Made America Famous'**, he becomes one of Harry's unsung heroes. The song also features Don Tropea on lead guitar and Big John, Tom and Steve on backing vocals. It is released as the flip-side to the single **'Star Tripper'** in Feb 1976 but like many others fails to chart.

From the cheap seats

Simone Moore - *I love this song! Yet another example to me of how Harry saw through the fakery in our country to the core of our real problems and was not afraid to call out the bullshit when he saw it. Just sad that he is not here to keep reminding us, and sad so many of the problems are worse than ever.*

Cliff Geisma - *Harry's counterpoint to Dylan's 'The Times They are a Changin'. Storytelling as a commentary on society at its best.*

Gerry Naughton - *'The Rock' is capitalism eroding away at our social fabric and the environment.*

Rick Gilmartin - *My take, and it might be too corny so hold on, was Harry stood with the little guy. The little guys know and should be listened to. Not laughed at, rejected, ignored, or sent away... It's the little guys that care for the most and sacrifice the most for all of us.*

Sandy ****

The title says it all. Harry pouring out his feelings for his wife in a three-verse song even more endearing for its innate simplicity. Perhaps evolving from an early poem, it is included on the demo tape Harry sends to Elektra in 1971, prior to signing the contract, but not chosen for an album until now. Like in many of Harry's love songs the passing seasons figure prominently. Not as lyrically outstanding as **'She Sings Songs Without Words'** on the previous album, it is still a heartfelt and tender tribute to his wife (now of six years), beautifully decanted, and deserving a place on what after all is chiefly his family's tribute album. Mike Masters is the preferred cellist on this recording, with Big John providing the angelic backing vocals toward the end. It is chosen as the flip-side to the single **'Dreams Go By'** in July, and at the Tribute Concert at Carnegie Hall is beautifully performed by Graham Nash.

169

From the cheap seats
Mark Charlesworth - *The most beautiful song ever, but wouldn't it be great if everyone could see everyone in the same way.*

Dirt Gets Under Your Fingernails *
Disappointingly weak song and really not worthy of gracing such an otherwise fine album. Basically, it's just an 'O Henry'-style tale of irony, with a grease monkey of a car mechanic and his hard-working wife who has dreams of being a painter. The payoff at the end comes as no surprise, but the one thing that saves it is the lyric, typically tongue-in-cheek Chapin. However, the chorus lacks the punch found in so many other songs about domestic relationships. Chosen as the flip-side to the single **'Tangled Up Puppet'** when released in October.

Bummer ****
Where the song **'Sniper'** is inspired by a real-life event, this is actually a near-factual account of one, although no names are mentioned and some poetic license is in evidence. It tells the story of a man who grows up abused, gets in trouble with the law, is then drafted for service in Vietnam, wins the Medal of Honor, and upon his return finds it hard not to get back into his former habits and is ultimately killed. The story mirrors the life of Dwight Hal "Skip" Johnson, born without knowing who his father is in a Detroit housing project in 1947. Drafted into the US Army he serves as a tank driver in Company B, 1st Battalion, 69th Armored Regiment, 4th Infantry Division, and in mid-1968, a matter of days before the infamous Tet Offensive begins, his regiment receives a call to go to the aid of a front-line infantry platoon that is outnumbered and under attack. The medal citation describes what happens next:

For conspicuous gallantry and intrepidity at the risk of his life above and beyond the call of duty. Specialist 5 Johnson, a tank driver with Company B, was a member of a reaction force moving to aid other elements of his platoon, which was in heavy contact with a battalion size North Vietnamese force. Specialist Johnson's tank, upon reaching the point of contact, threw a track and became immobilized. Realizing that he could do no more as a driver, he climbed out of the vehicle, armed only with a .45 caliber pistol. Despite intense hostile fire, Specialist Johnson killed several enemy soldiers before he had expended his ammunition. Returning to his tank through a heavy volume of antitank rocket, small arms and automatic weapons fire, he obtained a sub-machine gun with which to continue his fight against the advancing enemy. Armed with this weapon, Specialist Johnson again braved deadly enemy fire to return to the center of the ambush site where he courageously eliminated more of the determined foe. Engaged in extremely close combat when the last of his ammunition was expended, he killed an enemy soldier with the stock end of his submachine gun. Now weaponless, Specialist Johnson ignored the enemy fire around him, climbed into his platoon sergeant's tank, extricated a wounded crewmember and carried him to an armored personnel carrier. He then returned to the same tank and assisted in firing the main gun until it jammed. In a magnificent display of courage, Specialist Johnson exited the tank and again armed only with a .45 caliber pistol, he engaged several North Vietnamese troops in close proximity to the vehicle. Fighting his way through devastating fire and remounting his own immobilized tank, he remained fully exposed to the enemy as he bravely and skillfully engaged them with the tanks externally-mounted .50 caliber machine gun; where he remained until the situation was brought under control. Specialist Johnson's profound concern for his fellow soldiers, at the risk of his life above and beyond the call of duty are in keeping with the highest traditions of the military service and reflect great credit upon himself and the United States Army.

On his return from Vietnam Johnson finds it difficult to adjust to civilian life, unable to find work, and getting into debt. Returning to the army as a recruiter after being awarded the medal, he is later diagnosed with PTSD. In 1971 he walks into a store while a robbery is taking place and is shot four times by the store owner, believing him to be one of the perpetrators. He is buried in Arlington Cemetery.

With an atmospheric musical introduction of nearly two minutes, Leka pulls out all the stops with his strings and horn section (recorded separately at Whitney Recording Studio in Glendale) before we hear Harry's voice introducing the nameless lead character. Straight away we get the picture of a baby born into an environment without love, living in squalor, physically abused, just a *"laid-back lump in the cradle chewing the paint chips that fell from the ceiling."* A few years pass and we see failures in education and a gradual decline into a world of drugs and debauchery, leading inevitably to incarceration that does nothing more than fuel a burning hatred and label him as a no-hoper who will ultimately end up being killed. Out of prison, he returns to a life of crime until he gets his draft papers, which probably end up saving his life, at least for now. What follows is a more-or-less retelling of Johnson's own experience, although in this story he is badly wounded. Now out of the army, our hero's life almost parallels that of Johnson, except that it has him doing the actual robbery and getting killed by the cops.

The song, of course, is a biting condemnation of how the country treats African-American males from the inner cities in the 70s and even later. But it is being related by the master storyteller, who, without taking sides, cleverly puts his point across. Like the gunman in **'Sniper'**, the character in this song is damaged goods, with a head full of demons, and with motive enough to hit out at a society that should have given him a fair crack at life, but instead ignored the warning signs that were already there. Both loners, both unloved. Perpetrators or victims? Harry leaves that for us to decide.

171

From the cheap seats

Alan L Geraci - *In 'Bummer', the life of a black man growing up an accident child from two drifting parents whose lost souls produce an unloved child. Adrift in the system, existing in a societal drug culture, poverty, prison and adjunct societal apathy, the boy is groomed for society's disposal system, a default military existence. Now the unloved child of societal apathy, whose country groomed him to kill, found his reason to exist, to kill with impunity. But instead of dying in the honor of the kill, he survives and is put back in society where he ends where he began: Without love, a chance to be loved or a country who valued his black life.*

Stop Singing Those Sad Songs **

Following on from the trauma of **'Bummer'**, we have a last-minute addition to close the album, and, like **'Star Tripper'**, it's another attempt by Harry at some self-criticism. Although lyrically rather trite, it has an up-beat melody that does create a nice bookend to **'Dreams Go By'**, the opening track.

Modest Success Once More

Portrait Gallery is released on September 27th 1975, finally reaching a modest #53 on the *Billboard* 200. Of the three singles culled from the album, only **'Dreams Go By'** will break into the charts. With the timing, the hard slog of the recording, the issues with Leka, and the last-minute selection of songs, it becomes one of the least successful studio albums of Harry's career. Ironically, it also contains some of Harry's finest lyrical work and two of his most dramatic story songs in **'The Rock'** and **'Bummer'**. Although some critics had been won over with the previous album, there seems to be a backlash with *Portrait Gallery*. *"Mundane," "overblown," "vacuous,"* and *"cliché-ridden"* are just some of the comments that Harry has to face. Even **'Tangled Up Puppet'**, one of the best songs on the album, is slated as being *"abysmal,"* and accuses Sandy as co-writer of sinking to her husband's level. Phil Sutcliffe of *Sounds* writes on December 13th that apart from three decent tracks, the rest are simply moralizing *"dross."* One other contributing factor for the album's lack of success is the departure from Elektra that fall of Jac Holzman and Ann Purtill, longtime champions of Harry's work. The new boss David Geffen is not a visionary like Holzman. He is an out and out businessman whose chief interests lie in making vast sums of money, and not in a love of music. He can see *Portrait Gallery* is not going to be as successful as the last album. He is expecting another hit song, another **'Cat's in the Cradle'**. With that unlikely to happen, he will now push Harry into making a greatest hits album. Ironically, it will result in the most successful album of Harry's career.

172

Three Chapin boys: left to right - Harry, Tom and Steve *(©. Chapin Archives)*

Chapin Music! - Harry, Tom and Steve *(©. Chapin Archives)*

"And I see her in the twilight and that radiant sunset there....." (©. *Chapin Archives*)

Harry (©. *Chapin Archives*)

Film making (©. *Chapin Archives*)

174

Harry and Sandy with Jono, Jaime and Josh
(©. Chapin Archives)

Harry with Bill Ayres
(©. Chapin Archives)

Harry with John Wallace, Tim Scott and Ron Palmer c1972 *(©. Chapin Archives)*

175

Harry with his son Josh at the Lively Arts Festival in Huntington. *(©. Chapin Archives)*

Harry with Ron Palmer, Mike Masters and John Wallace c1975 *(©. Chapin Archives)*

© Steve Stout

© Steve Stout

177

"Hello honey, it's me..." © *Steve Stout*

© *Steve Stout*

178

Greatest Stories Live

"For four and a half years, people have been coming up to me and saying 'you're so much better live.'"

"Zeus Did Not Illuminate My Brain"

For Harry, the fall of 1975 sees completion of *Portrait Gallery* and a rapid return to nationwide touring, in which he can showcase some of the new songs and do his self-promoting bit to increase album sales. On September 9th the band appear once again on *The Tonight Show with Johnny Carson*, in which a performance of **'Tangled Up Puppet'** is taped at the Burbank studios in LA between 4.30 and 6pm for an 11.30pm screening. This is followed a week later with two shows at the Performing Arts Center in Milwaukee, concerts at Richmond's Eastern Kentucky University and the Celebrity Theater in Phoenix, and on the 21st an emotional return to the USAF Academy in Colorado Springs for a reunion with some of the people who said he would have no successful career outside the Air Force. The following day he begins a week-long engagement on *The Mike Douglas Show* with singer Eddie Fisher co-hosting, before returning closer to home to end the month with concerts in Rhode Island and Connecticut. October is also a memorable month for the band with another concert across the border in Toronto and their first visit to "Bananatown" - Scranton, Pennsylvania - and a first chance to sing **'Bananas'** in front of a raucous audience, whose town Harry has made famous. After a series of dates in the Midwest they return to New York City on October 19th to play two concerts at the Avery Fisher Hall.

In an interview given in October 1975 Harry gives an insight into his writing craft: *"One advantage I've had as a writer is that I've learned my craft over the fact that I've spent about ten years writing 400 songs that nobody paid any attention for one simple reason. Basically, they stank. I'll say one thing, doing that kind of homework you start thinking I'm not a genius by any means. I'm a person who's done a lot of hard work and I've learned a lot from my grandfather, who's a writer. They call him Tricks, and I've learned a lot of the techniques, the craftsmanship of putting together a good lyric. A lot of people write in different ways. Most people write what I call attitudinal songs other than story songs or situational songs, but I've learned a various method of doing it, mostly from trial and error...Zeus did not illuminate my brain, I've had no divine inspiration. I think the songwriting craft is just a lot of qualified decisions the same way a bricklayer does it or somebody cooking a soufflé at home, or whatever. It just got to do with past knowledge and an accurate eye and an accurate ear..."*

179

Snags With The Recording

Taking a short break, Harry gets label boss Geffen to agree that the greatest hits album he has in mind should be a collection of live performances. After all, Geffen is well aware of the impact Harry has in front of a live audience, and he sees a live album has strong commercial viability. Steve Chapin also sees first-hand that live performing is the secret to Harry's success, and always believes his performances are better in concert than on record: *"Harry would get caught up in the moment of it all and never got cranked up in the recording studio the way he did performing live. That way people always got their money's worth."*

In an interview two years later, Harry reflects: *"Elektra wanted us to think about doing a Greatest Hits album at some point. I had been told by a lot of people that some of the things we do live have never been captured on record. I didn't want to put out re-takes of the old tracks, so I thought it would combine three things at once. It seemed like the best thing to do."*

But where to record the songs? The band's November itinerary has them playing four dates in California, one in Idaho, two in Washington State, and two in Oregon, before returning to the East Coast for the remainder of the year. As an added bonus Tom Chapin has come west to join the tour. Harry writes: *"For four and a half years, people have been coming up to me and saying 'you're so much better live'- 'when are you going to do a live album?'- 'your records don't capture the emotion you generate in a concert.' It was frustrating, but also challenging. We had to try it someday. Of course, I kept wanting to try the new music. But then it was time to release what they call in the trades a 'Greatest Hits' album. I suddenly thought – how about combining the two – live recordings of the best of what we had done before? After some meeting we were on."*

Rather than selecting the best songs from recordings of each show, which would work out quite expensive for the label, Elektra limit it to the first three shows on consecutive nights - San Diego Civic Auditorium (Nov 7th), Santa Monica Civic Auditorium (Nov 8th) and Berkeley Community Theatre (Nov 9th). As the decision from Elektra comes at short notice, it results in makeshift preparations for the sound recordings. The company Wally Heider handle the job at all three concerts, but due to some setbacks with the audio equipment, the finished job is, as Harry would put it, *"not up to professional contemporary standards."* He recalls some of the problems:

"Of course, there were all of the usual problems and then some. On short notice, was Wally Heider Recording available to do the live recording? With the great reputation those guys have, and the subsequent busy schedule, we were relieved to find that they would do it. Then, during the first recording-concert in San Diego, some local radio station decided to join us on stage through the auspices of Doug Walker's amp. If you hear a hair spray

180

commercial in the middle of one of the songs, that's the source. Then, for the first time in at least 100 consecutive concerts, the PA system went bananas – the San Diego crowd was so great – I owe a special thanks to them for staying with us and allowing some of those performances to be used on the album. Next day we passed up the option of flying and drove up to LA. The concert was a joy and our PA and radio problems were solved. It was only on returning to the hotel that we discovered the friendly San Diego to LA airline we had not used had pushed the button and cancelled all transportation for the balance of the tour. At 4.00am, after hours on the phone, flights were put together again and the pressure of possibly missing sold out concerts and recording them for this album were relieved. The crowds at Berkeley, the PA and Wally Heider Recording had given us what we needed to finish up the album. Quick mixing sounded reasonably reasonable and we decided to go with what we had."

Harry decides to re-record many of the songs back in the Elektra Sound Recorders Studio in LA, with guitars and cello parts redone by the band members. The mixing is handled once again by Bruce Morgan, with a final mix of the live and re-recorded versions carried out by John Stewart at Phase 1 Recording Studio in Toronto, ably assisted by Steve Chapin. The end result is outstanding.

Apart from **'Sniper'**, some of the other live songs not making the cut are **'Short Stories'**, **'Could You Put Your Light On, Please'**, **'On the Road to Kingdom Come'**, and **'Someone Keeps Calling My Name'**. Either Harry or Elektra see fit to include on the live album three studio recorded songs. Relatively unknown to the keenest of fans, the three titles - **'She is Always Seventeen'**, **'Love is Just Another Word'** and **'The Shortest Story'** - are all songs arranged and produced by Paul Leka during the *Portrait Gallery* sessions, but all failing to make it onto the album (certainly not because they are considered weak songs. In hindsight all three of them would surely have given that album greater impact by replacing what could be considered average songs such as **'Dirt Gets Under Your Fingernails'** and **'Stop Singing Those Sad Songs'**). The choice of live recordings doesn't please everyone. Drummer Howie Fields recalls: *"I always felt it was a huge blunder to omit from the LP the powerful version of 'Sniper' that we performed during those live sessions...someday perhaps it will see the light of day. In place of that, three studio tracks left over from the Portrait Gallery sessions were chosen."*

As well as Harry, Steve, and Mike Masters, the session musicians on the studio tracks are John Tropea (electric guitar), Alan Schwartzberg (drums), Don Payne (bass), Tim Moore (piano), Paul Leka (piano & clarinet), Bob Springer (conga, chimes & castanets) and Ron Bacchiocchi (synthesizer & clarinet). Background vocals are by Big John, brothers George & Frank Simms, Christine Faith, Dave Kondziela, Mary Mundy, Betse Wager, Sue

181

White and Kathy Ramos. Thanks to Harry, two live performances of his brothers' songs are also included to showcase their talents as songwriters - Tom's **'Saturday Morning'** and Steve's **'Let Time Go Lightly'** (the latter becoming a regular addition to future live concerts).

Despite *Greatest Stories Live* being a double album and the inclusion of three studio songs, there are only eleven live tracks, just two more tracks than *Heads and Tales* has. All five previous albums are covered, with one from *Heads and Tales*, two from *Sniper and Other Love Songs*, two from *Short Stories*, four from *Verities & Balderdash*, and one from *Portrait Gallery*. All the most popular songs are here, **'Taxi'**, **'Cat's in the Cradle'**, **'I Wanna Learn a Love Song'**, **'Mr Tanner'**, **'W.O.L.D.'**, **'Dreams Go By'**, and **'Circle'**. Two other songs are the ones Harry will refer to as the fans' choice, and an essential part of any live album - a superb rendition of **'Better Place To Be'** clocking in at 9.17 minutes, and perhaps the definitive live version of **'Bananas'**, for some at an unbearable length of 10.45 minutes. Disappointingly for the fans, for the first time on his albums, there will be no lyrics, not even for the three new songs.

Greatest Stories Live (1976) *****
Elektra 7E-2009
Recorded -
    live material: Nov 7-9 1975 by Wally Heider Recording
    studio material: Summer 1975
US Release Date: April 23rd 1976
Producer: Steve Chapin & Fred Kewley (live)
          Paul Leka (studio)
Engineer: Greg Calbi (live)
         Ron Bacchiocchi (studio)

She is Always Seventeen *****
The first significant appearance of political writing in Harry's albums, recounting the turbulent events of the 60s and early 70s, from "Camelot" (the Kennedy administration), the student killings at Kent State University, to the fall of President Nixon, and how the country reacts to them. The focus of the song is how the "love generation" is so much a part of those events. In some ways it is a recycled version of **'What Made America Famous'**. The "She" referred to in the song is the youthful idealism, which Harry sees retaining the spirit of a 17-year-old. The song begins with just two lines sung in close harmony.

She has no fear of failure, she's not bent with broken dreams.
For the future's just beginning when you're always seventeen

182

With this we then travel back in time to Washington in 1961, with the narrator listening to President John F Kennedy making his inaugural speech, and sharing his "Camelot" vision for the country and how that vision is to be spread around the world during his term in office. Two years later we are back in the city to witness the great Civil Rights march with Martin Luther King, and barely "six months" after that (in reality it was only three) they hear the tragic news from Dallas, that that one brief shining light has been snuffed out:

It was nineteen sixty-one when we went to Washington,
She put her arms around me and said, "Camelot's begun."
We listened to his visions of how our land should be;
We gave him our hearts and minds to send across the sea.
Nineteen sixty-three, white and black upon the land;
She brought me to the monuments and made us all join hands.
And scarcely six months later she held me through the night
When we heard what had happened in that brutal Dallas light.

In the chorus that follows the narrator hopes that the current generation will hold on to that youthful idealism, if its dream of a better country is ever to be attained:

Oh, she is always seventeen,
She has a dream that she will lend us and a love that we can borrow.
There is so much joy inside her she will even share her sorrow;
She's our past, our present, and our promise of tomorrow.
Oh, truly she's the only hope I've seen, and she is always seventeen.

Time moves on and we are now in the mid 60s, with racial violence and rioting sweeping from city to city, along with anti-Vietnam demonstrations. But he still sees a glimmer of hope with the love-children of the late 60s.

It was nineteen sixty-five and we were marching once more
From the burning cities against a crazy war.
Memphis, L.A. and Chicago we bled through sixty-eight
Till she took me up to Woodstock saying with love it's not too late.

The narrator next makes a reference to Denver, Colorado, and for many first listeners to the song, this probably has them reaching for the history books to find out what happened there. In fact, it had all started in Phoenix, Arizona, in 1966, with the "housewives' revolt" - women homemakers, angered by bread prices shooting up in supermarkets, decided to boycott the commercial bakeries and start baking their own. Within weeks the boycott had spread to other locations, and in Denver it escalated to an all-out war between supermarkets and the "mad housewives" over price hikes. Before long protests were organized across the country and even in Canada, and it even came to the attention of the Johnson administration. Prices did eventually come down, maybe due to public pressure or simply supply and demand, no one can be really sure. But the movement had a lasting legacy, and for the legion of American women who had never thought of protesting before, they had now found their voice.

We started out the seventies living off the land;
She was sowing seeds in Denver trying to make me understand
That mankind is woman and woman is man,
And until we free each other we cannot free the land.

The song ends with the revelation of the Watergate Scandal and the fall of Nixon, *"the crooked king,"* with a final sentiment about the plight of starving children.

Nineteen seventy-two, I'm at the end of my rope,
But she was picketing the White House chanting,
"The truth's the only hope."
In nineteen seventy-five when the crooked king was gone
She was feeding starving children saying the dream must go on.

Underpinned by superlative guitar, once again played by John Tropea, this is perhaps one of Harry's most underrated songs and requires repeated listening to fully appreciate its musical and lyrical complexities. Without the lyrics, some listeners, like me, misheard the line *"Oh, truly, she's the only hope I've seen"* for being *"Oh, Julie"* and it being another one of Harry's odes to an ex-girlfriend, perhaps....

From the cheap seats
Scott Sivakoff - *I initially didn't relate to this song when I first heard it. It came right after all of the greatest of Harry's catalog on* **GSL** *and seemed to cover events that occurred before I was even born. However, the more I listened to it, I found additional meaning. To me, this song is essentially a person witnessing 'her'... the 'she'. 'She' seems to be saying, 'Look, we can affect our environment by getting involved. We can support, and even succeed in having positive outcomes if we get involved. Yes, it's hard. Yes, there are setbacks. Yes, there are failures, but there are also successes.' To survive we have to remember and try to see the world with some level of innocence and positive hope while also trying to deal with a world without that innocence. It's a hard balance. Again, just my interpretation here. I will also say that it would have been nice to have this song along with the other outtakes on*

184

Portrait Gallery and then have extra live tracks on GSL. I'd love to hear some of other live cuts that didn't make GSL.

Bill Nash - *And a perfect folk song... this song could obviously be added to by other songwriters. At least chronologically... it could be at least 48 verses long!*

Love Is Just Another Word ****

A hit single that never was. In this bitter companion to **'She is Always Seventeen'**, Harry is at his cynical best, deriding the so-called "love generation" of the late 60s for selling out its conscience in the 70s, a decade when the demand for social improvement is needed more than ever. The narrator first gives his view on the escalation of the Black Power Movement and its advocates who believe in racial pride and equality for all African-Americans. Next comes a jibe at the feminist movements and their quests for equal rights, followed by a subject now so dear to Harry's heart - starving children - this is one of just a handful of songs in which Harry brings the topic up. The chorus then ties it all together. This most underrated song is surely the kind of record Elektra should have been looking for as a potential hit single, but never considered. It has all the ingredients - a powerful lead vocal with strong meaningful lyrics, a thumping musical track, and wonderful backing vocals. Paul Leka's solid production and John Tropea's funky guitar elevate the song to make it fit nicely in with what are considered the type of hip songs dominating the charts at the time, and at a modest 4.37 minutes it would surely get airplay on radio. We will never know. Maybe the reason is the sensitive subject matter, and Harry, being Harry, never holds back on his views, views that probably shake a few heads and raise eyebrows in Elektra's boardroom.

The Shortest Story *****

There has never been a more moving song written. Period. Harry manages to encapsulate in song the plight of world hunger in what is a graphic portrayal seen through the eyes of a dying child. In just three verses and a little over two minutes we go from birth to death in just twenty short days - a short story indeed. For many Chapin fans in an age when the word vinyl only applied to a type of flooring, these three thought-provoking studio songs remained largely unknown for many years, as the subsequent CD release of the album does not include them (an oversight by Elektra maybe, but probably due to time limitations or someone's insistence that the live tracks take priority). As it is, **'The Shortest Story'** remains frozen in time, perhaps never performed in concert. Harry has expressed his point in a song. He will now use his powerful rhetoric and gritty determination to hammer that point home.

The song certainly lives up to its name, as it is the shortest recorded song of Harry's career, clocking in at a just 2.27 minutes. With the world's attention finally focused on world hunger three years after Harry's death in 1984 the question must be asked what role, if any, Harry would have played in events such as Live Aid and USA For Africa?

From the cheap seats

Frank Walker – *With I think Harry probably would have been one of the coordinators! In some ways, he was! Because his manager put together things like 'We Are The World', Harry's influence was already there. Harry always talked about getting high profile people involved & Bruce Springsteen tells that great story about Harry being relentless with him. I think with Live Aid, he would have taken full advantage of having these people there, applaud them for what they did that day, then say to them, "OK now what can you do tomorrow?"*

Patricia Ehrich - *I have no doubt that Harry would be up front and center.... he would have been one of the primary forces behind it, I'm sure!*

Walter Lechowski - *I think Harry would be the 1st one Bob Geldof would ask to appear.*

The Zinger Musical

During the early part of 1976 Harry and Sandy begin work on writing a new rock musical called **The Zinger**, which will be shown as one of the new productions at the PAF Playhouse in Huntington. It is set inside a futuristic recording studio in the next century. With the writing beginning shortly after Christmas, the production goes through many revisions over the next three months, with the help of Brother Jonathan Ringkamp, a Franciscan monk and longtime associate of PAF. The cast of relatively unknown artists chosen for the roles include Beverly D'Angelo, Pat Benatar, Christine Lahti, and Ben Vereen, and they all spend a short time at Harry's home auditioning and rehearsing the material, some of which is still in the process of writing. Steve Chapin is also on hand to act as musical arranger. The writing team begin to have issues when Ringkamp objects to Harry's continued absence, and with just four days to go before the premiere, he walks out on the project.

22-year-old future superstar Pat Benatar had been performing as a cabaret singer in local pubs and clubs when Harry invites her for an audition. During the Tribute Concert for Harry in December 1987, she recalls that time:

*"I met Harry in 1975 in a small pub in Huntington, Long Island, where I was singing cabaret songs and trying to make a living. He said, 'Kid, why don't you come back, we're having auditions for the show that I'm doing at the PAF Playhouse.' I said, 'Sure, I've never seen a famous person that close before.' So I went over there and the show was **The Zinger**, and **The Zinger** took place in a futuristic time. It was kind of futuristic rock 'n' roll. The character I played was Zephyr and she was a kind of rough and tough rock*

186

'n' roll singer of the future. The problem was I hadn't really learned how to sing rock 'n' roll, so I was a little out of place. I remember at rehearsals they would come back, Harry and Steve and everybody, and they'd say, 'You're doing really great, but you've got to rough it up a little. You gotta get this a little tougher.' I said, 'Okay, okay.' So, Harry. I know you're listening and probably smiling, but I finally got it...We miss you!'"

Many of the performers complain about the lack of rehearsing. Beverly D'Angelo, an accomplished Broadway performer, comments: *"We have been so rushed for time, with so much rewriting going on that the actors really haven't had much opportunity to concentrate on performing. Much more is left up to us and we have been creating almost as much as the writer and director. That's brand new for me."*

Harry explains the inspiration behind the new play is through his disappointment with **The Night That Made America Famous**: *"I wanted to do something else right away, using what I had learned from that experience. The first time around I think I was awed by working on Broadway and never took advantage of my own potential, my own instincts. I came away from that with several ideas. I wanted to do a book musical, but not one in which all of a sudden, a character breaks away from the action and starts singing. And I wanted the sound quality to be unlike anything heard previously in a theater."*

Ringkamp also gives his opinion: *"The play is set in the future, because it is a valid way of approaching something of political intent. Taking it out of your time and place allows for objectivity and lets one explore a subject without becoming emotionally involved with the political forces that exist today, without requiring the audience to play guessing games to identify names and faces. It is built on the premise that nothing changes in terms of human nature and a man's attempts to deal with his environment and political struggles... The future won't look so different."* Harry disagrees about it being futuristic: *"The TV networks are doing that today - not just with possible programs to see what newspaper or magazine listings can capture a potential viewer's interest... And who's to say that some things we have today won't be kept."* Despite Harry's frantic schedule and the last-minute revisions, **The Zinger** eventually opens at the PAF Playhouse on March 19th 1976, but only for a six-week run. Although performing to a full house most nights, most of the audience consists of friends and families of Long Island corporations that are involved in PAF.

Cry For My Country

During the winter months Harry has also taken part in a couple of specials for television. At the end of February 1977, he co-hosts and performs songs on ABC's Bicentennial Sunday afternoon show, *Conscience of America*, along with news reporter Frank Reynolds, former anchor of ABC Evening News. One of the songs, **'Cry For My Country'**, sounds like a sure-fire hit. Harry's lyrics are a stinging critique of the government's current apathy:

I can hear my country crying
For the dreams of yesterday
It's the sound of something dying
Saying we lost our way

In the silence I hear whispers
They gather in the night
And then they echo in the dawn
As were lookin' for the light

I can hear my country crying
From the dark that's in our eyes
It reflects in dirty water
And the wasted lives

Our tears are in our smokestacks
And the clouds that fill our skies
They wash on down their gutters
As an old dream goes dry

So we cry for our country
We weep for our land
We take off her arms
But we don't take her in hand
Do we take to the road
And make tomorrow today
Or take to our heels boys
And watch her fade away

I can hear my country crying
It's a sound she cannot hide
We've leveled all her heroes
And the myths died
She's lost in the homeless wanderer
And exiled on her knees
Like a flower wrenched out from her roots
And cast adrift at sea

Yes I can hear my country crying

For some hands to turn the tide
Will someone stand alone
And take that trail untried
Our country should be singing
A song beyond the walls
Through the open roads and the skyways
Is where our future goes

So we cry for our country
We weep for our land
When we take off her arms
We don't take her in hand
Do we take to the road
And make tomorrow today
Or take to our heels boys
And watch her fade away

As good as it is, and seen as a strong contender for inclusion on the next album, it is never released. On March 12th Harry is also invited to introduce a ninety-minute late-night special for NBC called *Friends*, in which he chats with celebrity comedians Henry Winkler (The Fonz of the hugely successful sitcom *Happy Days*), Peter Sellers, and Bill Cosby in the comfort of their homes. Harry also writes the title song. Most of the reviews are positive and all point to Harry as a TV star in the making:

One reviewer is impressed with Harry: *"The find of the show, however, was composer-singer Harry Chapin as the interviewer. Possessed of enough fame of his own...Chapin was quite obviously accepted as an equal by his subjects and this led to the kind of penetrating questions and answers that are extremely rare on talk and interview shows. Through all this, Chapin projected an affable manner that was easy to take. He may have added a whole new facet to his career by this one-shot special. A performer with credentials acceptable to the wide spectrum of rock-folk fans who can also create rapport with the television audience on the latter's terms has long been a commodity in scarce supply – and Chapin's winning performance in Friends was a sterile showcase of tv-wise ability that should be pursued further by both performer and NBC."*

The song **'Laugh Man'**, which features on his next album **On the Road to Kingdom Come**, is actually written for the pilot but never used, and the proposed season of shows is later cancelled. That same year Harry also writes the theme song for the short-lived CBS sitcom *Ball Four*, a failed attempt by ex-pitcher Jim Bouton to bring his bestselling book about a fictitious minor league baseball team to the television screen.

189

Apart from the disappointment of *The Zinger*, the new productions put on at the PAF Playhouse in Huntington that spring are receiving good reviews, and as a result Harry continues to get more support from the corporate community. Also, Jay Broad's ten-year-old art-in-education program now has 122 schools across Long Island, involving some 130,000 children. In June Harry chairs PAF's first annual board meeting, and it is attended by a variety of corporate heads and politicians who all pledge to raise $10,000 in funds to support the arts and establish a better quality of life for all Long Islanders. Disillusioned with presidents, his peers, and society as a whole, Harry chooses this time to get involved in the political progress, and in the summer is elected as a one of the Long Island delegates to support Mo Udall at the Democratic Convention in New York, although Udall will ultimately lose out to Jimmy Carter. Harry is no politician, but he has the support of not only Sandy, but also his brother James, now a college professor in US politics, and who was, is, and forever will be, his guiding light.

Harry is living up to his promise. His commitment to Sandy and her own agenda is now total.

On the Road to Kingdom Come

"I think it's going to be the best thing I've done so far. It's got some major new story songs; it has some interesting new combinations of different kinds of sounds that the group is making and we've gotten to the point where we're really playing well together"

Masters Quits The Band

For the first six months of 1976, the Bicentennial year and also a Presidential election year, Harry is kept away from a recording studio, his frantic schedule divided between commitments to PAF and W.H.Y., getting involved in politics, and taking to the road with his band. On January 3rd he invites his good friend and folk singer, Pete Seeger, to join him and Tom in a benefit concert for PAF at Huntington High School, and then for the next two months takes the band on a whirlwind tour with dates in Indiana, Ohio, Michigan, Tennessee, and Florida. On February 22nd they return east to appear at the State University of New York in Brockport and perform the following setlist: Short Stories, On the Road to Kingdom Come, Cat's in the Cradle, Mr Tanner, 30,000 Pounds of Bananas, If My Mary Were Here, Circle, Someone Keeps Calling My Name, Could You Put the Light On, Please. Three days later Harry flies out to California to do a solo benefit at Stanford University for the Bureau of Western Mythology before returning east to perform at Princeton University on the 27th, followed next day with Harry and Tom giving solo concerts at Vassar College in New York, sharing the billing with Don McLean. The second show is interrupted by a bomb threat, and rather than sending everyone home, the evening is completed on the lawn outside without microphones.

The following month, while *The Zinger* finally gets under way back in Huntington, Harry remains close to home with performances in Boston and New York, even entertaining an enthusiastic audience in Watertown, the place he has made famous for being the inspiration for **'Better Place To Be'**, and the butt of his oft-quoted, "I spent a week there one afternoon." The next month brings more shows in the Midwest, including a solo benefit on April 4th at a Dance Marathon for Mental Retardation at the University of Illinois in Champaign, which is broadcast live on the campus radio station. May sees concerts much nearer to home, before culminating with two performances in Canada. On May 23rd they perform at the Westchester Premier Theater in Tarrytown, New York with the following setlist: Dreams Go By, W.O.L.D., Better Place To Be, Six String Orchestra, Tangled Up Puppet, 30,000 Pounds of Bananas, Mr Tanner, Let Time Go Lightly (Steve), Cat's in the Cradle, Taxi, Circle, Sniper.

On June 5th Tom Chapin is the last brother to marry when he weds Bonnie Craven, who had previously been married to film director Wes Craven. In addition to Bonnie's two children with Wes, Jonathan and Jessica, Tom and Bonnie go on to have two daughters, Abigail and Lily, and the three sisters will later go on to perform together as The Chapin Sisters. Harry attends the wedding before flying out to do a solo concert in Omaha, Nebraska, where he arrives an hour late but still gives a wonderful intimate performance. The next few days take in concerts across Indiana and Kentucky. With Harry continuing to put new material together and try it out before live audiences, he decides to start the recording process. With Leka now out of the picture, and with that the Bridgeport studios, this will take place at Elektra's studios in LA with Steve Chapin now at the helm. But before all of this starts, there is one issue Harry has to deal with.

Cellist Michael Masters has been with the band since the *Short Stories* days, but he has developed an ego as big as Harry's and sees himself on an equal footing when it comes to stage presence. Visibly unhappy with his lot, often disrespectful to Harry, he is emanating negative vibes and it is having an effect on the rest of the band. After hundreds of live performances, and in particular his wonderful cello work on **'Tangled Up Puppet'** and **'Babysitter'** on the last studio album, he is asked to leave the band. Masters will be paid to remain with the band for two more months, mainly to train the new cellist in playing the new material. He is twenty-year-old Ron Evanuik, an accomplished musician who has mastered his art at the Cleveland Institute of Music. Although Evanuik will be credited as cellist on the new album, according to drummer Howie Fields, three LA session cellists are drafted in to play.

"The Best Thing I've Done So Far…"

Steve Chapin will produce and arrange the new album, to be called *On the Road to Kingdom Come*, and he and Harry both agree that it will be more band-orientated, with less use of session musicians. That will mean new experiences for Doug Walker and Howie Fields, their first contributions to a studio-recorded album of new material. The engineer is John James Stewart, who has recently worked on Elton John's *Blue Moves* album. Having worked successfully on the mixing for *Greatest Stories Live*, Stewart now seems to recording supervisor Kewley the right person to engineer the new album. Right from the start there are problems. To begin with, Stewart is unfamiliar with the new 24-track recording equipment at Elektra Sound and finds it difficult to operate. If that's not bad enough, there is infighting between Fred

192

and Steve. Where Fred is looking for a low-key, vocal-driven production, as on the first three albums, Steve sees the focus should be more on the music, but without losing the power of the vocals, and more like the professionalism evident on *Verities & Balderdash*. But Steve, despite having the edge on Kewley when it comes to production talent, is once again overshadowed, and it falls in Kewley's favor, which many believe is the wrong decision.

Another problem is with Harry himself, his attention diverted to spending more time with Sandy and the kids, who have been brought over to LA, instead of focusing on the recordings. According to Fred, Harry even writes songs on his way to the studio, and fears that he is not spending enough time and effort to craft songs that will raise the standard of what's gone before - a standard that his record-buying fans have come to expect. Sandy puts it down to the fact that he is churning out material too much, too fast, amassing a large amount of material and always pushing the label for that elusive double album. Brother Tom believes that although Harry is trying to write the best material he can, his other commitments are now taking up much of his time and pulling him in different directions, with music no longer seen as his first priority. After making his first few albums, it seems Harry has lost interest in being in a recording studio.

Despite that, recording of *On the Road to Kingdom Come* commences on June 15th and carries on, intermittently, until July 8th. After the first three-day session, Harry goes down to the Civic Auditorium in San Diego for a one-off show before flying back east to perform at the outdoor Merriweather Post Pavilion in Columbia, Maryland, where Led Zeppelin and The Who had famously shared billing back in 1969. Recording resumes on the 21st and after four days is again put on hold for the best part of two weeks to keep to his touring schedule. Despite reservations about Kewley's involvement in the recording, his handling of the tour logistics is impressive, with flights and accommodation bookings taking in thousands of miles and concerts ranging from Florida, New York, Virginia and North Carolina. On June 30th Harry makes a return appearance at the Mississippi River Festival in Edwardsville, Illinois. The final three days of recording commence on July 6th, with additional recording carried out at the Hit Factory in New York, and the final mixing process once again done at Phase 1 Recording in Toronto.

Harry's sixth studio album will need to impress Elektra, still smarting from the disappointing sales of *Portrait Gallery*. No gatefold sleeve this time, but the cover features a line-sketch by Harry's uncle, Michael Burke, depicting a coastal village, with castle and burned-out cottages, and the outline of one of Harry's eyes encompassing the silhouette of a ship on the horizon. On the rear cover is a photo of a relaxed Harry taken by David Gahr at the Huntington home. Once again, as on previous studio albums, full lyrics are enclosed, a bonus for listeners, as it will include two of Harry's finest story songs. This is a complete departure from *Portrait Gallery*, with very few

193

references to family members in the songs, but Harry is optimistic: *"I think it's going to be the best thing I've done so far. It's got some major new songs; it has some interesting new combinations of different sounds that the group is making and we've gotten to the point where we're really playing well together. So, there's a kind of quality that a group of people who have played songs live has when they record, that's different from even the best studio musicians."*

On the Road to Kingdom Come (1976) ****
Elektra 7E-1082
Recorded: Elektra Sound Recorders, Los Angeles & The Hit Factory, New York June-July 1976
US Release Date: October 23rd 1976
Producer: Steve Chapin
Engineer: John James Stewart

On the Road to Kingdom Come *
Apparently written by Harry during a weather-induced three-hour-plus layover at Kansas City Airport on the way to performing a Ralph Nader benefit at the KSU McCain Auditorium in Manhattan, Kansas, and sung that night while reading the words scribbled down on a piece of paper lying on his knee. Harry is in a cynical mood. At the time of the presidential primaries, the news of a sex scandal involving Ohio Democratic nominee Wayne Hays and his mistress Elizabeth Ray has just broken in the *Washington Post*, forcing his resignation as chairman of the Committee on House Administration in June 1976. Whatever faith Harry has in the administration has been eroded, and it results in a tirade against everything from politics to religion. He says later: *"I read about disaster after disaster in the morning paper and how our politicians had such holier-than-thou attitudes which were being exhibited by both Ford and Carter. And I just thought I should write an ode to all our hypocrisy."* Originally written as an eleven-verse statement, Harry eventually condenses it to just six, but still retains its impact. He begins with the hypocrisy of religion, a subject till now that has escaped his attention; then it's unelected Republican President Gerald Ford's turn, and even the military's top brass and the music industry get stinging rebukes.

From the cheap seats
Alan L. Geraci - *On the Road To Kingdom Come forces the listeners to confront the paradox of God and human existence in several vignettes. Ultimately, "we are all just travelers" pins all of us with the reality of mortality against all spirituality.*
Jim G Phynn - *I always saw it as an attempt to write a song in the vein of "Stuck inside of Mobile with the Memphis Blues Again" by Bob Dylan, peppered with social-political jabs. (Hypocrisy of clergy and warmongering*

194

military men, his disdain for Gerald Ford and, to a lesser degree, Ted Kennedy, etc.)

The Parade's Still Passing By ****
Harry's fitting tribute to one of his heroes, singer Phil Ochs, who had previously been referenced in the song '**Changes**' on the *Short Stories* album. Born in El Paso, Texas, two years before Harry, Ochs once described himself as a "singing journalist," and arrived in Harry's neighborhood of Greenwich Village in the early 60s, performing in local clubs and rapidly becoming an integral part of the Village counter-culture scene. With his sharp wit and insightfulness, he wrote and sang passionately about war, civil rights, and injustice, although referring to them as just "topical songs." His Guthrie-style delivery won the praise of his contemporaries, and he performed regularly at demonstrations and rallies. After a prolific period in which he recorded eight albums for Elektra, each one deemed progressively better than the one before, by the 70s Ochs began having mental health issues, including alcoholism and a bipolar disorder. In 1976 he took his own life, looked on by Harry as a selfish act, for he believed he should have persevered with his music. Like Guthrie and Seeger, Harry sees him as a forerunner in the protest movement, more so than Dylan. Harry always praised Ochs for maintaining his moral stance, comparing his social commitment to those who had long since forgotten the phrase, name-checking Och's seminal composition, 'There But For Fortune' (a chart hit for Joan Baez in 1965), and admiring him for not selling out like so many others.

From the cheap seats
Gerry Naughton - *That such a great wordsmith, musician and humanitarian as Harry Chapin wrote such a poignant tribute to Phil Ochs is the highest possible commendation. This is probably Chapin's most underrated song, because its essence is lost in the fact that Ochs is such an unknown singer-songwriter...Both Harry and Phil died far too young, but the parade of appreciation will be passing by forever.*

The Mayor of Candor Lied *****
Like '**Taxi**', this is another song inspired by Harry's relationship with Clare McIntyre. Back in the summer of 1963, Clare had suddenly gone off to Europe, leaving Harry distraught. In the back of his mind he believes it was her father's idea, to get her away from a man who he looks upon as a no-hoper. For his fictional tale based on that episode Harry chooses the real town of Candor, New York, which he remembers from his college days at Cornell in nearby Ithaca. The narrator of the story is the young son of a farmer, and in the very first verse he learns there is a secret to be revealed. The young man

195

is in love with a girl who we later find out is called Coleen (substituting for Clare), the well-bred daughter of the local mayor:

In the little town of Candor in the last year of my youth
I learned the final lesson of the levels to the truth
My father was a farmer he'd go tilling in the ground
My mother was a neighbor, she'd go visiting around.
But I didn't care.
For I had found the answer to a plowboy's lonely prayer.
She was the daughter of the Mayor.

To this young farmer boy, this girl means everything and does not fear the inevitable consequences. But, of course, there will be consequences, and the mayor does his best to end their clandestine relationship. But as they continue to see each other, Coleen does her best to soothe the young man's temper, and in doing so drops a subtle hint of what is to transpire:

The Mayor fought my courtship for he'd made other plans
He saw her married to a better man than a boy with farmer's hands.
I said - I hate your father, it's so hard not to strike him.
She said - You know I love you because you're so much like him.
And so I'd go sneaking in the evening
And there she'd stand a crying in the dawn as I was leaving

In the chorus that follows we get to learn what will happen later, maybe a bit of a spoiler, but another hint all the same:

But the Mayor of Candor lied
When he offered me his only daughter
The Mayor of Candor tried
To take her across the water
What a thing to do to a young man in love
What a thing to do to your daughter.

Now we come to the first 'unexpected' twist in the tale, perhaps not quite the shock some are expecting, as the narrator finds his mother in the arms of the mayor. For all those who have lived and breathed Sunday afternoon mini-movies on TV, they can probably write the script for what follows.

One day with father on his tractor and mother off again
I go to find the Mayor and work out what I can
But he is not at his office, he is not at his home
When I find him in the countryside he is not alone

196

He is holding a woman and imagine my surprise
As she jumps back from his arms I look into my mother's eyes,
The Mayor of Candor lied.

With the cat out of the bag, as far as the storyline goes, now it begins to get more interesting, and suddenly the thought of blackmail rears its ugly head. Although we hear nothing from his mother, the real perpetrator of this drama, she does seem more horrified with the blackmail issue than she does being caught in an uncompromising position. Apparently, his love for Coleen is so great he seems to forget about the effect his mother's infidelity will have on his father, back home quietly tilling the land. But we all know different by now, don't we?

All my thoughts of outrage, embarrassment and pain
Were washed away by what came roaring through my brain
The Mayor's at my mercy and I hear my own voice say -
Your run for re-election is just one month away.
And the world will never know of what I've seen here sir
But I'll be with your daughter, is my meaning clear, sir?

My mother looks in horror at the compromise we made
But the Mayor's rueful smile says this piper must be paid
I had a month of joy in heaven from this deal I'd made in hell
What was to happen then my friend, a prophet could not tell

And so, to keep things as close to Clare's story as possible, Coleen goes off to an *"unseen"* foreign shore for a few months, leaving the poor young man lamenting on their separation, highlighted by Big John's wonderful falsetto.

The day after his re-election and the victory celebration
The mayor takes his family on a month-long foreign vacation
Oh Coleen - you know how much I love you
There is no one I'd ever place above you
Oh Coleen - you don't even know me
To have you there's nothing that's below me.
Oh Coleen....
But time always passes after all
And as the summer follows spring so does the winter follow fall

The nail-biting climax to the story is at hand. Unlike Clare, who does eventually come back, we never do see Coleen again, and of course, according to the mayor, it's all her decision. He has called the boy's bluff and doesn't

197

give a damn about the young man's mother (we never do get to hear what happens to her):

The day that they return I stand waiting on the road
I watch the car drive up, I watch the passengers unload
Of course she is 't there, of course I should have known
The Mayor says that she has stayed, the decision was her own.

I spit out my hatred and my fury at his lies
When he says you tried to blackmail me, you're just as bad as I
He says - Go do your damnedest, boy, throw your mother to the streets
You know it's been too many years, I had to be discreet

As they stand there arguing, the mayor gives away one final clue. If the penny hasn't dropped yet, it is left to the last line of the last verse.

And as he stands there saying we're just two of a kind
It hits me like a thunderbolt exploding in my mind
As I look into his leering, aged, wrinkled mirror of my own face
He laughs and sneers and says - Of course dear son
Where do you think you came from in the first place?

Some will admit, "Well. I never saw that coming," others have worked it out long before; but either way, they have just experienced the climax to one of Harry's greatest story-songs, a gripping melodrama which, like '**Taxi**', ultimately leads to film producers scrambling over each other for potential screenplays.

From the cheap seats
Ronald J Dold - *Harry told the story about the song at a concert I attended in Houston. He was driving through NY and came across a directional sign for (blank) Free School and asked himself "I wonder if it costs $$ to go to (blank) Free School?" He continued down the road and saw a directional sign for Candor and asked himself "I wonder if the Mayor of Candor lies?" At least that's the story he told as I remember.*

Lucy Lambert - *As always, Harry had a way with double meanings and twists on a phrase and shades of meaning. That's why we all loved his music. The Mayor, a politician, worked events to his benefit just as the young man tried to do. As always though, there must be others around one to help hide a lie. The Mayor isn't the only one at fault. Harry illuminates the human condition once again!*

Joe Cyr - *A masterful tale of love versus hate and a youthful realization that all is not as it seems. There are no winners in this song, only victims.*

198

Charlotte Light - *I like to count the clues when people hear it for the first time. When they hear the ending, the smile of understanding dawns. Priceless.*

Melba Davis Nickoles - *I remember the first time I ever heard the song. Yes, that was a long time ago, but it seems like it just happened. I was a teenager, and was appalled, shocked, and angry at the 'mayor'. I was innocent back then and this just blew my mind.*

Laugh Man **

Written by Harry for the pilot of the show called *Friends*, in which he interviews celebrity comics, but never used, as all further shows are cancelled. The song takes an emotional look at the fading career of a comedian.

Corey's Coming *****

According to Harry a song about *"an old man with a dream and a young man who buys it"* - words quite familiar to all of Harry's fans. Like **'Better Place To Be'**, it's often cited by the singer as one of his favorite compositions, and tells the story of John Joseph, an old man living in a broken-down old railroad yard, a place Harry refers to in concert as one of the most evocative places he can imagine. The narrator is the young man in question and he tells of the times he goes to visit the old man to listen to his stories:

Old John Joseph was a man with two first names
They left him in the railroad yard when they took away the trains
And only one run a week comes on roaring down that line
So all he's got to worry 'bout is time.
I come by in the evening to hear 'bout where he's been
He says – "Come on sit down Kid, where shall I begin?"
He starts telling me the stories of the glories of his past
But he always saves the story of his Corey for the last.

The simple chorus has John Joseph describing his mystical Corey, maybe even singing it to the narrator:

And he says my Corey's coming. No more sad stories coming
My midnight-moonlight-morning-glory's coming aren't you girl?
And like I told you, when she holds you
She enfolds you in her world.

Although he has never seen this woman, the young man is keen to find out more and asks the townsfolk if they know of her.

I was quite surprised to find out all the places that he knew
And so I asked the townsfolk if his stories were true

199

Well they said old John was born here, he's lived here all his life
He's never had a woman, let alone a wife.

To his surprise no one has even known the old man to have a woman in his life. Next time he sees the old man and challenges him, he gets an unexpected reply. Once again in the chorus, John Joseph repeats the claim that Corey is on her way.

And very soon you'll find out as you check around
That no one named Corey's ever lived in this town
So I chided the old man 'bout the truth that I had heard
But he smiled and said reality is only just a word.

But in the next verse, the tone of the music grows sombre and the narrator finds the old man has died in his sleep.

I came by one evening but he did not hear my shout
I looked in the window and I saw the fire was out
When he would not wake up, I forced in the door
And I saw that Old John Joseph would tell stories no more.

The scene at the graveyard, just three of us were there
Me and the gravedigger we heard the parson's prayer
He said - We need not grieve for this man,
For we know that God cares!

In the next scene a mysterious woman appears at the graveside. Of course, we have all guessed who she is, but the following lines always manage to remain achingly poignant.

They put the cold dirt over him, left me on my own
And when at last I looked up I saw I was not alone
So I said if you're a relative, he had a peaceful end.
That's when she said my name is Corey you can say I'm just a friend.

In the extended version of the song found on the 1979 album *Legends of the Lost and Found,* Harry changes these last two lines and adds a whole new verse:

They put the cold dirt over him and left me on my own
And when at last I looked up I saw I was not alone
Standing there in silence with a shawl around her head
Was a beautiful young woman, I remember what she said,

"Is that John Joseph there?"
I nodded my head, "Yes."
That brought a soft smile to her.
She said, "It's time he got some rest."
So I said, "If you're a relative, he had a peaceful end,"
That's when she said, "My name is Corey,
You can say I'm just a friend."

The chorus is repeated, but no longer the upbeat optimism we had heard from the old man. For the narrator he realizes that John Joseph's dream is in fact a flesh and blood reality, and the softness of the voice maybe indicates the young man is now captivated too by this woman's mysterious aura. As the song draws to an end the young man is found to have taken John Joseph's place in more ways than one and will now be the one to carry on his stories, especially the one about Corey:

So that's the old man's story, I'm glad you came tonight
You see a busted down old railroad yard sure makes a lonely sight
You may wonder why a young man would work out here alone
Well the job pays enough to keep some flesh on my bones.
And I confess I get to missing the old man a bit
And there's one other reason I guess I should admit...

Written in March 1976, this is the second great story song on the album, and rightly regarded as among one of his finest compositions. Some sources claim that the story is inspired by Harry's longtime friend Zeke Marsden, a brakeman on the B&O Railroad in Boston. When originally written it was some twelve minutes long, and eventually edited down to a more single-friendly 5.38 minutes. At a concert in Frankfurt, Germany in 1977 Harry introduces the song by saying: *"Of all the songs I've written it's the least true, and yet if I had the ability to make one of my songs completely literal, I would like to make this one."*

According to Harry's daughter Jen: *"The family used to go to a restaurant in Huntington called The Hungry Bear where a singer/songwriter named John Joseph cast quite a romantic shadow over the place. Other than that, there is more here about dreams and overcoming the cynicism of reality. I also see elements of the folk tradition and the value of storytelling coming into play."* One story has the name of Corey being taken from a fan in the early days, who had stayed with Harry on the road when he had been a struggling artist.

Even though on the inside jacket of the album Harry writes: *"Thanks to real life singer-songwriter John Joseph for his help with 'Corey's Coming',"* for many listeners Corey remains an imaginary character in the old man's head. Others interpret Corey as being the angel of death "coming" to take John

201

Joseph as it will soon be his time. Whatever it may be, it remains a beautiful song, and any song that is left open to conjecture and mixed interpretations is a sign of a master storyteller. The song is released as a single coupled with '**If My Mary Were Here**' but fails to chart.

From the cheap seats

Melba Davis Nickoles - *In my mind, as a teenager, it became like a romance novel. A Mystery Romance. Harry had such a great imagination. I felt a kinship with his imaginings. I read all the time, as a teenager, so listening to Harry, was like reading a new book. A new story.*

Kelly Barry - *Firstly, it's a guy telling a story about an old man telling a story. I always admired how clever that idea is. Then of course, the story is positive in nature - one of belief and trust and a bit supernatural. I always tear up in the graveyard - never fails. The setting of the story is so vivid - I can see it now. It always will be in my top 3 of Harry's songs.*

Cliff Geismar - *One man's dream is not readily understood and accepted by another. Old John Joseph had a dream that was real and that made him happy. That's all that any of us need. A very special song that works on many levels.*

Karen Spall - *The opening verse is so emotive. As for the imagery of a man alone being visited by this fantasy figure who loves him and makes him whole, that is romantic and beautiful and speaks to the truth that reality is fluid and what we make it.*

Ellen Gordon Klein - *I always loved this song. For me it's about hope, and having something to look forward to, which makes you want to get on with life. It can be imaginary or real, but it doesn't matter as long as it makes them happy.*

Karla Dixon Britt - *The whole song is a movie in my head. It is such a lovely story about the friendship between two men of different generations but with the same spirit. Harry could tell a story.*

If My Mary Were Here ****

At first glance this is spirited ballad about the loneliness of missing the one you love, but Harry has a different interpretation. This goes back to a time when Harry considered himself a fool or villain by *"waging sexual wars and losing often."* At a Knoxville concert in 1979 he confesses: *"This is a song about the male species feeling sorry for himself for no good f*****g reason. It's another song which I put a verse and chorus back into it. It's amazing how there's been some key moments in my life when I've been as real s.o.b. and it doesn't turn out well, and then I go back and ask some to have pity on me..."* Later, at the Bottom Line concert in 1981, he introduces the song a different way: *"People tend to see in others their own faults. So, this is a pure example of me being as real bastard in such a situation. Any relationship that any of*

202

you men have here, purely coincidental, do not feel threatened in the very least, because it's just Harry Chapin being an asshole."

So, it's all about feeling sorry for yourself and asking for pity, but it's also another example of Harry's lyrical craft, honed here to perfection. Along with **'Fall in Love with Him'**, this is an attempt to prove to himself and his critics that there is more to him than the story songs, and that he can still write three to four minute love songs without much effort. The song is quite puzzling. Who is this Mary? Where has she gone? And who is the narrator phoning to tell his story? Maybe we don't need to know the answers, but all the same we are still left with a beautifully worded song that trips along at a nice pace. It is later considered suitable enough to be chosen as the flip-side to the single of **'Corey's Coming'**.

Fall In Love With Him ****

Like the previous track, this is an exercise in writing craft rather than feeling, and also another song that should have been released as a single. Notable for Doug Walker's excellent guitar riff and the backing vocals provided by the trio of excellent session singers, Donna Fein, Sharon "Muffy" Hendrix and Carolyn Dennis (ex-wife of Bob Dylan).

Caroline *****

This may be Harry's tribute to one of his ex-girlfriends, but surprisingly, it has lyrics co-written with Sandy, leading one to be unsure of just when it was written. Nevertheless, between them they have produced a wonderful character portrait of a mysterious girl who may have figured in Harry's life at one time or another. Very similar in style to **'She Sings Songs Without Words'**, Harry's sublime love letter to his wife, this is another lyrical masterpiece. Some commentators believe that it was actually written with Sandy in mind, with a three-syllable name like Caroline substituted to better suit the flow of the lyrics. And the lyrics flow like heaven-sent ambrosia.

Caroline is young, spontaneous, and unsure of what she wants from a relationship. A little naïve perhaps, but totally seductive, flirting, teasing, and seemingly keeping her frustrated lover at bay. In each verse Harry's voice gets progressively higher, as if heightening the passion that is building up inside him, and only subsides a little with the chorus. Certainly, one of Harry's most arousing and seductive songs.

From the cheap seats
Melba Davis Nickoles - *It is still a love song. You don't know who he wrote it about. I don't know what year he wrote it. That might determine who it is about. It goes so perfectly with the melody, maybe he just came upon a name that went with that melody. I don't believe, even though he wrote historically accurate songs, that all of them had to be about a specific person.*

Just a beautiful name with an equally beautiful melody. If this song was written during the time he was married to Sandy, and I believe she was his muse, it was probably about her. With every song writer, something comes first, the lyric or the melody. If the melody came first, this was the perfect name to go with it, and was about Sandy, but had a beautiful name to go with that melody.

Roll Down the River **

A song in which the narrator tells his soon-to-be-leaving-him girlfriend just what he thinks of her.

Harry Fires Fred Kewley

With the album not due for release until October, Elektra are apprehensive of issuing any singles, despite there being several suitable radio-friendly candidates. Within days of the final recording, Harry is back on the road, with four shows in Charlotte, North Carolina, a spot at the Temple Music Festival in Ambler, Pennsylvania on July 12th, and then back to LA for two performances at the Greek Theater and one at Sea World in San Diego. Two days later he crosses the country to appear at the Westbury Music Fair in New York and also a return to the Schaefer Music Festival in Central Park on August 4th, in which Michael Masters makes his final appearance with the band.

In late August Harry decides not to renew Fred Kewley's contract as manager, partly due to his involvement with the poor production work on the new album, and partly because of Fred's attitude toward benefit concerts, which he feels are eroding the markets for paid appearances. Not only that, he doesn't receive payment himself for the benefits and sometimes even forgets to book them in advance. For Fred it is always about the money earned, not the money given away. Harry will always look on him as a good guy and loyal friend, but this attitude is letting him down. He is no hustler. Good hard work has given way to laziness, and Harry now feels that for what Fred is being paid, it is time for a real professional to run his affairs. Harry even talks to Fred about making certain changes with management, but according to him, he never comes to any decision, and he only learns of his firing when a letter comes from Harry's lawyer. After a partnership of more than five years, and after seven albums and numerous concert dates, it all comes to an acrimonious end. In the resultant lawsuit that stretches over four years, Kewley sues Harry for all lost income through all of Harry's benefits and even money owing through a clause in the contract that links him to Harry's royalties. Attempts at an out-of-court agreement come to nothing, and in a final hearing in 1980 Kewley wins the case and receives $100,000 including legal expenses.

Under New Management

Harry has lost a good friend, but he gains another, and one who will have an even greater impact on his future career. His name is Ken Kragen, a 40-year-old son of a professional violinist, currently in the employment of Jerry Weintraub, head of Management Three, who is one of the music industry's most powerful talent scouts and tour managers, whose clients include John Denver, Neil Diamond and Elvis Presley. Although Harry initially wants Weintraub himself on board, he is paired with Kragen, who has his roots in folk music, having already managed The Kingston Trio, and who will later start his own company and make a superstar out of country singer Kenny Rogers.

As part of the Management Three organization Harry sees big opportunities. Weintraub also owns Concerts West, which may result in Harry having to perform fewer benefits for more money, and with Weintraub's roster of high-profile artists it could very well add input into helping raise funds for both PAF and W.H.Y. It is Kragen who suggests to Harry the idea of concession sales at his concerts, whether benefit or otherwise. He points out that many artists sell concessions and sign autographs at their concerts to make extra money. Harry could do just that to raise money for his charities. Harry realizes now that he could have been doing that for the past two years. Why didn't Fred Kewley ever think of that?

Another change comes in the shape of Harry's stepbrother, Jeb Hart, who he now brings on board to take charge of organizing the benefit concerts. Along with Bob Hinkle, Hart has been managing Tom Chapin's solo career and promoting his first album, *Life is Like That*, which is released on the Fantasy label that year. Not only that, they have secured for him the support act to Janis Ian's upcoming 114-date tour. One of the highlights of Tom's debut album is the song **'Number One'**, a fond tribute to Harry with sublime moving lyrics.

By the end of the summer the Management Three organization gets to work on Harry. Arrangements are made for a major solo tour of European countries in mid-October and merchandise is ordered to be sold at concession stalls at concerts.

On September 2nd, Ron Evanuik makes his concert debut with the band in front of a sell-out 15,000 crowd at the outdoor amphitheater at Pine Knob in Clarkston, Michigan. But the frantic schedules are taking their toll on Harry. Prior to the Pine Knob concert Harry misses his scheduled flight from New York to Detroit and has to take the next one. Arriving late, the promoters have him flown by helicopter to the venue to make a late but dramatic entrance. On the 7th he is also late for a morning flight from New York to LA, where he is scheduled to tape a performance for Don Kirshner's *Rock Concert* television show, and is pulled up by a highway cop for speeding and driving on a revoked license. For the foreseeable future he will be hiring a driver. The end of the month brings an impressive show at the 3,000-seater DAR Constitution Hall in Washington DC before heading off to Canada for two concerts in Winnipeg and Calgary.

Meanwhile, it is becoming apparent that the whole benefit process now calls for better control, and that's where his new management team rises to the occasion. Out of the 230 concerts so far this year, 130 have been benefits for one good cause or another. From earnings in excess of $1 million, some $600,000 is given away, of which 30% is taxed. That means Harry is giving away some $350,000 of his own money. Hundreds of requests keep coming in for him to help out with different charities and fundraisers, and it becomes the task of Susan Gensel, his new secretary, to sift through all the requests and try giving priority to the ones she feels need help the most. Anything that helps prevent sickness or death through malnourishment or disease is always put ahead of raising money for dance classes or things like that, but even so, Harry finds it hard to turn anything down. Once Harry decides to do it (and he seldom refuses), he leaves it to Jeb Hart to make the necessary booking. There are also reciprocal benefits with fellow artists. Where Harry invites willing friends like Don McLean, Pete Seeger, Oscar Brand and Richie Havens to play concerts at Huntington and around Long Island, he also returns the favor and takes part in concerts for some of their own charities.

Big John Wallace realizes only too well the strain the number of benefits is having on the band, but recalls there is never any resentment. How can there be? What can anyone possibly say to this man who is leading by example with his tireless energy and commitment to such worthy causes? All this work doesn't go without recognition, and on September 18th Harry is nominated for Outstanding Public Service at the second annual Rock Music Awards in LA, but despite the immense contribution he has given, which outdoes all the illustrious nominees, the award goes to Lynard Skynyrd for their work in saving Atlanta's Fox Theater. It takes a long time for Harry to come to terms with this.

In October Harry performs across the country, as well as the ten-day solo tour of Europe organized by Kragen (mostly UK dates), but with the presidential elections coming up in the following month he increases the number of benefits to support political candidates who happen to share his views. Although Harry is a confirmed Democrat, he helps candidates across all parties, as long as they are reading from the same hymn sheet as he is. Apart from this, he also needs to boost funds for PAF, which is suffering cash flow issues, so he and Sandy hit on the idea of holding seafront barbecues outside their Huntington home, with Harry performing mini-concerts for $25 a ticket. Some days thousands of people attend.

On October 23rd the new album, *On the Road to Kingdom Come*, is finally released, and everyone can see that Kewley's ill-advice on the production has resulted in a work of lesser quality. Harry's voice is, as you expect, in top form, but problems with the mixing lead to some of the instruments being almost inaudible, drowned out by bass and drums. Also, with no suitable singles being released, Elektra keep the album's promotion low-key. They expected another *Verities & Balderdash*, another hit single like '**Cat's**', but what they get is a weak album which in their eyes has all the hallmarks of being a failure. Once again chart success eludes it, and it peaks at a dismal #87 on the *Billboard* 200 chart. Could it be that Harry is getting tired of taking chances with his music? While critics will always use evaluation and self-analysis to find the answers, maybe Harry has his own answer in the metaphor - these roads are meant to take you to and from places.

Melody Maker has a scathing review: "*It is a strange fact of life that people with little talent for singing insist on singing, to the discomfort of all within earshot. There are whole lists of performers with actively unpleasant voices, who, through some baffling quirk of their own fancy, seem convinced the rest of the world should share their inadequacies...The voice is suitably quavery, croaky, clumsy and artless...And, of course, non-singers always proudly bear aloft their lyrics, usually wry observations on this funny old world, admonitions to a whole string of long-suffering girlfriends, and cautionary tales spun from a great storehouse of wisdom. Non-singers surround themselves with devoted session musicians who pick away at acoustic guitars, various strings and horns, are deeply honoured to be associated with such a project. Non-singers also draw vast armies of devoted fans who cheer loudly at the first line of one of their most obscure songs is hinted at while the glass of water goes down on stage.... A work of rare artistry for some, utter tedium for the rest of us.*"

Other reviews are a little more positive: "*Compared to some of his earlier work, which was often dry and dour, these songs are vigorous and saturated in sound...As a musical storyteller, Chapin has few peers...*"

Apart from the strength of the two main story songs and the glowing tribute to Ochs, Harry agrees with many of the comments he receives from his fans that the general feel of the album lacks his emotional commitment; that it's more an exercise in musical and lyrical craft rather than feeling. In essence, what they are saying is that when art becomes craft, there's no communication, and it's no longer art.

Harry takes all this on board. The next album will be so much different.

Dance Band on the Titanic

"I think all of us should be very hungry, very greedy, because the only thing we know for sure is that we're alive now and if we don't take it now, we're going to lose out. I never want to be sixty-five and say 'I wish I had done this.' To me, that is the saddest admission any human being can make"

Iceberg Ahead - The Beginning of a Great Year

In the process of reevaluating his musical direction, Harry looks for ways of finding out where the focus should be. By the fall of 1976 he hosts half a dozen songwriting workshops at PAF in Huntington, getting into conversations with the students that might encourage and foster new ideas for his songwriting. And something surely rubs off. Over the next two or three months, Harry writes something like thirty new songs, many of which will be considered among his best work since *Verities & Balderdash*. On September 25th Harry co-hosts a first Hungerthon on Washington's WASH-FM radio station. In between this and the flurry of writing new material, the touring continues at an even more frantic pace, with two shows per evening becoming more frequent, such as the ones in November at Cape Girardeau, Miami and Toronto.

Following an appearance on *Good Morning America* on November 10th, Harry plays once again at Avery Fisher Hall in New York and at the USN Academy in Annapolis. The month ends with two shows at the Aerie Crown Theatre in Chicago. On November 28th Harry co-hosts another Hungerthon on WNEW-FM radio in New York and it proves an even bigger success than the first one. This time he has among his guests Tom Chapin, Ralph Nader, Pete Seeger, and a very moody Patti Smith. Four days later Harry is honored for his Hungerthons with an award for Broadcast Excellence at the annual International Radio Programming Forum in New York. Hungerthons are becoming fashionable, and within days of the award ceremony WMWR-FM in Philadelphia holds its very own, including a live radio broadcast of two of Harry's benefit concerts at the Dick Clark Westchester Theater in Tarrytown, New York, which are also aired on its sister station WNEW-FM. At the beginning of December, the band play four consecutive nights (five shows) at the Valley Forge Music Fair in Devon, Pennsylvania, followed by Harry performing with Tom at the University of Illinois in Urbana. In the run up to Christmas concerts are closer to home, including a nostalgic return to Brooklyn College on the 17th, before winding up the season the following day with two shows at the Chrysler Hall in Norfolk, Virginia.

The Need for a Successful Album

With Christmas out of the way Harry is keen to get his new songs recorded. Out of all the new material he has written, thirteen songs will eventually be chosen for the new album, which will have a conceptual theme and be called *Dance Band on the Titanic*, his statement on the lack of social concern in the 70s that is dooming the country, by using the analogy of passengers of the famous ship partying away to a band's feel-good tunes which only serve to deflect attention away from the death-dealing horror awaiting them.

Harry recalls: *"I believe the music of the seventies and most of the art world is functioning like the dance band on the Titanic and there are icebergs all-around of our own making. The music industry's job is to divert attention in the ballroom so that people aren't worrying about the icebergs outside and promote business as usual...."*

Elektra president Mel Posner, perhaps missing the point that Harry is actually criticizing his industry, is keen to have this new album produce at least one hit single, and suggests that to make it happen Harry gets another top producer on board to avoid the issues Steve Chapin had on the last album. Harry is tasked with the job and talks are held with Jon Landau, ex-*Rolling Stone* music critic and now Bruce Springsteen's successful producer, but although interest is shown Landau has to decline due to other commitments. In the end Harry settles with Steve. After all, he decides, he doesn't need a smash hit single, he just needs it to be a great fast-selling album to appease Posner. To facilitate its success the experienced Jack Malken is drafted in as engineer. But how does Harry keep coming up with his story-songs, and how is it that very few of his contemporaries are doing the same?

In a 1977 interview he explains that the first story song he ever heard was an eleven-minute one written by his father Jim Chapin called 'Stonewall Jackson', about the Confederate general, and continues: *"I think the only reason that no one else has written story songs is because they're not dumb enough. Its not a very economical way of writing in both ways. Most of it is too long for AM radio; also, it takes a long time to write a story song, both in terms of effort and in that you can't tell a story like 'Taxi' in three minutes. Nobody has proved apart from me that it can be commercially viable. I guess 'Ode to Billie Joe' was one song like that. Then there's always stories. I'm living and always experiencing things. The exciting thing for me is that I've become a category – in a recent review of an Elton John album it said it contains a 'Chapinesque' tune, and when they sort of use you as an adjective, it's sort of flattering, right?"*

Recording of *Dance Band* commences on January 19th at Elektra's Secret Sound Studios in New York, chosen by Harry mainly because he wants to remain near home, and also because brother Tom had recorded his first solo album there just a few months before and will be on hand again to play on some of the songs. There will also be a new cellist on board (the fourth), as Ron Evanuik's six-month stint comes to an end. Never quite living up to expectations with the band, Evanuik is replaced with the more accomplished (George) Kim Scholes.

The first two days in the studio sees the recording of a mini-epic called **'Mercenaries'**, while the following two days Harry has another stab at an old song called **'Seasons & the Sky (So They Sail)'** which didn't quite work out last time. Work also begins on **'Paint a Picture of Yourself (Michael)'** which is completed the next day. After a day off, recording commences on the 24th with two songs, **'Country Dreams'** and **'Mismatch'**, followed over the next couple of days with two more, **'The Time To Listen'** and **'My Old Lady'**, the latter resurrected from the *Kingdom Come* sessions. Three more songs are recorded in the next three sessions, **'I Wonder What Happened To Him'**, **'She Always Said'**, and **'Odd Job Man'**, as well as completion of **'Manhood'** and commencement on the album's title track. Work resumes on **'Dance Band'** on the 31st, together with **'We Grew Up a Little Bit'**, while the whole of the next day sees a final try at **'Seasons & the Sky'**. Over the next two days the title track is finally wrapped up, as well as the slow-tempo part of Kenneth Burke's contribution, **'One Light in a Dark Valley'**. In a grueling nineteen-hour long session on the 4th the 14-minute magnum opus **'There Only Was One Choice'** is completed after ten takes. Over the last six sessions **'Why Should People Stay the Same'**, **'Bluesman'** and **'I Do It For You Jane'** are all recorded, with the up-tempo segment of **'One Light in a Dark Valley'** bringing the recording of the album to a close on March 8th.

The Chapin Musical

Meanwhile on January 30th a cabaret-style musical called *Chapin* has opened at the Improvised Theatre in Los Angeles. Conceived by actor and theatre producer Joseph Stern, and co-produced and directed by actor William Devane, it resembles the style of *Jacques Brel Is Alive and Well and Living in Paris* and consists of some twenty-one interpretations of Harry's songs, including many of the classics, as well as one or two from his last studio album. The five singers are Wings Hauser, Barbara Illey, Jennifer Darling, Scott Jarvis and one of the stars of the Jacques Brel revue, George Ball. The songs performed are as follows:

Act I
'Sunday Morning Sunshine', 'Dreams Go By', 'W.O.L.D.', 'Barefoot Boy', 'On the Road to Kingdom Come', '30,000 Pounds of Bananas', 'You're Still My Boy', 'The Mayor of Candor Lied', 'Cat's in the Cradle', 'Sniper'

210

Act II

'Stop Singing Those Sad Songs', 'Six String Orchestra', 'Corey's Coming', 'Mr Tanner', 'Taxi', 'Dogtown', 'Halfway to Heaven', 'A Better Place To Be', 'Someone Keeps Calling My Name', 'Circle'

Co-producer Stern comments on Harry's work: *"He's basically a balladeer in the old tradition. He takes amazingly simple incidents and tells stories and makes it all work. A year and a half ago I went to a Broadway play called **The Night That Made America Famous**, a non-book musical directed by Gene Frankel which featured Chapin's songs. The show wasn't working because it was all crazy lights and whirling dervishes. It was a hype. All wrong. After the performance Chapin came out onstage sat on a stool and played his music simply. He had everybody hypnotized. I can't think of any other writer who composes so naturally for the theater. His songs are about specific kinds of people; cleaners, aging disc jockeys, people who want to be ballplayers, blue-collar types. He has great range and his text is usually up to something..."*

In the critically-acclaimed show the singers step up to the mark and deliver some remarkable performances. Barbara Illey summons both emotion and terror in her rendition of **'Dogtown'** as well as a memorable performance of **'You Are Still My Boy'**, a song later to resurface in 1981's **Cotton Patch Gospel**. Scott Jarvis is immensely touching as the aging deejay in **'W.O.L.D.'**, and Sam Weisman shows both a rare humorous side in **'Six-String Orchestra'** while at the same time turning in a dramatic performance with **'The Mayor of Candor Lied'**. George Ball has the audience in hysterics with **'Bananas'** before teaming up with Jennifer Darling in the second act for a moving **'Better Place To Be'**. Darling also duets with Weisman on **'Taxi'**, one of the show's many highlights.

One reviewer is amazed at the setting for the performance of **'Sniper'**: *"The viscerally disturbing number occupies precisely the right spot, closing the first half of a show that is less a cabaret entertainment than potent musical theatre in the form of a song revue. Russell Pyle has stretched a cloth resembling a parachute across the stage, a simple and imaginative solution to the problem of scenery, and Ward Carlisle has painted it with beautiful lighting."*

Harry has found unexpected success in performances of his songs, even without him being there to sing them. That shows the impact and strength of his writing. The show runs for over seven months and is a critical success. It also breaks new ground, with Harry becoming the first contemporary American artist to have a theatrical production made in his honor consisting entirely of songs he himself has written (apparently, Harry had given Stern the rights to use his songs with a contract written on the back of a paper plate). Harry and Sandy finally get to see one of the shows in May and are impressed,

211

but Harry can't resist going backstage to give the cast some tips on performing his songs.

Meanwhile, in between the recording sessions for *Dance Band,* Harry continues with the touring schedule, with concerts held in Indiana, New York, and New Jersey, and even one up in Ontario on March 4th. The remainder of that month sees a return to the Midwest and a welcome return to the Brooklyn Academy of Music in New York. On March 22nd Harry does two benefit shows at the University of Michigan in Flint for Michael Moore, an ex-student and now the young editor of a struggling radical left-wing newspaper *The Michigan Voice,* which had started out as *The Flint Voice.* Apparently, Moore went backstage after a recent concert and asked Harry to do a benefit show to keep the paper going. In fact, Harry will go on to make Flint concerts an annual event, and for his efforts Moore presents him with an inscribed gold pocket watch before going on a decade later to become a successful documentary film maker himself. On the 27th Harry returns to Champaign, Illinois, for a solo concert at the University of Illinois's Huff Gym, recorded on local radio. The setlist is as follows: Paint a Picture of Yourself Michael, Odd Job Man, W.O.L.D., They Call Her Easy, 30,000 Pounds of Bananas, Tangled Up Puppet, Mr Tanner, Dreams Go By, Cat's in the Cradle, Taxi, Circle, Someone Keeps Calling My Name. Steve Chapin misses a number of these March shows as he is busy in New York with the production of the new album.

Around this time, Harry gets a phone call from his friend John Denver, who has recently watched one of Harry's documentaries on world hunger. To his surprise and somewhat puzzlement, Harry is told that the singer is planning to hold a meeting with some White House officials about his ideas on solving world hunger. The meeting actually involves the President's son, Chip Carter, and Denver proposes to start giving 20% of his concerts' takings to combat hunger issues, but also suggests that they get in touch with Harry, as he is the one person totally committed to the problem.

Making His Mark In Europe

On April 4th, the band begin a nine-day, nine-city tour of Europe, with a rousing concert in Dublin, and this time, unlike last October, he has taken Sandy and the kids along for the ride. The following night he plays Belfast, before a two-date short tour of England, performing in front of his enthusiastic English fans at the Apollo and New Victoria Theatres in London. The latter show receives a glowing review:

"Chapin sings in a clear, pleasant voice, using unfussy melodies and arrangements played by a small backing group within which a cello provides haunting counterpoints. His stage personality is captivating. He did as he wished with Thursday's audience. As he hunched dumpily in his chair,

212

tousling his hair, talking wittily and relevantly about the circumstances of his songs, himself, and his musicians, not a soul stirred, except to laugh or applaud. The final standing ovation was spring-heeled and genuine. London will see no more absorbing concert this year."

Melody Maker also reviews the concert, one of the best he ever receives: *"His concert at London's New Victoria last Thursday was one of those momentous occasions which happens only too rarely when an artist of unique talent, who has been on the rise for several years through thoughtful albums, transcends the climbing process to establish himself at the top of the ladder. Chapin played probably the best concert of his life, dramatically reliving the pungent songs he'd written so long ago and which have come across with staleness in a lesser talent... Chapin could not be said to be plying his voice or personality of any significance, and he relies totally on rapier-like observations of city and suburban life to make his mark. His stage presence, slightly self-deprecating and pleasingly engaging, has a neat line in how-this-song-came-about... This was one of those exhilarating, moving concerts one remembers forever. Rare and touching, honest and searing. Not comfortable, but probing. Amazing. Enthralling. If you missed it, don't dare skip Chapin next time."*

The *New Musical Express* echoes the praise, despite pointing out the blocks of empty seats: *"The Harry Chapin cult, if such it can be called in Britain, received a considerable shot in the arm during his brief tour immediately before Easter. With a proliferation of other gigs, perhaps to expect even a respectable number to come to the New Vic was ambitious - but as it turned out, just about every Chapin freak in the south of England was there... Word of mouth alone will ensure that upon their return (scheduled for the autumn) Harry and his group will have a completely full house with people standing."*

Reading this, Harry must feel ten feet tall. The British music press seem to have fallen in love with Harry and his music. Following a concert in Amsterdam, Harry and the band play at the two-day Great Easter Rock and Blues Express Festival in Munich, along with fellow artists Status Quo, The Small Faces, The Scorpions, Dr Feelgood and John Mayall. The show is repeated the next day in Dortmund, and following their afternoon performance, Harry flies down to Naples where his brother Tom joins him on stage for a concert. Returning to Germany the next day, April 11th, their performance in Bremen is recorded for local radio, while the following afternoon they tape a short concert at WDR Studio in Cologne in front of a quiet and reserved audience for the television show *Rockpalast*. The setlist is as follows: Shooting Star, W.O.L.D., Mr Tanner, Dance Band on the Titanic, Taxi, Six String Orchestra, Corey's Coming, Bluesman, Mail Order Annie, 30,000 Pounds of Bananas, Cat's in the Cradle, Circle, Odd Job Man, I Wanna Learn a Love Song.

213

When performing in these non-English speaking countries the language barrier often prevents Harry's wonderful lyrics from receiving the appreciation they merit. But they enjoy the music. Few of the new songs are performed on the tour, with Harry relying on what he considers his greatest hits to satisfy the expectant audiences. In an interview Harry explains why he's still keen to break the European market: *"Because I know I'm not a significant factor here. I got $30,000 for a one-nighter in Chicago. Last year I went to a club in Copenhagen and the singer didn't show, so I did a little bit. The owner liked me so much that he offered me $20 plus the chance to work regularly at a similar fee! I was so excited I could have given up my day job. But seriously, I want to pay my dues and win an audience. The language barrier is going to be a healthy challenge. We tried it out in Germany with no problems. Things didn't work out perfectly, but audiences understand imperfection. If the audience understands, period, you've communicated..."*

The Touring Takes Its Toll

The sheer volume of benefit concerts is steadily wearing Harry out, and he's beginning to realize that they are in danger of becoming counter-productive. There have to be less strenuous ways of raising money. Some of the benefits he agrees to do are in small two-star towns, towns with small venues and small audiences, and the takings are consequently small. He sees this as wasted time and now believes that it can be better spent by him becoming more directly involved in politics, by continuing to lobby and put pressure on the government to take action, by organizing and co-hosting more Hungerthons around the country, and at the same time, by making more hit records that can raise funds from their sale. As a result, he discusses the problem with his management team, and by the middle of the year the number of solo and group benefit concerts are drastically reduced. There are signs that Harry just might be turning his back on a music career to becoming a full-time political campaigner.

Meanwhile the extensive tour of the West continues, including another visit to the Burbank studios for an appearance on *The Tonight Show with Johnny Carson*, in which he performs **'Cat's in the Cradle'** and a television debut of **'Dance Band on the Titanic'**. The last two weeks of April see concert dates in Oregon, Washington and Vancouver, as well as down in Arizona and New Mexico. This is followed in early May by a week of performances in California, including guesting once again on the popular *Merv Griffin Show*, in which Harry appears with members of the cast of **Chapin** to perform **'Mr Tanner'**. During rehearsals he also performs an early version of a new song, **'Flowers Are Red'**, which he hopes to persuade Griffin to sing with him later on the show (he declines the invitation). Harry

214

also does four shows in two days at the Circle Star in San Carlos, followed by several more dates in the Midwest and New Jersey before returning home for a short break. In June the hectic summer schedule gets underway with three more dates in Canada and two benefits in Huntington with friends Tom Paxton, Peter Yarrow and Josh White Jr.

Harry is again in Europe with the band on the 27th to do a filmed concert in Copenhagen for Danish television, performing some of his best-known songs, as well as fine renditions of **'If My Mary Were Here'** and **'Six-String Orchestra'**. During the month Harry is also presented with a Humanitarian Award by the Music and Performing Arts Lodge of B'nai Brith in New York, a ceremony attended by Elektra's boss Mel Posner. During the night Sandy tells Posner what a contribution Harry is making to the music industry, and it appears to resonate with him. Within days Elektra host a lavish $10,000 pre-release press party for *Dance Band* on a yacht. Their faith in its success proves to be short lived. July brings a welcome return to the Pine Knob outdoor amphitheater in Michigan and an appearance at the Temple University Music Festival in Ambler, Pennsylvania. A return to the newly-named Dr Pepper Summer Music Festival in Central Park rounds off the month, although the first two days' performances are rained off. Once again, the show is opened by Jim Chapin's Jazz Three band. Harry's choice of songs meets with some approval by one reviewer who describes them as *"demonstrably proletarian in tone, narrative in structure, and full of the sort of sentimental plot and not really-surprising denouncements that one encounters in ersatz O Henry short stories."* Despite viewed by some as being overworked and lacking originality, the songs' appeal is undeniable.

A Double Studio Album at Last

Despite mixed reviews for some of his new songs, Harry's mind is now fixed on achieving his next goal, and that will take the considerable efforts of a number of people to make it happen. With the recording of the songs in the can, Harry now pushes his management team to persuade Elektra to agree on a double album. One of the key songs Harry has written is over fourteen minutes long and will take up almost the whole of one side. To keep the integrity of what he is attempting to accomplish, it has to be double album. Harry's team get to work and Jerry Weintraub holds a meeting in LA with the label's new head, Joe Smith, who is dead against the idea, and by way of changing Harry's mind offers to give him $200,000 of promotion work for a single album. Even Harry's old friend Ann Purtill is brought in to try and get him to change his mind, but, as always, Harry doesn't listen. He has already noted the success of the recent double album *Frampton Comes Alive* and even the triple album *Wings Over America*. There's no changing his mind. He has written and recorded enough good songs and considers the production to be first class. It will be a double album or nothing! Eventually Harry gets Smith to agree.

The new album has a gatefold sleeve with the cover designed by Tony Lane and Suzy Rice complementing the album's 1912 Edwardian theme. Harry and his band, along with other members of the team, are pictured in a framed sepia photograph posing as the band members of the ill-fated ship, along with a steward and two officers, and all standing on the deck in front of one of the iconic lifeboats. The framed picture is resting on top of a period-looking suitcase which is adorned with contemporary stickers, each with the name of one of the album's songs. The inside jacket has silhouettes of the band in front of a drawing of the ship's deserted dining room, set at an angle to depict the listing vessel. Once again lyric sheets are included. That cover will be responsible for a great deal of the album's success, with many people buying it simply because of its title and the historical significance, and in doing so they are probably being introduced to the artist for the very first time (particularly in Europe). For some it will take a long time to understand its real context. But there is a hint - on the inside cover is a comment from Harry: *A familiar name is being etched on the bow of Space Ship Earth. There are icebergs up ahead but life goes on as usual. Down in the cramped quarters of steerage up to the sumptuous salons of first class the ever-multiple variations of oft-repeated themes making a dancing counterpoint to the long low melancholy dirge of the fog horn.* Harry will go to great lengths to expand on his interpretation of the new album in the many interviews and concerts he conducts in the following months.

Dance Band on the Titanic (1977) *****
Elektra 9E-301
Recorded: Secret Sound Studios, New York Jan-Mar 1977
Additional recording at Producer's Studio, New York & Minot Studios, White Plains NY
US Release Date: September 10th 1977
Producer: Steve Chapin
Engineer: Jack Malken

The album is the longest of Harry's career, clocking in at over 74 minutes. Side one, perhaps the weakest on the album, features the title track followed by the moral of **'Why Should People Stay the Same'** and the bouncy **'My Old Lady'**, before it finishes with one of the album's first story songs, **'We Grew Up a Little Bit'**. Side two opens with the ultra-funky **'Bluesman'**, then calms down with the paean to realtors in **'Country Dreams'**, a love song for someone else's wife in **'I Do It For You, Jane'**, and the heart-wrenching ballad, **'I Wonder What Happened to Him'**. Side three has a tribute to

216

Harry's uncle Michael Burke in **'Paint a Picture of Yourself (Michael)'**, which precedes three fine examples of Harry's lyrical craft, with **'Mismatch'** and **'Manhood'** bookending the epic **'Mercenaries'**, arguably the album's finest track. The final side has just two tracks, **'One Light in a Dark Valley'**, composed by Kenneth Burke, and the mammoth 14-minute saga that is **'There Only Was One Choice'**.

Dance Band on the Titanic ****

The title track in some way sets the context of the album, an allegory about how he felt the current socio-political apathy was dooming the country and could be compared to the ill-fated ship's dance band who continued playing as a way to divert the passengers' attention from the impending threat of the death-dealing iceberg that awaited them.

Back in April 1912 the White Star liner *Titanic*, while on its maiden voyage from Southampton to New York, struck an iceberg mid-Atlantic and sank with the loss of 1,500 lives. With the ship's eight-piece band being told to play on as it began to sink, the third-class steerage passengers below raced topside to get into lifeboats, but when they got there were ordered to go back down to the third level to get their own lifeboats. There is the rub, which Harry points out in an April interview: *"Except there were no lifeboats on the third deck, and that's what's happening now. The rich on the top deck are getting richer and richer. And the bottom two thirds are in worse shape than ever. So, we're all hiding in our first-class cabins thinking we're safe. People say there is no reason to be an activist. Stay in your cabin, decorate it to your heart's content and convince yourself there's no iceberg..."*

In another interview Harry sums up the song and album in fewer words: *"The dance band played as the Titanic went down, and that's maybe what the world is about. Maybe music helps to camouflage the bad things and make things seem better than they really are, but in the end an iceberg is bound to come and cave us in."*

The song begins with what will be the chorus, and references the famous song that the band were reputedly playing as the ship sank (although some eyewitness accounts claim it was the hymn 'Autumn'). But already Harry has set the tone for the song with a casual but caustic remark.

We then follow the ship's journey, a ship so modern and so huge that it has been dubbed "unsinkable." The key line here is *"Even God couldn't sink this ship,"* as it shows the kind of attitude people can adopt when everything around them is going okay, so blasé about the potential problems there might be. The ship is now three days out at sea, and the band is playing, drowning out the sounds of danger ahead. Unlike the ship's band, which consisted of violins, cellos, bass and piano, Harry sees it more as a kind of jazz club band, with the narrator being a guitarist. As disaster strikes in the night the lifeboats are ordered filled, with the captain finding it hard to believe what has befallen

217

his ship. Even the ship's chaplain, the one person who should instill some hope and faith in the passengers, becomes a victim to Harry's sardonic wit. The chaplain has taken the role of the first-class passengers. As the lifeboats are filled and pull away, the band remains on board, resigning themselves to the fact that they now have a new onlooker. As the end is near, it seems just the band and the radio operator remain on board, tapping out a message to the only person who can save them now. The chorus is then repeated until it fades out, voices sounding like those of drowning men as the ship disappears beneath the waves...

For the title track Harry and Steve bring in extra session musicians for the recording, with Steve Gadd on drums, Neil Jason on bass guitar, Buzz Brauner on tenor sax, and Harry DiVito on trombone. Backing singers on the track consist of Jeff Gross, Mike Solomon, and Barbara Lindquist.

From the cheap seats
Jason Colannino - *Not so long ago in a Galaxy not so far away there was a time where music reflected what was going on in society. Harry said often that if you wanted to know what was really going on in the country you would listen to The Beatles, Bob Dylan or Pete Seeger. Nowadays music is a way to forget about what's really happening as the iceberg punches a hole into the hull of our country.*

Patricia LoTurco - *I interpreted it as Harry's message to the world about the state of affairs and how music is a reflection of the times.*

Why Should People Stay the Same? ***
With the opening song setting the scene, what follows are kind of vignettes of what could be looked on as individual passengers and their stories. In this song Harry is showing his insecurity over his relationship with Sandy and how his past behavior has jeopardized their marriage, very much like the sentiments in **'Star Tripper'** on the *Portrait Gallery* album. Doug Walker is given the chance to play bass guitar.

My Old Lady **
A song originally recorded for the *On the Road to Kingdom Come* album, this is a tongue-in-cheek look at feminist one-upwomanship. The narrator is the male chauvinist pig here. One reviewer writes: *"The MCP (Male Chauvinist Pig) of this song is befuddled: 'You see, my old lady took herself a young man last night / It got me crazy when she said Baby don't you get uptight.' The humor is self-directed, and the self-mocking tone is further captured by the funky sound - kind of a cross between a jug band and a calliope. The result, musically, is a clownish indignation; and the irony is complete."* The humor of the song is indeed self-directed. The narrator's wife has found herself a younger man, and despite his own infidelity (at least inside

218

his head), he sees it as a challenge to his image of how a good woman should behave. It is released as a unsuccessful single backed with '**I Do It For You Jane**'.

We Grew Up a Little Bit ****
Much like a prequel to '**Halfway To Heaven**' on *Verities & Balderdash*, this is another story of a fragile marriage on the verge of break-up, but with the workaholic husband telling his neglected and almost forgotten wife that they should learn from the past to save their future. In eight verses he picks through the bones of their relationship in a desperate attempt to keep their marriage alive. The husband is the narrator and it begins with a premature baby, maybe forcing their marriage, and his young bride is left alone day and night to care for the child as he pursues an education to further his career. All the time it means they have both to adjust to the changes that are beginning to put a strain on their relationship (strains of '**Cat's in the Cradle**', perhaps). As his career as an electrical engineer takes off, they buy a new house in Shaker Heights (a suburb of Cleveland, Ohio), have more children, and perhaps spend more money than they can afford. The years go by and both become frustrated, he with his job and she with her domestic solitude. But things now change. They begin to socialize separately, and he becomes suspicious of her apparent flirting. The conversations dry up and he hides behind a veil of infidelity as they both look to alcohol for answers. Events now conspire to bring it all to a head, with heated words, and a regrettable act of violence. But it's not the end, and as they sit together and talk things over, he ponders what must be done to save their marriage.

Session man Elliot Randall plays acoustic guitar. Harry also recorded an engaging slow version of the song with slightly different lyrics, including having the town of Pleasantville substituting for Shaker Heights.

Bluesman ***
Inspired by the time Harry had traveled up to Harlem with Tom to learn blues guitar from the blind but energetic Reverend Gary Davis. For the song he has a Brooklyn medical student ("the kid") who hops on a Greyhound bus bound for Alabama in the hope of being taught blues guitar by an aging (nameless) father of American Blues. Through an engaging dialogue between the kid (Harry) and the bluesman, voiced by Big John, along with some interesting instrumental interplay, the result is a bouncy blues-flavored song with nice guitar licks from Doug Walker, and with Tom Chapin on hand to play acoustic guitar. Harry also makes reference to the subject in '**There Only Was One Choice**'.

219

Country Dreams *****

When you thought that a motel owner, the subject of **'Vacancy'**, was a touch random for subject matter, Harry now writes about the tribulations of another seemingly mundane occupation - that of a realtor. Here the narrator slips into the shoes of a hard-working man who hates his job working for the Pocono Land Development Company (selling real estate in the Pocono Mountains region of Pennsylvania, *"just two hours from New York City"*). He is phoning his wife and trying to convince her that at least the job is paying the bills. The chorus takes the form of his usual sales pitch, one he knows by heart. But the lifestyle he has for sale is also the very thing that he has a dream to achieve for his family, a dream both he and his wife have shared since their time together at college. He is now selling their dream to someone else, a fading dream that is beyond their financial means. Coming to terms with his lot, he resigns himself to the fact that their dream will never be realized and sees the irony of it all. But he tells his wife not to give up, he'll make sure it will all work out in the end...

Steve Chapin must take a lot of credit here for its wonderful sing-along track, bouncy musical intro, and perhaps the best melodic chorus since **'Cat's in the Cradle'**. Unlike the similar subject matter of **'Vacancy'** on *Verities & Balderdash*, it does not portray the abject loneliness felt by the motel owner in his sad little world. Instead, the realtor here is in constant touch with his dream of a better life, but unable to grab it with both hands. He's doing the best he can, he just needs a little more time. One newspaper review describes the song as follows: *"It examines how our dreams have a way of dissipating like so much dust. Here the fictional dream was simple – like a contented life in the country with his loved ones. The problem with 'Country Dreams', however, is Chapin's unwillingness to let the song be general. Chapin hammers out the theme, making it rigid and as a result he leaves the listener's imagination out in the cold."*

I Do It For You, Jane ****

During Harry's association with Management Three, he is asked by company boss Jerry Weintraub to write a song for his wife Jane, a former singer, in what appears to be a troubled marriage. The result is another fine love song, perhaps Harry's first and only one written to order. Supplied with some background information, Harry comes up with a lyrical gem. Chosen as the flip-side to the single **'My Old Lady'**.

I Wonder What Happened To Him *****

A heartfelt, bittersweet plunge into despair, with simple and straightforward lyrics and oozing with emotion. Without doubt one of Harry's finest ballads and, despite the mammoth production values evident in many of the meatier songs found here, this gentle paean to insecurity is the most

220

compelling song on the album. One critic dubs it *"a neurotic's neurotic love song,"* and it's hard to disagree. With Harry's acoustic guitar, along with cello and violins conducted by concertmaster Guy Lumia, the narrator in the song is asking his girl about her past romances, and how long it will be before he too becomes her past. A fictional tale, maybe, but this is wholly based on Harry's own insecurity over whether Sandy's ex-husband Jim Cashmore still figures in her life, perhaps brought about by her never talking about him, almost erasing him from her mind. But it's more than that, it shows how deeply in love he is with Sandy, and that to lose her now will be too hard for him to accept. The song is chosen as the ideal flip-side to the **'Dance Band on the Titanic'** single release.

From the cheap seats
Carlton Anderson - *My favorite Chapin song of them all. Such a longing in his heart to fully understand this woman, "that drawer of your old photographs sits there like detective's leads, and that packet full of letters that I do not dare to read. And then there is that negligee that was made for candlelight. You know I've never seen you wear it. Was it used on 'other' nights,"* but ultimately a legitimate fear, *"will I too disappear like I've never ever been?"*

Paint a Picture of Yourself (Michael) **
Song inspired by Harry's uncle Michael Burke, son of Kenneth, who will go down in history as the person credited for getting Harry, Tom and Steve into music. When Harry is just 15 years old, his 18-year old uncle gives him a store-bought cheap guitar, and the rest, as they say, is history. But Michael is very much like Harry, never quite knowing which career path to follow, and in the song Harry takes a nostalgic and light-hearted look back at that earlier time. Debuting the song at a concert in Chicago in 1977 Harry tells the audience about his uncle: *"Every time he gets good at something, he changes. For example, he went to Harvard in architecture, graduated. For three years started a brilliant career. Just about the time things were going well, he quit. Then he started tracking satellites for the Smithsonian Institute in Hawaii, then quit. Then he got married, got good at that, quit, and now after another five careers, he's finally become an artist, and I asked him to do the cover of the* **On the Road to Kingdom Come** *album, which he did."* Tom Chapin provides additional vocals on the track, and Elliot Randall once again plays acoustic guitar.

Mismatch *****
A song that could have been written about Clare MacIntyre, the **'Taxi'** girl, but in hindsight is probably not. Reminiscing about his late teens, Harry often relates in concert about how he is attracted to the untouchable girls from

221

affluent Scarsdale, New York, seemingly a world away from those in his own Brooklyn neighborhood. At the Bottom Line concert in New York in January 1981, with much ribbing from Big John, he introduces the song as follows:

"The girls of Scarsdale New York seemed to have all the magical, mystical qualities that I did not have and knew I never would have. But somehow, they seemed so beautiful, so sophisticated, so worldly, so stimulating, and most of all, sadly enough, completely unavailable. But still I fantasied... And then the summer of my 19th year, after finishing my first full year at Cornell University, I was working in the construction industry for the summer. All of a sudden as I was working, there she was, and she was from Scarsdale, and she was beautiful, and she was stimulating, and she was lovely, and worldly, and charming. Most of all, thank God, completely available. So anyway, the sad truth is that real-life things don't often turn out the way you had hoped, and indeed, that was the case this particular summer, and I wrote a song about our experience."

In the song the mismatch could not be more apparent, as we find the narrator, an out-and-out sentimentalist, married to what can only be described as a sadomasochistic woman. It may at first come across as quite shocking, but the song's warm tenderness transcends any cause for ridicule, and we are left with what is just a sad and tender love song.

Mercenaries *****

As Harry would say it, a song about *"the two oldest professions in the world."* In April 1977 the band play at the Paradiso Club in Amsterdam and following the performance take time to visit the infamous but popular red-light district in the early hours of the morning. Apart from the obvious, Harry also sees groups of soldiers and sailors there, and thinks of the juxtaposition of these two old professions. The following month the band play in San Diego, home of the US Navy's Pacific fleet, and once again it triggers in Harry's mind the psychological questions about war, violence, and the love and war between the sexes. The story takes place in an unnamed war zone with a soldier on leave - a mercenary with a back pocket full of *"blood money"* - roaming the seedy streets of a town one night, and looking for sexual pleasure as a brief respite for what he has just been through and what he is yet to face:

It's a slow-motion night in the hot city lights
Past time when the good folks are snoring in bed
On a loose-jointed cruise to recolor your blues
With illegal notions alive, alive in your head

You are back from some war that you've been fighting for
Some old blue blood bastard in a dark pinstripe suit

222

and the word from your loins has your mind in your groin
And your back pocket burning with blood, blood money loot

Along the way he witnesses some unpleasant, even sickening, sights that must abhor him, but at the same time still having those *"illegal notions"* on his mind.

So, you walk past the glow of the flicker-picture shows
Where the raincoat men wait for a child to come by
And the women in doorways who have nothing to say
'Cause your money is talking to the ones that you would try

He visits a brothel and pays to have sex with a prostitute, and for a fleeting moment he remembers what it's like to feel the warmth and tenderness of a woman, albeit a woman of the night.

She owns the block with the dead pawnshop clock
She's the answer to dreams that you pay to come true
She's got no heart of gold, but that's not what she's sold,
She just sees herself doing what she, what she has to do

And she's all that you're hoping as her coat falls open
Give her bread, she leads you to a bed on the floor
Where for ten million years and through ten billion tears
The armies of bootmen have marched back from their wars

She's in that state of grace before time finds her face
With a mind of old wisdoms and a body still young
And she tastes as sweet as a child's chocolate
Before the butts and the whiskey had wasted the taste of your tongue

Play the music again of the grey-stubble men
That groaning blue symphony moans evermore
And you watch as she fakes it, and of course you just take it
She's better than others you never paid money for.

But it is all too fleeting, and he finds himself out of there, with the woman waiting for her next customer to come along. Harry's lyrics highlight the cold reality of what has just transpired:

You've used up your booty, the girl's done her duty
The turnstile has turned and you learn you are done

223

You're back on the street joining fresh marching feet
You see more soldiers coming, and your girl chooses one

Soon, he's back on the firing line, taking the customary precautions, and joking with others about his experience. But maybe his joking is a rather thin disguise for how he really sees the parallels in their two professions. In his dreams, he wonders what it would be like for soldiers like him to be like that woman, and having love, not fighting, as their trade:

And the medic has brought shots for what you have caught
Your leave is all over, you're back on the line
And you joke in the trenches of the hot-blooded wenches
And the things that you'll do when they next give you the time.

And you're back in your army, back shedding red blood
And you dream of the girl as you sleep in the mud
And you know you'd swap with her, if the deal could be made
'Cause you'd rather be working at love,
Love as your trade

Do we look on the woman as being a mercenary too? We know nothing about her apart from what she does; not why she does it, or what circumstances have placed her here. We would like to think that the money she receives is hers to keep, but the sad reality is that it probably isn't, and that, like so many, she is just being used as a sex slave, a commodity, and being forced into doing this by some heavy-handed employer with ugly threats hanging over her head if she fails to comply. Mercenaries have a choice in what they do. Maybe this soldier who looks on *"love as a trade"* has no conception of what in sad reality is something in which some women have no choice.

From the cheap seats
Tony Bentivegna - *Harry's great 'War Is Hell' song... You can tell they spent a lot of time polishing the songs.*

Manhood ***
A song about the shifting poles between adolescence and adulthood, much in the same vein as **'Babysitter'** on the *Portrait Gallery* album. The narrator here is a young man having his first sexual encounter with a woman who has much more experience, and although afterwards he is keen to start again, she simply tells him: *"You know, you never can."*

One Light in a Dark Valley (An Imitation Spiritual) **

In tribute to his maternal grandfather Kenneth Burke, the literary theorist, poet and novelist, Harry sings one of his compositions.

There Only Was One Choice *****

Bookending the album after eleven or so character studies, we return to Harry himself, and a wonderful autobiographical look back at his career, life-choices, the aging process, the music industry, and his ongoing frustration with what he sees as an apathetic country selling out its soul. Arguably considered his pièce de résistance, just the sheer complexity of its composition make it stand head and shoulders above all that's gone before. This is Harry showboating his lyrical craft to the extent that it can justifiably be called art. With its sudden and unexpected changes in tempo and melody, it's like listening to fragments of different songs cobbled together, songs within a song, and because of that, it shouldn't work on so many levels, but it actually does, and it's all down to Harry and his brother Steve - one, the master wordsmith and imagery maker, and the other, a producer and arranger rising to the occasion and getting the very best from what is basically just Harry's band, with no session musicians in sight, apart from the wonderful Pittsburgh Memorial Choir providing those angelic backing vocals. The lyrics are said to have been written down in a notebook over the best part of a year, with Harry revisiting them from time to time, picking up inspiration from the ever-changing political and social landscape. Analyzing those lyrics has always been as mind blowing as watching him perform them in concert, and they are open to various interpretations. This one has had wordsmiths scrambling through their lexicons and thesauruses for many years, but without Harry here to explain, we are left to decide for ourselves to see what may be lurking between those cryptic lines. I'm sure Harry will be laughing now at the very thought of it.

For an appraisal of the lyrics I also have to thank fellow Chapin fan Gerry Naughton for his invaluable insight.

In the opening verses we hear from the narrator describing in the third person how he becomes a singer, learning to play guitar at an early age, and being influenced by artists such as Guthrie, Seeger, the Beatles, the Rolling Stones, and Dylan. He also makes reference to the time he learns "a little black and blues" from the old Reverend Gary Davis, the Bluesman himself:

There's a kid out on my corner, hear him strumming like a fool
Shivering in his dungarees, but still he's going to school
His cheeks are made of peach fuzz - his hopes may be the same
But he's signed up as a soldier out to play the music game

225

There are fake patches on his jacket - he's used bleach to fade his jeans
With a brand-new stay pressed shirt - and some creased and wrinkled dreams
His face a blemish garden - but his eyes are virgin clear
His voice is Chicken Little's - But he's hearing Paul Revere

When he catches himself giggling - he forces up a sneer
Though he'd rather have a milk shake - he keeps forcing down the beer
Just another folkie - late in coming down the pike
Riding his guitar - he left Kid brother with his bike

And he's got Guthrie running in his bones
He's the hobo kid who's left his home
And his Beatles records and the Rolling Stones
This boy is staying acoustic

There's Seeger singing in his heart
He hopes his songs will somehow start
To heal the cracks that split apart
America gone plastic

And now there's Dylan dripping from his mouth
He's hitching himself way down south
To learn a little black and blues
From old street men who paid their dues
'Cause they knew they had nothing to lose
They knew it, so they just got to it

With cracked old Gibsons and red clay shoes
Playing 1-4-5 chords like good news
And cursed with skin that calls for blood
They put their face and feet in mud
But oh they learned the music from way down there
The real ones learn it somewhere

The verse that follows will be repeated at the end of the song:

Ah, strum your guitar - sing it kid
Just write about your feelings - not the things you never did
Inexperience - it once had cursed me
But your youth is no handicap - it's what makes you thirsty
Hey, kid

226

In the next couple of verses, the narrator has a stab at the current music industry, which he sees as being a cultural problem: the music moguls and the instant stars they create now churning out lucrative disco and pop dross to the masses, living their lives of limousines and Lear jets, so unlike the 60s, when music identified with the country's social and political issues.

You know you can hear your footsteps as you're kicking up the dust
And the rustling in the shadows tells you secrets you can trust
The capturing of whispers is the way to write a song
It's when you get to microphones the music can go wrong

You can't see the audience with spotlights in your eyes
Your feet can't feel the highway from where the Lear jet flies
When you glide in silent splendor in your padded limousines
Only you are crying there behind the silver screen
Now you battle dragons - but they'll all turn into frogs
When you grab the wheel of fortune - you get caught up in the cogs

He then derides the music critics - the *"jackals"* - who thrive on seeing artists who write meaningful songs have their careers falter, while at the same time showering plaudits on those instant pop stars making fast bucks for their respective labels:

First your art turns into craft - then the yahoos start to laugh
Then you'll hear the jackals howl 'cause they love to watch the fall
They're the lost ones out there feeding on the wounded and the bleeding
They always are the first to see the cracks upon the walls

Following these few verses of reflection, the narrator now switches to first-person as he views the aging process in what becomes chillingly prophetic for the listener. Predicting his own death will come soon, he emulates his hero Phil Ochs's own prophetic song, 'When I'm Gone'.

When I started this song I was still thirty-three
The age that Mozart died and sweet Jesus was set free
Keats and Shelley too soon finished, Charley Parker would be
And I fantasized some tragedy'd be soon curtailing me

Well just today I had my birthday - I made it thirty-four
Mere mortal, not immortal, not star-crossed anymore
I've got this problem with my aging I no longer can ignore
A tame and toothless tabby can't produce a lion's roar

227

His mind is plagued by his lack of chart success and the fears of the music industry going into a recession, and that time is quickly running out for him to make his mark and have an impact on political and social issues that concern him the most:

And I can't help being frightened on these midnight afternoons
When I ask the loaded questions - Why does winter come so soon?
And where are all the golden girls that I was singing for
The daybreak chorus of my dreams serenades no more

Yeah, the minute man is going soft - the mirror's on the shelf
Only when the truth's up there - can you fool yourself
I am the aged jester - who won't gracefully retire
A clumsy clown without a net caught staggering on the high wire

With that, we now have an abrupt change in the tempo as the narrator reflects on the reasons which made him love his country:

Hello my Country
I once came to tell everyone your story
Your passion was my poetry
And your past my most potent glory
Your promise was my prayer
Your hypocrisy my nightmare
And your problems fill my present
Are we both going somewhere?

But now he vents his anger, and like a carnival barker, uses his country's Bicentennial Year to hammer home his thoughts on its failures. The dog food reference comes from a government statistic that claims a quarter of all dog and cat food sold in the US is bought by old people to feed themselves and that some 25 million Americans, mainly children, go to bed hungry. The *"pirates"* are the propagandists - the lying moguls and politicians who never fulfill their promises. *"While blood's the only language"* is a reference to the overseas conflicts brought about by the country's foreign policy rather than dealing with social matters at home.

Step right up young lady - Your two hundred birthdays make you old if not senile
And we see the symptoms there in your rigor mortis smile
With your old folks eating dog food and your children eating paint
While the pirates own the flag and sell us sermons on restraint

228

And while blood's the only language that your deaf old ears can hear
And still you will not answer with that message coming clear
Does it mean there's no more ripples in your tired old glory stream
And the buzzards own the carcass of your dream?

The flow of the lyrics suddenly becomes unhinged, maybe not all that unexpected in one of Harry's songs, but for a fleeting second, we are not sure what we are listening to. Actually, *"B.U.Y Centennial"* is a subtle hint at the commercialism that's eroding America's old-fashioned values, while *"American Perennial"* refers to the ongoing problem of politicians and others putting self-interests first.

B*U*Y Centennial
Sell 'em pre-canned laughter
American Perennial
Sing happy ever after

Then it seems we have been taken back to the beginning of the album with a blast of the familiar chorus from the song **'Dance Band on the Titanic'**, but nevertheless a brief statement of the dangers that society faces when the rich are getting richer and the poor remaining poor. But, of course, we've heard this all before....

There's a Dance Band on the Titanic
Singing Nearer My God to Thee
And the iceberg's on the starboard bow
Won't you dance with me

The narrator now focuses on the false hopes and propaganda dominating the media:

Yes, I read it in the New York Times
That was on the stands today
It said that dreams were out of fashion
We'll hear no more empty promises
There'll be no more wasted passions
To clutter up our play

It really was a good sign
The words went on to say
It shows that we are growing up
In oh so many healthy ways

229

And I told myself this is
Exactly where I'm at
But I don't much like thinking about that

But his conscience suddenly begins to ask him questions, dismantling the propaganda machine:

Harry - are you really so naive
You can honestly believe
That the country's getting better
When all you do is let her alone

Harry - Can you really be surprised
When it's there before your eyes
When you hold the knife that carves her
You live the life that starves her to the bone

In the next four verses the narrator is angrily calling for action - it's not good enough to dream of a better world in our sleep; where is the help and support when he feels alone with his overwhelming sense of responsibility?

Good dreams don't come cheap
You've got to pay for them
If you just dream when you're asleep
There is no way for them
To come alive, to survive

It's not enough to listen - it's not enough to see
When the hurricane is coming on it's not enough to flee
It's not enough to be in love - we hide behind that word
It's not enough to be alive when your future's been deferred

What I've run through my body, what I've run through my mind
My breath's the only rhythm - and the tempo is my time
My enemy is hopelessness - my ally honest doubt
The answer is a question that I never will find out

He questions his own self-evaluation, whether he should sacrifice his music career and give in to the lure of populism. How do his priorities with his music career and tireless campaigning affect his marriage and family life? Is it all worthwhile?

Is music propaganda - should I boogie, Rock and Roll
Or just an early warning system hitched up to my soul
Am I observer or participant or huckster of belief
Making too much of a life so mercifully brief?

But in that evaluation, he knows his place. He realizes that his life and career have made a difference and has used his craft to benefit so many good causes, unlike what was being said in the boardrooms:

So, I stride down sunny streets and the band plays back my song
They're applauding at my shadow long after I am gone
Should I hold this wistful notion that the journey is worthwhile
Or tiptoe cross the chasm with a song and a smile

Well I got up this morning - I don't need to know no more
It evaporated nightmares that had boiled the night before
With every new day's dawning my kid climbs in my bed
And tells the cynics of the board room your language is dead

Despite all this despair Harry is satisfied that he has made the right choice in following a musical career and not selling out to pop stardom. He could have been many things – pilot, film-maker, architect, even a politician – but in the end there was only one choice, and it's a gift and legacy that he can pass on to his children, telling them they should write about their feelings and not let inexperience deny the learning of the craft:

And as I wander with my music through the jungles of despair
My kid will learn guitar and find his street corner somewhere
There he'll make the silence listen to the dream behind the voice
And show his minstrel Hamlet daddy that there only was one choice

Strum your guitar - sing it kid
Just write about your feelings - not the things you never did
Inexperience - it once had cursed me
But your youth is no handicap - it's what makes you thirsty, hey kid
Strum your guitar - sing it kid
Just write about your feelings - not the things you never did

One reviewer comments on the song: *"At the album's end, in the explicitly autobiographical 'There Only was One Choice', the underlying themes of ambivalence and self-doubt about career and life choices reach their climax. It's a lament for the loss of youthful idealism and for the compromises one is forced to make as success comes into conflict with a preferred lifestyle. But*

231

the song ends with a realization that after all, there was only one choice - one that had to be made - and it suggests that through the next generation the cyclical pattern of life and life's choices will continue."

From the cheap seats
David Wollman - *Good dreams don't come cheap. You have to pay for them. If you just dream when you're asleep there is no way for them to come alive to survive.*

Steve Baratta - *At a concert in Chicago, Harry said they were going to do one more song then take an intermission. Some people went out to beat the crowd for refreshments or for the restroom. They came back to find this song still being played.*

Europe Once More

Touring from one side of the country to the other continues. On July 24th the band play Warwick Music Theater in Rhode Island with the following impressive setlist: And The Baby Never Cries, Corey's Coming, Dirty Old Man, Babysitter, 30,000 Pounds of Bananas, Dance Band on the Titanic, Circle, Six String Orchestra, Cat's in the Cradle, Taxi, If My Mary Were Here, Better Place To Be, Bluesman, Horniest Rock Drummer (Howie), Blow Up Woman (Doug), Mercenaries, My Old Lady, W.O.L.D., Mismatch, Odd Job Man, Tangled Up Puppet, Dogtown.
    Following dates in Chicago and St Paul, Harry flies to Los Angeles to appear one more time on *The Tonight Show with Johnny Carson*, where he performs **'Bluesman'** and **'I Wonder What Happened To Him'** for guest host Gabe Kaplin. The following day, August 11th, he takes the band into a studio to tape a short interview with BBC radio presenter "Whispering" Bob Harris and perform **'Dance Band'** and **'Mercenaries'** for a later showing on Britain's long-running music show *The Old Grey Whistle Test* (so-called from an old Tin Pan Alley phrase, when first pressings of records were heard by the doormen - "the old greys" - and if they were heard whistling the tune the next day, it had passed the "whistle test" and was a sign of being a success). It is aired in Britain on October 4th. Three decades later the clip of **'Mercenaries'** will resurface in the archive series *Singer Songwriters* at the BBC.
    Following two shows at Los Angeles' Greek Theater, Harry and the band return east to play two shows in Connecticut and two in Holmdel, New York, before embarking in early September for a nine-day tour of England and Ireland. On the 3rd they perform an impressive setlist to a sell-out audience at London's Rainbow Theatre, including blistering performances in a show that's also recorded for the *King Biscuit* radio program. The whole set is as follows: I Wonder What Happened To Him, Mercenaries, My Old Lady, Mr

Tanner, W.O.L.D., Halfway To Heaven, I Wanna Learn a Love Song, Tangled Up Puppet, Taxi, Sniper, There Only Was One Choice, Cat's in the Cradle, Bluesman, Odd Job Man, Dogtown, Mail Order Annie, Let Time Go Highly (Steve), 30,000 Pounds of Bananas, Dance Band on the Titanic, Circle.

Angie Errigo of the *New Musical Express* is there to see the performance and writes her review on the 10th that Harry is *"so overwhelmingly American in that open, larger than life, 'concerned' sort of way that he is predictably big in the States with moderately hip, middle class, liberal-thinking, sort of sensitive and aware 25-35 year olds. Yet he went down a storm with a full house of people to whom I would have thought both the material and the approach was alien... He comes across as one hell of a nice man."*

Although not too impressed by the set as a whole, Errigo goes on to say that, *"sometimes others, such as the sad 'Taxi'...and the very chilling 'Sniper' are very real, articulate and dramatic portraits ... I'm not putting down Harry Chapin at all, honest. He does what he does with charm and strength and obviously strikes a chord of recognition in his fans. It was just uncannily like walking into the wrong party, that's all...or waking up in the wrong country."*

The tour continues with shows in Manchester, Dublin, Belfast, Sheffield, Southport, and Glasgow, before culminating in Newcastle on September 11th, the day after the album *Dance Band on the Titanic* is finally released. Within a month it peaks at #58 on the *Billboard* 200 chart, not at all impressive, but a definite improvement on recent albums. It will go on to sell half a million copies and be certified gold. Elektra also put out a single that month, with the album's title track backed with **'I Wonder What Happened To Him'**, but despite all the advance promotional work it fails to chart. What Harry considers is his best work to date is not resulting in the sales numbers he anticipates.

Harry loves the British audiences, but not as much as he loves the British music press. On the day of the album's release, and following Harry's performance at the Rainbow Theatre in London, *Melody Maker* gives its review: *"He has become a star and deservedly so, with little of the media hype that has managed to pack our major concert halls. He has done it. Let it be said, on his talent alone...Success has not spoiled either Chapin or the band, though it has made them both a hundred times more powerful than they ever used to be. At times, the sheer confidence radiating from the stage becomes just a mite too powerful, and one has the impression that he could sing the telephone directory right now and get away with it. This is a dangerous position for an artist to be in, though naturally he's got to ride the wave while it's in flood. There were one or two danger signs on Saturday: a tendency to oversell the songs so that his voice grew well-nigh incomprehensible, occasional weaknesses creeping into the lyrics, and tunes reminiscent of past successes. But the best of his new songs are the best he has written..."*

233

The following month brings another positive review: *"Chapin's music can't be pigeonholed so easily. Though he does have a predictable element, it is less in his music and lyrics and more in the form his artistic expression takes...With the material from this album added to his repertoire, Chapin in concert can only be better."*

But not all British critics are warming to Harry: *"I really can't make my mind up about this guy Harry Chapin. On one level he is totally crass and on another he is totally brilliant... except being crass is Chapin's real strength. He inhabits a world of wives and kids and clean shirts and electricity bills and Sunday morning car cleaning. But he is anything but trite. He's a fatalist. He accepts the existence of pain. He realises the necessity of change."*

"The Best Job in the World"

Although the album may be looked upon as Harry's high-water mark, it seems lost in its decade, aching for a life outside of the pop-froth that's swamping the charts in the late 70s. No other album in Harry's career has received so much from the music press, nor has Harry conducted so many interviews explaining its concept. But on the whole reviewers on both sides of the Atlantic are warming to it. This is after all the double studio album he has craved since signing with Elektra, and the songs he considers among his finest work. Many fans as well as music commentators will look on the *Dance Band on the Titanic* as the dividing line between Harry's earlier work and what will come later. The remainder of September finds Harry and the band with concert dates in Florida, Louisiana, and the Midwest, as well as another performance for the cadets at the USAF Academy in Colorado Springs and at the famous Kiel Opera House in St Louis. The following month many of the concerts are held closer to home, with a string of performances in the New York area.

The final two months of the year see no let-up for the band, and include concerts throughout the country and also several more dates in Canada. Many of the bookings are for back-to-back shows, with eleven performances held in less than a week in the middle of December. They also make another appearance at the three-day Valley Forge Music Fair in Devon, Pennsylvania, where they are supported by singer-songwriter Karla Bonoff. On November 27th Harry holds a benefit for W.H.Y. at Fordham University in New York and the show is broadcast live on WNEW radio. The wonderfully long setlist is as follows: Dance Band On the Titanic, Babysitter, Mr Tanner, Paint a Picture of Yourself Michael, I Wonder What Happened To Him, W.O.L.D., It's Only Love (Tom), Crystal Green (Tom), Magic Man (Tom), We Grew Up a Little Bit, And the Baby Never Cries, Odd Job Man, Burning Herself, Let Time Go Lightly (Steve), Six String Orchestra, Taxi, Monday Sun Don't Shine (Tom), Saturday Morning (Tom), My Name is Morgan (But It Ain't

234

J.P.) (Tom & Doug), Make a Wish (Tom), Number One (Tom), Bluesman, Mail Order Annie, Love Is Not In Season (Steve), The Horniest Drummer (Howie), Blow Up Woman (Doug), 30,000 Pounds of Bananas, Taxi, Circle.

On December 20th Harry appears once more on *The Tonight Show with Johnny Carson* to perform **'Mismatch'** and **'Flowers in Red'**, and an impromptu rendition of '**Dirty Old Man'** while being interviewed by guest host John Davidson. On Boxing Day, BBC Radio 1 airs an interview that Harry recorded during his September visit to London with presenter Noel Edmonds, their very own "morning DJ" who in 1974 had plugged **'W.O.L.D.'** on his show and got it into the charts. In between playing a selection of his songs, Harry takes a philosophical look at his writing:

"I try to write songs where humanity is under stress. People have had their dreams and their expectations coming into conflict with realities and not necessarily all of them solving all of the problems that come up. All the people I write about are desperately questing towards life, just as I am. I have found some more socially acceptable ways of questing...I think all of us should be very hungry, very greedy, because the only thing we know for sure is that we're alive now and if we don't take it now we're going to lose out. I never want to be sixty-five and say 'I wish I had done this.' To me, that is the most sad admission any human being can make...The fact is, I've got the best job in the world and I'm frightened that someday somebody's gonna wake me up and say 'Harry we've found you out, you have to go and get a real job now.' Because I've got the best job. I make an awful lot of money. I have tremendous ego gratification from an awful lot of people. I define my own product. I'm not selling toilet paper that people wanted before. No one wanted Chapin music before I did it. I define the times I work, and I can do a tremendous amount of it, if I do a qualitative job, of seducing people with some of my ideas."

The BBC have come to see Harry as the consummate interviewee, and they invite him back in February 1981 for another chat with Edmonds, this time accompanied by young Jenny and Josh.

1977 has brought mixed fortunes for Harry. On the music side of his career, the reception for his new album has not been as positive as he anticipated, despite the quality of the songs and the promotional work involved. His fans even look on the album as a transitional triumph for him. Both personal and humanitarian goals have been achieved, the Presidential Commission seems to be on track, and he is honored as one of the Ten Outstanding Young Americans (TOYA) for "human improvement." Not only that, he also receives The Rockies' Public Service Award for the second year running, the Long Island Association's Man of the Year, the Junior Achievement of New York's Man of the Year, and finally an award presented on national television for outstanding public service at the 3rd Annual Rock Music Awards.

The following year will bring more changes and greater challenges.

235

Living Room Suite

"Millions of dollars have been raised for things I believe in. Telling stories of our time, building a lasting body of work, new songs, new records, new audiences, new challenges, and still that painfully exciting process of growth that can make one's life into a richly woven tapestry."

Plotkin and a Change in Style

January 1978 finds Harry split between spending more time with his family up at their new vacation home in Vermont, and down in New York recording songs for his next album, *Living Room Suite*. This time Harry will return to his family for inspiration, much like he did on *Portrait Gallery*. The children are growing up fast – Jono and Jason young teenagers, Jaime set to go to Hamilton College in the fall, and Jen and Josh going on seven and six respectively. There will be no long story songs, a first for Harry, but a collection of personal observations of parenthood with some advice for the future. His love for his wife and family has been fully restored, and from now on there will be no more wallowing in self-pity as some see all too evident on previous albums. Harry is a wiser and happier man now.

Thoroughly disappointed with Elektra's attitude toward *Dance Band*, which Harry considers his best work, he realizes that no matter what he comes up with next, they will treat it with the same disdain. This will be the last album of the ten-album deal, but it now seems that their relationship is close to breaking point. Elektra are again calling for a more professional producer on the new album. Although Harry is willing to let Steve continue the work successfully done on *Dance Band*, he agrees with his brother to call their bluff by letting them have their way. On Jon Landau's recommendation, and with Steve's agreement, Harry hires Chuck Plotkin, currently the head of A&R at Elektra, and who will later achieve great success working with Bruce Springsteen and Bob Dylan.

The first meeting Harry has with the new producer is during the first day of a vicious ice storm that will grip the northeastern states for days to come. Two days later Harry will perform an impromptu concert for hundreds of Huntington's displaced residents at the cot-filled YMCA hall. Plotkin is a visionary producer and aims to bring a fresh approach to the recording, with no lavish arrangements and fewer takes. Jack Malken, Michael Barry, Toby Scott, Jay Krugman, and Jim Niper will all have a share in the engineering. Steve Chapin will remain on hand as keyboard player and music arranger. As well as Harry's regular band being involved, Tom Chapin is invited to play most of the acoustic guitar parts to enable Harry to concentrate on his vocals.

236

Plotkin also brings in session guitarist Lou Volpe, drummers Andy Newmark and Jimmy Keltner, and Neil Jason on bass. He also introduces a horn section and even the services of esteemed vocal groups The Cowsills and the Dixie Hummingbirds to provide harmony vocals.

Recording is due to begin at the Secret Sound Studios in New York on January 15th but a power cut at Harry's house keeps him away, and the band are left to rehearse on their own. The following day, with Harry now in attendance, work begins on **'Flowers Are Red'**, **'Poor Damned Fool'** and **'Seasons & the Sky (So They Sail)'**, one of the songs left over from the *Dance Band* sessions. On the 17th vocals are tried out for **'I Wonder What Would Happen To This World'** and Plotkin decides to get Jim Keltner in for future recording, with Howie Fields moved over to percussion. Two more days are spent perfecting **'Poor Damned Fool'** and recording a final take of **'Seasons & the Sky'**. On the 21st **'Dancin' Boy'** and a basic track of **'I Wonder What Would Happen To This World'** are completed. On the 23rd work commences on **'Why Do Little Girls'** with session drummer Andy Newmark stepping in for Keltner, who has a prior arrangement, and the following day sees takes of **'It Seems You Only Love Me When It Rains'**. Over the next several days work is completed on **'Oh My Jenny'** and **'Somebody Said'**.

Harry sums up the last four years: *"This commitment to end world hunger, and my music and story songs, are ways of dealing with the world as I see it. I'm playing 200 concerts a year – half of them benefits – all of them attempts at getting across the footlights to people I would enjoy spending time with in non-concert situations. And over the past 4 years of musical fun, millions of dollars have been raised for things I believe in. Telling stories of our time, building a lasting body of work, new songs, new records, new audiences, new challenges, and still that painfully exciting process of growth that can make one's life into a richly woven tapestry."*

Meanwhile for Harry, early February brings a string of concerts in Ontario, interrupted by an appearance on the *Merv Griffin Show* on the 3rd, along with fellow guest, actor David Soul, who has himself been enjoying a brief but successful musical career. For the next two months Harry and the band appear at venues all across the Midwest and northeastern states. On April 1st they play two concerts at the Paramount Theater in Austin, Texas, before returning to the studio next day to do re-work on **'Flowers Are Red'**, only to fly out west again the following day to do a string of concerts in Arizona and Nevada, including one at the Aladdin Theater in Las Vegas. The remainder of April sees concerts at Long Beach and San Carlos in California, followed by their first-ever trip to Alaska, with shows in Anchorage and Fairbanks, before making another concert debut, this time in Honolulu on the 23rd. On April 6th *Rolling Stone*'s Dave Marsh, a longtime critic of Harry's music, writes an article about Harry's humanitarian work called 'Singing for the World's

237

Supper' and also notes Harry's conviction that the music industry and the music press have a dislike for him on account of his "sermonizing." May has a full program of concerts across the country, stretching from Florida to Virginia. On May 13th at the Fox Theater in Atlanta, the band perform another fine setlist: Dancin' Boy, Flowers Are Red, Paint a Picture of Yourself Michael, Babysitter, Dreams Go By, Burning Herself, Better Place To Be, The Mayor of Candor Lied, Old Greasy Spoon, Star Tripper, They Call Her Easy, Halfway to Heaven, Love Is Not In Season (Steve), Sniper, W.O.L.D., Dirty Old Man, If My Mary Were Here, Caroline, Mr Tanner, I Wonder What Happened To Him, Tangled Up Puppet, Six String Orchestra, Taxi, Dance Band on the Titanic, Any Old Kind of Day, Jenny.

While Steve remains behind to assist in the mixing of the new album, Harry and Tom head off to Europe for their most extensive tour to date of Ireland and the UK, with concerts in Southport, Glasgow, Sheffield, Belfast, Dublin, Bradford, Newcastle, Manchester, London, Birmingham and finally Croydon. Returning to the States, on June 7th Harry performs a benefit with Joan Baez, Peter Yarrow and Holly Near at the Civic Center in Santa Monica. The remainder of the month finds the band doing another show in Toronto and three consecutive nights at the Oakdale Music Theatre in Wallingford, Connecticut.

After additional recording is carried out at the Sound Factory and Clover Studios in LA, as well as at the Record Plant in New York, and with final mixing completed at the LA studios by Plotkin, Niper and Thomas, the new album is considered complete. But not everyone will be happy. The album cover features a photograph by Reid Miles of Harry sitting on a cozy couch and playing his guitar with just a ginger cat for company, and surrounded by a random collection of living room-friendly ornaments, children's toys, umbrellas and crutches. A clock on the wall has the time 3.25. The back cover is of the same scene half an hour later, but with Harry now gone, leaving just the cat and guitar on the chair, and the clock now showing the time as 3.55. All symbolic perhaps. A lyric sheet is also included.

Living Room Suite (1978) ***
Elektra 6E-142
Recorded: Secret Sound Studios, New York Jan 1978
Additional recording by Jim Niper at Sound Factory, LA; Corky Stasiak & Jay Krugman at The Record Plant, New York, and Bobby Thomas at Clover Studios, LA
US Release Date: June 1978
Producer: Chuck Plotkin
Engineer: Jack Malken, Michael Barry, Toby Scott, Jay Krugman & Jim Niper

In the liner notes on the album, Harry explains: *"Webster's dictionary says, 'a SUITE is a series or a set.' The songs do seem to fit together in a way slightly different than any of the other eight albums. Maybe somewhat less story-oriented – though just as strongly felt. And yet the feeling of a LIVING ROOM is what we try to create when the group and I sing in the two hundred or so concerts we do each year."*

Dancin' Boy ***
Harry's song for his six-year-old son Josh is a seemingly happy ode to fatherhood and inspired by Josh's behavior when Harry is at home working on new songs. And of course that's Harry indulging himself on harmonica.

If You Want To Feel ****
Wonderful feel-good song that addresses the reluctance of a romantic partner to make a full commitment due to them being hurt by others in the past. Released as a single in June 1978 backed with **'I Wonder What Would Happen To This World'**. Among the session musicians are Ernie Watts on saxophone, oboe, clarinet and flute, and backing vocals are provided by The Cowsills.

Poor Damned Fool ***
A tribute to Sandy in one sense, but more about self-depreciating love and loosely based on Jim Cashmore, Sandy's ex-husband, who had died a few months earlier. Where **'I Wonder What Happened To Him'** was about Harry's insecurity brought about by his belief that his relationship with Sandy could go the same way it had done with Jim, this is the realization that Jim was a fool to let such a woman slip away. As he says in concert: *"As the years go by I'm more and more grateful he was such an idiot."* Often misquoted as "Poor Damn Fool."

I Wonder What Would Happen To This World ***
Harry's brief venture into gospel music, close to but not quite the real thing. Providing the inspirational backing vocals are The Dixie Hummingbirds and Joe Russell and Herbert Rhoad of The Persuasions. Chosen as the flip-side to the single **'If You Want To Feel'**, the song title is chosen for Harry's final epitaph.

Jenny ***
Harry's ode to his seven-year-old daughter, originally titled 'Oh My Jenny'. In Country-style fashion he admits to her he is still the **'Cat's in the Cradle'** father he promised not to be when he wrote that song about her younger brother Josh four years before. Full of apologies, he spells out what she really means to him and basically what an idiot he continues to be.

239

Unsuccessfully re-recorded by Harry in November for possible release as a single along with **'Flowers Are Red'**.

It Seems You Only Love Me When It Rains **
In a similar vein to **'If You Want to Feel'**, but with a slower tempo, the main character criticizes his partner for her defensiveness, alluding to the fact she has been burned before, while believing that she truly loves him because she's *"not afraid to hold the pain."*

Why Do Little Girls **
Another song inspired by daughter Jenny and an in-your-face lyrical reference to female discrimination in society and how it starts at an early age and by adulthood women are forced by culture into subordinate roles. A great chance for Harry to show off his banjo skills.

Flowers Are Red ****
One of Harry's most popular songs and a look at how conformity can crush creativity. Harry states in various interviews (and often in concert) that the inspiration for the song is a report card his secretary Susan Gensel shows him for her eldest "Huck Finn-type" son Robbie, which reads *"Robbie started the year marching to a different drummer, but he is gradually joining the parade."* The song, however, is partly inspired by a poem Sandy was given by a first-grade teacher who had received it from an education course instructor, saying how things should be done.

Perturbed at the blanket push for conformity without any attempt to understand or even encourage the young boy's obvious enthusiasm, Harry writes about a young artistic boy who is summarily punished for showing creativity and forced to conform. At the end of the song, just when it appears the boy may have found a more nurturing teacher after moving to a new town, we are left the sad reveal that the boy no longer wishes to pursue his individuality: he's been taught conformity at all costs and even with encouragement he simply follows the standard with no creativity.

In concert Chapin often adds as an ending, "there must be a way to help our children say..." and then repeats the seemingly happy chorus the boy echoes early in the song. No such happy ending here. Unfortunately, the subject matter is too serious to make it a chart hit when released in September with **'Why Do Little Girls'** as the flip-side. 13-year-old future actress Sarah Jessica Parker supplies uncredited vocals on the record.

From the cheap seats
Cliff Geismar - *The quintessential educational lesson. Harry reminded educators what we already know. Creativity should not be restricted or handicapped.*

240

Simone Moore - *Makes me cry every time I hear it because it is such a pervasive and negative part of the teaching environment and our society in general. Taught it to my kids and am proud to say they understood it and grew up to be able to express their creativity and individuality because of it!*

Deborah Miller Brenner - *The national anthem of every special education teacher and art teacher that ever was.*

Beth Waggenspack - *I typically use it when teaching. When students ask me about what they can write for a final project in Communication and Gender, I tell them exactly those lines.*

Lucy Lambert - *A great comment on the educational system, teaching to tests, no individuality. I remember subbing in a kindergarten class and bringing the whole class to the window to see how many colors of green we could see. I was channeling Harry at the time for sure.*

Somebody Said **

Uptempo song of social commentary about the direction of American music and a derivative of the **'Dance Band'** theme. It is a tale of a disenfranchised character struggling to believe in good, seeing too much selfishness and greed, and worrying about the drift toward being left isolated by society.

Another Chart Failure

The album is another relative failure, peaking at #133 in the *Billboard* 100 chart at the end of July. Two unsuccessful singles are finally issued, with **'If You Want To Feel'** released in June, and **'Flowers Are Red'** held back until September. The album will eventually go on to sell some 350,000 copies, equaling the sales of *Sniper*, *Portrait Gallery* and *Legends of the Lost and Found*. The main reason is that most of the songs just don't have that emotional connection with the listener. Although the lyrics are certainly not among Harry's finest, the main problem lies with the music and Plotkin's slaphazard production. The end result is clearly not what Harry or Elektra have in mind from the so-called "big-gun" producer they thought they had found in Plotkin. In fact, on June 21st, just days after the album's first pressing is released, Harry is back in the New York studio to spend several more days trying to re-record **'Flowers Are Red'** and **'Jenny'**, but it doesn't work out. Within days of the album's release Plotkin has left Elektra, leaving behind him what some critics consider one of the worst albums of the year. Harry now seriously considers his future with the label. This has been a great blow to him, and as the *Dance Band* album was considered his artistic comeback, to have it followed with what is not just a commercial failure, but with production shortcomings as well, is a bitter pill to swallow.

Rolling Stone has mixed feelings on the album but sees that its virtues lie in Harry for once coming down from his pulpit to bring an intimacy to the songs. Otherwise, his *"grandiose showmanship"* often returns to drown out any well-meaning sentiments. On June 10th, *Melody Maker* strikes another blow when reviewing Harry's recent concert at London's Rainbow Theatre:

"Harry Chapin occupies a highly individual niche in the singer-songwriter league, and there has always been something penetrating and vital about all of his work, on the nine albums he has made. But at the Rainbow, London, last Wednesday, a disturbing tendency to talk far too much between songs, to virtually lecture the audience on his admirable new cause (world hunger) and a trend towards maudlin new songs about his children marred Harry's hitherto articulate material. On stage he resembles a campfire entertainer who looks and dresses as if he's entertaining the troops; but his songs are much too personalised, invariably aimed at real people who have marked his life, for him to be considered extrovert...Harry finds it hard to get away from sentimentality to make his marks. As if to demonstrate his self-consciousness, Chapin seemed to feel it necessary to explain his raison d'être for every song with a long preamble. Occasionally, of course, this is fine – but overdone, it tends to be a bore. The songs should stand up on their own...Summing up, it's impossible not to warm to Chapin, but there seemed real dangers last week that the man may stray too far from making the incisive points that have marked his best works. Let's hope not..."

With promotion for the new album almost non-existent, the touring commences in earnest. By the end of July Harry and the band return to the West Coast for dates at the Greek Theater in LA and an appearance on *The Tonight Show with Johnny Carson*, hosted by Bob Newhart, in which he performs **'Poor Damned Fool'** and **'Tangled Up Puppet'**. This is followed by an outdoor concert at San Diego University before returning east to perform in a string of summer music festivals, beginning with the four-day Westbury Music Theater in New York, followed with the two-day Temple Music Festival in Ambler, Pennsylvania, before attending the annual Mississippi River Festival at the Southern Illinois University in Edwardsville. Fortunately for Sandy and the family, the remainder of the month involves concerts closer to home. On August 17th Harry stages a benefit performance at the Merriwhether Post Pavilion in Columbia, Maryland, in aid of the Food Policy Center, and it is attended by a host of friends and officials, there to celebrate the creation of the Presidential Commission. The touring continues throughout August, including two shows at the Cape Cod Melody Tent in Hyannis, Massachusetts, and a return appearance at the Dr Pepper Summer Music Festival in Central Park on the 23rd, which is recorded on WNEW radio, and features a rare live performance of **'Bummer'**. The full setlist is as follows: Shooting Star, If You Want to Feel, W.O.L.D., Poor Damned Fool, I Wanna Learn a Love Song, Flowers Are Red, Bummer, Cat's in the Cradle, Love Is

Not In Season (Steve), Tangled Up Puppet, Why Do Little Girls, Mr Tanner, They Call Her Easy, Halfway to Heaven, Caroline, My Old Lady, Better Place To Be, Bluesman, 30,000 Pounds of Bananas, Circle. Also, that month, they play two shows at the Grand Opera House in Wilmington, Delaware.

During September the band are once again in the Midwest, including return visits to the Pine Knob Music Theater in Michigan. On October 21st Harry performs a benefit at the Capitol Theater in Passaic, New Jersey for ex-basketball star Bill Bradley, who is now running for US Senator. Also appearing on the bill are actors Dustin Hoffman and Chevy Chase. At the beginning of November Harry and the band spend a week doing concerts in Florida before returning north for shows in New Jersey and New England. On the 18th they tape songs for another appearance on the televised *Don Kirschner Rock Concert*, with a setlist that includes **'Dancin' Boy'**, **'Jenny'**, **'Mr Tanner'**, **'Flowers Are Red'**, **'Better Place To Be'**, and **'Poor Damned Fool'**, as well as a couple of songs from Tom and Steve. On the 21st they travel up to Canada to perform two shows in Ottawa.

Challenges In Harry's Own Backyard

Although Harry will never stop raising money and is always on hand as a fund raiser, he now sees that the focus for his humanitarian efforts should be through the Commission, and he attends their bimonthly meetings around the country (the only member to actually attend all the meetings). The final Hungerthon he participates in takes place in Los Angeles on Thanksgiving Day, November 23rd. At one of the Commission's bimonthly meetings someone poses a question to Harry that if he feels he can find a solution to ending world hunger, how come he can't do the same to the problem *"in your own backyard?"* Harry faces that challenge head-on and before long establishes New York's first food bank called Long Island Cares, whose chief aims are *"to improve food security for families, sponsor programs that help families achieve self-sufficiency, and educate the general public about the causes and consequences of hunger on Long Island. Our vision is 'A Hunger Free Long Island'."*

Harry will still continue his efforts to raise funds for PAF, although not personally being involved in its day-to-day running. He establishes and oversees a board of corporate executives to finance the merger of two of Long Island's established symphony orchestras, the Suffolk and Nassau, into what becomes the Long Island Philharmonic. He also continues to invite some of Long Island's top businessmen and political figures to charity dinners and concerts, but his efforts to attract some of the top names in the music business to perform is disheartening, as many decline for one reason or another. Harry also goes out of his way to support the struggling Clearwater project set up by

243

his old friend Pete Seeger, now a spritely 60 years old, and performs a benefit concert for him in Tarrytown, New York. He also organizes a 'Challenge 79' benefit concert held at the Nassau Coliseum to support Long Island's famous Eglevsky Ballet, and with the help of performers that include Gordon Lightfoot, Dave Mason and Waylon Jennings manages to raise some $90,000 to help get it back on its feet following the death of its founder. In order to keep this and many other Long Island art institutions alive, Harry pledges to set out challenges through more Hungerthons to raise money for what he calls Long Island's cultural cornerstones – theater, dance and symphony, as well as the building of what will become the Long Island Cultural Center.

The beginning of December sees the band returning to the Aerie Crown Theater in Chicago as well as performing at the four-day Valley Forge Music Festival in Devon, Pennsylvania. But Harry is once again ready to record some new material, and this time it will finally bring an end to his almost ten-year-long relationship with Elektra.

Legends of the Lost and Found

"I was insecure about the whole business. I was insecure about whether I had a career that was going to be in trouble. Everybody was telling me the music business was in disaster."

Time For Another Live Album

As the year 1978 is drawing to a close, Harry feels the time is right to record a new album. He has written some new songs, as well as now wanting to resurrect some old ones that failed to make previous albums. But he also feels that his record-buying audience is due another live double album. Submitting the idea to Elektra, there is no objection. After all, in their mind this will be his last album with them and he's sure to sign with another label. They let him have his way, but promoting it will be another matter. Harry also realizes that due to copyright law none of his back catalogue of songs can be recorded again for a minimum of five years if he goes with a new label. That means another 'greatest hits live' album will have to wait if he leaves Elektra. So, it is decided. This will be a double live album – with ten brand new songs and six definitive versions of some of his classic songs which, when previously sung live, had some lines edited out. Harry agrees that the live recordings will be done during their March concerts in Tennessee and during April performances in Texas and Arizona.

In order to try them out he gets the band together for rehearsals at the Full Tilt Studio in New York, beginning December 14th, with initial work done on two songs, a disco-inspired **'Goodbye to the 70s'** and one with a working title of **'Pretzel Land'**, on which drummer Howie Fields contributes one line to the lyric. The following day they work on another old song called **'Seasons & the Sky'** as well as new songs **'Copper and the Penny'** and **'Old Folkie'**, the latter a tribute to Pete Seeger. After two more sessions at Full Tilt, rehearsals resume on Boxing Day at a house on Smith Street in Brooklyn. That night they move to Elektra's Secret Sound Studios where for the next two days they lay down some basic tracks for the songs already rehearsed. Although more rehearsal dates at Full Tilt are penciled in for early January, Harry fails to tell the band he has decided to take his family on vacation, and only manages to get back for a session on the 7th, much to the band's consternation. On January 17th the tour schedule commences with a trip up to Canada, beginning with two concerts in Hamilton, Ontario, followed by ones in Kingston (in which Harry arrives two and a half hours late), London and Toronto. The remainder of the month has performances in New England.

245

February sees a string of dates in the Midwest, including Cincinnati's Music Hall and the University of Michigan in Ann Arbor. During sound checks at these concerts Harry and the band rehearse and later try them out to gauge audience reactions. Some of the concerts are also recorded by their sound team for the band to listen to afterward. Some of his new songs are **'Legends of the Lost and Found'**, **'Get On With It'**, **'We Were Three'**, **'Stranger with the Melodies'**, **'Odd Job Man'**, and revised versions of **'Copper'** and the re-named **'Pretzel Man'**. Tension grows within the band as Harry begins to miss sound checks due to prior commitments, and with just days to go before recording is due to commence there is a strong need for harmony. On February 26th a planned rehearsal of **'Goodbye to the 70s'** at Secret Sound Studio again takes place without Harry, leaving the disgruntled band to work on the new song **'Stranger With the Melodies'** instead. On March 4th the band travel to Tennessee for what will be the three recorded concerts from which songs for the new album will be selected. The mobile recording unit for the shows is handled by Filmways/Heider Recording Studios. The first recorded show takes place at the Orpheum Theater in Memphis, which includes sound checking and rehearsals prior to the concert.

Two nights later on the 6th they play the Memorial Auditorium in Chattanooga, after which the band listen to the recordings of this and the previous show. The following night sees their performance at the Memorial Auditorium in Knoxville, with a recorded setlist that has pleasing results: Jenny, Poor Damned Fool, Corey's Coming, If My Mary Were Here, Tangled Up Puppet, Mail Order Annie, Old Folkie, The Day They Closed the Factory Down, Get On With It, Copper, Cat's in the Cradle, Flowers Are Red, Salt and Pepper, Stranger With the Melodies, Pretzel Man, Legends of the Lost and Found, Love Is Not In Season (Steve), Odd Job Man, 30,000 Pounds of Bananas, Taxi, You Are the Only Song.

The remainder of March and early April has the band performing across the country, from West Virginia to Florida, New England to Indiana, and Louisiana to Oklahoma. The next batch of recorded concerts commences at the Paramount Theater in Austin, Texas, on April 10th, followed next day at the University of Texas in Houston, then the Southern Methodist University in Dallas on the 12th, before moving on to Arizona two days later for two shows at the Celebrity Theater in Phoenix on the 14th and at the Community Theater in Tucson the next day. At which venues the selected songs are chosen has never been established.

Meanwhile, with the recordings now in the hands of the engineers and mixers at Secret Sound, the band continue with their busy touring schedule, which takes in the northwest states and Canada, followed by more dates in the Midwest. On May 22nd they begin a six-date tour of England and Scotland at the Apollo Theatre in Manchester, with a return to the Rainbow Theatre in London on the 28th. Tom Chapin joins him for most of the dates. While in

London Harry is again invited by the BBC to take part in a radio show called *Star Special*, in which artists get the chance to play at DJ and choose some of the records that have inspired them over the years, and some that he admits he would have liked to have written himself. The show is broadcast on August 26th 1979 and Harry chooses songs from Pete Seeger, The Beatles, Jim Croce, John Prine, Don McLean, James Taylor, Joni Mitchell, Steve Goodman, Bob Dylan, Gordon Lightfoot and many others. The British tour ends in Newcastle on the 31st.

Back on home turf, the band's June itinerary sees return dates in Wallingford, Tarrytown and Holmdel, as well as another appearance at the Mississippi River Festival in Edwardsville, Illinois, and two shows at Pine Knob in Clarkston, Michigan. The following month brings concerts in San Diego and LA, as well as return trips to Hawaii and Alaska for one-off shows. On the 27th Harry performs three concerts in Austin, Texas, the last one being an emotional solo performance. On July 23rd, during a solo concert at the Civic Theater in New Orleans, Harry invites some of the overcrowded audience to sit on the stage with him during the performance, and as a result a notebook of his goes missing, a notebook that not only contains chords and lyrics to some new songs, but also 22 poems he has written for what will be his second poetry book, called *The Book of Eyes*. At the end of August Harry undergoes a tiring one-off trip to Australia for four solo performances in Melbourne and Sydney.

On October 26th, while back performing in New Orleans at the Saenger Performing Arts Center in New Orleans, Harry gets word that there is a drugged-up man in the hall who claims he has his notebook and is demanding $2,250 for it. On meeting him Harry offers to write him a cheque for $1,000, and even though Harry could have summoned over nearby cops, he hands over the cheque, takes the notebook, and lets him go. More grateful than angry, Harry now realizes that his second book of poetry, together with lyrics and new song ideas, are all back on track.

Hart and Hinkle Take Over The Reins

The hectic touring schedule continues throughout the fall, but it brings several changes for Harry and the band. To begin with, after changing his concert booking agent several times, Harry settles for one of the largest players in the music business, International Creative Management (ICM). He also severs links with Management Three now that their three-year contract has expired. For one thing Ken Kragen has left the company to turn Kenny Rogers's fortunes around in a spectacular way, and another reason is that Weintraub has been unsuccessful in getting some of Harry's story songs made into films. Even though $25,000 was offered for a screenplay for a television movie based on **'Cat's in the Cradle'**, it never materializes. From this moment the trusted pair of Jeb Hart and Bob Hinkle take on the role of management. Some of these changes result in tension among the band members, who have not been involved in any of the decisions Harry has made. There is a distinct lack of communication, but Harry senses their growing dissension and agrees to hold discussions with the band in future to allow them to input ideas of their own.

But it's not all bad news. Soon after leaving Management Three an offer comes in from ABC for them to use some of his songs in an upcoming TV movie called *Mother and Daughter – The Loving War*, loosely based on **'Tangled Up Puppet'**, about a divorcee called Lillie, played by actress Tuesday Weld, and her struggle to raise her pregnant daughter (Frances Sternhagen). The songs chosen include re-recorded versions of **'Woman Child'**, **'Circle'**, and **'Tangled Up Puppet'**, and four new ones, co-written with Sandy, **'I Don't Belong'**, **'Another Day to Dance Upon'**, **'A Loving War'**, and **'Make It a Holiday'**. Directed by Burt Brinckerhoff, the movie also features Harry as Lillie's ex-husband, who not only narrates the story in the opening scene but has a brief cameo at the end of the movie, his one and only acting role, in which his only line is "Welcome back, beautiful" as he kisses Tuesday Weld. The movie airs on January 25th 1980.

On October 16th another drastic change occurs when during a concert at The Palladium club in Dallas, cellist Kim Scholes suddenly walks off stage. Drummer Howie Fields recalls what happens:

"This Dallas gig, that was booked between dates in Lincoln NE and Denver CO, was one that our sound company, Maryland Sound, could not get to. The time/distance element was just impossible. The dirty laundry of the situation was simply that Harry pushed for this gig (and many others) to help raise money for a variety of causes that he was committed to and responsible for. His solution: if our sound company couldn't make it, we'd just get a local company. There were many other gigs that fell into this scenario and this was one of the things that drove the band crazy because the quality element of the show was severely diminished when we didn't have our own sound and band equipment. Harry however was never concerned about this and, around this time, it was a heated and ongoing discussion we'd have with him.

"In any event, on this night, Kim, who played ARP synthesizer and Fender Rhodes piano on a couple of songs, found himself playing a ARP that was busted. He was not at all happy. The last straw came when Harry called **'Dogtown'** *which we hadn't played in a dog's age. It was at this point that Kim calmly slid the ARP console off of the Fender Rhodes. It crashed to the floor whereupon Kim quietly left the stage for the last time as an official member of the Chapin band. I saw the event and knew that he was a goner at that moment."*

248

Howie Fields's setlist for that evening has the penultimate song entitled 'Son of Taxi', an obvious reference to a very early untitled performance of what will become **'Sequel'**. The full list is a follows: Story of a Life, Shooting Star, Stranger With the Melodies, Copper, They Call Her Easy, Dogtown, Cat's in the Cradle, Bluesman, Any Old Kind of Day, W.O.L.D., If My Mary Were Here, 30,000 Pounds of Bananas, Better Place To Be, Flowers Are Red, Son of Taxi (Sequel), Circle.

Yvonne Cable Joins the Band

Scholes has been Harry's cellist for two years and three albums, memorable for his fine playing on songs such as **'I Wonder What Happened To Him'** and the live versions of **'Tangled Up Puppet'** and **'Mail Order Annie'**. Harry is unhappy with his sudden departure, but it highlights the band's current dissatisfaction. With the other band members in admiration of Scholes' stand, Harry agrees to let him continue his role as the unofficial travel agent and sometime music arranger and conductor. To recruit a new cellist Harry once again places an ad in the *Village Voice* as well as several music establishments around New York, and Steve Chapin and Scholes are given the task of holding the auditions. Out of nearly fifty candidates, the talented 33-year-old Yvonne Cable, from Lima, Ohio, is finally chosen. Apparently, Harry balks at the idea of a woman in his all-male band, but is quickly won over by her talent and commitment, and she brings a whole new dimension to the live concerts.

Yvonne recalls later: *"Playing with Harry and touring with the band was an amazing experience. When a friend told me that there was an opening for cello with the group, I started learning the songs. When the auditions were over and the band picked me for the cello position, Harry was not sure that he wanted a woman in his group. Maybe he thought that he would have to change his on-stage routine that he had used for years. What actually happened, however, was that fans started to write to him to congratulate him for adding a woman to the group. He realized that he had an asset rather than a liability, and ran with it and the rest is history!"*

The new album **Legends of the Lost and Found – Greatest Stories Live** is released in October. The artwork for the gatefold sleeve is again impressive, with the front cover photograph taken by Harry of a piece of 3D artwork by his uncle Michael Burke that involved a building up of elements with dripping wax. The inside jacket has an illustration by the talented Ron Dilg depicting characters and scenes from some of the songs, while the back cover has a photo of the band taken by Daryl Pitt at the end of their concert at Pine Knob in Clarkston, Michigan on June 30th 1979. Once again full lyrics to both old and new songs are included. Side one comprises four great new story songs,

249

'Stranger With the Melodies', 'Copper', 'The Day They Closed the Factory Down' and 'Pretzel Man', while side two has a longer version of 'If My Mary Were Here', and three new songs, 'Old Folkie', 'Get On With It' and 'We Were Three'. Side three has a revival of 'Odd Job Man', once slated for the *Dance Band* album, and three "definitive" live versions of 'Poor Damned Fool', 'Flowers Are Red' and 'Mail Order Annie', with the final side having, beside the title track, revised versions of 'Tangled Up Puppet' and 'Corey's Coming', and one more new track, 'You Are the Only Song'. None of the new live songs have studio versions recorded.

Legends of the Lost and Found – New Greatest Stories Live (1979) ****
Elektra BB-703
Recorded: Chattanooga, Memphis, Knoxville, Austin, Houston, Dallas, Phoenix & Tucson, March-April 1979
US Release Date: October 1979
Engineer: Jack Malken & Michael Barry

Stranger With the Melodies *****
Written in the fall of 1978 and demoed in concerts at the time with slightly different lyrics to the final recorded version. We find the narrator spending his first night in a boarding house when the silence of his room is broken by the sound of a hoarse voice and a guitar coming from the next room, a monotonous melody with what seem like nonsense lyrics - just naming the chords he is playing. Rather than complaining, the narrator lies back in his bed, almost seduced by this *"soft and sinking sound"* as the stranger begins to hum and whistle the refrain. He finds it hard to get to sleep, and with daylight just a couple of hours away, he finally bangs on the wall for the stranger to stop. After a short silence he hears a voice telling him that it wasn't all that long ago that he was being paid to play his music. He continues by saying that he needs to do this in the dark solitude of the night as drugs or drink don't give him the satisfaction he craves. He's not singing to remember, but singing to forget. The narrator is curious why he only sings this one song and it's then that the stranger opens his heart and tells him his story of a rocky relationship he had in which he wrote the melody and his partner wrote the words to create the most wonderful songs that *"angels must have heard."* But without giving any more details, even of who is to blame, their relationship had come to an end, leaving him with the realization that a song doesn't have any meaning *"when it don't have nothing to say."* Something about his voice, or what he says, rings a bell with the narrator and he tells the stranger that he sounds like someone he knows, to which the stranger admits he is. With that the stranger returns to his playing and the narrator eventually falls asleep, not sure when he awakes whether he has dreamt all of this.

250

Surely one of Harry's most moving songs, although his inspiration for the story has never been determined. Harry has written songs about other singers before, most notably in **'Old Folkie'** and **'Bluesman'**, but this song is performed with such conviction and passion that is stands out as one of Harry's finest moments.

From the cheap seats
Mark Charlesworth - *In life you pay your dues and someone else gets the reward. That for me is what this song is about. Really for me one of Harry's sadder songs.*
Alan L Geraci - *This is the musical version of 'Circle' where you always end where you begin. 'You sound like what's-his-name'. He said, 'That's who I am.' The stranger was an incomplete version of himself as he rolled through his chords, over and over again. By letting his partner go and not being set free put him in this feedback loop of loneliness.*
Julian Chase - *The first song that ever made me shed a tear.*

Copper ***
Originally called **'Copper and the Penny'**, this is about what Harry calls *"the great American tradition"* – the crooked cop, and inspired by a 12-page letter he receives from Rochester, New York. In the song the narrator is a cop, the father of a thirteen-year-old boy, whose mother had run off with a salesman ten years ago to leave him to bring him up on his own. His son looks up to him, aspiring to follow in his footsteps and be a cop too one day. Over the years the narrator confesses that the bitterness of his wife leaving him has changed him from a straight and honest man into a dishonest *"two-bit grifter,"* and with all the *"smart cops on the make"* he is taking a piece of the same pie as they are doing, *"learning the trade from the gutter parade"* and turning a blind eye to criminals in return for taking bribes. And that bribe money will go toward paying the bills and putting his son through college to achieve his ambition. In the song he angrily warns an associate called Lou not to give him his $10 weekly bribe money when his son is with him, as it will destroy that hero-like image he has of his father. Instead he can pay him double the following week...

The Day They Closed the Factory Down ****
Recorded at one of the two concerts performed in Texas, the inspiration for this touching song is unclear. The narrator is a woman whose father has been killed in a furnace blast at a clothing factory in the town and who is now left to look after her mother and raise her baby brother on the $10 a week payout that has been settled in court. Maybe she is having a relationship with the factory owner, hence becoming the talk of the town, and the man is looked on by some as *"rake"* and a *"fake."* When he tells her one night that he is

going to relocate the business, but won't see the old town die, she doesn't believe him and knows their relationship will also come to an end. Not a concert regular, but still one of Harry's strongest and clearest vocals.

From the cheap seats
Robert Cupples - *My take is that there is, indeed, an affair going on (an affair of convenience - that will soon end when the factory closes) - but that is the sub-plot ... the real story is the devastation that is about to happen when this "one-horse-town" loses its only horse.*

Scott Sivakoff – *I think this whole song centers around the concept of the one-horse town and the people who center their lives and families around the company (factory). One accident can shut down the factory and then leave people who live in the town in a tough spot. I think the song is trying to capture that environment. I don't think that there is an affair going on here. At least not in the traditional sense. The guy in the first verse is kind of a rock star at the factory... but by the second verse he appears to be gone and we start to explore what happens to the family, the factory and ultimately the town.*

Jim G Phynn - *I love this song. When I first heard it, I admit that I had difficulty following the story itself, but once I "got" that it became really moving and emotionally charged. I consider it a part of the "awesome trilogy" of songs on the* **Legends of the Lost and Found** *album (the other two being* **'Stranger with the Melodies'** *and* **'We Were Three')**

Pretzel Man *
Nonsense song originally called **'Pretzel Land'**. A low point in Harry's music career.

Old Folkie ***
Harry's tribute to his old friend Pete Seeger (1919-2014), the *"man who put the meaning in the music book,"* and a song originally entitled **'Old Smoothie'**. Harry sees him as carrying forward the torch that was lit by the late Woody Guthrie, and in what at the time was a 40-year career as a social activist and ardent campaigner for a better world, he is simply referred to as just an *"old folkie,"* when the reality is he was so much more…

Get On With It **
With a waltz-like feel to it, this song is about two sides of a relationship, and two opposite points of view. When performed live always guaranteed to get reactions from the audience. In what appears to be their first date, the narrator is in a rush to seize the moment, do what he believes is the inevitable thing and get her into bed. But she prefers to take it more slowly, saying that time goes too quickly. They move in together and there's the making of a permanent relationship. He suggests they get married straight away without

252

wasting any more time. But for some reason it all goes wrong and she asks him to move out and at least remain friends before it's too late. And now it's his turn to see take it slowly, don't be hasty and give up without giving it a chance. After all, time goes so fast...

We Were Three ***
A sad story about a couple who believe that any permanency in their relationship is reliant on things around them never changing, in this case an old lady, perhaps homeless, feeding birds on the park bench the day they first met each other who returns there on the first day of spring and remains there all summer. As long as she is there his partner believed their relationship would continue as well. She cares for the old lady, even giving her treats and the gift of an umbrella, something her partner finds it hard to understand. But three years later, come the first day of spring, he notices out the window the old lady is no longer there, never to return, and we now realize that the relationship too has ended, leaving him wondering where she has gone...

Odd Job Man *
Another audience favorite and, after **'Bananas'**, Harry's second stab at a country & western song, and performed half sung-half spoken in the style of Charlie Daniels. The song is inspired by the time when money was tight and Harry was doing extra gigs to earn more cash. The narrator of the story works at a gas station and is asked by a rich businessman to do some work for him while he's out of town for a month. The man looks down on him and treats him like dirt, but he needs the money and puts up with it. When he comes to the house next day the businessman's beautiful wife answers the door and takes him through to her husband, who gives him a list of jobs that need doing, but when he goes to discuss payment the man tells him, *"When you're dealing with a gentleman, you get just what you earn."* With her husband gone, he starts on the jobs, but all the while conscious that this beautiful lady is watching him and passing compliments. A month goes by, the jobs are finished, and he's back at the gas station when the man turns up and gives him $100 – a measly buck an hour for the month's work. But he doesn't react, and knows in his mind that justice has been done - what this man has just done to him, he has been doing the same to his wife all the time he'd been away....

Legends of the Lost and Found ****
Harry's one and only stab at prog-rock, sounding at times very much like Genesis and The Moody Blues, and seemingly out of place on the album apart from being the title track. In a whirlwind of evocation and sensual phrasing he puts together a seductive love letter to the woman in his life, or one he craves to become part of his life. Lyrically powerful, it showcases Doug Walker's

253

excellent guitar work, the collective harmonies of Harry, Steve, John and Doug, and finally John's excellent falsetto vocal on the last verse.

You Are the Only Song ****
Full of wonderful sentiments, this is Harry's tribute to his fans and an alternative encore to close his concerts, although often leading into a shortened rendition of 'Circle'.

Goodbye To Elektra

Of the six updated live versions of classic songs on the album, all considered definitive: 'Corey's Coming' has a verse added to the graveyard scene; 'Flowers Are Red' has additional lyrics; 'Tangled Up Puppet' begins with the first verse instead of the chorus; 'If My Mary Were Here' has verses switched around; 'Poor Damned Fool' is as the original version, although listed here as 'Poor Damn Fool', and a wonderful slower version of 'Mail Order Annie' has Harry on harmonica.

In 2005 *Legends of the Lost and Found* becomes the last of Harry's vinyl albums to be released on CD when the Chapin family acquire the rights to the music. The new version is remixed from the original multi-track recordings with Josh Chapin as executive producer and Chapin Foundation board member Jason Dermer as producer and engineer. While making every effort to stay true to Steve Chapin's original mix of the songs, this new version features enhanced vocals, less overdubbing, and a revised track order to produce a better feel for a live concert.

Despite being a live album, the original *Legends* fails to repeat the commercial success of the first live album released three years before, mainly due to the label's reluctance to promote it, and it peaks at a poor #163 on the *Billboard* 100 charts in November. Many of Harry's fans are not even aware of its existence until many months later. Another tangible reason is the current state of the music industry. With the country still suffering the effects of an economic recession that had begun in the fall of 1978, subsequent tax increases and surging oil prices are having a marked effect on disposable income. Fewer people are now buying records, and many are recording songs and albums off the radio onto tape recorders instead of going to record stores, and, unlike before, those stores can now return unsold albums to the record label for refunds. Some retailers are even buying and selling counterfeit albums to offset their losses. This is just the beginning of what for decades to come will be a gradual financial disaster for the music industry. Harry, his mind already made up about leaving Elektra, is understandably worried in this changing climate. Not only is he insecure about the whole music business, he believes his career could be in jeopardy. Without a hit record in four years

254

there is little chance of gaining a big record contract. To keep the money coming in Harry and the band continue to work hard, taking every gig they can grab, no matter where.

As well as retrieving his lost notebook in New Orleans, October also brings concert dates in Colorado, including Denver and a return to the USAF Academy, as well as shows in Phoenix and Lincoln. The setlist for the Uptown Theater in Kansas City on the 12th is as follows: Bluesman, God Babe You've Been Good To Me, Cat's in the Cradle, Story of a Life, If My Mary Were Here, Taxi, Copper, Let Time Go Lightly (Steve), Mail Order Annie, The Day They Closed the Factory Down, Mr Tanner, W.O.L.D., Better Place To Be, We Were Three, 30,000 Pounds of Bananas, Old Folkie.

On November 1st Yvonne Cable accompanies the band for the first time at the show in Jacksonville, Florida, where she watches Kim Scholes play his final concert, and then makes her debut as cellist the following night at the first of two shows at the Gusman Theater in Miami. Scholes will remain with the band to coach her for the next two shows in Sarasota and Orlando. Ten days later the band fly back to LA following a concert in Alabama to tape songs for *The Tonight Show with Johnny Carson*, in which they perform '**Mail Order Annie**' and '**Get On With It**' for guest host and up-and-coming presenter David Letterman, before catching another flight to Georgia the next day to play at the Civic Center in Atlanta. Following their regular appearance at the three-day Valley Forge Music Fair in Devon, Pennsylvania, they spend the remainder of the month with performances closer to home. On December 11th, after the show at Butler University in Indianapolis, Harry, in his usual style, informs the band members that in a week's time they will be recording songs for the new album and for a new record label, and to top it all, will be recording it down in Miami, Florida.

Although Elektra have offered Harry a contract to remain with them, Harry has already been in talks with another label, Casablanca Records, a former subsidiary of Warner, and founded as an independent label back in 1973 by Neil Bogart, former head of Buddah Records. Three years later it had merged with Peter Guber's indie-film company Filmworks. Casablanca specializes in disco music, signing the likes of Donna Summer, Cher, Bill Withers, Village People and Lipps Inc, as well as the bands Kiss and Parliament. As far back as March, when Casablanca's vice president Irv Biegel gets word that Harry is not going to renew his Elektra contract, they are eager to sign him up. Biegel goes to see him in several concerts and is impressed with the singer and the audience's reaction. He gets in touch with Monte Morris, Harry's attorney, and arranges a meeting with the singer. The meeting between Harry and Biegel takes place in Casablanca's New York office, and during the meeting Harry gets to hear more about 36-year-old Bogart. He already knows him through his long track record of being a man of vision and creative ability, much like Jac Holzman. Biegel tells him that

255

both he and Bogart see Harry as reaching his full potential as a singer in the coming decade, writing the kind of songs that could reverberate around the world, much like Dylan's had done the decade before. They also see in him a man with strong commitments, totally dedicated to matters he believes in. With Harry, they believe his best is yet to come.

To record his music Biegel arranges for Harry to meet two of the best record producers in the business, brothers Howard and Ron Albert of the small independent company Fat Albert Productions. Based in Miami, the brothers are minority stockholders in Criteria Recording Studios, and on their roster of successes are Derek & the Dominoes' massive album *Layla and Other Assorted Love Songs* and Crosby, Stills and Nash's *CSN*. When they meet with Harry in Miami that first week of December, the brothers fall in love with his personality and the feeling Harry gets in return is mutually uplifting. They can't wait to begin working together. Harry has been writing new songs throughout the fall and early winter of 1979. He already has an idea for the new album, and has been showcasing early versions of the songs in live concerts for the last couple of months. He now feels everything is falling into place. Even before the ink has hardly dried on the contract papers, he is ready to start recording again. All he has to do now is tell the band…

Sequel

*"Most writers write attitude songs. I write about the situation that
creates the attitude"*

Looking to the Past

It seems like Harry has never looked forward to recording an album as much
as he does with this one. On December 13th, the day after informing the band
following the concert at Butler University in Indianapolis, they are back in
New York to begin rehearsing the new songs at Star Sound Studios. Drummer
Fields recalls:

*"Harry was late for rehearsal and then a phone call came in just as I
happened to be out near the rehearsal studio desk. It was Harry, so I took the
call whereupon he said he was sorry, but that he was not going to be able to
make it to the rehearsal. Then he very excitedly proceeded to read to me the
lyrics he had just completed which was the song 'Sequel'. I was speechless
and remember what I said to the band when I returned to the studio... 'You
guys aren't gonna believe this.... Harry wrote a sequel to 'Taxi'.' At the outset
the band's take on this was that it was a desperate effort to get some press and
get back on the charts but I have to say that, in time, we all got interested and
involved in the song. So, it was on that night and in that way that we learned
that the LP we would soon be recording would be entitled Sequel."*
(*Circle*, Fall 2004)

For a number of years Sandy has been urging Harry to write a follow-up to
'Taxi', but it isn't until recently that he has that idea in mind, and it begins as
a lyrical poem which he sometimes recites and part-sings at the end of concerts
to gauge the audience's response, which is incredible. One of the reasons that
spurs him on is the fact that after seven years he has met up again with Clare
MacIntyre, the **'Taxi'** girl herself. Instigated by Clare, they agree to meet up
in a New York restaurant. Although speaking on the phone with her on a
number of occasions over the preceding years, it is only now that Harry learns
what has been happening in her life. After living in South America, she is now
long divorced from a husband who was both quick-tempered and a playboy.
In the meantime, she has had physical and emotional problems, even suffering
a stroke that left her in a coma. Now she is working in New York and living
alone in an apartment. She feels the problems lie with her father, the former
mayor of Scarsdale, and asks Harry if he can talk to him. He agrees to, and the
two of them meet up, and in an amicable discussion her father shows his
admiration for how Harry has gone on to fulfill his potential. But that's where

257

it ends. Even though they chat occasionally on the phone, Harry never sees Clare again. Whatever feelings he had for her are long gone. But where the story ends, a song has just begun.

During more rehearsals at Star Sound on December 14th Harry informs the band that they will be leaving for Miami in just two days' time, Sunday the 16th, four days earlier than had been planned. After a couple of days of frantic organizing, the band arrive at the studios at 1755 NE 149th Street. This is looked upon as almost hallowed ground, where the likes of Eric Clapton, The Eagles and The Bee Gees have recently recorded some of their best work. There they meet up with the Albert brothers and engineer Don Gheman. For the new album the Albert brothers draft in just a couple of session musicians, with Joe Lala on percussion and Howard Albert himself on synthesizer. Tom Chapin is also on hand to provide his acoustic guitar and banjo expertise. Also brought in is accomplished backing vocalist Chuck Kirkpatrick as well as the top soulful backing singers Rhodes, Chalmers & Rhodes, consisting of Charlie Chalmers and sisters Donna and Sandra Rhodes, probably best known for their work on Al Green's *Lets Stay Together*.

The next day, December 17th, recording work begins in earnest with some fifteen takes for **'Story of a Life'** and work commencing on **'Northwest 222'**. On the 18th, the tracking is completed on **'Story of a Life'** and begun on **'I Finally Found It Sandy'** and **'Salt and Pepper'**. Over the next couple of days recording commences on **'Sequel'** and **'God Babe You've Been Good to Me'**, with the whole session on the 23rd taken up with laying the basic track for **'Sequel'**. Further work at Criteria is then cancelled as Harry and the band return home for Christmas and prepare for the New Year concert dates in Canada. As a result, it is decided that the next recording sessions will take place at Nimbus 9 Studios in Toronto. After a short Christmas break, Harry goes to Secret Sound Studios in New York on the 27th to record the handful of songs that will feature on the soundtrack to the TV movie *Mother and Daughter –The Loving War*.

The first week of 1980 is as frantic as ever, as Harry and the band flit between recording in the studio from 10am to 4pm and doing live performances in the evening commencing at 8pm. Harry misses the recording schedule on January 2nd, but is on hand that night for the first of thirteen concerts in Toronto, Hamilton, London, Guelph, Ottawa and Kingston. On January 3rd recording commences on **'I Miss America'**, with Harry interrupting proceedings by attending interviews. The following day the old chestnut **'Seasons & the Sky'** is tried out once again, having failed to make the last two albums, and tracking begins on **'Up On the Shelf'**. Another new song called **'All The Time You Knew'** is tried out the following day. After a short break a lighter version of **'Story of a Life'** is tried out on the 8th, as well as a session for **'Remember When the Music'**. On the 9th the master take of **'God Babe You've Been So Good To Me'** is completed, and two days later

258

the Nimbus sessions come to an end. The album is on schedule to be released in late spring.

After a well-earned break the band members assemble near Huntington on the 23rd for a photo shoot for the new album (although it's never used). The photographer is Ruth Bernal. Howie Fields recalls: *"The idea was to depict the affluent surrounding of what Sue (the girl in 'Taxi') had become in 'Sequel'. The photo shoot took place at a gorgeous mansion somewhere out near Harry's hometown of in Huntington, Long Island. Cellist Yvonne Cable was dressed as a French maid, Doug Walker & I as gardeners, I think John was a taxi driver and Harry was the passenger in the taxi about to visit his long-lost love. I think Steve was a butler but the memories are vague. There was definitely a taxi there for the shoot however."*

On January 27th Harry performs a solo benefit with Tom and Pete Seeger at Huntington High School before the touring schedule once again gets underway in earnest. Their setlist is as follows: God Babe You've Been So Good To Me, Salt and Pepper, Stoopid, Dancing Boy, Grandma's Farm, I Know An Old Lady, Story of a Life, I Wanna Learn a Love Song, Cat's in the Cradle, Taxi, Flowers Are Red, When Moses Was, Tangled Up Puppet, Circle. But before January comes to an end there are big changes afoot. In the blink of an eye Harry now has a new record label.

Bogart and Boardwalk

Neil Bogart has decided to sell his financial interest in his label to the Polygram Record Group, who three years before had acquired a 50% stake in Casablanca for an estimated $15 million. As the bosses of Polygram see things, there had been overspending and accounting irregularities with Bogart's company, and they also see him as the reason they have just lost Donna Summer, one of their biggest artists, to rival company Geffen Records, due to his failure on agreeing which direction she should take in her musical career. As a result, they decide to ease Bogart out. Filmworks, the movie division, is separated from Casablanca and renamed Polygram Pictures. With the dust settled, Bogart and Biegel between them form a new company called Boardwalk Entertainment. But will they persuade Harry to go with them? Their mutual love affair wins the day, and after hearing the final mix of the new album the decision is made, and Harry once again puts pen to paper and signs a one-album contract. There are risks, of course, but at least it will mean he will be the label's leading artist, with all the attention focused on his music. Bogart and Biegel see Harry as spearheading the label's new creative image and breaking away from their old disco days. Geffen can keep their disco queen - they have got the **'Taxi'** man.

With all the unsettling changes going on, the release date for the new album is postponed until July, while the new label has to start from scratch building up its organization. Tom Chapin is also signed to the label, but it is a short-lived affair, and the songs for his next album *In the City Of Mercy* are not well-received by Bogart. As a result, it is decided not to release it. It is, however, later taken up by another label.

Harry also has to deal with the bad vibes and bickering that seem to be more prevalent among his band members and road crew. Since giving the band more say in the decisions that have to be made, Harry now realizes that it is having a negative effect on their main roles. Brother Tom has seen it for himself and warns Harry about the consequences. He gives it to him straight – he needs to take back charge. One thing that helps bring about some harmony within the band is the departure of road manager Jeff Gross, often seen as the one most likely to stir up trouble. After five years in the role, he quits the job due to personal reasons, not least having a recent drug problem. As a replacement Harry takes on board his friend and former charter pilot Rich Imperato. In a time of unreliability and inconsistency within the world of promoting concerts, Harry remains the consummate reliable and consistent professional. Promoters see in him an unselfish easy-going artist not driven by greed. He has become one of the nicest men in the business and they are now queuing up to get him concert deals. Last year saw him do some 200 performances around the country, bringing in some $1.75 million. 1980 will see that increase by 25% with what will be a record number of concerts. That record is well on the way as February sees solo and band performances at venues across the Midwest and also a solo concert for the Winter Olympic Games at Lake Placid on the 21st. March has the band returning to Florida for dates in Orlando, St Petersburg, and Miami, followed by dates in Tennessee and Illinois. The last few days of the month find them back east with performances in New York, New Jersey, Pennsylvania and New Hampshire.

But that month also brings sad news for Harry when 51-year-old Al Lowenstein, one of his political idols, is tragically gunned down in his New York office on the 14th by a crazed co-worker. After years of tireless campaigning, Lowenstein has been living a lonely life these last few years, divorced from his wife, with her and their children now living with someone else. Harry cannot escape the relevance here, for he himself has come close to losing it all by putting work ahead of family. But he had seen the dangers and reacted. For his friend, it is all too late. Within hours Harry will dedicate his new song **'Remember When the Music'** in his honor. That spring Harry performs a solo benefit for Fight World Hunger at the Michigan Theater in Ann Arbor, followed by more dates in Canada, this time in New Brunswick and Nova Scotia. A string of performances in the northeastern states include a concert at Carnegie Hall on April 17th.

The final week in April takes the band from Iowa down to Lousiana and Texas, with a return visit to Austin for two shows. During the month of May the schedule continues with concerts along the West Coast, starting in California, before heading north for dates in Oregon and Washington State. Several shows across Canada follow, as well as two performances in Williamsburg, Virginia, before they take a well-earned month's break. Only a handful of concerts are played during June, including one in Dayton, Ohio, on the 18th, where a moving **'Mr Tanner'** is received with wild enthusiasm by the town the song has made famous. On July 16th Bogart has the band return to Criteria Studios in Miami to begin a couple of days doing final work on the new album. On that first day they record the four-minute version of **'Sequel'** that ultimately appears on the album. This is followed by the band performing at Meadowlands in East Rutherford, New Jersey, and then concerts in California, supported by Arlo Guthrie, who at the Greek Theater in LA on the 22nd performs the iconic 'Alice's Restaurant' for the first time in ten years. Their setlist is as follows: Shooting Star, Mercenaries, Stranger With the Melodies, Up on the Shelf, W.O.L.D., Cat's in the Cradle, Corey's Coming, Mr Tanner, The Mayor of Candor Lied, Taxi, Sequel (spoken), Better Place To Be, Story of a Life, Flowers Are Red, Let Time Go Lightly (Steve), 30,000 Pounds of Bananas, Remember When the Music, Circle.

Two days later the band are back in Miami for the final recording sessions for the album. On the 24th Bogart himself is on hand to watch the up-tempo version of **'Remember When the Music'** being recorded, with finishing touches to that song completed the next day.

The beginning of August has the band touring New England, with concerts at Hyannis, Hampton, and the PAF in Saratoga, as well as a return to the Merriwhether Post Pavilion in Columbia, Maryland, where they are supported by Janis Ian. On August 14th they appear at the Poplar Creek Music Theater in Chicago, again supported by Arlo Guthrie. Following the concert in Chicago, one newspaper review on August 20th dubs Harry the *"Geoffrey Chaucer of the Now Generation,"* and his bittersweet songs akin to modern *Canterbury Tales*: *"His heroes are old toilers living in a world they don't understand and trying to make sense of the hollow senselessness of individuals struggling against one another to find fulfillment. Their search for the good life creates new emotional gaps that leave them lonely, afraid and unhappy with themselves...."*

Following more shows in Omaha and Minneapolis, Harry and the band make another appearance in Hamilton, Ontario, on the 19th, a show that is filmed and released later on VHS as *The Final Concert*. The setlist is as follows: Story of a Life, Shooting Star, Taxi, Mr Tanner, W.O.L.D., Better Place To Be, Cat's in the Cradle, Flowers Are Red, Mail Order Annie, They Call Her Easy (edited from the film), 30,000 Pounds of Bananas, Sequel, You Are the Only Song, Circle. The following day Harry makes an appearance on

261

the daytime TV show *Dinah and Friends*, before going on to give performances in Iowa, Ohio and Michigan.

On the 25th the band perform at the Garden State Art Center in Holmdel, New Jersey. One critic writes: *"Harry Chapin takes life at full tilt, combining music, social activism, like a one-man cyclone, and still finding time for his fans…He comes on stage like a friend you haven't seen in some time, who tells you stories, plays some music, jokes around and fills you in on his life. There's an intimacy and an intensity when Chapin performs and an easy rapport with the band."* That fall brings the pinnacle of the year's touring schedule, with 25 concerts in September and an incredible 33 in October. At least two-thirds of these are benefits, many of them in support of Democrat politicians fighting what seems to be a losing battle in the upcoming presidential election. October has the band performing nine concerts in Florida, with others in Georgia, Alabama and Lousiana. Also, that fall, apart from being reunited with his lost notebook, he is also reunited with his old friend Ken Kragen, who he invites back as his manager to work alongside Jeb Hart and Bob Hinkle.

Following final mixing by the Albert brothers and engineer Don Gehman, the new album *Sequel* is finally released on the Boardwalk Entertainment label in mid-October. The front cover, designed by Christopher Whorf, features the roof of an Orange County taxi cab showing its call number 81A7 outside a Boardwalk Theater with the neon sign displaying 'Harry Chapin in Sequel.' The rear cover is reminiscent of *Heads and Tales* with a photo by Ron Slenzak of Harry casually standing by the open rear door of a yellow cab. Many years later some look on the taxi's call sign as somewhat prophetically indicating July of 1981.

Sequel (1980) *****
Boardwalk FW-36872
Recorded: Criteria Recording Studios, Miami & Nimbus 9 Recording Studios, Toronto, Jan, May & July 1980
US Release Date: Mid-October 1980
Producer: Howard Albert & Ron Albert (The Fat Albert Boys)
Engineer: Don Gehman & Chuck Kirkpatrick

Sequel *****
Nine years after **'Taxi'** takes the country and cab drivers in particular by storm, the long-awaited and much-anticipated follow-up is here for all to enjoy. It may have deserved a more fitting title, but at least it gives some indication of what listeners might expect, even though there are many who don't see the connection until they begin to listen to it or read the lyrics. It could quite easily have been a sequel to half a dozen songs from Harry's back catalog, songs such as **'Better Place To Be'**, **'Mail Order Annie'** and **'Corey's Coming'**, all of which could be tagged with the label "to be

262

continued…" Up till now there had been very few hit songs with sequels - Buddy Holly's 'Peggy Sue' / 'Peggy Sue Got Married'; Leslie Gore's 'It's My Party' / 'Judy's Turn to Cry', and more recently David Bowie's 'Space Oddity' / 'Ashes to Ashes' (which had only just been released a month before, almost with an identical timescale). For an encore at a concert with Tom in Norwich, Connecticut, the previous year, Harry had read out the lyrics to this new song from a napkin on his knee and had received a fantastic response. Harry has actually performed concerts in San Francisco, back in October 1979, the very place where real-life Clare, his girlfriend at the time, had packed her bags and gone off to university, triggering what would be the breakup of their relationship. Maybe being there has rekindled memories of her in Harry's mind. At the time it was just a lyric without music, and it takes Harry months to turn it into a song, finally spurred on by his decision to have it ready for the new album. With a collection of other tracks that turn a nostalgic eye back to earlier times, perhaps it is only fitting that it finds its way onto what will turn out to be Harry's last completed studio album.

We left Harry and Sue (real-life Clare MacIntyre) back in 1972 on the debut album *Heads and Tales*, and despite a resounding live version found on *Greatest Stories Live* four years later, for many fans that was the end of it. A sad tale of lost love, never to be rekindled, with both parties either "acting happy" or "flying high" in acceptance of their current lives. So the story goes. But what if?

Harry recalls the idea for a follow-up from Sandy: *"For years she had been saying I should do a sequel to 'Taxi', yet it's not that simple. She said that life keeps changing, people keep changing, and if you put them together again, you'll find there'll be a different reaction. But I was afraid the song would diminish 'Taxi'."* With his focus now on setting the lyrics to music, Harry eventually decides to retain most of the original melody, along with some new ones in order not to make it too identical. The result is an outstanding song that some see as not just a sequel, but the next chapter in an ongoing melodrama, the outcome of which, as Harry indicates at the end of the song, "only time will tell". If there is another installment, time is one thing Harry will not have…

The sequel is set ten years on (six in the original lyric), and Harry, ex-taxi driver but now a successful singer, is back in San Francisco, the setting for the original song, and is there to play a concert. The very first lines are repeated from the last verse of **'Taxi'**, so anyone in doubt about where this is going is now put at ease:

So here she's actin' happy inside her handsome home
And me, I'm flyin' in my taxi, takin' tips and gettin' stoned
I got into town a little early
Had eight hours to kill before the show

263

First I thought about heading up north of the bay
Then I knew where I had to go

We know who he's looking for, and we also realize that in the intervening years the narrator has now gone "straight" (off drugs) and made a success of his singing career, choosing to take a taxi rather than the customary limo. Lovely touch here by Harry. When he last saw Sue, she had achieved her dream and had become a successful actress living the high-life in the city by the bay. Now he can tell her that he too has achieved success.

I thought about taking a limousine
Or at least a fancy car
But I ended up taking a taxi
'Cause that's how I got this far
You see, ten years ago it was the front seat
Drivin' stoned and feelin' no pain
Now here I am straight and sittin' in the back
Hitting Sixteen Parkside Lane

Realizing that Sue no longer lives in her posh gated house with fine trimmed lawns, he finds out she now resides in an old apartment block in the city.

The driveway was the same as I remembered
And a butler came and answered the door
He just shook his head when I asked for her
And said "She doesn't live here anymore"
But he offered to give me the address
That they were forwarding her letters to
I just took it and returned to the cabbie
And said "I got one more fare for you"
And so we rolled back into the city
Up to a five-story old brownstone
I rang the bell that had her name on the mailbox
The buzzer said somebody's home

When they finally meet it brings a smile to her face. She tells him how she has heard his songs on the radio, although he plays it down by saying it's better when you don't get to realize your dreams (of flying):

And the look on her face as she opened the door
Was like an old joke told by a friend

264

It'd taken ten more years but she'd found her smile
And I watched the corners start to bend
And she said, "How are you Harry?
Haven't we played this scene before?"
I said "It's so good to see you, Sue
Had to play it out just once more"
Play it out just once more
She said I've heard you flying high on my radio
I answered "It's not all it seems"
That's when she laughed and she said, "It's better sometimes
When we don't get to touch our dreams"

He then asks her about her dreams of becoming an actress, but she simply tells him that was somebody else, and that she has finally likes herself, not the person she was:

That's when I asked her where was that actress
She said "That was somebody else"
And then I asked her why she looked so happy now
She said "I finally like myself, at last I like myself"
So we talked all through that afternoon
Talking about where we'd been
We talked of the tiny difference
Between ending and starting to begin
We talked because talking tells you things
Like what you really are thinking about
But sometimes you can't find what you're feeling
Till all the words run out

After a brief conversation about their dreams and aspirations, he asks her to come and see him at the concert, but she tells him she works at night, leaving some to wonder about what she actually does.

So I asked her to come to the concert
She said "No, I work at night"
I said, "We've gotten too damn good at leaving, Sue"
She said, "Harry, you're right"

The rest of the story is left for us to surmise.

Don't ask me if I made love to her
Or which one of us started to cry

Don't ask me why she wouldn't take the money that I left
If I answered at all I'd lie
So I thought about her as I sang that night
And how the circle keeps rolling around
How I act as I'm facing the footlights
And how she's flying with both feet on the ground
I guess it's a sequel to our story
From the journey 'tween heaven and hell
With half the time thinking of what might have been
and half thinkin' just as well
I guess only time will tell

Harry at his teasing best. But if there is to be another installment, time is one thing that Harry will not have.

The original lyrics were actually recorded and appear as the 'Gehman Mix' on the Chapin Productions CD-release of the *Sequel* album. Here's where the lyrics differ from those originally written, and the following verse describing how Harry arrives at Sue's apartment was edited out of the final version:

It was three flights up to her apartment
But that wasn't why I breathed so fast
You see nothing can set off your heartbeat
As when you return your heart to your past

The next few verses contain much of the original lyric as Harry and Sue exchange greetings. Then we have another verse that is edited out from the original:

She asked me how I tracked her down
I said, "We were supposed to get together someday,"
I said, "Think of all our memories"
She said, "Most people leave it that way."

This revised verse is an expansion of the original. We share their last moments together, but are left to guess what happens next. Harry at his teasing best. But apparently Harry sees fit to change it slightly, and in doing so adding that special Chapin touch. Like in **'Taxi'**, Big John is given a few lines to sing in his wonderful high voice, following the verse ending *"Till all the words run out"*:

Your silence is the spring of which the wisdom grows like moss / You have saved me from the darkness and the legend of the lost / Your laughter is the

266

liquid that makes emptiness seem strange / and your tears can almost make the seasons change ... change

For Harry and Sue, the tables have turned. It all comes down to self-worth. In Harry's case, he couldn't achieve it until he could prove to himself that he could make a successful career, while Sue has now discovered her own self-worth by no longer sacrificing her feelings or moral self while maintaining her success. Therefore, we find the two of them personally ending up in the same place in life, while at the same time going in completely opposite directions. Where in **'Taxi'** Harry is questioning his worth by a lack of success that leaves his life unfulfilled, Sue appears to be unhappy and unsatisfied despite having all the trappings of success.

Radio stations across the country embrace **'Sequel'** like they did with **'Taxi'**. Although managing to just miss out on breaking into the **Billboard** Hot 100 Top 20, peaking at #23 on December 13th, it becomes the fastest-selling single of Harry's career, as well as being the best-selling one since **'Cat's in the Cradle'**, six years earlier. Harry believes that with all the hard work put into crafting it, the song doesn't diminish **'Taxi'** at all, and often quips that Sandy suggests he now makes it a trilogy of songs and by calling the next one 'Hearse', in which Harry is finally carried away.

From the cheap seats

Cliff Geismar - *A wonderful song. A masterpiece of a sequel. Isn't a favorite of mine, I love it immensely but don't cherish it like other jewels of his. He had so much more to give us all. With* **'Sequel'**, *Harry was jettisoning the past and bridging to the future, which we were never to benefit from.*

Bruce Morgan - *I remember the first time I heard* **'Sequel'**. *It blew my mind how he continued the story. The lyrics touched anyone who lost a love then found them again. However, it's not a happy ending. Harry always knew how to touch people. Rest in Peace Harry.*

Miranda Riddle - *There's a comfort and ease in* **'Sequel'** *that isn't in place yet in* **'Taxi'**. *The lyrics flow more easily, the melody is "prettier". It's a perfect representation of the journey that this semi fictional version of Harry has been through. I'd argue* **'Sequel'** *is a more complete and complex song, and, in some ways, I prefer it. The bridge, "we talked all through that afternoon..." is among the most poignant words and music Harry has ever written. Up there with* **'Better Place to Be'**.

Dawn Herrmann - *When I have a great book and it ends, it breaks my heart a little.* **'Sequel'** *gave me a chance to revisit a story I loved and brought it full circle.*

267

I Miss America ***

Harry at his cynical best with one of his pet gripes - America's lost values - and having a go at everything from beauty contestants to football coaches and television executives. In the first verse the narrator is a young teenage girl being persuaded by what can only be described as a degenerate lecher of a competition judge to enter the "ultimate" Miss America pageant, with the guarantee of winning, but only if she is prepared to sleep with him, which she obviously does. Only when she wins does she reflect on what's she's done to get her there. Hence the tears. Without naming names, Harry next has a dig at Woody Hayes, the former coach of the Ohio State Buckeyes football team, who after the Gator Bowl in 1978 had been dismissed for hitting Charlie Bauman from the opposing Clemson Tigers for interrupting a Buckeye pass that could have won his team the game with just two and a half minutes left on the clock. The incident triggered a pitch side brawl. Hayes already had a history of bad conduct in the sport. All he had to say about the incident was: *"Nobody despises to lose more than I do. That's got me into trouble over the years, but it also made a man of mediocre ability into a pretty good coach."* For the third verse the narrator looks at the unreality of the American dream as seen on television. For this Harry points at television executive Fred Silverman, who during the 70s had brought to the screen some of the most top-rated and best-remembered soaps, serials and sitcoms, all with a distorted and sanitized image of family life "as it should be," but in reality, nothing like it. Everything appears fake, even down to the canned laughter that prompts you to think something's funny when actually it's not. Finally, Harry brings it all home with his young son Josh asking for the chance to share his dad's vision of the American Dream, only if it is just that, a dream...

The prominent synthesizer in the song comes courtesy of Howard Albert. The song is also chosen as the flip-side to the 1987 CD-single of **'Remember When the Music'** released on the Dunhill label.

Story of a Life *****

Depending on what concert some fans have attended, Harry wrote this song either on a plane or waiting for a plane. One version has him at Buffalo airport, waiting for a flight to Youngstown, Ohio, in September 1979, but the most popular version is that after a concert at the Paramount Theater in Austin, Texas, on April 10th 1979, he takes a flight to Dallas at the time when a tornado rips through the Red River Valley and destroys the town of Wichita Falls. In an interview with BBC radio presenter Noel Edmonds in February 1981 he introduces the song with another version of how it comes about:

"I'm in this little Piper Club flying towards Dallas when, all of a sudden, we are getting bounced, jounced around. I mean a 400 feet wind shear up and down in half a second. The plane feels like it's falling apart. So, all of a sudden, the whole thing about when you panic your whole life flashes in front

268

of your eyes. Well my life is flashing in front of my eyes, but I swear it was coming in rhymed couplets...Somehow, I didn't think of what could be about to happen, so I pulled out a sick bag cause there was nothing else to write on and a pen and started to write lyrics. So by the time I landed in Dallas I'd finished the song...I think it's one of the best lyrics I've ever written, so I hope you like it. If you don't, screw ya."

When it was, or wherever it was, Harry has truly put down some of the finest lyrics he has ever written. Showing an amazing sense of maturity for someone still in his mid-thirties, he ponders over the many changes he has endured throughout his life and how all his goals and aspirations have also changed with time while in the process of seeking his greatest accomplishment and finding true happiness in what matters to him the most, his wife Sandy. The strings and horns are beautifully arranged by brother Steve.

The evocative lyrics speak for themselves:

I can see myself it's a golden sunrise
Young boy open up your eyes
It's supposed to be your day.
Now off you go horizon bound
And you won't stop until you've found
Your own kind of way.

And the wind will whip your tousled hair,
The sun, the rain, the sweet despair,
Great tales of love and strife.
And somewhere on your path to glory
You will write your story of a life.

And all the towns that you walk through
And all the people that you talk to
Sing you their songs.
And there are times you change your stride,
There are times you can't decide
Still you go on.

And then the young girls dance their gypsy tunes
And share the secrets of the moon
So soon you find a wife.
And though she sees your dreams go poorly
Still she joins your story of a life.

So you settle down and the children come
And you find a place that you come from.

269

Your wandering is done.
And all your dreams of open spaces
You find in your children's faces
One by one.

And all the trips you know you missed
And all the lips you never kissed
Cut through you like a knife.
And now you see stretched out before thee
Just another story of a life.

So what do you do now?
When she looks at you now?
You know those same old jokes all the jesters tell
You tell them to her now.
And all the same old songs all the minstrels sang
You sing 'em to her now.
But it don't matter anyhow
'Cause she knows by now.

So every chance you take don't mean a thing.
What variations can you bring
To this shop-worn melody.
And every year goes by like a tollin' bell.
It's battered merchandise you sell.
Not well, she can see.

And though she's heard it all a thousand times
Couched in your attempted rhymes
She'll march to your drum and fife.
But the question echoes up before me
Where's the magic story of a life?

Now sometimes words can serve me well
Sometimes words can go to hell
For all that they do.
And for every dream that took me high
There's been a dream that's passed me by.
I know it's so true

And I can see it clear out to the end
And I'll whisper to her now again
Because she shared my life.

270

For more than all the ghosts of glory
She makes up the story,
She's the only story of my life.

From the cheap seats
Fred Kearns - *My favorite of all songs, any song, play it almost every time I pick up my guitar, have played it at anniversary parties and post my video of me playing when I have had a close relative pass as they had left an impact on me as did Harry.*

Kelly Barry - *Don't think there is a more poignant song in Harry's repertoire. To me, it means more as we age - not sure a young person could fully appreciate it. How someone in his mid-thirties could write this is baffling, but I can tell you that someone in his mid-sixties gets it completely.*

Remember When the Music ****
A song about lost youth and idealism from a simpler time in society which had more sense of unity and togetherness. This is the original upbeat song that is also recorded in a much slower version as the closing track of the album (see **'Remember When the Music- Reprise'**). As the story goes Harry writes it on the day following the death of his friend and hero Al Lowenstein on March 14th 1980; but as we know, the song was actually written prior to January 1980, so although the story fits the song, the date of the song, sadly, doesn't quite fit the story. On December 15th Harry appears on an edition of the *Mike Douglas Show* that had been taped on November 4th, and he performs a moving rendition of the song, introducing it as follows:

"This year has been the best year we've ever had. This last April (actually March) I had a sort of melancholy duty. One of my three heroes, a guy named Al Lowenstein, got shot. For those who don't remember who he was, the fact is in the early sixties he more than anyone else got young white America involved in a quest for racial justice. Later on in the 60s he went to see Bobby Kennedy and asked him if he'd run against President Johnson and end the Vietnam War. Bobby said no. Then he went and saw Gene McCarthy, and he said yes, and the rest is history. Early seventies Al was in Congress himself. Mid-seventies he was ambassador for Human Rights at the United Nations. In 1980 he saw a kid who no one else would see. He put seven bullets into him. Spent the night hoping he'd pull through. He died before midnight, and I wrote this song the next morning when I got up..."

In subsequent concerts Harry also dedicates the song to John Lennon, who was killed on December 8th 1980. For this record and the reprise version that rounds off side two Harry prefers Tom to play acoustic guitar to save him from his *"stumble, bumble fingers,"* and also employs Chuck Kirkpatrick on electric guitar and additional background vocals. Meanwhile Steve Chapin does an excellent job arranging the strings and horns.

271

Quoting a line from the song in a tribute to the singer following his death, *Rolling Stone*'s Dave Marsh writes: *"Harry Chapin may have been naive to think things could be that simple again, but only a real fool would deny that this dream is at the heart of what drew us all to music. This is one of those times when the line gets drawn."*

Up on the Shelf *****
Certainly, one of the underrated highlights of the album, this is another wonderful slice of tongue-in-cheek nostalgia from Harry, in which he contemplates life, music, politics, religious beliefs, and his marriage - all with derisive comments from Big John and Doug thrown in for good measure - and he also gets a rare chance to play trumpet.

From the cheap seats
Anne Tiffen Taylor - *"You've lived yourself a good life, but a blind one."* *Definitely more complicated than upbeat in my opinion. It's an enigma: deep, reflective lyrics set to an upbeat melody and beat.*

Salt and Pepper **
An uptempo and light-hearted tale of an old sailor who misses his adventures at sea but now finds happiness and salvation in his wife, despite the rough and tough demanding demeanor she shows to others – the *"pepper"* to his *"salt,"* especially to his friends in the bar from which he relates the story. But he assures them what she really means to him.

God Babe, You've Been So Good To Me ***
Another tribute to Sandy, which reflects on the early days of their relationship. In a radio-broadcast concert at the Agora Ballroom in Cleveland, he introduces the song as follows: *"This is a song I wrote about five weeks ago on the way to New Orleans. I've been in a very romantic mood lately. I haven't copyrighted it yet so turn on your tape recorders and steal it from me if you like it."*

Northwest 222 **
Inspired by the name of the Minneapolis to New York mail-run night flight that Harry often takes when heading back home from Midwest concerts. When the mail contract is lost in late 1979, Harry puts his feelings into words. Tom Chapin plays banjo on the track.

I Finally Found It Sandy *****
The third of three songs on the album dedicated to Sandy. Unlike most of his tributes to her, this is joyfully upbeat and reflects in Harry his sheer love for not only his wife, but for life itself.

Remember When the Music – Reprise *****

Highlighted by Tom Chapin's evocative acoustic guitar and with strings arranged by Steve, this is a sublime finale to what will become Harry's last completed album. Tom Chapin takes up the story: *"This came about during the sessions. We had worked hard and long in recording the faster version, and I was sitting alone on a couch with my guitar outside the studio when I found the slow riff that opens this version. 'Hey, Harry! Come here and listen to this.' I thought it worked better this way, honoring the lovely melody and giving more time to hear the evocative lyric. Harry & the Alberts liked it, so we recorded it and ended up using both versions, this as the ending song."*

Following the death of John Lennon in December 1980, this was the preferred version sung in concert. In other performances he dedicates it to his friend Al Lowenstein who had recently been killed by a gunman. For this final song, one of the bridges of the uptempo version is omitted, and it changes the whole feel of the song from a happy nostalgic look back at days gone by into a sombre and melancholy epitaph for something more profound that has now gone, maybe never to return. But we can dream there is still hope.

Harry's Comeback Album?

Unlike the fate of the **Legends of the Lost** album, promotion work for this album goes into full swing, with radio stations being bombarded with all the customary hype. For many it is seen as Harry's comeback album, and within weeks Harry is back in LA doing the rounds of the TV and radio stations, conducting performances and interviews, often seizing the opportunity to showcase his political and humanitarian concerns. Not surprisingly the album meets with mixed reviews, with the interest mainly focused on the title track. Chart-wise it manages to emulate *Dance Band*'s moderate success and peaks at #58 on the *Billboard* 100 chart in December and goes on to sell half a million copies. The record label releases several singles, the first being the title track, backed with **'I Finally Found It Sandy'**, and it reaches #23 on the *Billboard* 100, the highest chart position since **'Cat's in the Cradle'**, and one place better than the original **'Taxi'** single. In time it will sell over a million copies and receive platinum status, the fourth and last of Harry's singles to do so. The following year two more singles are lifted from the album. In April **'Remember When the Music'**, backed with **'Northwest 222'**, fails to chart, and the following August **'Story of a Life'**, backed with **'Salt and Pepper'**, is issued with similar results. The album is re-released in 1987 as *Remember When the Music* on the Dunhill Label and includes two unreleased tracks, **'Hokey Pokey'** and a gorgeous Sandy-penned ballad called **'Oh Man'**, culled from the sessions and originally written to provide a voice to the female

273

counterpart in the movie soundtrack for *The Last Protest Singer*. In 1999 a further re-release is issued as *Storyteller* with the ten original tracks.

Meanwhile the touring schedule has to continue. Early November sees performances in Norfolk and Philadelphia, with a whistle-stop flight to LA on the 3rd to tape appearances on the *Mike Douglas* and *Merv Griffin* television shows for screening in December. On November 9th they are in Ithaca, New York, performing two shows at Harry's old alma mater, Cornell University. On December 12th the band appear at the Mill Run Theater in Niles, Illinois and perform the following: Stranger With the Melodies, Up on the Shelf, Dogtown, W.O.L.D., Mercenaries, Cat's in the Cradle, Corey's Coming, Mr Tanner, The Mayor of Candor Lied, Taxi, Better Place To Be, Story of a Life, Flowers Are Red, Let Time Go Lightly (Steve), Sequel, 30,000 Pounds of Bananas, Remember When the Music, Circle.

Three days later there is another afternoon appearance on *The Mike Douglas Show*, followed the next day by taping several songs with the band for an edition of *The Midnight Special* which he will also host. Screened on January 9th, he performs outstanding versions of **'Sequel'**, **'Remember When the Music'** and **'Story of a Life'**. He also makes an appearance on the December 19th edition of the show, hosted by The Pointer Sisters.

It looks like 1981 will be a pivotal year for Harry Chapin. Not only is he in the process of writing new songs and screenplays for TV projects, he will be working on a new album; looking forward to seeing his second book of poetry completed; getting even more involved in supporting the struggling Long Island performing arts; dealing with a new government that could pose a real threat to the very existence of his much-cherished Presidential Commission on world hunger; and, on top of all this, undertaking what looks like being a record-breaking tour schedule at home and abroad.

In December Harry celebrates his 38th birthday, having accomplished in ten years what some artists take a lifetime to achieve. But he is as hungry as ever. There will be no slowing down. For him, it has always been onwards and upwards.

One More Tomorrow

"I was working on the external agenda of being an institutionalized good guy. I realized I wasn't solving my personal questions. I realized you can be a hero to the world, profit the multitudes and still be a louse or nonfactor in terms of home"

Unfinished Business

Harry is looking forward to 1981, but he also needs to look back. These last few months of being constantly on the road touring and promoting his new album, writing poetry and new material for songs and screenplays, and attending meetings near and far, have also had an effect on his family, particularly Sandy. In her eyes he has once again become the **'Cat's in the Cradle'** husband and father. Sandy puts it to him that all the danger signs for their relationship are back again, but it is his twenty-year-old daughter Jaime who puts it across the best. In a meeting with her father back in November she urges him to ease back on his work. While he is out there rectifying other people's problems, he is not solving his own. Once more he is putting his career ahead of his marriage and family. It's another wakeup call. He needs to strike a balance, and with the coming year he will strive to aspire to not just what they want him to be, but what he himself should be.

Harry can see it plainly: *"I was working on the external agenda of being an institutionalized good guy. But I realized I wasn't solving my personal questions. I realized you can be a hero to the world, profit the multitudes and still be a louse or nonfactor in terms of home. It's the participant-observer question again. Career, family, marriage – what's the right balance?"*

Harry's and Sandy's ideas of relaxation cannot be more different. She recalls how their short family vacations, intending to be a relaxing break for all, become for Harry 'working vacations,' with him constantly on the phone in the departure lounge, writing while on the beach or in the hotel room, and then again on the phone once back at the airport. Harry's daughter Jen later admits that every single day Harry had to live with the heavy burden of hypocrisy brought about by **'Cat's in the Cradle'** hanging heavily on his shoulders, and then trying his best to make up for it when he was at home. But Harry is trying to make amends, and starts off the New Year by employing someone to handle the funding of the social causes he is involved with. He also commits himself to reducing the tour dates come the fall so he can work closer to home on some of his other projects, both old and new. Apart from **Cotton Patch Gospel** there are plans to write a screenplay about Cuban revolutionary Che Guevara, and also a plan to resurrect a draft abandoned

275

back in 1977 for a novel based on the song **'The Mayor of Candor Lied'**. But it doesn't stop there. His creative juices are about to overflow. Closer to home he is in talks with the director of the Eglevsky Ballet to incorporate some of his songs into what he calls *Ballads for Ballet*. Apart from seeing the possibilities of his songs **'Taxi'** and **'Sequel'** adapted for a movie, he also begins writing a two-part play called *Goddess of a Woman*, and even a book focusing on his beliefs. And that's not even touching on his political concerns.

Then there's *The Last Protest Singer*. Sandy recalls: *"Harry was thinking more and more of transitioning to film. He was concerned about staff, performer, road crews, etc being dependent on him financially."* Part of Harry's Boardwalk deal includes money for developing a feature film, and as far back as 1978 he has had ideas for a movie based partly on the life of his hero Phil Ochs, but in his own words: *"The man is called Willie Seine, but he is also Wolf Biermann, and Victor Jara and Pete Seeger and Theodorakis and Maria Farantouri and Bulat Okudsava and Ramon and Woody Guthrie and Paul Robeson and Phil Ochs."* Apart from Seeger and Guthrie, for those unfamiliar with some of the other names, Biermann is a German singer-songwriter and former East German dissident best known for his song 'Ermutigung' (encouragement); Jara was a Chilean singer-songwriter and political activist tortured and killed during the Pinochet dictatorship in 1973; Farantouri is a Greek singer and political and cultural activist who collaborated with Miris Theodorakis to record protest songs during the Greek military junta of the late 60s and early 70s; Okudsava is a former Soviet singer-songwriter whose songs presented a subtle challenge to Soviet authority without being overtly political; and Robeson was a black singer famous for his bass baritone as well as his cultural and political activism, and whose Soviet sympathies had him blacklisted during the McCarthy era. With all this in mind, Harry begins to write songs - lots of songs - all intended for the score for his screenplay, and even asks Sandy to write songs for the female lead.

So that's Harry's agenda for 1981. But what about Sandy? Neglected for so long, he now urges her to follow her dream of becoming a teacher. To see this gifted and ambitious woman forever being labelled as just Harry Chapin's wife is shameful. From now on he will give her all the motivation and support to make it happen. He realizes there are two creative people in this relationship and come the spring she will begin teaching a course on Creative Process/Social Issues at Hofstra University on Long Island. Now it's this woman's turn to shine.

Even though come the fall, the initial plan is for the number of tour dates to be curtailed, the year kicks off on January 8th with six shows over three consecutive nights at the historic Bottom Line club in Greenwich Village, as a celebration to mark Harry's 2,000th concert (although largely symbolic, as it's almost impossible to determine the actual number). The band remains the

276

same – Big John, Doug, Steve, Howie and Yvonne. The songs performed over the six shows are: Taxi, Up on the Shelf, Story of a Life, I Miss America, Mercenaries, Better Place To Be, I Wanna Learn a Love Song, Mr Tanner, W.O.L.D., Cat's in the Cradle, Mismatch, Old Folkie, Let Time Go Lightly, Star Tripper, Bluesman, If My Mary Were Here, Paint a Picture of Yourself Michael, Mail Order Annie, Dreams Go By, Poor Damned Fool, Sniper, Remember When the Music, Flowers Are Red, 30,000 Pounds of Bananas, Sequel, You Are the Only Song, Circle.

The shows on the whole are well received by the New York press, although one reviewer criticizes the monotonous similarity of the songs, both in melodic structure and arrangement. The remainder of January brings four concerts in Bloomington, Minnesota and four in Green Bay, Wisconsin, followed by shows in Michigan. On the 24th and 25th the band play four shows in Monroeville, Pennsylvania, and round off the month with two shows in Providence, R.I.

Touring Overseas for the Last Time

A few days later Harry and the band embark on a two-week tour of the UK and Ireland, beginning at the Fairfield Hall in Croydon, just north of London, on February 1st. The local paper reviews the show:

"His ability to put his caustic comment and acute observation of human nature into a form of cameo stories is undoubtedly his most personal gift. Yet a lack of economy and self-discipline in his writing makes his songs long - often to the point of tedium. Length can be justified - but only if development takes place and if colours change - and they don't in many of Harry's numbers.... I shouldn't worry. Harry says and sings what he wants to. He must expect others to do the same."

Over the next few days, the band play in Reading, Manchester and Southport, followed by performing to their enthusiastic Irish fans in Belfast, Dublin and Cork. Returning to England they appear in Birmingham and at two venues in London, the last being the Dominion Theatre on the 11th.

While in London Harry once again takes the opportunity of appearing on BBC radio for a Sunday morning special hosted by his old friend Noel Edmonds. Accompanying him on the tour are Jenny and Josh, who, required by their school to keep journals of their visit, do their very best to steal the show. When Noel asks Josh what his dad is really like, Josh immediately replies, "I don't know, he's away too much." During the show Harry performs **'W.O.L.D.'**, **'Salt and Pepper'**, and **'Story of a Life'** before the kids (and Noel) join him in an impromptu rendition of **'Flowers Are Red'**. The next two days find Harry in the north of the country with concerts in Leeds, York and Newcastle. A final show in Edinburgh on the 15th brings the UK and Ireland tour to a satisfactory end.

When Harry returns to Secret Sound Studio in late June 1981 some twenty-one songs have been written and eventually demoed, including a version of **'Last Stand'** with Big John on lead vocals. There are also cuts made of Steve's **'Love Is Not In Season'** and Tom's **'Number One'**. The plan is to meet up again later in the summer to actually record the album. A record of the songs taped at the sessions include the following: **'The Last Protest Singer'**; **'November Rains'**; **'Basic Protest Song'**; **'Last Stand'** (with Harry on lead vocal); **'Last Stand'** (with Big John on lead vocal); **'Sounds Like America To Me'**; **'Word Wizard (Word Seller)'**; **'Anthem'**; **'A Quiet Little Love Affair'**; **'I Don't Want to Be President'**; **'Silly Little Girl'**; **'You Own the Only Light'**; **'Love Is Not in Season'** (Steve on lead vocal); **'Number One'** (Tom on lead vocal); **'Hokey Pokey'**; **'Watch Me Drown'**; **'Tomorrow is Today'** (originally written for the *Sequel* album); **'Wind Coming Up'**; **'Oh Man'** and **'My Brother John'**.

These demo tapes become the only musical documentation of Harry's new songs. The proposed album is dubbed *"music to accompany the truth,"* but some fans will be disappointed to see a marked change to what they have heard previously. In fact, with these new songs and Harry's political state of mind, Harry could be putting his hard-fought reputation on the line. It's hard to see that this album will endear him to many of his devoted fans. In 1988, seven years after Harry's death, the tapes, now in Sandy's possession, are handed over to producers Keith Walsh and Clair Marlo to be worked on and cleaned up. At Secret Sound Studio they begin the process of mixing and mastering what are considered the most completed songs. With additional musicians including Grant Geissman (guitar), Jon Cobert and Pat Coil (synth & acoustic piano), Bill Lanphier (bass), and M B Gordy (drums), work is carried out to embellish the tracks, with Harry's voice then overdubbed. Additional work is done at Counterpoint Studio in New York, and Record One and Juniper Studios in Los Angeles, with mixing completed by Walsh at Media Sound, New York, and final mastering at Future Disc Systems in Hollywood by Steve Hoffman.

The Last Protest Singer (1988) ***
Dunhill Compact Classics DZL 041
Recorded from demo tapes: Secret Sound Studio & Counterpoint, New York; Record One & Juniper Studios L.A, September 1988
US Release date: November 30th 1988
Producer: Keith Walsh & Clair Marlo

The eleven chosen songs are perhaps the best that could have been selected, but some fans believe that Tom's **'Number One'** and Steve's **'Love**

278

Is Not in Season' should have been chosen over what may be considered lackluster tracks. Also failing to make the cut is Big John's version of **'Last Stand'**, allegedly the one Harry intended to use. However, the tracks finally chosen have been completed *"in a way that honors Harry's intent."* Unfortunately, we'll never know what Harry's real intent was.

Apart from there being no poignant story songs, there is, as the title of the album suggests, an almost complete collection of political statements - Harry's last stab at a country and government whose political trends he feels so unhappy with - which are filled with both cynicism and mockery. Was this heralding a new direction for Harry? Just one of the many nagging questions that can never be answered. There are echoes of the Farley Higgins character from *Sniper and Other Love Songs*, but here we have Willie Seine, a man Harry sees as a composite of the great American protest singers like Woody Guthrie and Pete Seeger, and through the course of the eleven songs we follow his journey. The problem here is getting the feel for the album that Harry intended. With no clues as to what the final track order was to be, there is no narrative structure; no bigger picture; and there's a rawness in Harry's vocal that may betray a possible fractured weariness.

For the eleven songs I will let my friend and fellow fan Scott Sivakoff, a fine musician in his own right, give his own interpretations as an interesting counterpoint to my own views.

Last of the Protest Singers ***

Willy Seine, the narrator, laments on the fact that nobody protests about anything anymore and that he is being looked on as some kind of 'novelty act.'

Scott Sivakoff - *To me, this song seems a little autobiographical. Harry was always putting himself out there to try to save the world. In this song he seems to ask if it's worth it. The line "Should I just play some rock and roll, 'cause nobody really gives a damn" makes me wonder if he was questioning whether the good fight was all worth it. I think in his heart of hearts he knew that he was making such a difference and his efforts were worth it. The song, to me, is an interesting reflection on that.*

November Rains ***

A love song of sorts, but also a portent of death. There's a roughness in Harry's voice that sets it apart from the gorgeous love ballads found on previous albums. Whatever happened to that angelic voice that graced **'Old College Avenue'** some seven years before?

Scott Sivakoff - *I wonder if this song is a metaphor to the way people were feeling at the time given the state of the country and the world. The song*

279

does have elements of hope in there: "November Rains! Why don't you shine your warm sun on down? November Rains! Why don't you keep me warm past sun down? Why don't you rain your warm sun down? Down on me?" There is some pleading, even some hope there.

Basic Protest Song *
For me not one of Harry's finest moments. It just doesn't hold up amongst the rest of the songs here and should have been left in the box of demo tapes. Harry almost growls out the lyrics, maybe intentionally, but it leaves you to wonder if it's just a symptom of a growing tiredness in what he's doing.

Scott Sivakoff - *This song is very interesting. I like it for two reasons. First, I love the music and the style. The music is powerful and the style is a little different from what we are used to from Harry. Second, the message is great! I love how there is the juxtaposition of moving through life and doing the normal things that we all do as if there is some great formula we should all follow and all the while learning and asking questions until some of us wind up at that age where we look back and realize that in the pursuit of that formulated life, we forgot about those lessons and the things we questioned. Really wonderful stuff.*

Last Stand ****
Possibly intended to be the final track on the album. Before being led off to torture and a welcome death Willie recognizes that this time it's him that's on the line and he dies understanding it's *"too late to find that one last face waiting in the rain."* The song is inspired by the news of the assassination attempt on President Reagan in March 1981. Even with Harry singing this, it is undoubtedly the most sing-along track on the album, and perhaps the best-known song, allegedly the last one Harry ever writes that goes on to be recorded.

Scott Sivakoff - *I like this song a lot as it appears to tell us that we should always fight right up to the end. I think that Harry did that. From what I have heard and read, the man almost never rested. Some have speculated that Harry must have though his time was short and therefore was pushing for everything he could all the time. In that respect "when you hear the sound of taps played by the one man band, you know this is where you have to make your last stand."*

Sounds Like America to Me ****
Compared to the more raucous political statements on the album, this is Harry in a mellower mood but still making a point as he attacks the country's vanishing values and shames almost any American that is listening to it.

Scott Sivakoff - *I think this song is like* **'Dance Band On the Titanic'** *or* **'The Rock'** *in that it talks about distraction. It's very easy to get distracted with easy things: new taste-sensation; simple questions we can all understand, etc. I think that Harry saw a different kind of America (or at least hoped to see a different kind of America) and this song illustrates that. The chorus is almost shaming the listener...*

Word Wizard ***
Willie's wife (maybe) reflecting on his journey and how she should react on his return. Wonderful music track makes this stand out.

Scott Sivakoff - *I can't say for certain, but I think that this song is almost like the narrator (not necessarily, but could be Harry himself) looking back at him or herself and questioning what he/she sees. The person on the outside almost appears to be describing someone who is not paying attention to them, but that they are sticking by anyway because they feel such a strong connection that even though they are being fed these (possibly) made up stories they still stick by and move forward. (Interesting side note: I think that this song was originally titled* **'Word Seller'** *and had slightly different lyrics which are on the original demos).*

Anthem **
Willie sings about a young actress he meets, and he dies singing one of his popular songs, having *"never found the music to accompany the truth."* One of the songs that is dropped for the Chapin Productions re-release.

Scott Sivakoff - *I think that this is one of those songs that attempts to describe the state of the world at the time. A lot of what it says is still true today. The song does it through the eyes of the "old man" who is looking for the best of what this country has to offer, but is also finding that in some way (many ways) it comes up short. In the end, I think the realization is that no one is perfect (not even the country) and sometimes you have to just take the compromise.*

A Quiet Little Love Affair **
Willie sings about why he is losing faith with the country he once loved. This song is also dropped for the Chapin Productions re-release.

Scott Sivakoff - *In the same context as* **'Basic Protest Song'**, *I find this song interesting because it starts off on a very positive note. If you take the literal approach to this, the guy in the story starts off his relationship with this country like the start of a love affair with another person. It's all fun, rainbows and unicorns at the beginning. But relationships take a lot of work and the*

281

lesson here is that if you don't work at your relationships (with people, your country or whatever), usually those relationships will fall apart. I have heard Harry say that we live in a participatory democracy. You can't just vote every two or four years, do nothing else and expect the love affair to stay fresh and good.

I Don't Want to Be President **
Willie meets the power brokers - the *"men who own the sky and the soil."*

Scott Sivakoff - *Another song about doing what you are expected to do versus doing what you want or what is best. Also, this song is a bit about compromise as well. The person in this story just wants to help and be as helpful as possible. He is not power hungry or ambitious, but I think he understands that sometimes having that power thrust upon you is the best way to be effective. Great leaders usually don't seek power, but rather power is thrust upon them. Had Harry gone into politics, I believe that he would have done so to be more effective and I believe that he would have been a great leader.*

Silly Little Girl ***
As Willie Seine packs his knapsack to head off on his journey his wife warns him that when he returns, she won't be there.

Scott Sivakoff - *Harry was out touring, trying to "save the world", make time for family, etc. Sometimes you have to slow down and pay attention to what's important so that you are not dealing with a silly little girl, but rather are back in the world dealing with mature relationships.*

You Own the Only Light ****
Harry's final love song to Sandy? Perhaps, but still an unexpected finale (if that is what it was meant to be) to what is mainly a politically-themed album, and it begs to wonder if this would have actually made the final album, as it seems quite out of place with the other songs. Having said that, we must be thankful that it was considered near complete and so was included here. A wonderful ballad.

Scott Sivakoff - *A wonderful bookend to this album. A real love song! I am not sure if the person Harry is singing to is a real person, an idea, the country, etc. However, this song leaves the listener with a positive feeling. If you can share your light with someone/something you can have a real relationship and get something good out of it.*

Somethin's Brewin' in Gainesville

During the fall of 1980 Harry had been approached to write music for a one-man show called *Somethin's Brewin' in Gainesville*, based on the late Dr Clarence Jordan's book *Cotton Patch Version of Matthew and John*. Jordan, a theologian and minister, was a farmer and New Testament Greek scholar, who in 1942 had founded Koinonia Farm, a small but highly influential interracial farming community at Americus in southwestern Georgia. While studying at college he had come to believe that the roots of poverty were spiritual as well as economic. When the farm became a target for repeated violence and an economic boycott throughout the 50s and 60s, President Eisenhower refused to intervene, nor did the state governor, a firm supporter of racial segregation, who went as far as investigating Jordan and his partners for purported Communist ties. Before his death in 1969, with hostility now subsiding, Jordan focused his efforts on writing, and among his most celebrated work was the *Cotton Patch* series, a paraphrase of the New Testament, in which he translated the context of scripture by using American analogies. As a result, Rome is substituted by Washington, Judaea becomes Georgia, Jerusalem becomes Atlanta, and Bethlehem becomes Gainesville. The story has Christ's birth in 1980s Gainesville, and portrays the effects it has on him growing up in the Deep South, with some passages from his translations. Not only does the book go on to sell over 300,000 copies, it comes to the attention of a promising Atlanta-based young actor and singer called Tom Key, who takes the book to heart and begins visiting divinity schools and colleges in the south, performing a one-man show based on the stories, playing over thirty characters with his wonderful baritone voice. He doesn't take long to get noticed, and while performing at a college in Alabama in the fall of 1980 he is approached by stage director Russell Treyz and invited to come to New York and perform to some important people in the business, including acclaimed producer Phillip Getter. Getter is amazed at what he sees and as a result Treyz and Key write a new book and two-act play called *Somethin's Brewin' in Gainesville*.

After Harry is approached by Getter to contribute a couple of songs, he goes to see the play in New York and is impressed with the whole concept and its outrageous anachronism, even taking a fresh look at Jesus Christ as being a *"genuine revolutionary."* Instead of contributing a couple of songs, he offers to write a whole bunch of songs for the show - some thirty in fact – and help with the adaptation, which delves even further into the Southern vernacular than Jordan's original. Harry also gets his brother Tom on board as musical director. The style of the show is radically changed, and where once it was a one-man show, a four-piece band known as The Cotton Pickers is introduced, consisting of Pete Corum (bass fiddle), Michael Mark (guitar and mandolin), Scott Ainsle (fiddle, banjo, mandolin, dobro) and Jim Lauderdale. As the setting is rural Georgia, it gives the show a fresh country and western/bluegrass feel, and Harry writes songs with that in mind. Of the songs Harry contributes, sixteen are finally chosen. Twelve are new compositions, as well as two taken from the Broadway show, *The Night That Made America Famous*, (**'When I Look Up'** and **'You Are Still My Boy'**), and two from previous albums, **'I Wonder (What Would Happen To This World)'**, from *Living Room Suite*, the lyric of which ends up on Harry's tombstone; and, at Sandy's suggestion, a re-working of **'Everybody's Lonely'** from *Heads and Tales* to be called **'One More Tomorrow'**.

Rehearsals for the new show begin at the 500-odd seat Charles Playhouse in Boston in late May, with six previews commencing June 4th and the opening show on the 10th. It is a low-budget affair without stage props, and the plan is for a five-week run in Boston before hopefully transferring it to Broadway. Although the previews are mainly performed to a half-empty hall, come opening night there is standing room only, thanks to the efforts of Harry and his friend Zeke Marsden, who offer free tickets to all and sundry.

The songs in the show are as follows:

Act I

'Somethin's Brewin' in Gainesville'; 'Baby Born to God'; 'I Did It'; 'Mama is Here / I Did it (reprise)'; 'It Isn't Easy'; 'Sho'Nuff'; 'Turn It Around'; 'When I Look Up'; 'Ain't No Busy Signals'; 'Spitball'; 'Miracle on Stone Mountain'; 'Love the Lord Your God'; 'Blind Date'; 'Goin' to Atlanta'

Act II

'Are We Ready?'; 'You Are Still My Boy'; 'We Gotta Get Organized'; 'We're Gonna Love It While It Lasts'; 'Jubilation'; 'Dangerous Man'; 'Jud'; 'Hey, What's Goin' On?'; 'Jud (reprise)'; 'Thank God For Governor Pilate'; 'One More Tomorrow'; 'I Wonder (with Jubilation reprise)'; 'Somethin's Brewin' in Gainesville (reprise)'

But this is a progressive show in a conservative Boston, and it brings a mixed bag of reviews, with *Boston Globe*'s Kevin Kelly saying *"Somethin's Brewin' is Really Sumpin' Awful."* Within a few days the show closes, and with it, Harry's participation. The show will eventually go on to achieve great success as *Cotton Patch Gospel*, but sadly Harry won't be there to see it.

Cotton Patch Gospel

On October 21st 1981, three months after Harry's death, a tightened and revitalized version of *Somethin's Brewin'*, now with the catchier title *Cotton Patch Gospel*, opens off-Broadway at Lambs Theatre 130, West 44th St. and

284

runs for 193 performances. Produced by Phil Getter and directed by Russell Treyz, with Tom Chapin as musical director, it stars Tom Key and the Cotton Pickers band, consisting of Scott Ainsle, Michael Mark, Pete Corum and Jim Lauderdale. Drama critics love the show and so do many religious commentators. *Contemporary Christian Music* call it: *"A dream come true. A breath of fresh air."* The *American Baptist Magazine* is also impressed by the *"powerful drama and joyous celebration."* The *Messenger* concludes with a *"rollicking foot-stomping, hand-clapping new musical."*

Tom Key is undoubtedly the star of the show, playing a multitude of characters ranging from Jesus to 'Governor' Pilate. The production's country songs move the characters through the stages of Jesus's earthly ministry, most of which occurs in Georgia. Like Jordan's original, the musical adaptation is intended to offer people a fresh perspective on Jesus's life and provide a modern twist on the Gospel message. The satirical flavor of the show is highlighted by a monologue filled with food references and jokes about the Bible and scenes that wouldn't look out of place in a Monty Python sketch. When Jesus is born to *"God and a Georgia girl,"* three angels appear bearing cheese-dogs, while Mary begins writing in her baby book. As Jesus reaches adulthood he goes on a tour with the Bible like a preacher until he falls in with a band of cronies that include Jack, Jim, Rock and Jud. In another scene Jesus pretends to walk on water while feeding the masses with five boxes of Nabiscos and two cans of sardines. The scene later switches to Atlanta and Jesus ends up being lynched, not crucified, by the Ku Klux Klan and Governor Pilate.

A Head Full of New Ideas

The show goes on to play to packed houses around the country over the next four decades and receives unanimous critical praise along the way. It even becomes the only off-Broadway show to receive praise from both music and religious publications. In the decades to come following his untimely death, Harry's name will be shining brightly in theaters and playhouses all across the country. Although praised by the critics, the show's songs divide opinions among his many fans. Had he lived, some see this as a turning point in Harry's music career, and a gradual shift from recording to musical theater. After all the negativity heaped on previous shows like **The Night That Made America Famous**, **The Zinger** and **Chapin**, the plaudits for **Cotton Patch Gospel** would have been for Harry like a shot of adrenalin and maybe would have convinced him, and producers alike, that musical theater was the way forward. The demands of constant touring with the band were no doubt causing a strain on Harry and his family. His voice was changing, with a sometimes rasping and almost growling vocal evident in some of the last concerts he did and the demos he made for ***The Last Protest Singer***. In interviews conducted after live shows that sometimes go on for three hours or more, he often appears physically drained, but he still manages to retain the determination to put his views across, almost robotically, in his own inimitable style.

Harry is not the same man he was ten years before. The energy is still there, for sure, the charismatic charm evident in abundance, but the rigors of recording music seem to be getting in the way of his real ambitions. Less focused now in the studio, he seems to be in a quandary over what should take priority. Although in the previous twelve months he has performed a record number of concerts, there appears to be no let-up and he is already planning an extensive late-summer tour. The failure of PAF is a bitter blow for him and Sandy, but the concert stage and the ability to raise funds for good causes is still the place where he feels he can do the most good, although the conflict between being on the road or at home with his growing family will no doubt remain a constant issue. His head is filled with new ideas for songs, shows and revues, and maybe these will for a time take precedence over any more studio albums.

But this of course is all supposition. Harry is still the consummate entertainer, and performing his lifeblood. For an artist who has already made half a dozen stellar albums, he is following in the footsteps of his contemporaries, many of whom have produced what is considered their best work in their earlier years. But Harry has many strings to his bow. While he excels as a writer and performer, he is also a great communicator who can reach out to people in a way few others can ever hope to. He is a pain-in-the-ass activist who antagonizes some; wins the lifelong respect of many. As an award-winning but underrated film producer he can quite easily turn his hand to making movies, maybe even bringing some of his story songs to the big screen. Like the ones he faced so many times in his past, there will be more crossroads to come; more decisions over which direction to take. What can be certain is, whichever path Harry will choose to travel, it will no doubt bring more demands and challenges, but ultimately it will also lead to success and personal gratification. Maybe he just needs a little more time to do it… maybe just one more tomorrow.

Last Stand

"Harry once said to me that if there is a God, it must be a God who recognizes our weaknesses and then hugs us. Well, now Harry knows who God is. He beat us on that one, too." (Bill Ayres)

More Problems Closer to Home

The touring schedule continues into March with two shows in Dallas and Phoenix before hitting the West Coast. Following a show at the Dorothy Chandler Pavilion in Los Angeles the band play a week of 50-minute shows at the Sahara Tahoe Hotel in South Lake Tahoe, Nevada, commencing on the 3rd (the time restriction imposed due to loss of revenue by people not gambling). The schedule continues with a performance in Portland, followed on the 14th with Harry making a solo appearance on the *Solid Gold* television show at the Paramount Theater in Seattle. Co-hosted by singer Leo Sayer, he performs another top-notch performance of **'Remember When the Music'**, dedicating it to both Al Lowenstein and the late John Lennon. The remainder of March sees shows in Michigan, Minnesota, and North Dakota, as well as a visit to Canada for concerts in Winnipeg, Regina, Banff and Saskatoon. Before the start of the last performance on the 30th, Harry and the band are watching the news in their hotel room showing the attempted assassination of President Reagan. Inspired by the events of the day, Harry begins putting together a song he calls **'Last Stand'**, and, during the soundcheck that evening, he begins working on the arrangement with Big John in mind as lead vocalist. For the next three weeks the concerts bring Harry and the band closer to home, with dates in Massachusetts, New Jersey, Pennsylvania, New York and Connecticut.

On April 1st the band play the Walter Brown Arena in Boston and have the following setlist: Mercenaries, They Call Her Easy, Mr Tanner, Cat's in the Cradle, Remember When the Music, Dreams Go By, Taxi, Corey's Coming, Flowers Are Red, Mail Order Annie, Let Time Go Lightly (Steve), Better Place To Be, 30,000 Pounds of Bananas, Sequel, You are the Only Song, Circle. A week later they begin the first of three days performing at the annual Valley Forge Music Fair in Devon, Pennsylvania, followed on the 12th by a concert at Fairfield University in Connecticut. The following day Harry takes the band to Secret Sound Studio in New York to start rehearsing and recording demos for some of the new songs he has written for the next album, *The Last Protest Singer*. The remainder of April includes concerts in Kentucky, Indiana, Michigan, Illinois and Iowa.

287

That spring Harry establishes the Democratic Project, a think tank which will outline a new economic agenda for the party in light of the Republican success in the election. This not only threatens Harry's Presidential Hunger Commission, but also the sustainability of PAF, the Eglevsky Ballet, and the Long Island Philharmonic, which are all barely keeping their heads above water. Harry promises to donate the proceeds of one concert a month to the project and appoints Mark Green as executive director. For much of May Harry and the band perform shows around New York, Pennsylvania, and Massachusetts, with a final visit to Canada to do four concerts at the new O'Keefe Center in Toronto on the 16th and 17th. In between concerts Harry continues writing songs for the next album.

On May 26th the band are back at Secret Sound in New York along with new producer Brooks Arthur recording demos of new songs slated for the new album and possible soundtrack for the proposed movie. They include 'Last Stand', with Harry now singing lead vocal, although he still has Big John in mind for the final version. Arthur is already a well-established engineer and producer, having worked alongside Janis Ian on her Grammy-winning album *Between the Lines* and the hit single 'At Seventeen'.

It has been a tough start to the year for PAF in Huntington. With subscriptions having fallen below 4,000, it now has a record deficit of $550,000. Harry is not joking when he tells the papers he is broke. He has been giving away more money than he's been making, and it's finally caught up with him. He hasn't even the funds to pay for an ad in the *Long Island Newsday* paper to make a plea for public support to save PAF. Only through the help of his friend David Laventhol, the paper's publisher, does he manage to buy time and get the ads put in on a six-month payment plan. However, no offers of financial help come, and in February PAF files for bankruptcy, although allowed to operate for another six months as long as no further debts are incurred. Shows have to be cancelled and cutbacks made with personnel, and even two benefit concerts at Huntington High School with Pete Seeger only manage to raise $20,000, just enough to keep the playhouse open for a week, and consequently well short of the intended target. It sounds the death knell and by the end of the year PAF will cease for good.

With Harry's spring tour coming to an end on May 31st at Chateau Deville in Framingham, near Boston, it's time for him to take it easy, and only a handful of concerts are held throughout June, beginning with two shows in Charlotte, North Carolina, on the 2nd; a solo concert at the 8th Annual Lively Arts Festival on the 7th; a performance at the Broome County Arena in Binghampton, New York, on the 12th; and ending with two shows at the Dr Pepper Summer Music Festival in New York on June 24th and 25th. Now in its 16th season, it is held this year at the city's Pier 84, while Central Park's Wollman Skating Rink is under renovation. In front of a capacity 8,000-strong audience that includes Mayor Ed Koch, Harry and the band perform what will be their last major public concert. On June 25th Harry tapes another appearance on the television show *Solid Gold* with fellow guests Carol Bayer Sager and Dionne Warwick. During the show he and Tom perform **'Circle'** together. It is not aired nationally until August 1st, making it Harry's last ever television appearance. The day after the Dr Pepper shows he is back at Secret Sound doing more work on the demo tapes for *The Last Protest Singer*. With an empty schedule ahead of him, Harry takes his family on a well-earned vacation to Hawaii, returning to Huntington on Monday, July 13th, refreshed and eager to get back to performing and finishing the new album.

Long Island Expressway, Thursday July 16th

Plans are soon underway to commence a late-summer tour schedule, beginning in three days' time with a free concert at the Lakeside Theater in Eisenhower Park, East Meadow, Long Island, followed the next night with a performance at the Hampton Beach Casino in New Hampshire, and a few days later a return to the Garden State Arts Center (PNC) in Holmdel, New Jersey.

On the morning of Thursday, July 16th, the day of the Lakeside concert, Harry is up and about early, making calls and checking his appointments for the day, which include a couple of afternoon business meetings in Manhattan. One is with manager Jeb Hart at the EMI offices to plan a more sensible concert schedule, while the other is a meeting to discuss his role in the upcoming PBS film *Working*, based on Louis "Studs" Terkel's book *Working: People Talk About What They Do All Day and How They Feel About What They Do*, recently adapted as a play on Broadway. That morning Harry also learns that his friend Kenny Rogers will make a major financial commitment for ten years and sponsor the World Hunger Media Awards, which goes to journalists who write about hunger issues. Setting off around noon in Jaime's blue 1975 VW Rabbit (apparently because the tape deck in his van isn't working), Harry stops ten minutes later for coffee and a snack cake at the Halesite Bay Deli along Huntington's New York Avenue. Philip Purpura, owner of the deli, recalls the following day: *"He stopped in here an hour before he died, and offered to save me a front row seat at his concert last night. He walked behind the counter and took his own coffee and custard, just like he always did. That was at 12.10..."* Harry then heads off, taking his usual shortcut to get on the busy Long Island Expressway (Interstate 495) at Exit 45A. Once there Harry keeps in the left-hand lane at a steady 65mph.

What happens next is reliant on witness statements. Some 25 miles short of his destination, Harry suddenly turns on his emergency lights, perhaps due to mechanical or a medical problem. At around 12.27pm, approaching Exit 40 in Jericho, his car slows right down to about 15mph and in what could be his efforts to get off the highway his car veers across into the centre lane, almost striking another car. Veering left and right Harry's car is hit from behind by a 38-wheel flatbed tractor-trailer traveling over 50mph, and unable to apply its brakes in time. As they collide, the truck mounts Harry's car, ruptures a gas tank, and explodes in flames. Robert Eggleton, the truck driver, together with another trucker, manage to cut the seat belt and drag the unconscious Harry out of the burning car through the broken window, and within minutes he is taken by police helicopter to Nassau County Medical Centre, where for half an hour a team of doctors try to revive him. All attempts fail and Harry is pronounced dead at 1.05pm. He was 38 years old.

Dr Minouri Araki, Nassau County's deputy chief medical examiner, reports that Harry's aorta was lacerated by the impact and as a result he died of massive internal hemorrhaging in his chest cavity. He rules out a possible heart attack at the wheel, but states that he suffered a cardiac arrest due to his severe injuries. An autopsy reveals that his heart was in very good condition. It is also reported that Harry had been driving without a valid license, having already had it revoked due to previous traffic violations. Tom is the first family member to receive the news, and although shocked he is not really surprised by what's happened. At his home in Brooklyn, where he shares an apartment block with Harry's managers Jeb Hart and Bob Hinkle, he is asked by their secretary to go up to their office and take a telephone call from the police concerning Harry. At the time Jeb and Bob are in Manhattan waiting for Harry to arrive for their scheduled meeting. After hearing the news, Tom has a conversation with the police about trying to confirm Harry's identify, and he remembers that Harry often wears an inscribed gold pocket watch given to him by his friend Michael Moore for doing several benefits for his struggling newspaper. The police are also able to verify his name through a license plate check. Tom then gives Jeb a call and between them they begin phoning around to break the news.

That afternoon Harry and his family had been invited to a birthday barbecue at the home of his personal assistant Don Ruthig in the neighboring town to Huntington. Sandy is already there helping set up, with the kids coming a little later. As usual Harry is late. For some reason Sandy has to return home to pick something up, and while she's gone Don gets the call from Jeb. Don then has to go over to Sandy's house to break the terrible news to her. Howie Fields is also at Don's house when the news comes through:

"We were supposed to play a free concert that evening at Eisenhower Park in Hempstead, Long Island, which was very close to Huntington, Long Island where Harry lived. Don Ruthig was the fellow in charge of Harry's office and he decided to have a party/barbecue at his house that afternoon so there we were swimming in the pool, eating, drinking, having a good time. At one point I took a walk inside the house and I was in there with Don, Ann Chapin (Steve Chapin's now ex-wife), and a couple of other people. Don was very quietly sitting close to the phone and after several minutes the phone rang

290

and he picked it up, exchanged a few words with someone, hung up the phone and, in tears, said 'He's dead.' That's how I found out. John Wallace showed up shortly after that and that's when he found out I believe. Then at some point we made our way over to the concert site where there were already a few hundred people assembled. I believe it was concert promoter John Scher who took the stage and informed the crowd that 'Harry Chapin was involved in a fatal car accident.' After that we all convened at Harry's house and stayed till quite late. I drove guitarist Doug Walker to Brooklyn and then went home."

That evening, out at East Meadow on the grassy knoll above Lakeside Theater, thousands of Harry's fans have already made themselves comfortable in readiness for the evening show. By 6.30pm word is passed around by the security guards' walkie-talkies: *"All traffic out. No concert."* The tragic news of the accident that happened six hours earlier soon spreads. Stunned and bewildered, many fans who have come to watch the free concert scheduled to begin at 8pm refuse to leave the park, and remain on their blankets drinking and talking quietly. Some gather together and spontaneously start singing his songs. Ethel Fleiss of Huntington, who had arrived with her daughter at 4pm to claim a front-row seat, recalls: *"We were his friends, anyone in Huntington was his friend. He was one of those guys who would rush up to you in the supermarket and kiss you even if he didn't know your name, but he knew he'd seen you before and he knew you were from Huntington."* At 8.25pm, when the stage crews had dismantled the equipment and left, several thousand of the expected 25,000 are still there, gathered together in groups and singing, passing lighted candles around the circles. Young 17-year-old Nancy Heller of East Northport, playing her guitar in one of the groups, recalls later: *"He inspired me to write my first song. I came up to him at a concert and said, 'Will you be my friend?' He said, 'Forever friends.' My God, how he touched me."*

John Rockwell of the *New York Times* reports Harry's death on July 17th with the simple headline: 'Harry Chapin, Singer, Killed in Crash'. The news is also announced in a United Press statement the following day.

The news of Harry's death reaches people at different times and in many different ways. Living in the UK, I was in the kitchen making breakfast for my two-year-old daughter the following morning when the news came on the radio. When my wife came home from work that evening, she couldn't understand why I had his albums scattered all over the floor, and the track I was playing at the time was **'Shooting Star'**. I thought that was very apt - that night Harry was the brightest star in the sky.

Barry Hochberg - *My wife and I (we saw two of his concerts together) had just returned from our honeymoon and our good friends called us to turn on the news. We went from the honeymoon high to a very sad low.*

Suzi Singleton - *I heard it on the car radio in CT, in the backseat of the car with my little sister. We were young but had sung along with* **Greatest Stories Live** *for what felt like forever. I remember us holding hands and crying. We got to the drive in. My stepfather told us to shut up. I remember so clearly looking at him and saying "don't you understand? Harry's dead, man!" My sister and I held each other and cried softly. I don't remember what movie we saw. I don't think we paid any attention.*

Jacky Hahl McCurdy - *I was working in a nursing home, in one of the back rooms and it came over the radio. I had to hold onto a bed rail to keep from collapsing. I cried, burst into tears. The only time I have ever cried over a celebrity's death. I went to the kitchen, and people asked me why I was crying. Believe it or not, some had never heard of him, some were like...oh ok...but I was devastated. We had tickets the following week to see him at Garden State Arts Center. He was such a part of my musical life...to this day, I sob when I sing* **'Corey's Coming'***.....Eyes are getting weepy as I think about that day...*

Tony Zimmerling - *I was at a record store earlier in the day. Went to dinner at my mom's. She told me Harry had died. I couldn't put any words together. I just pulled one of the just purchased albums out of my bag. It was Harry's* **On the Road to Kingdom Come***. Turns out I bought it about the exact time of Harry's death.*

Patricia Ehrich - *I was getting ready for work. Got a call from my mother-in-law telling me the horrible news. Needless to say, I did not go to work that evening. Went over to my daughter's babysitter's house and talked nonstop about Harry. I didn't want to be alone and could not believe this could be true. I was just devastated.*

Frederick Hintze - *I was out of the country having a great time on vacation. Picked up the USA Today and my heart sank.*

Eric Smith - *I was just out of college at a corporate training event in Malvern PA. I was planning to join my new friends for dinner and drinks when I heard the news. I was devastated and just stayed in my hotel room and reflected/mourned over the life and loss. In Harry's words, there was neon outside the window (that night) not the moon.*

Cliff Geismar - *I was in my car at the entrance to Eisenhower Park to get in to see Harry play. The man at the gate told us. My brother said he was kidding. I knew he wasn't. It was a very bad day... After we got into the park, I remember we sang* **'Circle'** *at the lake in Eisenhower Park.*

Michele Franco Perez - *My mother called me at work and told me so I wouldn't hear it on the radio on the way home. Mom was always thinking of my well-being. I was devastated.*

Jason Colannino - *My family and I just came back from the beach that day. It was a pretty average summer day, till I heard the news on WNEW, Bill*

292

Ayers and Pete Fornatale sharing stories and playing the music. Since then, summers have never really been the same.

Mary Jo McDonough - *My great aunt had died that morning, so my family was busy contacting other family members and friends. When I phoned my brother in Boston, he thought I was calling about Harry, whom I had not heard about yet. I immediately called a fellow Harry lover and we spent the entire night into morning sitting on my patio, drinking wine, reminiscing about Harry concerts we'd been to and listening to WNEW New York radio. It didn't seem real.*

Frank Walker - *I was getting ready to see him at Eisenhower Park that night when I heard it on the TV News. I went anyway & everyone was still there, shocked, singing his songs. I brought a poster I drew of him that I was hoping to give him & put on the brick wall in front of the stage. After walking around, I came back to the poster & it was surrounded by candles & one of the TV news stations was filming it.*

Gary Licker - *When I arrived at the Lakeside Theater on July 16, 1981, there were less than 20 people who had already shown up. It was 12 noon and I secured my front row seat. I basked in the sun for the next 8 hours listening to my boom box and watching the grounds fill with fans. This was to be my first time ever seeing Harry and I couldn't be more excited! As the sun was setting and the crowd was still increasing, there was a murmur that rippled through the field. Soon we would learn of Harry's fate and the concert that was not to be became a vigil.*

Eric Zahrn - *I was in Belleville Il at my wife's cousin's, watching TV with the sound off, and trying to keep our two sons asleep. When Harry's face came on TV I knew it wasn't good. Long sad ride back to Indiana the next day. Made sure all four sons and some of their friends grew up to 'Mr Tanner', 'Bummer', and all the others. A life-changing weekend!*

Gerry Naughton - *I was living in London at the time, but was back home in my native Ireland on holiday. The Evening Press came into my brother's house whilst I was visiting. After browsing the sports pages (always first), I turned to the news and saw a small article about Harry's death. My niece saw that my face went pale, because I had been to Harry's concert in London only a few months earlier and we spoke briefly...Harry's songs will live forever!*

On a Hillside in Huntington

On July 21st, on a little hillside at Huntington Rural Cemetery, overlooking the town, Harry is quietly laid to rest in a simple ceremony attended by some fifty mourners consisting mainly of just family and close friends. After reading a passage from the Bible, Ayres remembers: *"Harry once said to me that if there is a God, it must be a God who recognizes our weaknesses and then hugs*

293

us. Well, now Harry knows who God is. He beat us on that one, too." Standing by the solid oak casket, alongside Bill and the Reverend Goldie Sherrill, pastor of Grace Church, Sandy reads one of Harry's favorite poems, 'Sleep, My Beloved, Sleep' by Yevgeny Yevtushenko. The ceremony ends with everyone holding hands and joining Tom and Steve in singing **'Circle'**. The grave is marked by the planting of a tree and a large rock brought from the farm in Andover, a rock on which Harry and his brothers used to play. On a bronze plaque between two American flags are the words 'Harry Chapin 1942-1981' and below the name a simple epitaph, a line from one of his songs: *Oh if a man tried to take his time on earth and prove before he died what one man's life could be worth / I wonder what would happen to this world.*

Sandy remembers how Harry loved the water: *"We found a place as high as we could with a view of the water. And from here, alongside Route 110, you can see all of Huntington without any sign of different neighborhoods...We thought he'd like the symbolism. We thought he'd like the symbolism. Harry always to break down barriers between different sections and regions. He was always talking of erasing that road, the symbolic dividing line of Long Island. Harry wanted to bring all Long Islanders together."*

That day it seems all Long Islanders are there together in spirit on that breezy hill.

The Legacy

"Being a rock star is pointless. It's garbage. It's the most self-indulgent thing I can think of. I've got nothing against selling out. But let me sell out for something that counts. Not so Harry Chapin can be No 1 with a bullet, but so I can leave here thinking it mattered."

"Decency and Dignity"

Sandy once said of her husband: *"He runs until he sleeps. He used to be afraid of dying. That's why he makes so many double albums, so many appearances, so many benefits. He wants to leave something behind. He wants people to know that he was here."* And Harry would be the first to agree with her: *"My work is my coefficient against dying. I can say, 'Here it is. I've done it. C'mon, take a look at it.'"*

For one brief shining moment Harry Chapin had graced the world with his charismatic persona and a body of music that both baffled and bewitched fans and critics alike. With a heart as big as his ego, he will always be remembered as sitting on a stool in some concert hall, college gymnasium, or open air theater, with his guitar resting on his knee, tousling his hair, sharing friendly banter with Big John while at the same time trying to describe to a transfixed audience the story behind the song he's about to perform. But that was not unique, and he had contemporaries doing that same thing. What made him stand out was that he was not just a singer. He was the epitome of the traveling troubadour - a singing novelist who brought his stories to life through music; a playwright who turned scripts into melodramatic tapestries, and an artist who painted lyrical landscapes for his characters to act out their roles. It was an inbred talent fostered by a young life spent in the cultural surroundings shared by artists, musicians, and literary artisans.

Of course, many performers have devoted fans, but Harry's fans were of a different breed. Instead of seeing him as their idol, they looked upon him more as a friend, whether watching him perform or just listening to his music. His concerts were always intimate affairs, and for many who were lucky enough to catch a live performance it was like being invited into his Huntington home and sitting on a couch while being entertained. All that was missing were the tea and cakes. After the concerts Harry would always take time to mingle with his fans to sign autographs and raise money for his charities, and many of those fans would come away with their own story of how in some small but significant way he had managed to touch their lives, even for the briefest of moments. Harry's untimely death is in itself the kind of novel that he would have conjured up himself, a man whose life is cut short

295

before attaining his goal, falling just short of the finish line. Most of his critics rubbished his music, and although personally offended by it, he was never disheartened. When one music critic once commented on another performer as being *"a rich man's Harry Chapin,"* Harry retorted, *"Look at where they've got me. They've got me as a standard for comparison. If anyone is lower than me. He has to be at the very bottom of the ocean."*

The tributes Harry received were widespread and seemed to be as spontaneous as the standing ovations he often received as a performer. In Congress, nine senators and thirty congressmen paid tribute to him on the floor, an honor no other singer had ever received from the nation's legislators. Senator Robert Dole of Kansas, not a man who some would say possessed a political generosity of spirit, nevertheless concluded his speech by saying that Harry was *"a liberal, and a liberal in the best sense of the word. He possessed a spirit of generosity and optimism that carried him through his various commitments with a great sense of seriousness and purpose...What he was really committed to was decency and dignity."* Where it is still common when a person dies to make them appear greater in death than in life, that was never the case with Harry, and he lived up to Bob Dylan's admonition that *"he who is not busy being born is busy dying."* Harry's personal motto should be etched in stone: *"We all have the potential to move the world - and the world is ready to be moved!"*

Harry's commitment to his beliefs shone brightly at a time when any commitment to an ideal was often looked on with contemptuous derision, and that's what makes him such a rare human being. He was an unfaltering champion for saving the lives of those on the brink of death through starvation. If that alone is to be derided, now as it was then, we are still living in a world that has much to learn. The actor Robert Redford, who worked with Harry on Sun Day, a solar energy rally back in 1978, recalls: *"The kind of commitment Harry made is rare. In all my experiences in this business, I can honestly say that Harry was the most stand-up guy I ever met."*

On July 23rd, a week after Harry's death, family and friends gather at the Grace Church in Brooklyn for the first memorial service. The afternoon is one of tears, laughter, and fine singing, with speeches from people that range from Zeke Marsden, the Boston brakeman for the B&O Railroad, to two congressmen - young Long Island Democrat representative Tom Downey and Republican representative Ben Gilman, there through his work on the Presidential Commission. Also in attendance is Harry's close friend, Vermont's Democratic Senator Patrick Leahy, whose narrow victory the previous year he attributes to Harry's support. Brothers Tom and Steve are joined by Oscar Brand, Steve Goodman, Mary Travers, Peter Yarrow, Dolores Hall and Pete Seeger to perform songs old and new. John Wallace also sings **'Last Stand'**, the first public performance of Harry's last song.

But it is older brother James who sums up one of the reasons Harry had made his mark on so many people:

"Most great men appear greater because they maneuver to diminish other people. But if Harry was a great man, and I think he was, it's because he really did feel better when everybody else felt better. He always remembered that the average person isn't you or me or even an American worker but someone living in the slums of Rio or Bombay...It was Harry's greatest gift to inspire, and his death has not diminished that. Our job is not to attempt the impossible task of filling Harry's shoes, but rather to accept Harry's challenge to better fill our own."

The Harry Chapin Memorial Fund

Mourners like Ken Kragen and Harry's old friend Harry Belafonte take note of what James says, and during the service Kragen announces the formation of the Harry Chapin Memorial Fund to be launched with a $10,000 donation from Elektra, and on August 17th a benefit concert in aid of the fund will be hosted by Kenny Rogers, also managed by Kragen, at the Nassau Coliseum in Uniondale. Rock managers Irvin Azoff and Jerry Weintraub also volunteer their support. The show's promotor Ron Delsener sums up everyone's feelings: *"Harry did a benefit for everybody else, now it's time for us to do one for him."* In the meantime, across the country, thousands of fans who have bought advance tickets for Harry's late summer shows are refusing to have their money refunded.

On September 3rd Dave Marsh of *Rolling Stone*, longtime critic of Harry's music, writes a personal tribute. Full of admiration for the humanitarian work Harry had accomplished, he doesn't detract from words he had used in the past to describe the man – preachy, emotionally overwrought, didactic, simplistic – but he makes a point of saying that maybe not all of them were correct.

In donating so much money for good causes, Harry was so far ahead of his fellow artists that he overdrew his account. Nor did anyone give as much time and energy. Justice Holmes once remarked that if energy is genius, then Harry Chapin was a genius. He tried to be everywhere and do everything at once. If he got you cornered, he would harangue and cajole you on what needed to be done until convincing you that you had to do it. He took every opportunity in between singing to lecture a captive audience on everything that mattered to him, until it mattered to them too. And many times, he succeeded in doing just that.

But Harry also took risks in his music career. The long narratives such as **'Taxi'** and **'Better Place To Be'** were out of step with the fashion of the times and were coolly received by many critics. The amount of benefits he performed didn't always sit well with his band members and created friction as the years went by. Sandy recalled: *"There were concerts he had planned to do for himself that he turned into benefits because an organization suddenly couldn't make its payroll."* Due to other commitments, he also began to lose focus with the recording of his albums, and that too led to disharmony with the band. Bill Ayres recalled how Harry acted on his beliefs: *"He constantly talked about reinventing America. In his vision, the Constitution established a democratic process in which people who were being asked, not just to vote, but to be informed and involved."*

Harry lived his life with a love and vibrancy that is hard to match, and it was a life that certainly did matter. His energy was limitless, and it was an energy that came from the people he helped. Brother James commented: *"Harry enjoyed being rich, and famous. But he also wanted to be good. That was the paradox of his nature."* His personality and his generosity did so much to help struggling cultural organizations and inspired and persuaded others to participate in raising much-needed funds. Whenever the Long Island communities needed him, he was there to help. Sandy reflected on just how many things her husband had been committed to: *"Harry was supporting 17 relatives, 14 associations, seven foundations and 82 charities. Harry wasn't interested in saving money. He always said, 'Money is for people' so he gave it all away"* (actually more figurative than factual). In December 1980 Harry had confessed: *"I have an annual meeting with my accountant. Sandy has given up going with me because she always knows what they're going to say. They always say, 'Harry, there's good news and there's bad news. The good news is that you've made more money this year than ever before. The bad news is you ain't keeping it.'"*

In the months following Harry's death, members of the various charities and organizations hold regular meetings at his Huntington home to discuss and find ways to continue the causes which he supported. In the last six years of his life it is estimated that Harry raised more than $3 million. Sandy does her best to keep things on track. The Harry Chapin Foundation raises $200,000 in its first year alone, and the benefit concert hosted by Kenny Rogers raises a further $150,000. Members of the Chapin family become more involved and head some of Harry's ongoing projects. James becomes chair of W.H.Y., the organization closest to Harry's heart and now struggling to survive. He laments: *"We miss his ability to raise funds. What was unique about Harry was his ability to scatter seeds and see which ones would grow."*

In 1982 Kenny Rogers keeps his promise to Harry and, together with his wife Marianne, establishes the World Hunger Media Awards. At the first ceremony, held that year at the United Nations building in New York, Rogers also announces a special Achievement Award of $20,000 to establish two Congressional fellowships in memory of Harry.

Lies and Legends

In late 1983, as another tribute to the late singer, *Lies and Legends: The Musical Stories of Harry Chapin* premieres in the Apollo Theater in Chicago (although at this stage it's called *Legends and Lies*), and has a successful ten-month run. Based on an idea by theater impresario Joseph Stern, it showcases some of Harry's finest songs acted out by five accomplished singers. Directed by Sam Weisman, staged by Tracy Friedman, and with Tom and Steve as music directors, it also has Sandy as creative consultant. The original singers are George Ball, John Herrera, Anne Kerry, Amanda McBroom and Ron Orbach, and the music performed by Rokko Jans (piano and conductor), John Chappell (guitar), Jocelyn Davis (cello), Tom Mendel (bass) and Bill Hansen (percussion). What are deemed the most theatrical of Harry's songs are performed in a way that allows the stories within to develop their own dramatic shape. They are: 'Circle / Story of a Life'; 'Corey's Coming'; 'Salt and Pepper'; 'Mr Tanner'; 'Old College Avenue'; 'Taxi'; 'The Rock'; '30,000 Pounds of Bananas'; 'Get On With It'; 'Shooting Star'; 'Sniper'; 'Dance Band on the Titanic'; 'W.O.L.D.'; 'Dogtown'; 'Mail Order Annie'; 'Odd Job Man'; 'Dreams Go By'; 'Tangled Up Puppet'; 'Cat's in the Cradle'; 'Halfway to Heaven'; 'Oh Man'; 'Better Place to Be'; 'Winter Song'; 'You Are the Only Song / Circle'.

That same year a soundtrack album is released on the Titanic label. On April 24th the following year the show opens at New York's Village Gate and runs for 79 performances, and now has Big John Wallace playing bass guitar in what for him must be an emotional return to where for him it all began. The cast of performers now consists of John Herrera and Ron Orbach, along with two veteran Broadway comedy performers in Martin Vidnovic and Terri Klausner ably assisted by Joanna Glushak. Once again it is directed by Weisman and staged by Friedman, with Karl Jurman brought in as the new conductor. Some people are confused by the title given to the show. Why "Lies?" Steve and Tom agree that it could be a synonym for "stories," and according to Tracy Friedman that's exactly what the songs are, stories *"with beginnings, middles and endings, and lyrics like little movies and characters that are really there - ordinary people going through extraordinary situations."*

The show gives no biographical detail of Harry and there is no narration, thus giving a *"lie to a true-to-life interpretation of its intentions"*. The director allows the songs to sing for themselves, the performers dressed in drab costumes, with no elaborate sets or choreography; no indulgent interpretations of the songs. Even though Harry is no longer stage center, some critics still castigate many of the songs, seeing them as nothing more than *"wallowing in sentimentality while flaunting trite,"* like *"greeting-card verses,"* *"lumbering melodies,"* and even *"anti-intellectual."*

299

The following month the show moves to the Bluma Appel Theater in Toronto and runs from May 23rd to June 22nd with a performing cast of Vince Metcalfe, Kevin Hicks, Diane Stapley, Moira Walley and Alec Willows. Over the next two decades and more, performances continue around the regional theaters to mixed reviews and changing cast members, and even with alternating names such as *Harry Chapin's America: Lies and Legends* and *Harry Chapin and Friends.*

Live Aid and USA For Africa

In late 1984 the world finally sees for itself what Harry had been seeing for a decade. The seeds he had sown in the mid 70s are finally bearing fruit. Over in the UK, a BBC news report by Michael Buerk highlights a famine of biblical proportions in Ethiopia, and when beamed around the world the images shock millions of viewers. Before the year is out, singer Bob Geldof of the band The Boomtown Rats launches his Band Aid project, where dozens of artists get together to record a song called 'Do They Know Its Christmas (Feed the World)', which goes on to raise substantial amounts of money for famine relief. Inspired by its success, Harry Belafonte contacts Ken Kragen, and between them they organize their own version called USA for Africa, beginning with the release of an all-star anti-hunger anthem called 'We Are the World', which receives huge donations totaling $63 million, raises worldwide consciousness, and saves millions of lives in the process. Both Belafonte and Geldof make it known that it is Harry who *"provided much of the needed inspiration to bring artists together to join in the struggle."* Kragen is quoted as saying: *"I'm not an overly religious person but at that moment in time I felt Harry Chapin had crawled up inside of me. I really physically felt it happen and I said, 'You son of a gun, you're directing the whole thing.'"*

The following year they join up with Geldof to organize the two mammoth Live Aid concerts in London and Philadelphia, held on July 13th, which go on to raise $127 million through donations. On May 25th the following year the USA for Africa project continues with the Hands Across America event, where 6.5 million Americans symbolically join hands to form a human chain from coast to coast and help raise a net $15 million for local charities to fight hunger and homelessness and help those living in poverty. Kragen again remembers Harry's inspiration: *"I thought of Harry as I stood in the line and wished he was there. Harry would have loved this event. As much as anyone, he would have understood how to mobilize it, how to galvanize people into further action. He also understood the issues; he had the verbal skills and the charisma, as well as the hard-practical know-how to pull it off. Harry Chapin embodied all the best qualities needed to realize our goals."*

The first public recognition of Harry's work doesn't come until the American Music Awards in 1986, when Harry Belafonte accepts the special public service award for his work, but chastises the audience of music moguls that it is Harry Chapin who they should pay tribute to as being the inspiration behind it all. Harry's dream is being continued, although he may have had a word or two to say about the "event psychosis." That same year Harry receives the President's Award of Merit.

Carnegie Hall, December 7th 1987

A more fitting recognition of Harry's work comes on what would have been his 45th birthday, December 7th 1987, when Sandy is presented with a special Congressional Gold Medal on his behalf at a lavish charitable ceremony at New York's Carnegie Hall, which emulates the experience of one of Harry's concerts. Harry becomes the 115th recipient of the medal, following in the footsteps of George Washington, Thomas Edison and Robert Kennedy. Hosted by Harry's great friend Harry Belafonte, a host of stars are invited to perform songs, including Pete Seeger, Oscar Brand, Richie Havens, Paul Simon, Bruce Springsteen, Graham Nash, Judy Collins, Peter Paul and Mary and The Hooters.

In a short speech, due to her having laryngitis, Sandy Chapin pays tribute to her husband:

"I would like to say that Harry loved this country, and he used to say that more than anything else he believed in the Constitution of the United States and the fact that it stood for human rights and human needs, and he was going to make his life stand for carrying that out. And he loved the people of this country. He often said that what he was doing was he was working to try to eliminate hunger by working to promote arts because he thought that it brought out the humanity in people's lives. He called what he was doing selfish or enlightened self-interest because he felt that he was the one who gained because he used to quote Pete Seeger and say that every day he had to get up and go out to be with the live eyes, the live hearts and the live minds. He felt very strongly, as some of the witnesses have said, that each man should feel that he could make a difference and that his life did matter...More than anything else, Harry was trying to promote the idea of self-reliance, self-reliance in himself and self-reliance in the people whose lives he touched and self-reliance for the underprivileged in our country."

James Chapin, whose destiny had led him in a different direction, speaks fondly of his younger brother's commitment:

"...If the test of a person's greatness is when this person's life influenced others for the better, then Harry has passed this test. So, when you ask if Harry Chapin should be someone we honor, I say yes, he should be honored because

301

we define ourselves by who we choose to honor. When we talk about Harry Chapin, we are talking about a man who deserves to be honored, a great man and a good man. The two words should go together, but they often don't. In other words, there are many people we call great men who are not good men, and when you think about that, that is a very bad thing indeed. One of the reasons that Harry was a great man was that he felt better when other people felt good..."

Consumer advocate Ralph Nader described Harry as a *"whirlwind"* and a *"first-class Congressional lobbyist and civic strategist,"* adding that: *"When somebody unique passes away, we say we won't see his likes again. With Harry, we haven't seen anyone like him, with his consistency, generosity, and versatility. His death was a tremendous blow to the growth of democracy in America."* Bruce Springsteen, while singing **'Remember When the Music'**, speaks fondly of the singer, recalling how Harry pursued him everywhere - from recording studios to hotel lobbies - to enlist his support in the fight against hunger. He reflects on his unceasing energy and positive spirit, and his pragmatic approach to affecting social change: *"I think that Harry instinctively knew it was going to take a lot more than love to survive. That it was going to take a strong sense of purpose, of duty, and a good clear eye on the dirty ways of the world. So, in keeping with his promise to himself, he reminds us of our promises to ourselves and that tonight, alongside Harry, it's that promise that his spirit would have us remember and honor and recommit to. So, do something and may his song be sung."* In the years since that concert, Springsteen has quietly helped W.H.Y. and dozens of other organizations to raise millions of dollars to help people in need.

But the highlight of the star-studded evening is when the gold medal is presented to Harry's son Josh, who then walks across the stage to place it on an empty stool against which rests Harry's guitar.

And what of Harry's band? They continue to perform together for a couple of years after his death, and as The Strangers they release an album called *In the Night* before splitting to pursue solo projects. Tom Chapin makes a number of solo albums aimed at both the junior and adult markets, and also hosts the *National Geographic Explorer* TV show, winning along the way a string of awards for his music, including three Grammys. Steve Chapin gets involved in New York real estate and remains relatively quiet until the release of his debut solo album *Chapter 11 Rag* in 1990. John Wallace quits music for a time and dabbles in computers; Doug Walker joins a band called Wedge and plays the New York club circuit; Howie Fields remains a much sought-after drummer, playing for bands such as The New Riders of the Purple Sage, and Yvonne Cable puts her cello playing on hold to get involved in holistic medicine. From time to time the old band still come together to do benefit concerts in aid of W.H.Y. and then go their separate ways. Eventually the Steve Chapin Band is formed, with Steve on piano and lead vocals, Big John on bass, and Howie on drums. They have moderate success until calling it a day in 1994 (at least for the time being).

On November 21st 1993 Harry's grandfather and mentor Kenneth Burke dies of heart failure at his farm in Andover at the age of 96. His productive career continues to influence writers to this day.

"The Quintessential American"

In 1991, ten years after Harry's death, the Chapin family enter into discussions about making a movie about Harry's life. A screenplay has been written and Oliver Stone is said to be interested in directing it. Actors Kurt Russell and Jeff Bridges are both considered to play Harry. Sadly, nothing comes of it, and at the time of writing, just two years away from the 40th anniversary of the singer's passing, it is hoped that interest in a movie biopic will gain renewed interest.

During the remainder of the decade Sandy remains heavily involved in keeping Harry's projects alive, as much as she was in their origin. Often staying *"in the corner of the room, never in the middle of it,"* when Harry was alive, she still plays down her part. After all, she comments, Harry was a so politically motivated and energetic because he came from family of like-minded people. *"He raised the money. He had the vision, and he had all the imaginative ideas to keep the whole project going."*

Another ten years pass and Sandy's role is as important as ever, overseeing the Harry Chapin Foundation, which continues to fund projects like the Huntington Arts Council and the Long Island Philharmonic. Then there is also Long Island Cares, with its aim of fighting domestic hunger and poverty, and with a food bank that gives 2.8 million pounds of food a year to some 30,000 people in need. Bill Ayres administers World Hunger Year, the project he co-founded with Harry. Sandy is optimistic: *"The organization almost fell apart after Harry died. After all, he used to raise 85 per cent of the money. For two years we struggled. But with the help of family and friends, we're doing more now than when he was alive."*

For Long Islanders, Harry is remembered for much more than his music. The commitment he displayed in issues closer to home is immeasurable, and in making Long Island a kinder place by bringing communities together and supporting their educational and cultural fabric, he becomes in time the Island's conscience. Larry Austin, president of the Long Island Philharmonic, pays tribute to Harry: *"The Island would be different without Harry. Of all the people who've made an impact on Long Island, Harry is on top of the list."* Austin also recounts a time when Harry stood in pouring rain welcoming cars turning up for a benefit and getting stuck in the mud, while other officials stood in the dry under a tent. Harry knocked on the window of every car and said, "Hi, I'm Harry Chapin. Just park your car and don't worry about the rain. You're gonna have a great time." Unfortunately, the Long Island Philharmonic disbands in 2016.

At a gala dinner sponsored by the Long Island Association business group, Sandy receives their medal of honor for the Chapin family. During the evening Tom performs **'Cat's in the Cradle'**, and Harry's 20-year-old daughter Jen joins her uncle on stage to sing an emotional rendition of **'Sandy'**, the song Tom had performed at her parents' wedding. During the celebration Bill Ayres recalls: *"I miss his friendship. We were best friends, and I miss his incredible vitality. He was the quintessential American. If he saw a problem, he'd say, 'Let's do something about it'."*

But more than anyone else, it is Sandy, Harry's *"dream lover of a lady,"* who misses him the most. She reflects on their life together, a life so different to what they had planned: *"I thought we'd have a quiet life together as writers. Harry was always talking about taking time off from concerts to write a book. So, I had been quietly saving money for the past four years. Otherwise I might have had to borrow from friends."* With so many fans mourning the loss of Harry, it pales into significance with Sandy's loss. She still wears the wedding ring designed by her daughter Jaime: *"I miss him so much as a parent. My son Josh needed a coach for his soccer team. He asked me if I could do it. That just killed me. Lots of things I just do. If Harry were here, he'd get things moving more. His was the most interesting, stimulating mind I've ever come across. We worked so well together."* When asked if she still listens to Harry's albums, she often replies, *"I don't have to. I've lived them."*

And the Years Keep Rolling By....

The dawn of the new century also brings renewed interest in Harry's music. In July 2001, on the 20th anniversary of Harry's death, singer John McMenamin performs his tribute concert *Remembering Harry Chapin* at the Strand Theater in Lakewood, New Jersey, a show he has regularly staged at various venues each year since 1981 to help raise money for W.H.Y. For the Strand show McMenamin brings together three of Harry's band members - John, Howie and Yvonne - on stage for the first time in twenty years. In 2003 the *Circle* newsletter is launched, inspiring *"fans and friends to make a difference."* Sadly, that same year, Harry's older brother James dies aged 62, and six years later Harry's father Jim Chapin dies in Florida, just shy of his 90th birthday. In 2014 the Chapin family self-publish **Book of Eyes**, Harry's second collection of poems and lyrics, which also include paintings by his grandfather Big Jim.

Bringing the story right up to date, we find World Hunger Year continuing with its excellent work. Now called WhyHunger, it has become a national leader in its cause, and remains focused on its fundamental goals - combating the root causes of hunger, poverty and injustice, closely supporting grassroots solutions, and promoting self-reliance. It also receives the support of many established artists such as Bruce Springsteen and Yoko Ono. The Chapin Foundation also continues its tireless mission of supporting non-profit organizations that have *"demonstrated their ability to dramatically improve the lives and livelihood of people by helping them to become self-sufficient."* It focuses on helping small community organizations and programs which are overlooked by some of the larger organizations and to date has awarded some 600 grants and over $2 million.

Even though Harry has been taken from us, his music is alive and kicking. The Harry Chapin Band, with Big John, Steve and Howie, along with John's son Clark Wallace (electric guitar) and Steve's son Jonathan (acoustic guitar), perform songs by Harry and Steve to a whole new generation of enthusiastic fans. Tom Chapin, the consummate performer, is much sought after as always, and continues to record solo albums for both children and adults alike, as well as writing a series of storybooks. His daughters Abigail and Lily, along with stepdaughter Jessica, now perform as The Chapin Sisters, and since 2005 have garnered critical acclaim for their music. And then there's Harry daughter Jen, the apple of his eye who inherited her father's voice, and is not only a high school teacher but also an accomplished singer-songwriter in her own right, with a handful of well-received albums under her belt, and already being compared to the likes of Alanis Morissette and Tori Amos with her writing and performing. For generations to come the name Chapin will be associated with good quality music, both old and new.

"The World is Lost Without Him"

Harry was a prolific songwriter who, over a creative period that lasted almost two decades, composed hundreds of songs, only a fraction of which made it on to official albums. From **'Stars Tangled'** to **'Last Stand'**, arguably his first and last, they include some of the finest story-songs ever written; the most heartfelt and endearing compositions about family and lost love, and some of the most hard-hitting and biting protest songs of his generation. And for every song that made fans reach for a box of tissues, there were also those that could make you laugh out loud, make you bitter and depressed, or even shock you to the core. Whatever effect it had, it endeared him to an army of devoted fans, who to this day still look back on his life and work for moral guidance and inspiration. But winning over fans also alienated Harry in the eyes of many critics. Even so, for him chart success was not his ultimate goal, and even having one of his songs get into the lower reaches of the top forty was like having a number one hit in his eyes. But unlike the sporadic chart success, appreciation for his work meant much more to him, and his constant struggle to get critical acclaim was a seemingly never-ending fight. One minute he could be the biggest star in the country, a Grammy nominee with a number one single, and the next he could be like Mr Tanner.

Harry once said in an interview: *"Being a rock star is pointless. It's garbage. It's the most self-indulgent thing I can think of. I've got nothing against selling out. But let me sell out for something that counts. Not so Harry Chapin can be No 1 with a bullet, but so I can leave here thinking it mattered."* He could have chosen to do many things in his life, other than being a singer. His teen years were filled with hesitation, indecision, and disillusion, never really knowing what to do next. With so much conflicting advice and coaching by so many close friends and family members, all with his best interests at heart, he came to each crossroad, one after another, unsure of which direction to take. But in the end, he let his heart rule his head, and for this Brooklyn minstrel to achieve his destiny, there only was one choice.

But before bringing Harry's remarkable story to a close, it's only fitting to leave some of the final words to those in the cheap seats - his equally remarkable fans. What does Harry Chapin mean to them?

Mike Smith - *Harry was a musical, political, and personal hero to me. The constants in my life, aside from my family, have been music, activism, and trying to do something when I'm in doubt, and I owe that to Harry.*

Kenneth Cleys - *Harry was more than a songwriter and musician, he was a man with great compassion and empathy of things around him.*

Lucy Lambert - *Music was a vehicle for his compassion and need to do for mankind. Never another!*

Melba Davis Nickoles - *To watch him, his energy, bounding from place to place was a joy. I believe there could only ever be one. One Harry. Soft gentle Harry. Top of his lungs Harry....A gift to the world, lost too soon. Oh, how I wish he was still here.*

Susan Lee Cooper - *Harry was a close friend, a great father and a modern-day pied piper. His honest story telling first captured me in '***Mr. Tanner'*** and he wrote '***Flowers Are Red'*** for my son. I worked with him until he died, a piece of me went with him.*

Ellen Gordon Klein - *Harry was and is my idol. His songs touched me since my teens in ways no other songs ever could or have. Every one had such a wonderful story and so much emotion. In concert, it always felt like I was the only one there, just sitting in his living room listening. He was a good, giving charitable person, and most of all, he CARED.*

Steve Love - *My role model above all others.*

306

Sylvia Ryerson - *Harry was an extraordinary man. He gave so much of himself. His legacy will live on forever.*

Elaine Phillips Chamard - *The world is lost without him.*

Daniel Drew - *A great story teller with a great smile. Inspiration as how we should live - When in doubt do something.*

Colleen Marikje Barker - *His songs and stories are the soundtrack of my youth, and have remained my touchstone ever since. He is never to be duplicated in this world.*

Vicki Verbanovic Chalfant - *Not only were Harry's songs relatable, but as a fan he always took the time to make you feel like you mattered. Like it was important that you were there listening.*

Randal Tylin - *The only artist ever to make his songs relevant, a simple message and beautifully put to music.*

Bohan Donner - *There are days I cry sentimental tears listening to his songs. I always felt he left this earth willing his fans to do better by their neighbors.*

Mike Holper - *He was an inspiration, a role model of what passion and commitment to a cause looks like. My "story of a life" was irrevocably affected by Harry...and much for the better.*

Terera Honeycutt - *A beautiful humanitarian and one of the best story tellers of all time.*

Patricia LoTurco - *He was a dedicated humanitarian who used his fame to make the world a better place to live... He was much more than a talented musician. Harry was the most dedicated musician who gave back to society and is a true legend whose memory shall live on forever.*

Bruce Balbach - *Harry was (and still is) the greatest musical storyteller ever! His stories/songs were life changing because they were real! How blessed we are that Harry's legacy lives on through his family.*

Linda White - *He made a difference and will always be remembered. In my life and in my heart.*

Patricia Ehrich - *He put his money where his mouth is. Harry was the real deal. A genuine decent and kind human being. He will always be my role model and my hero.*

Alan L Geraci - *Harry's social conscience penetrated into the souls of all who knew him, heard his music, or felt his energy.*

Marc Lazarus - *A Harry Chaplin concert was like hanging out with a whole bunch of cool people and listening to music. Harry made it feel like he was just another member of the crowd and happened to be the one who brought the guitar along.*

Joan Mercer - *He was an amazing man who proved that even one person could make a difference. He just went way too soon.*

Doug Wood - *Harry was an inspiration for me to be a better version of myself. His energy was his own but he challenged us all to find our own areas of passion and to get off the couch.*

"An earth-changing human being"

Harry was not just a singer-songwriter, he was more than that. As a singer-actor he breathed life into his mini-movie songs with incredible vocalizations, and also dipped deeply into a well of empathy and poignancy, enabling him to create a wave of emotive power that washed over and seduced the most hard-hearted listeners. He wrote about ordinary people and compiled a gallery of vivid characters ranging from mass murderers to mail-order brides, from aging DJs to lonely waitresses, from desperate dreamers to unsung heroes. The epitome of a laid-back entertainer, his gifted voice enabled him to reach out and engage with people in ways that were endearingly unique, captivating and pulling them into his story with a voice that could be equally aggressive and angelic at the change of a chord.

And within the songs he would often abruptly alter the whole dynamic of the song, changing the vocal and music to totally detach it from what had gone before, almost creating a song within a song. Listening to one of his songs for the first time, it soon became a case of expect the unexpected. Harry was certainly one of the first singers of his generation to extensively use voices as an instrument, and he and his band, especially Big John, turned it into an art form. Seldom has a four or five piece band sounded like a mini-orchestra and church chorale all rolled into one. And that was down to Harry, with a little help from a succession of producers and arrangers, most notably his very own brother Steve.

Harry was also a much-underrated musician. Sometimes seemingly swallowed up by powerhouse lyrics, those beautiful melodies and sometimes challenging arrangements were as much a part of the songs' makeup as the subject matter itself. The way he nonchalantly played guitar finger-style made it seem so understated that it was easy to focus on the story and lyrics, and never really appreciate what was going on with his right hand. Even in the breaks between his vocals, Harry would use his guitar as if it had a voice of its own. And it's amazing to think that in the first four years of being on the road with the band, Harry never sought to use a drummer to keep time or help replicate the recorded sound of his music.

With all these qualities, it seems to be a cruel injustice that Harry has never been inducted into the Songwriters Hall of Fame, like so many of his contemporaries have been since it was introduced in 1969. Maybe the criticism that plagued his recording career for over ten years still lives on in an industry that now seems to puts image and dollars above art. Pete Seeger once said: *"Harry was a great songwriter and a master storyteller. He made up songs not to get famous but to analyze what it means to be human."* Music historian Dave Marsh, the perennial critic of Harry's music, perhaps gives the most fitting tribute to him: *"He was a person of the utmost faith. You run into someone so possessed by faith, unless you're spiritually stone blind, it's a powerful, inspiring experience. Harry Chapin may have been a journeyman pop star, but he was an earth-changing human being."*

So, what should Harry Chapin be most remembered for? A unique artist; an award-winning film editor and producer; an intellectual pessimist and political optimist; an inspirational spokesman for the myriad of strong beliefs that he held; a tireless and selfless fundraiser for countless charities and struggling cultural organizations; an ardent political lobbyist to bring change to what he saw as a tainted establishment; a first-rate American citizen? Yes, he was all of these, and more. But by a twist of fate it would be his musical path that would divert him in a whole new direction, with challenges he would meet head-on, fight tooth and nail, and with selfless commitment help to raise awareness of one of mankind's greatest failings.

Harry had always lived as if time was running out. Born into a world at war, he spent much of his short adult life waging his own war against world hunger, a war that even to this day is still to be won. But he would never have given up his crusade, and maybe if extra time on earth had been granted him, there would be more battles for him to fight and win. Although Harry's music had made him rich, he was never a rich man, and the money he selflessly gave away has helped to not only change many lives, but to save them too. In setting up a blueprint for a better and more sustainable world, he has truly made his mark, and in doing so gives us the answer to how he should be remembered. Harry Chapin was just an incredible human being. Maybe that had always been his destiny. In reality it has become his legacy.

HARRY CHAPIN
Albums

Heads and Tales (March 1972)

Sniper and Other Love Songs (October 1972)

Short Stories (December 1973)

Verities & Balderdash (August 1974)

Portrait Gallery (September 1975)

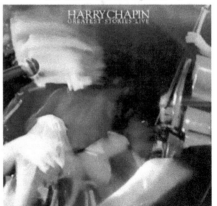

Greatest Stories Live (April 1976)

HARRY CHAPIN
Albums

On the Road to Kingdom Come (October 1976)

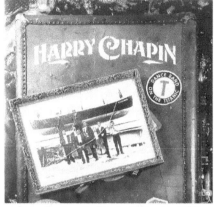

Dance Band on the Titanic (September 1977)

Living Room Suite (September 1978)

Legends of the Lost and Found (November 1979)

Sequel (March 1980)

The Last Protest Singer (November 1988)

For the Record

He lived for his music and now his music lives for him.
(Steve Stout)

The Albums

US – United States, UK – United Kingdom, CA – Canada, AU – Australia, NZ – New Zealand, NE – Netherlands, GE – Germany, SP – Spain, SA – South Africa, HK – Hong Kong, SC – Scandinavia, IT – Italy, EU – European Union

Heads and Tales
1972 US   Elektra EKS 75023 Vinyl LP (Promo for radio stations)
1972 US   Elektra 75023, EKS-75023 Vinyl LP
1972 US   Elektra TC-55023 Cassette
1972 UK   Elektra K42107 Vinyl LP
1972 CA   Elektra 75023, ERS 75023 Vinyl LP (red label)
1972 AU   Elektra EKS-75023 Vinyl LP
1972 GE   Elektra ELK 42 107 Vinyl LP
1972 NZ   Elektra EKS-75023 Vinyl LP
1976 US   Elektra 75023, EKS-75023 Vinyl LP re-issue
1976 UK   Elektra/Asylum EKS 75023 Vinyl LP re-issue
1987 US   Elektra 75023-2   CD
1990 US   Elektra e2-75023 CD (Club edition)
1990 US   Elektra CD75023 CD

Sniper and Other Love Songs
1972 US   Elektra EKS-75042 Vinyl LP (Promo for radio stations) white label
1972 US   Elektra EKS-75042 Vinyl LP
1972 US   Elektra TC-55042 Cassette
1972 AU   Elektra EKS-75042 Vinyl LP
1972 GE   Elektra ELK 42 125 Vinyl LP
1976 US   Elektra EKS-75042 Vinyl LP re-issue
1976 UK   Elektra K-42125 Vinyl LP re-issue
2002 US   Wounded Bird WOU 5042 CD

Short Stories
1973 US   Elektra EKS5065, 75065 Vinyl LP (Promo for radio stations) white label

312

1973 US Elektra EKS 75065, 75065 Vinyl LP
1973 US Elektra TC-55065 Cassette
1973 UK Elektra K-42155 Vinyl LP
1973 CA Elektra EKS 75065 Vinyl LP
1974 AU Elektra EKS 75065 Vinyl LP
1973 AU Elektra M5 75065 Cassette
1975 US Elektra EKS 75065, 75065 Vinyl LP re-issue
2002 US Flashback Records R2-76106 CD

Verities & Balderdash
1974 US Elektra 7E-1012 Vinyl LP (Promo for radio stations) white label
1974 US Elektra 7E-1012 Vinyl LP (Terre Haute pressing)
1974 US Elektra 7E-1012 Vinyl LP (Pitman pressing)
1974 US Elektra TC-51012 Cassette
1974 UK Elektra K52007, 7E-1012 Vinyl LP (labelled Verities and Balderdash)
1974 UK Elektra K52007 Vinyl LP (labelled Verities & Balderdash)
1974 UK Elektra K52007 Vinyl LP white label
1974 CA Elektra 7ES 1012 Vinyl LP
1974 AU Elektra 7E 1012 Vinyl LP
1974 AU Elektra M5E73 1012 Cassette
1974 GE Elektra ELK 52007, 7E-1012 Vinyl LP
1974 US Elektra 7E-1012 Vinyl LP (Santa Maria pressing)
1975 US Elektra 7E-1012 Vinyl LP (Speciality Records pressing)
1979 US Elektra 7E-1012 Vinyl LP (Speciality Records pressing) re-issue
1984 US Elektra 7E-1012 Vinyl LP re-issue
1990 US Elektra 1012-2 CD
1990 UK Elektra 60596 CD
1990 CA Elektra CD60596 CD

Portrait Gallery
1975 US Elektra 7E 1041, 7E-1041Vinyl LP (promo for radio stations)
1975 US Elektra 7E 1041, 7E-1041Vinyl LP (Santa Maria pressing)
1975 US Elektra 7E-1041Vinyl LP (CTH Pressing)
1975 US Elektra 7E-1041 Vinyl LP (Speciality Records pressing)
1975 US Elektra 7E-1041, 7E1041 Vinyl LP (Club edition)
1975 US Elektra TC-51041 Cassette
1975 UK Elektra K52023 Vinyl LP
1975 CA Elektra 7ES 1041 Vinyl LP
1975 AU Elektra 7E-1041 Vinyl LP
1975 NZ Elektra 7E-1041 Vinyl LP

1993 US/UK Elektra 9 60602-2 CD
2010 US   Wounded Bird WOU 1041

Greatest Stories Live
1976 US   Elektra 7E-2009 Vinyl DLP (Promo for radio stations)
1976 US   Elektra 7E-2009 Vinyl DLP
1976 US   Elektra 7E-2009 Vinyl LP (Club edition)
1976 US   Elektra C2-6003 Cassette
1976 UK   Elektra K62016 Vinyl DLP
1976 CA   Elektra 7E-2009 Vinyl DLP
1976 AU   Elektra 7E-2009 Vinyl DLP
1976 GE   Elektra ELK 62017 Vinyl DLP
1978 US   Elektra 8E-6003 Vinyl DLP re-issue
1990 US   Elektra E2 6003   2CD
1990 EU   Elektra 7559-60630   2CD
1991 CA   Elektra CEKJ-2009   2CD
?   AU   Elektra 9606302   2CD

On The Road to Kingdom Come
1976 US Elektra 7E-1082 Vinyl LP (Promo for radio stations) PRC
Richmond pressing
1976 US   Elektra 7E-1082 Vinyl LP (Promo for radio stations) Speciality
pressing
1976 US   Elektra 7E-1082 Vinyl LP
1976 US   Elektra TC-51082 Cassette
1976 UK   Elektra K 52040 Vinyl LP
1976 CA   Elektra 7ES 1082 Vinyl LP
1976 NZ   Elektra 7e-1082 Vinyl LP
1976 GE   Elektra ELK 52052 Vinyl LP
1970 US   Elektra 7e-1082 Vinyl LP re-issue
1990 US/UK Elektra 9-60613-2   CD

Dance Band on the Titanic
1977 US Elektra 9E-301 Vinyl DLP (Promo for radio stations)
1977 US Elektra 9E-301 Vinyl DLP
1977 US Elektra 9E-301 Vinyl DLP pressing PRC pressing
1977 US Elektra 9E-301 Vinyl DLP pressing CSM pressing
1977 US Elektra 9E-301 Vinyl DLP pressing Speciality Records pressing
1977 UK Elektra K62021 Vinyl DLP
1977 CA Elektra 9E-301 Vinyl DLP
1977 AU Elektra 9E-301 Vinyl DLP
1977 GE Elektra ELK 62021, 9E-301 Vinyl DLP
1977 NE Elektra ELK 62021, 9E-301 Vinyl DLP

314

1977 US Elektra K462021 Cassette
1990 US/UK Elektra 9 60549-2   2CD

Living Room Suite
1978 US   Elektra 6E-142 Vinyl LP (Promo for radio stations)
1978 US   Elektra 6E-142 Vinyl LP
1978 US   Elektra TC-8142 Cassette
1978 UK   Elektra K52089, 6E-142 Vinyl LP
1978 CA   Elektra 6E-142 Vinyl LP
1978 CA   Elektra ELK 6E-142A Vinyl LP
1978 AU   Elektra 6E-142 Vinyl LP
1978 GE   Elektra ELK 52 089 Vinyl LP
1993 US/UK Elektra 9 60528-2   CD

Legends of the Lost and Found: New Greatest Stories Live
1979 US   Elektra BB-703 Vinyl DLP (Promo for radio stations)
1979 US   Elektra BB-703 Vinyl DLP
1979 US   Elektra BC5 703 Cassette
1979 UK   Elektra K62025 Vinyl DLP
1979 CA   Elektra 2XBB-703, 2XBB703 Vinyl DLP
1979 AU   Elektra BB-703 Vinyl DLP
2005 US   Chapin Productions CPL2-5523   2CD (with revised track listing)

Sequel (also see *Remember When the Music*)
1980 US   Boardwalk FW 36872 Vinyl LP (Promo for radio stations)
1980 US   Boardwalk FW 36872 Vinyl LP
1980 US   Boardwalk FW-36872, FW36872 Vinyl LP (Santa Maria pressing)
1980 US   Boardwalk FW-36872 Cassette
1980 US/CAN Epic EPC 84996 Vinyl LP
1980 UK   Epic FW-36872 Vinyl LP
1980 CA   Epic FW-36872 Vinyl LP
1980 CA   Boardwalk FW 36872 Vinyl LP
1980 AU   CBS ELPS 4151 Vinyl LP
1980 GE   Boardwalk 26 16 001 Vinyl LP
1980 FR   Boardwalk 518001 Vinyl LP
1980 SC   Boardwalk FW 36872 Vinyl LP
1980 IT   Boardwalk LBW 17001 Vinyl LP
1999 HK   Boa Records BOA 1015 Vinyl LP * Issued as *STORYTELLER*
2001 US   Chapin Productions CD *with bonus tracks of Story of a Life, Remember When the Music and Sequel

315

Anthology of Harry Chapin
1985 US   Elektra 60413-1-E Vinyl LP (Promo for radio stations)
1985 US   Elektra 60413 Vinyl LP
1985 US   Elektra 60413-1-E Vinyl LP
1985 US   Elektra 60413-4-E Cassette
1985 UK/EU Elektra EKT16, 960413-1 Vinyl LP
1985 CA   Elektra 96 04131 Vinyl LP
1985 EU   Elektra 960 413-4, EKT16C Cassette

*Track list – W.O.L.D., Any Old Kind of Day, Cat's in the Cradle, 30,000 Pounds of Bananas, Taxi, She is Always Seventeen, Circle, Sunday Morning Sunshine, I Wanna Learn a Love Song, Better Place To Be, Song Man

Remember When the Music (re-issue of Sequel with bonus tracks)
1987 US   Dunhill Compact Classics GRL 335 Vinyl LP
1987 US   Dunhill Compact Classics GRC 335 Cassette
1987 US   Dunhill Compact Classics DZS035 CD
1987 AU   Dunhill Compact Classics 7559607732 CD
            *Bonus tracks – Hokey Pokey and Oh Man

The Gold Medal Collection
1988 US   Elektra 9 60773-2 2CD
1988 US   Elektra E2 60773 2CD (Club edition)
1988 US   Elektra 9 60773, CD773-2 2CD (Club edition)
1988 CA   Elektra 9 60773-2 2CD
1988 CA   Elektra CD60773 2CD (Club edition)

Track list – Taxi, Sunday Morning Sunshine, Old College Avenue, Dirty Old Man, I Wanna Learn a Love Song, Cat's in the Cradle, Tangled Up Puppet, Dancing Boy, Thanksgiving, Hunger Drives, Flowers Are Red, She Sings Songs Without Words, Shooting Star, Winter Song, Story of a Life, Commitment and Pete Seeger, There Only Was One Choice, A Better Place To Be, Mail Order Annie, Performing, W.O.L.D., Mr Tanner, Corey's Coming, A Child is Born, Sniper, Calluses, The Rock, Dance Band on the Titanic, I Wonder What Would Happen To This World, Sequel, My Grandfather, Remember When the Music (reprise), Circle

The Last Protest Singer
1988 US   Dunhill Compact Classics DZL 041 Vinyl LP
1988 US   Dunhill Compact Classics NEXMC101 Cassette
1988 UK   Sequel DZL 041 Cassette
1988 US   DCC Compact Classics DZS 041 CD
1988 UK   Sequel NEX CD101 CD

316

* The Sequel releases substitute the tracks Anthem and A Quiet Love Affair for Oh Man

Harry Chapin Tribute
1990 US   Relativity 88561-1047-2 Vinyl LP
1990 US   Relativity 88561-1047-4 Cassette
1990 US/CA Relativity ZK 90860   CD
1990 US   Relativity 88561-1047-2   CD
1990 US   Relativity 88561-1047-4   CD
1990 EU   Relativity 467726-1 Vinyl LP
1990 EU   Relativity 467726 2, 01-467726-10   CD

The Bottom Line Encore Collection
1997 US   Bottom Line Record Co BTL740   2CD
1998 US   Bottom Line Record Co 63440-47401-2   2CD
1998 US   Bottom Line Record Co 63440-47401-2   2CD (Club edition)
1998 AU   Bottom Line Record Co VEL 47401-2   2CD
1998 GE   Bottom Line Record Co VEL 79781-2   2CD

Track list – Taxi, Story of a Life, I Miss America, Mercenaries, A Better Place To Be, I Wanna Learn a Love Song, Mr Tanner, W.O.L.D., Cat's in the Cradle, Mismatch, Old Folkie, Let Time Go Lightly, 30,000 Pounds of Bananas, Sequel

Harry Chapin – Story of a Life
1999 US Elektra Traditions (Rhino) R2 75875   3CD box set + 76-page booklet
Track list – Taxi, Someone Keeps Calling My Name (Chapin Brothers), Empty, Greyhound, Any Old Kind of Day, Sunday Morning Sunshine, Sniper, Better Place to Be, They Call Her Easy, Mr Tanner, Mail Order Annie, W.O.L.D., Old College Avenue, Circle, Short Stories, Cat's in the Cradle, I Wanna Learn a Love Song, 30,000 Pounds of Bananas (live), Shooting Star, What Made America Famous, Vacancy, Dreams Go By, Tangled Up Puppet, The Rock, She is Always Seventeen, The Mayor of Candor Lied, Caroline, Laugh Man, Taxi (live), Corey's Coming, If My Mary Were Here, Dance Band on the Titanic, Mismatch, I Wonder What Happened to Him, Dancin' Boy, Flowers Are Red (live), Poor Damned Fool, Jenny. I Wonder What Would Happen To This World, Old Folkie (live), Remember When the Music (reprise), God Babe, You've Been So Good To Me, Story of a Life, November Rains, Sequel, Last Stand

Storyteller (Re-issue of the original 10-track *Sequel* album)
1999 HK Boa Records BOA 1015 Vinyl LP

317

Onwards and Upwards
2000 US Harry Chapin Foundation
VH1 Behind the Music: The Harry Chapin Collection
2001 CA   Elektra CR2 74344   CD
2001 SA   Elektra CDESP 088   CD
2001 EU   Elektra 8122 74344-2   CD
Track list: Taxi, I Wanna Learn a Love Song, Cat's in the Cradle, Sunday Morning Sunshine, Better Place To Be, Sequel, Circle, W.O.L.D., Corey's Coming, If My Mary Were Here, Sniper, Remember When the Music (reprise), 30,000 Pounds of Bananas

Harry Chapin - The Essentials
2002 US Elektra RS 76061   CD
Track list: Taxi, Sunday Morning Sunshine, W.O.L.D., Cat's in the Cradle, I Wanna Learn a Love Song, Better Place to Be, Dreams, Sniper, 30,000 Pounds of Bananas, Dance Band on the Titanic, Sequel, Remember When the Music (reprise)

A Better Place To Be – The Songs of Harry Chapin
2002 US Warner/Chappell RA-004 Promo CD
Track list: Taxi, Could You Put Your Light On Please, Sunday Morning Sunshine, A Better Place To Be, Circle, W.O.L.D., Mr Tanner, Cat's in the Cradle, Vacancy, I Wanna Learn a Love Song, Tangled Up Puppet, Corey's Coming, Flowers Are Red, Remember When the Music (reprise), Sequel, One More Tomorrow

Classic Hits of Harry Chapin
2003 US Elektra/Rhino CD
Track list – Taxi, Dreams Go By, Cat's in the Cradle, I Wanna Learn a Love Song, A Better Place to Be, Sunday Morning Sunshine, W.O.L.D., Sniper, Mr Tanner, She Is Always Seventeen, Dance Band on the Titanic, The Rock, Corey's Coming, Circle, Remember When the Music (reprise), Sequel

Heads and Tales / Sniper and Other Love Songs
2004 US Elektra 8122-76503-2   2CD of Harry's first two albums, with bonus tracks: Barefoot Boy (long 8.07 version), City Sweet, Halfway to Heaven (alternate version), Big Big City, Pigeon Run, Simple Song, Dirty Old Man, Songwriter's Woman.

Introducing Harry Chapin
2006 AU Rhino 8122787812 CD
Track list: Taxi, Could You Put Your Light on Please, Better Place To Be, W.O.L.D., Short Stories, Cat's in the Cradle, Tangled Up Puppet, Corey's

318

Coming, If My Mary Were Here, Dance Band on the Titanic, I Wonder What Happened to Him, Dancing Boy, I Wonder What Would Happen To This World, Flowers Are Red (live), Old Folkie (live), Circle

Harry Chapin – Original Album Series
2009 US Rhino Records / Elektra 8122 79836 3   5CD
Collection of the first five Elektra albums

Dance Band on the Titanic / Living Room Suite
2012 EU   Edsel / Rhino EDSD 2108   2CD
Two-album collection

Bottom Line Archive Series: Live 1981
2015 US Bottom Line Recording Co BLRCD001   3CD
Track list: Taxi, Story of a Life, I Miss America, Mercenaries, Better Place To Be, I Wanna Learn Love Song. Mr Tanner, W.O.L.D., Mismatch, Old Folkie, Let Time Go Lightly, Cat's in the Cradle, Remember When the Music, 30,000 Pounds of Bananas, Sequel. Up on the Shelf, Star Tripper, If My Mary Were Here, Bluesman, Flowers Are Red, Halfway to Heaven, Paint a Picture of Yourself, Mail Order Annie, Dreams Go By, Poor Damned Fool, Sniper, You Are the Only Song, Circle

Cat's in the Cradle – Live 77 (Huff Gym, University of Illinois, Champaign March 27th 1977)
2015 US Klondike KL2CD5033-1   2CD
Track list: Paint a Picture of Yourself (Michael), Odd Job Man, W.O.L.D., They Call Her Easy, 30,000 Pounds of Bananas, Tangled Up Puppet, Mr Tanner, Dreams Go By, Cat's in the Cradle, Taxi, Circle, Someone Keeps Calling My Name

Harry Chapin Live in New York 1978 (Wollman Rink, Central Park NY August 23rd 1978) * unofficial release
2016 UK Live Wire Productions LW2030   2CD
Track List: Shooting Star, If You Want To Feel, W.O.L.D., Poor Damned Fool, I Wanna Learn a Love Song, Flowers Are Red, Bummer, Cat's in the Cradle, Love is Not in Season, Tangled Up Puppet, Why Do Little Girls, Mr Tanner, They Call Her Easy, Halfway to Heaven, Caroline, My Old Lady, Better Place To Be, Bluesman, 30,000 Pounds of Bananas, Taxi, Circle

Drop the Needle on the Hits: The Best of Harry Chapin
2018 US Rhino RI-571891   Vinyl

Track list: Cat's in the Cradle, W.O.L.D., A Better Place to Be, Tangled Up Puppet, Taxi, If My Mary Were Here, Dance Band on the Titanic, Corey's Coming

Harry Chapin - The Singles A's and B's
2019 US Wounded Bird Records WOU6513   2CD
Track list: Taxi, Empty, Could You Put a Light on Please, Better Place To Be Pt 1, Better Place to Be Pt 2 , Sunday Morning Sunshine, Burning Herself, W.O.L.D., Short Stories, What Made America Famous, Cat's in the Cradle, Vacancy, Dreams Go By, Sandy, I Wanna Learn a Love Song, She Sings Songs Without Words, Tangled Up Puppet, Dirt Gets Under Your Fingernails, Corey's Coming, If My Mary Were Here, Dance Band on the Titanic, I Wonder What Happened To Him, My Old Lady, I Do It For You Jane, If You Want to Feel, I Wonder What Would Happen To This World, Flowers Are Red, Why Do Little Girls, Circle

The Singles (All Elektra unless otherwise stated)

US – United States, UK – United Kingdom, CA – Canada, AU – Australia, NZ – New Zealand, NE – Netherlands, GE – Germany, SP – Spain, SA – South Africa, FR – France. IR - Ireland

1972 US Taxi   EK45770-A Promo (one side stereo/one side mono)
1972 US Taxi / Empty   EK-45770 Single Feb 1972
1972 UK Taxi / Empty   K12044 Promo
1972 UK Taxi / Empty   K12044 Single
1972 CA Taxi / Empty   E45770 Single
1972 AU Taxi / Empty   ERM-45770 Single
1972 NZ Taxi / Empty   ERM-45770 Single
1972 NE Taxi / Empty   12.044 Single   picture sleeve
1975 US Taxi (6.40) / W.O.L.D (5.15) E45066 Spun Gold re-issue
?   CA   Taxi (6.40) / Cats in the Cradle   GS5508 Gold Standard reissue
1989 UK Taxi (6.40) / W.O.L.D (5.15) OG9907 Old Gold re-issue

1972 US Could You Put Your Light On, Please EK45792 Promo (one side stereo, one side mono)
1972 US Could You Put Your Light On, Please / Any Old Kind of Day K12060 Promo
1972 US Could You Put Your Light On, Please / Any Old Kind of Day EK-45792 Single June 1972
1972 US Could You Put Your Light On, Please / Any Old Kind of Day K12060 Single

320

1972 UK Could You Put Your Light On, Please SAM8 Promo
Taken from the concert at the Queen Elizabeth Hall in London, Oct 20th
1972 along with Plainsong's 'Amelia Earhart's Last Flight' and Mickey
Newbury's 'Remember the Good' on the A-side.
1972 CA Could You Put Your Light On, Please / Any Old Kind of Day
E-45792 Single
1972 NZ Could You Put Your Light On, Please / Any Old Kind of Day
EKM 43792 Single

1972 US Sunday Morning Sunshine EK-45811 Promo (one side stereo,
one side mono)
1972 US Sunday Morning Sunshine / Burning Herself EK-45811 Single
Sept 1972
1972 US Sunday Morning Sunshine / Burning Herself EK-45811 Single
1972 CA Sunday Morning Sunshine / Burning Herself E-45811 Single
1972 UK Sunday Morning Sunshine / Burning Herself K-12078 Promo
1972 NZ Sunday Morning Sunshine / Burning Herself EKM 45811
Single

1972 US Better Place To Be 8.55 E45327-A Promo (one side stereo /
one side mono) 12-inch with white label
1972 US Better Place To Be Pt 1 / Better Place To Be Pt 2 E45327-A
7-inch single with butterfly logo
1972 US Better Place To Be Pt 1 / Better Place To Be Pt 2 E45327-A
7-inch Single with red label
1972 US Better Place To Be 6.25 / Winter Song E45327 Single Dec
1972
1972 CA Better Place To Be 6.25 / Winter Song E45828 Single

1973 US W.O.L.D 5.15 / W.O.LD 3.56   EK-45874 Promo (A-side
stereo. B-side mono)
1973 US W.O.L.D 5.15 / Short Stories   EK-45874 Single Jan 1974
1973 CA W.O.L.D 5.15 / Short Stories   E-45874 Single
1973 GE W.O.L.D 4.02 / Short Stories   ELK 12133 Single   picture
sleeve
1973 NZ W.O.L.D 4.02 / Short Stories   ELM 45874 Single
1973 NE W.O.L.D 4.35 / Short Stories   ELK 45874 Single
1973 NE W.O.L.D 5.15 / Short Stories   ELK 45874 Single "Morning
DJ" picture sleeve
1974 UK W.O.L.D 4.02 / Short Stories   K-12133 Promo
1974 UK W.O.L.D 4.02 / Short Stories   K-12133 Single
1974 AU W.O.L.D 5.15 / Short Stories   K-12133 Single
1974 GE W.O.L.D 4.02 / Short Stories   K-12133 Single

1976 UK W.O.L.D 4.02 / Cat's in the Cradle K12224 Re-issue   picture sleeve
1974 US Cat's in the Cradle   E-45203 Promo (one side stereo / one side mono)
1974 US Cat's in the Cradle / Vacancy   E-45203 Single Aug 1974 picture sleeve
1974 US Cat's in the Cradle / Vacancy   E-45203 (CTH) Single
1974 CA Cat's in the Cradle / Vacancy   E-45203 Single
1974 AU Cat's in the Cradle / Vacancy   EKM-45203 Single
1974 NZ Cat's in the Cradle / Vacancy   EKM-45203 Single
1974 GE Cat's in the Cradle / Vacancy   ELK 12163 Single   picture sleeve
1974 SA Cat's in the Cradle / Vacancy   EKSEKS 638 Single
1974 SP Cat's in the Cradle / Vacancy   ELK 12163 Single (Hispavox label)
1974 IR Cat's in the Cradle / Shooting Star K12157 Single
1974 NE Cat's in the Cradle / Vacancy   ELK 12.163 Single   picture sleeve
1975 US Cat's in the Cradle / What Made America Famous? Elektra E-45067A Spun Gold re-issue
1977 GE Cat's in the Cradle / Dreams Go By   ELK 12 248 Single picture sleeve
1989 UK Cat's in the Cradle / W.O.L.D   OG-9907 Old Gold re-issue
1993 GE Cat's in the Cradle / Cats in the Cradle (live) PRO-817 Promo

1974 US I Wanna Learn a Love Song   E45236 Promo (one side stereo, one side mono)
1974 US I Wanna Learn a Love Song / She Sings Songs Without Words E45236 Single Feb 1975
1974 CA I Wanna Learn a Love Song / She Sings Songs Without Words E45236 Single
1974 AU I Wanna Learn a Love Song / She Sings Songs Without Words E45236 Single
1974 GE I Wanna Learn a Love Song / She Sings Songs Without Words E45236 Single   picture sleeve
1975 UK I Wanna Learn a Love Song / She Sings Songs Without Words E45236 Promo
1975 UK I Wanna Learn a Love Song / She Sings Songs Without Words E45236 Single
1975 NZ I Wanna Learn a Love Song / She Sings Songs Without Words EKM 45236 Single

1974 US What Made America Famous? E45893 Promo (one side stereo, one side mono) Theme from 'The Great Divide'
1974 US What Made America Famous? / Old College Avenue E45893 Single July 1974

1975 US Dreams Go By E45264 Promo (one side stereo, one side mono)
1975 US Dreams Go By / Sandy E45264 Single July 1975
1975 AU Dreams Go By / Sandy E45264 Single
1975 NZ Dreams Go By / Sandy E45264 Single
1975 GE Dreams Go By / Sandy ELK 12184 Single
1975 CA Dreams Go By / Stop Singing Those Sad Songs E45264 Single
1975 FR Dreams Go By / Stop Singing Those Sad Songs 12 191 Single

1975 US Tangled Up Puppet (A Song For My Daughter) E45285 Promo for radio stations (one side stereo, one side mono)
1975 US Tangled Up Puppet (A Song For My Daughter) / Dirt Gets Under the Fingernails E45285 Single Oct 1975
1976 NZ Tangled Up Puppet (A Song For My Daughter) / Dirt Gets Under the Fingernails E-45285 Single

1976 US Star Tripper / The Rock E45304 Single Feb 1976

1976 US A Better Place To Be Pts 1 & 2 E45327 (Taken from *Greatest Stories Live* album) Single June 1976
1976 NZ A Better Place To Be Pts 1 & 2 E-45327 Single

1976 US Corey's Coming / If My Mary Were Here E45368 Promo
1976 US Corey's Coming / If My Mary Were Here E45368 Single Nov 1976

1977 US Dance Band on the Titanic E-45426-A Promo for radio stations (one side stereo, one side mono)
1977 US Dance Band on the Titanic / I Wonder What Happened To Him E-45426 Single Aug 1977
1977 US Dance Band on the Titanic / I Wonder What Happened To Him E-45426 Single – red label
1977 UK Dance Band on the Titanic / I Wonder What Happened To Him K12271 Single
1977 CA Dance Band on the Titanic / I Wonder What Happened To Him E45426 Single
1977 AU Dance Band on the Titanic / I Wonder What Happened To Him E45426 Single

323

1977 GE Dance Band on the Titanic / My Old Lady ELK 12 273 Single
picture sleeve
1977 US My Old Lady   Elektra E45445   Promo for radio stations (one
side stereo, one side mono)
1977 US My Old Lady / I Do It For You, Jane   E45445 Single Nov 1977
red vinyl
1977 CA My Old Lady / I Do It For You, Jane   E45445 Single

1978 US If You Want to Feel   E45497 Promo for radio stations (one side
stereo, one side mono)
1978 US If You Want to Feel / I Wonder What Would Happen To This
World E45497 Single June 1978
1978 CA If You Want to Feel / I Wonder What Would Happen To This
World E45497 Single
1978 NZ If You Want to Feel / I Wonder What Would Happen To This
World E-45497 Single
1978 US Flowers Are Red   E45524   Promo for radio stations (one side
stereo / one side mono)
1978 US Flowers Are Red / Why Do Little Girls E45524 Single Sept 1978
1978 UK Flowers Are Red / Why Do Little Girls K12361 Single

1980 US Sequel   Boardwalk WS8 5700   Promo for radio stations (one
side stereo, one side mono)
1980 US I Finally Found It Sandy   Boardwalk WS8 5700 Promo (one
side stereo, one side mono)
1980 US Sequel / I Finally Found It Sandy   Boardwalk WS8 5700 Single
Oct 1980
1980 UK Sequel / I Finally Found It Sandy   Boardwalk FWS1 Single
picture sleeve
1980 CA Sequel / I Finally Found It Sandy   Epic WS8 5700 Single
1980 AU Sequel / I Finally Found It Sandy   CBS ES550 Single
1980 GE Sequel / I Finally Found It Sandy   Boardwalk 10 07 049 Single
1980 FR Sequel / I Finally Found It Sandy   Vogue 101403 Single
1980 NZ Sequel / I Finally Found It Sandy   Epic ES550 Single
1980 US Remember When the Music   Boardwalk WS8 5705 Promo
(both sides identical, reading 'stereo' and 'Side 1')
1980 US Remember When the Music / Northwest 222   Boardwalk WS8
5705 Single Feb 1981
1980 CA Remember When the Music / Northwest 222   Boardwalk WS8
5705 Single
1980 AU Remember When the Music / Northwest 222   CBS ES590
Single

1981 UK Remember When the Music / Northwest 222   Epic EPC A1168 Promo
1981 UK Remember When the Music / Northwest 222   Epic EPC A1168 Single
1981 GE Remember When the Music / Northwest 222   Boardwalk 100-07-068 Single   picture sleeve
1987 US   Remember When the Music / I Miss America   Dunhill DZ545001 CD Mini-Single
1981 US Story of a Life   Boardwalk NB7-11-119   Promo for radio stations (one side stereo, one side mono)
1981 US Story of a Life / Salt and Pepper Boardwalk NB7-11-119 Single Aug 1981
1981 IR Circle / Flowers Are Red K12587 Single

1988 US I Don't Want to be President Dunhill ZS45 – PROMO-1 Promo (one side stereo, one side mono)   red vinyl

Album Chart History

Heads and Tales
#60 *Billboard* Hot 200
Sales – 1,100,000 Gold

Sniper and Other Love Songs
#160 *Billboard* Hot 200
Sales – 350,000

Short Stories
#61 *Billboard* Hot 200
Sales – 1,100,000 Gold

Verities & Balderdash
#4 *Billboard* Hot 200
Sales – 2,700,000 Double Platinum

Portrait Gallery
#53 *Billboard* Hot 200
Sales – 350,000

Greatest Stories Live
#48 *Billboard* Hot 200
Sales – 2,100,000 Double Platinum

On the Road to Kingdom Come
#87 *Billboard* Hot 200
Sales – 350,000

Dance Band on the Titanic
#58 *Billboard* Hot 200
Sales – 500,000 Gold

Living Room Suite
#133 *Billboard* Hot 200
Sales – 350,000

Legends of the Lost and Found
#163 *Billboard* Hot 200
Sales – 250,000

Sequel
#58 *Billboard* Hot 200
Sales – 500,000 Gold

The Last Protest Singer
Did not chart
Sales – 250,000

Gold Medal Collection
Did not chart
Sales – 1,000,000 Platinum

Singles Chart History

Taxi
#24 *Billboard* Hot 100
#20 Cashbox Top 100
Sales – 1,000,000 Platinum

Could You Put Your Light On Please
#81 Cashbox Top 100
Sales – 50,000

Sunday Morning Sunshine
#75 *Billboard* Hot 100
#30 *Billboard* Adult Contemporary

#77 Cashbox Top 100
Sales – 50,000

Better Place To Be (1972)
#118 *Billboard* Hot 100
Sales - 50,000

W.O.L.D.
#36 *Billboard* Hot 100
#37 *Billboard* Adult Contemporary
#26 Cashbox Top 100
#30 UK *NME* Top 40
Sales – 1,000,000 Platinum

Cat's in the Cradle
#1 *Billboard* Hot 100
#6 *Billboard* Adult Contemporary
#1 Cashbox Top 100
Sales – 1,500,000 Platinum

I Wanna Learn a Love Song
#44 *Billboard* Hot 100
#7 *Billboard* Adult Contemporary
#40 Cashbox Top 100
Sales – 100,000

What Made America Famous
#87 Cashbox Top 100
Sales – 50,000

Dreams Go By
#33 *Billboard* Adult Contemporary
Sales – 100,000

Better Place To Be Pt 1 & 2
#86 *Billboard* Hot 100
#76 Cashbox Top 100
Sales – 200,000

Dance Band on the Titanic
Did not chart
Sales – 50,000

Sequel
#23 *Billboard* Hot 100
#37 *Billboard* Adult Contemporary
#34 Cashbox Top 100
Sales – 1,000,000 Platinum

Remember When the Music
#47 *Billboard* Adult Contemporary
Sales – 100,000

From the Cheap Seats – The Fans' Favorites

In May 2019 the Harry Chapin Fans Facebook group of over 1,000 members were asked by this author to name their favorite song and album of Harry's. The final list was as follows:

Albums
1. Greatest Stories Live
2. Verities & Balderdash
3. Dance Band on the Titanic
4. Short Stories
5. Legends of the Lost and Found
6. On the Road to Kingdom Come
7. Sniper and Other Love Songs
8. Portrait Gallery
9. Heads and Tales
10. Living Room Suite

Songs
1. Better Place To Be (live)
2. Mr Tanner
3. The Mayor of Candor Lied
4. Sniper
5. W.O.L.D.
6. There Only Was One Choice
7. Corey's Coming
8. Stranger With the Melodies
9. Taxi
10. What Made America Famous

Selected Television Appearances 1965-81

04-08-65 The Merv Griffin Show (as The Chapin Brothers) *unconfirmed date
14-10-65 Let's Sing Out (as the Chapin Brothers)
19-10-65 The Merv Griffin Show (as the Chapin Brothers)
21-10-65 Let's Sing Out (as the Chapin Brothers)
03-04-72 The Dick Cavett Show
05-06-72 The Dick Cavett Show
28-06-72 The David Frost Show
06-07-72 The Tonight Show With Johnny Carson
07-07-72 The Tonight Show With Johnny Carson
03-08-72 The Tonight Show With Johnny Carson
19-08-72 American Bandstand
19-08-72 The Midnight Special (pilot)
31-10-72 The Old Grey Whistle Test (UK)
13-11-72 The Tonight Show With Johnny Carson
24-01-73 The Tonight Show With Johnny Carson
23-02-73 The Midnight Special
23-02-73 The Tonight Show With Johnny Carson
03-03-73 15th Annual Grammy Awards, New York
19-04-73 The Mike Douglas Show
09-05-73 The Tonight Show With Johnny Carson
20-09-73 The Tonight Show With Johnny Carson
02-01-74 The Tonight Show With Johnny Carson
14-02-74 The Mike Douglas Show
21-05-74 The Mike Douglas Show
11-07-74 The Mike Douglas Show
10-10-74 Good Night America
04-11-74 The Mike Douglas Show (five nights)
03-12-74 Soundstage (PBS)
23-01-75 The Mike Douglas Show
01-03-75 17th Grammy Awards
26-03-75 The Mike Douglas Show
02-04-75 The Mike Douglas Show
26-05-75 The Mike Douglas Show (four nights)
30-06-75 The Mike Douglas Show (five nights)
09-09-75 The Tonight Show With Johnny Carson
22-09-75 The Mike Douglas Show (five nights)
10-11-75 Don Kirshner's Rock Concert
03-12-75 The Mike Douglas Show
19-09-76 2nd Annual Rock Music Awards
24-09-76 Don Kirshner's Rock Concert

10-11-76 Good Morning America
07-01-77 Friday Night With Steve Edwards
02-77   The Conscience of America
12-04-77 Rockpalast (W Germany)
20-04-77 The Tonight Show With Johnny Carson
02-05-77 The Merv Griffin Show
27-06-77 Liedercircus, Copenhagen
10-08-77 The Tonight Show With Johnny Carson
31-10-77 The Old Grey Whistle Test (UK)
20-12-77 The Tonight Show With Johnny Carson
03-02-78 The Merv Griffin Show
31-07-78 The Tonight Show With Johnny Carson
18-11-78 Don Kirchner's Rock Concert
12-11-79 The Tonight Show With Johnny Carson
20-08-80 Dinah and Friends
03-11-80 The Merv Griffin Show
15-12-80 The Mike Douglas Show
19-12-80 The Midnight Special
09-01-81 The Midnight Special
14-03-81 Solid Gold
25-06-81 Solid Gold (aired Aug 1)

Printed in the USA
CPSIA information can be obtained
at www.ICGtesting.com
LVHW022229200924
791680LV00001B/159